DATE DUE

The Unpredictable Constitution

The Unpredictable Constitution

EDITED BY

Norman Dorsen

New York University Press

NEW YORK AND LONDON

NEW YORK UNIVERSITY PRESS
New York and London

Library of Congress Cataloguing-in Publication Data
The unpredictable constitution / edited by Norman Dorsen.
p. cm.
Includes index.
ISBN 0–8147–1948–1 (cloth : acid-free)
1. Constitutional law—United States.   2. Constitutional law.
I. Dorsen, Norman
KF4550.A2 U57 2002
342.73'02—dc21   2001004923

New York University Press books are printed on acid-free paper,
and their binding materials are chosen for strength and durability.

Manufactured in the United States of America
10 9 8 7 6 5 4 3 2 1

Contents

Acknowledgments

For assistance in arranging the James Madison lectures that became the chapters in this book, and for help in its preparation, I am grateful to Bobbie Glover, the impressario of the events, to Karen Johnson for her imaginative and careful editing, to Andras Pap for his aid in formatting the articles, and to my hard-working secretaries Evelyn Palmquist and LuAnn Rolley.

I am also indebted to Dean John Sexton for his unflagging support for the Madison lecture program and so much else and to several faculty colleagues for their advice on which justices and judges to invite to deliver these prestigious lectures.

N.D.

Introduction

Norman Dorsen

It would have been hard to foretell, or even to imagine, a more startling constitutional event than the Supreme Court decisions in *Bush v. Gore*, which were rendered as this book was being prepared for press. The rulings determined the 2000 presidential election, in a scenario that was almost unthinkable to those familiar with the Court's history and practices. The case is a perfect prelude to a book dedicated to the "unpredictable" Constitution.

It was not merely that the case was "political" in the sense that it decisively affected the political direction of the country for at least the next four years. Nor merely that the Court's intervention lacked judicial precedent. But also that the rationales provided by two separate parts of the five-person majority—one resting on the asserted requirements of the electoral college provision of the Constitution and the other on "problems" under the equal protection clause of the Fourteenth Amendment—were so novel in their constitutional backing that many observers were persuaded that the opinions were driven by an unswervable desire to reach a particular result.

The four-person minority was also divided in its reasoning, two justices acknowledging the equality problems but unconvinced that they required judicial intervention and the others concluding that there was no federal question in the case and therefore it should have been left to the Florida courts to decide.

My purpose here is not to present a full analysis of *Bush v. Gore*, but rather to point to the case as a way of underscoring the Constitution's unpredictability.

This was the pattern from the beginning. *Marbury v. Madison*,[1] the first case in which the Court, in 1803, invalidated a congressional statute, seemed to present merely a narrow issue of entitlement to a federal judgeship rather than the momentous issue of the power of judicial review. And it would have been a bold seer who would have predicted, prior to the 1856 decision in *Dred Scott v. Sandford*,[2] the second time the Supreme Court struck down a federal law, that it would intervene so aggressively (and futilely) in the hypercharged political dispute whether to extend slavery to America's western territories.

An important reason that Supreme Court decisions such as these are so hard to predict is that, unlike other institutions, the Court can react only to controversies that are brought to it by the parties and must do so in the form in which they are presented.

The early cases are matched in their unpredictability by more recent rulings. While *Brown v. Board of Education*[3] was foreshadowed by a series of earlier desegregation cases involving higher education, the other leading Warren Court initiatives—such as the legislative apportionment,[4] criminal justice,[5] and school prayer decisions[6]—came to many as bolts from the blue, as did *Roe v. Wade* a few years later.[7] More recently, the Rehnquist Court has reversed sixty years of precedent by curbing congressional power based on a narrow reading of Congress's authority under the Commerce Clause[8] and by imposing federalism-related limits on legislation that seeks to regulate certain activities of the fifty states.[9]

We can be confident that further surprises are in store, that the only certainty is that there cannot be certainty about the constitutional course of the country. Among other things, the terrible events of September 11 surely will spawn novel constitutional questions that the Supreme Court will have to resolve, often no doubt in unpredictable ways.

It is therefore appropriate that the James Madison lectures presented in this volume address issues that underscore the pivotal role of the courts and suggest new directions that the judiciary may take. Four of the essays concern the administration of justice. Judge Jon O. Newman in writing about the enforceability of the "reasonable doubt" standard of proof in criminal cases and Judge Harry T. Edwards in examining the "harmless error" doctrine in criminal law both take big cuts at these two important and perplexing questions. New judicial pronouncements on these matters, whether or not "predictable," would have momentous consequences for the criminal justice system.

Judge Betty B. Fletcher and Judge Stephen Reinhardt write on the death penalty in the United States. Judge Fletcher addresses the narrowing availability of habeas corpus review in capital cases and the always present danger of executing innocent people; she concludes that the "system has it backward" by expending immense resources during appellate review but too often failing to provide adequate representation to defendants at trial. As if to prove Judge Fletcher's thesis, Judge Reinhardt's lecture provides a firsthand and searching account—literally a case study—of the execution of a man without a prior criminal record, although there was substantial doubt about his guilt. Despite these powerful testaments, it is not likely that the Supreme Court will invalidate the death penalty in the near future even though the United States is virtually isolated among developed countries in permitting this form of punishment.

Four articles consider issues of discrimination. The late Judge A. Leon Higginbotham, whose lecture was delivered in 1986 before the South African apartheid regime was dismantled, compares the American and South African experiences of racial bias within their judicial systems and suggests ways in which South Africa through enlightened statesmanship and civil rights activism could alter its oppressive system—a development that came sooner and more comprehensively than anyone could imagine at the time.

Three essays of varying types address women's rights and, more broadly, sex discrimination, as a natural sequel to popular movements supporting gender equality. Justice Sandra Day O'Connor provides a moving and perceptive glimpse of the legal world she witnessed as an honors graduate of Stanford Law School who could gain employment only as a legal secretary. She also questions the validity of a "new feminism" that posits that women and men have particular ways of looking at the world, regarding it as a throwback to the "myths we have struggled to put behind us." Justice Ruth Bader Ginsburg, who was the leading women's rights lawyer in the country while litigating for the American Civil Liberties Union, examines *Roe v. Wade* from the perspective of "judicial voice," concluding that the sweeping opinion in that case should be contrasted with the more restrained approach in contemporaneous decisions involving explicitly gender-based discrimination. And Judge Martha Craig Daughtrey traces the history of the women's rights movement and the Equal Rights Amendment from its passage by Congress to its eventual failure in the state ratification process, and she analyzes the parallel development of an equal rights jurisprudence based on the Equal Protection Clause of the Fourteenth Amendment.

Three lectures introduce additional elements to this book. Judge Richard S. Arnold explores the subject of constitutional interpretation as practiced by James Madison, showing how Madison often refused during later controversies to rely on his own formative contributions to the Constitution but nevertheless developed a consistent, yet flexible, view of interpretation that can still enlighten today's constitutional debates. Judge Richard A. Posner, in sharp disagreement with two recent Supreme Court decisions safeguarding the rights of women and homosexuals, criticizes constitutional theorists who conceal normative goals in vague and unworkable principles of interpretation. He argues that the two opinions lack the empirical support crucial to sound decision making. And Judge Patricia M. Wald questions when a state which provides numerous governmental programs for the benefit of its citizens and denies access to such a program to particular individuals can be held constitutionally accountable. Judge Wald focuses on cases involving the provision of welfare services to an abused child and a death row defendant's challenge to the composition of the jury that sentenced him to death, but her analysis has broader implications, such as in current cases in which a government seeks to withdraw support for art museums because of the content of some of their pictures.

The final essay departs from the norm. Until the lecture in October 2000 delivered by Lord Irving of Lairg, the Lord Chancellor of Great Britain, all Madison lecturers were either a justice of the U.S. Supreme Court or a judge of the U.S. Court of Appeals. In commemoration of the fortieth anniversary of the James Madison lectures and in recognition of the increasingly global nature of law, including constitutional law, it was decided to invite a distinguished foreign jurist to deliver a lecture.

Lord Irvine did not disappoint us. He shows in vivid detail how the American system of constitutional supremacy and judicial review shares many common features with the British unwritten constitution's emphasis on parliamentary sovereignty without judicial review. He concludes that both systems translate substantially identical commitments to popular sovereignty into distinct, yet related, approaches to constitutionalism.

The James Madison Lectures were inaugurated at the New York University School of Law "to enhance the appreciation of civil liberty and strengthen the national purpose." The first four lectures were published in book form in 1963, in *The Great Rights*, edited by the first director of the series, Edmond Cahn. It contained lectures by Supreme Court Justice Hugo Black, Justice William J. Brennan, Jr., Chief Justice Earl Warren, and Justice William O. Douglas on the general philosophy of constitutional liberty. It also included a perceptive essay on "The Madison Heritage," by the historian Irving Brant, which reminded us of Madison's many contributions to the principles of liberty, including the drafting of the Bill of Rights itself.

Fourteen of the succeeding lectures were published in book form in 1987 (paperback in 1989) under the title *The Evolving Constitution*.[10] The book included a masterful introduction by Archibald Cox, "Storm Over the Supreme Court," in which Professor Cox examined earlier controversies that had enveloped the Court, discussed the changes in doctrine and role that took place in the years following *Brown v. Board of Education*, and related these events and ideas to the disputes swirling around the Court in the late 1980s.

Despite the broad range of subjects they have canvassed, the thirty-two James Madison lecturers have not exhausted the opportunities for creative approaches to civil liberty, on matters as diverse as the rights of gays and lesbians, campaign finance reform, the religion clauses of the First Amendment, the decriminalization of certain narcotic drugs, the protections accorded poor people in our society, and constitutional problems associated with immigration, cyberspace, and the rise of terrorism. In each of these areas the unpredictable is waiting to happen and to be digested in thoughtful Madison lectures to come.

NOTES

1. 5 U.S. 137 (1803).

2. 60 U.S. 393 (1856).

3. 347 U.S. 483 (1954).

4. See *Baker v. Carr*, 369 U.S. 186 (1962); *Reynolds v. Sims*, 377 U.S. 533 (1964).

5. E.g., *Mapp v. Ohio*, 367 U.S. 643 (1961); *Gideon v. Wainright*, 372 U.S. 335 (1963); *Miranda v. Arizona*, 384 U.S. 436 (1966).

6. *Engel v. Vitale*, 370 U.S. 421 (1962); *Abington School Dist. v. Schempp*, 374 U.S. 203 (1963).

7. 410 U.S. 113 (1973).

8. E.g., *United States v. Lopez*, 514 U.S. 549 (1995); *United States v. Morrison* 120 S.Ct. 1740 (2000).

9. E.g., *Printz v. United States*, 521 U.S. 898 (1997); cf. *Alden v. Maine*, 119 S.Ct. 2240 (1999) (constitutional doctrine of sovereign immunity bars private actions against nonconsenting states in state courts).

10. The James Madison Lectures that have been published in the previous books and in this book have all appeared in the *New York University Law Review*, to which grateful acknowledgment is made for permission to republish.

Chapter 1

Government Benefits
A New Look at an Old Gift Horse

Patricia M. Wald

Tonight I am going to talk about an old problem in constitutional law: the volatile relationship between constitutional rights and government benefits. In my view, the jury-rigged doctrine of rights and benefits we are now living with deserves serious reconsideration. One aspect of that doctrine—unconstitutional conditions—may still be in flux but is moving swiftly backwards; another—fourteenth amendment procedural due process rights—seems static for the moment, mired in unattractive premises. In the current climate, many civil libertarians dread the idea of unsettling precedent. They would, in Hamlet's words, "rather bear the ills we have, than fly to others that we know not of."[1] Yet that attitude may be too timorous. As we pass through the bicentennial and enter the twenty-first century, we should not be afraid to propose changes in law or doctrine we believe are necessary—we must not accept as irreversible the battles we have lost in the past.

I begin with two recent Supreme Court decisions. The first, decided in the 1989 term, is *DeShaney v. Winnebago County Department of Social Services*,[2] a suit for damages under section 1983.[3] The facts were these:[4] infant Joshua DeShaney, placed in his father's custody after his parents' divorce, was physically beaten so regularly and so badly that he suffered permanent brain damage. Officials of the county Department of Social Services regularly received distress calls from neighbors and emergency room attendants

This lecture was delivered on October 26, 1989, and appeared in 65 N.Y.U.L. Rev. 247 (1990).

that Joshua was being abused by his father. At one point the Department temporarily placed the boy in custodial care, but shortly returned him to his father. His social worker kept orderly records of the calls and of suspicious conditions in the home but did not again try to remove the boy. "I just knew," she said later, "the phone would ring someday and Joshua would be dead."[5] After his final beating, Joshua's mother sued the county, its Department of Social Services, and various department employees, contending that Joshua had been deprived of his liberty in violation of the due process guarantee of the fourteenth amendment.

The Supreme Court affirmed the trial court's dismissal, holding that Joshua's loss of liberty could not be attributed to any unconstitutional action by the state.[6] The due process clause, the Court announced, "is phrased as a limitation on the State's power to act, not as a guarantee of certain minimal levels of safety and security."[7] The Court reasoned that, since the county had no obligation to provide child welfare services in the first place, it could not be held liable when the Department of Social Services failed to provide protection to the child, no matter how vulnerable he was known to be or how inevitable the tragedy. The county's sin was inaction, not action. It simply failed to do something helpful for Joshua; it did not do anything injurious to him, and that difference, the Court said, made all the difference for constitutional purposes.[8]

The second case, *Ross v. Oklahoma,*[9] decided the Term before *DeShaney,* involved a death row defendant's challenge to the composition of the jury which had sentenced him to death. The trial court had declined to excuse for cause a prospective juror who stated during voir dire that he would vote for a death sentence if the defendant were convicted; the defense instead had to use one of its nine peremptory challenges. The defendant contended on appeal that the trial court's error deprived him of one of his scarce peremptory challenges in violation of the fourteenth amendment.[10]

The Supreme Court unanimously agreed that the trial court had erred in failing to strike the juror for cause, but a majority of the Court held that the error had no constitutional significance.[11] Since the challenged juror did not sit on the panel which convicted and sentenced the defendant, the majority reasoned, the only injury to the defendant lay in the loss of a peremptory challenge; and "[b]ecause peremptory challenges are a creature of statute and are not required by the Constitution, it is for the state to determine the number of peremptory challenges allowed and to define their purpose and the manner of their exercise."[12] The defendant, in the Court's words, had "received all that Oklahoma law allowed him,"[13] and that in turn was all that the Constitution guaranteed. He had, in short, only been denied a benefit the state could have withheld in the first place.

Though the link between these two cases may not be immediately apparent, *DeShaney* and *Ross* were decided on common premises for due process purposes: both presumed that the denial or dilution of a mere privilege (as opposed to a right) properly can be characterized as government inaction, not action, and that there is a fundamental distinction between government inaction and government action that affirmatively harms an individual—that puts her in a worse position than she would have been in had government not acted. In *DeShaney,* that distinction was explicit: the Court said that the state's failure to protect a child—even one it knew was in danger—did not constitute a deprivation of liberty. "While the State may have been aware of the dangers that Joshua faced in the free world, it played no part in their creation, nor did it do anything to render him any more vulnerable to them."[14] The *Ross* Court's reliance on this distinction was less obvious, but no less real. Since the state was not constitutionally required to allow peremptory challenges, the defendant simply had been denied a gratuitous state benefit when he was forced to use a peremptory challenge to remedy an erroneous ruling on a challenge for cause.

In both *Ross* and *DeShaney,* the Court, critically, characterized the benefit the state failed to provide as a "gratuity" rather than a right. Thus, whether it is a "gratuitous" benefit or service that the state denied, or failed to provide, appears today to be the litmus test for whether constitutional harm has occurred. This mode of analysis has profound implications for our jurisprudence.

Over the years, the courts have developed several different verbal formulations for framing the issue. Sometimes it has been posed in terms of "rights" and "privileges": a constitutional difference exists between the state's power to infringe upon a right and its power to deny a mere privilege.[15] The same distinction appears at other times under the rubric of "burden" and "benefit": is the challenged government action a burden on the exercise of a citizen's right or just a restriction on a benefit the government was not compelled to bestow?[16] For certain kinds of benefits, the touchstone is "unconstitutional conditions": was the individual's access to government benefits conditioned upon his renunciation of constitutional rights?[17]

Whatever the verbal formulation, the premise remains the same: the Constitution enters at the point where the state constricts the individual's freedom to pursue protected private activity. But when the state simply declines to confer a benefit upon an individual, it is far less clear when or if constitutional principles apply. An example: it is obvious that my first amendment rights are not violated if the government refuses to provide me with a copy of *Ulysses*. Even if I am indigent, no one else will give me the book, and the government's refusal has the practical effect of denying me the opportunity to read it. The result will be no different even if the state institutes, then discontinues, a program of "*Ulysses* for the poor"; the mere fact that the government decides to provide a particular benefit does not create any vested right to its continued availability.

Yet, it is frightening to think that because something is a discretionary benefit in the first place, its denial on any grounds or in any circumstance has no constitutional significance. The Constitution, after all, imposes virtually no affirmative obligations upon the states.[18] A state is probably required to establish a judicial system, and perhaps to provide police protection, but that is about it. Virtually every other service that government offers could be characterized as a privilege, in the sense that the government could withdraw it entirely. If the characterization of a government program as a privilege or gratuity removes it entirely from constitutional scrutiny, then government possesses almost infinite power to control and manipulate every aspect of our daily lives.

In fact, as government expands its role in the lives of citizens—supplying food, jobs, travel, communication, information, housing, student loans—it can no longer plausibly be contended that their loss is simply the loss of a "windfall." Questions concerning the dispersal of government largesse that once were at the periphery of constitutional adjudication today lie at its core.

My worry is that the Supreme Court, especially in recent years, has dealt with these issues in mechanical, even casual, ways, that cumulatively could significantly diminish our constitutional protections from arbitrary or even malevolent government action or inaction. In two groups of cases—those in which the Court considers alleged "unconstitutional conditions" that have been imposed on the delivery of government services or benefits, and those in which the Court tries to define government actions giving rise to procedural protections under the due process clause of the fourteenth amendment—the Court has developed a highly formalistic jurisprudence. It applies constitutional protections on the basis of whether the government withholds a service or benefit awarded to others or effectively takes away something from a citizen that belonged to him to begin with. This distinction means little in the real world; it now means everything in constitutional terms. How did we arrive at this paradox?

I. Unconstitutional Conditions

A. Historical Evolution of the Problem

At the turn of the century, prevailing doctrine held that access to government benefit programs was a privilege which the state could grant or withhold on virtually any terms it chose. In *McAuliffe v. Mayor of New Bedford* in 1892,[19] Justice Holmes, while still on the Massachusetts Supreme Judicial Court, rejected a policeman's challenge to his dismissal for violation of a regulation limiting his political activities.[20] Said Holmes, "The petitioner may have a constitutional right to talk politics, but he has no constitutional right to be a policeman."[21] In one sense, Holmes's analysis was stunningly unresponsive. McAuliffe had not contended that he had a constitutional right to be a policeman. His claim was that his constitutional right to freedom of speech was infringed by his dismissal. Holmes's rationale makes sense only if we accept a second, unspoken, premise: that an unconstitutional infringement of speech occurs only if the sanction for exercising free speech is the deprivation of some other right, such as the right to liberty or property, rather than just the denial of a government benefit.

In *Hamilton v. Regents of the University of California*,[22] forty-two years later, the Supreme Court echoed the same view. In that case, male students challenged on religious grounds the university's requirement that they complete a course in military science and tactics. "California," the Court held, "has not drafted or called them to attend the university. They are seeking education offered by the State and at the same time insisting that they be excluded from the prescribed course solely upon grounds of their religious beliefs and conscientious objections to war."[23] In the Court's view, California had satisfied the Constitution's requirements by affording its citizens a choice between adherence to religious beliefs and access to higher public education.

B. The Midcentury Shift

Yet, in 1958, less than twenty-five years later, the Supreme Court had acknowledged that constitutional difficulties may inhere in the selective provision or withdrawal of government largesse. In *Speiser v. Randall*,[24] the Court upheld a challenge to the state's denial of veterans' tax exemptions because the claimants refused to take an oath that they did not advocate the overthrow of the government by violent means. Rejecting the state's contention that the tax exemption was a mere privilege, and that its withdrawal therefore was not tantamount to a penalty on the exercise of the plaintiffs' freedom of expression, the Court said:

> To deny an exemption to claimants who engage in certain forms of speech is in effect to penalize them for such speech. Its deterrent effect is the same as if the State were to fine them for this speech. The appellees are plainly mistaken in their argument that, because a tax exemption is a "privilege" or "bounty," its denial may not infringe speech.[25]

Five years later, in *Sherbert v. Verner*,[26] the Court applied essentially the same reasoning to the claim of a Seventh-Day Adventist denied unemployment benefits by South Carolina because of her religiously based refusal to accept Saturday employment. The Court stated:

> Governmental imposition of such a choice puts the same kind of burden upon the free exercise of religion as would a fine imposed against appellant for her Saturday worship. . . . It is too late in the day to doubt that the liberties of religion and expression may be infringed by the denial of or placing of conditions upon a benefit or privilege.[27]

Although traces of the old "right" versus "privilege" distinction continued to linger,[28] by 1968 the Court seemed to have shifted from its earlier broad-based approval of unlimited conditions on government benefits. That year, in a widely cited article in the *Harvard Law Review*, Professor William W. Van Alstyne proclaimed "The Demise of the Right-Privilege Distinction in Constitutional Law."[29] And in 1971, in *Graham v. Richardson*,[30] the Supreme Court declared that it had "rejected the concept that constitutional rights turn upon whether a governmental benefit is characterized as a 'right' or as a 'privilege.'"[31]

C. The Most Recent Trend

Since the 1970s, the pendulum has swung back once again. The Court has shown renewed reluctance to recognize that denial of a benefit can be tantamount to a penalty for exercising a protected right. While the Court has not stated explicitly that it is changing course, there has been a perceptible shift, with significant consequences.

In *Buckley v. Valeo* in 1976,[32] the Court struck down federal limits on campaign expenditures by political candidates and their organizations as violative of the first amendment. "In the free society ordained by our

Constitution," the Court said, "it is not the government, but the people . . . who must retain control over the quantity and range of debate on public issues in a political campaign."[33] But, almost without discussion, the Court held that such limitations could be enforced as a condition of a candidate's receipt of public financing. The Court asserted that "[j]ust as a candidate may voluntarily limit the size of the contributions he chooses to accept, he may decide to forgo private fundraising and accept public funding."[34] The Court made no effort to explain why a candidate should be compelled to make the choice between public funding and the exercise of constitutional rights, any more than Sherbert could be compelled to choose between her religion and unemployment compensation.

In *Maher v. Roe*,[35] the Court sustained a Connecticut law which provided state funding for childbirth but not for abortion, stating:

> The Connecticut regulation places no obstacles—absolute or otherwise— in the pregnant woman's path to an abortion. An indigent woman who desires an abortion suffers no disadvantage as a consequence of Connecticut's decision to fund childbirth; she continues as before to be dependent on private sources for the service she desires.[36]

Three years later, in *Harris v. McRae*,[37] the Court relied on the same reasoning in upholding a federal ban on funding for medically necessary abortions, asserting: "A refusal to fund protected activity, without more, cannot be equated with the imposition of a 'penalty' on that activity."[38] And in 1989 in *Webster v. Reproductive Health Services*,[39] the Court reaffirmed that same view with respect to the restrictive conditions a state could attach to the use of publicly funded hospital facilities or personnel for abortions.

Similarly, in *Selective Service System v. Minnesota Public Interest Research Group*,[40] the Court held that since no one has a right to federal student loan benefits, the government may condition such loans on the recipient's willingness to certify that he has registered for the draft;[41] this even though the fifth amendment would prevent the government from compelling anyone to say whether he is registered. Finally, in *South Dakota v. Dole*,[42] the Court held that even if Congress were barred by the twenty-first amendment from enacting a mandatory national drinking age, Congress could condition federal highway funding on a state's willingness to enact and enforce a drinking age of twenty-one years.[43] The Court noted that "the constitutional limitations on Congress when exercising its spending power are less exacting than those on its authority to regulate directly."[44]

Whether these decisions were ultimately right or wrong (I do disagree with some of them), I believe all of them would have been reasoned differently before 1970. The Court has continued to apply *Sherbert* in a narrow range of cases—those involving public benefits (generally unemployment compensation) from which members of particular religions are effectively excluded. But the Court has not given broad application to the more general insight on which *Sherbert* was based: the recognition that an individual who is deprived of government benefits as a result of constitutionally protected activity in effect has been penalized for his exercise of constitutional rights. Indeed, the Court has stated explicitly that *Sherbert* is "inapposite" in contexts other than religion clause claims.[45] In these less favored contexts, the Supreme Court has indicated that it will look far more skeptically at the likelihood of a constitutional violation if a "mere" denial of benefits is involved than if a bona fide right is involved.

D. An Alternative Approach

If government need not establish a benefits program at all, what is the constitutional harm or danger in denying benefits? One answer, of course, is coercion. As Professor Kathleen Sullivan pointed out in a recent article, through adroit manipulation of government largesse the state may coerce renunciation of constitutional rights in a way which it could not compel directly.[46] When conditions are attached to essential public benefits—benefits which citizens cannot, as a practical matter, do without—this reasoning seems particularly persuasive. Suppose, for example, that members of one political party were forbidden to obtain driver's licenses. The state, of course, is not constitutionally required to issue driver's licenses; nor does the law oblige any individual to obtain one. As a practical matter, though, the condition is plainly coercive: in our society, a "choice" between a driver's license and continued membership in the party amounts to very little choice at all.

But many—perhaps most—public benefits are not of this sort. Conditions placed on nonessential benefit programs are not likely to "coerce" an individual to forgo the exercise of a fundamental right. An example both demonstrates the limitations of the coercion rationale and suggests an alternative and, I think, ultimately stronger rationale for challenging the reinvigoration of the right-privilege distinction.

Suppose that a government program provided a grant of ten dollars to every citizen who signed a form attesting that she had not attended a religious service during the previous year. All of us would agree that such a program would be unconstitutional. But does the program have significant coercive potential? It does not seem likely that large numbers of churchgoers would forsake their religious tradition for ten dollars. Indeed, we can assume that most religious citizens would reject the condition and accordingly would be denied benefits that others received. And that is the infirmity in the scheme: the free exercise of religion results in disparate treatment and so is constitutionally suspect under equal protection guarantees of the fifth and fourteenth amendments. Why should the situation be any different when people are treated differently based on the exercise of other constitutionally protected freedoms?

I suggest that every constitutional right carries within it an equal protection norm and that any governmental program that limits or conditions benefits when a constitutional right is exercised creates a suspect category that must be justified under a heightened standard of review. The state should have to show that the denial of benefits to people who exercise constitutional rights is substantially related to important purposes of the benefit program itself. An equal protection type of analysis would avoid the deceptive, so-called neutral baseline of governmental inaction now used to identify an unconstitutional condition and would concentrate instead on whether there is a valid reason to distinguish between one who receives the benefit and one who does not.

The coercion rationale imbedded in the doctrine of unconstitutional conditions focuses concern on the individual who accepts the government's offer and forgoes the exercise of her constitutional rights. The equal protection approach, by contrast, focuses on the individual who engages in constitutionally protected activity and is thereby deprived of benefits which others receive. It recognizes that a deprivation of benefits others receive constitutes a penalty enforced only upon the exercise of constitutionally protected rights.

Of course, often an individual's legitimate qualifications for government largesse cannot be assessed accurately without consideration of his exercise of constitutional freedoms. To give an example: as a private citizen, I have a constitutional right to criticize the government's conduct of foreign policy. But if I am the National Security Advisor, my tenure is likely to be brief if I insist upon my right to decry the administration's geopolitical blunders. That government post, in short, can be conditioned on my willingness to forgo exercise of my constitutional right to speak out. In this sort of case, when an individual seeks government benefits despite the fact that his constitutionally protected activities render him unqualified, he is asking in effect that he be treated more favorably than other unqualified persons. It is then accurate to say that he is asking for a subsidy of his constitutional rights.

Frequently, of course, there may be honest disagreement concerning the relevance of constitutionally protected activity in light of a government program's underlying purpose. My concern is not with the Court's answer to this question in close cases, but with the fact that the Court fails to ask the question at all. The Court tends instead to assert that no constitutional right is implicated at all unless the government acts affirmatively to place an individual in a position worse than that he would have occupied if government had stayed out of the picture entirely.

Let me reiterate the difference between the present analysis used by the Court and my proposed equal protection approach by looking at some recent cases. In *Lyng v. International Union, UAW* in 1988,[47] the Court upheld a federal law which denied food stamps to any household whose members included a worker on strike. The plaintiff strikers argued that the food stamp denials unconstitutionally burdened their free association rights. Acknowledging that the right of association was implicated, the Court held that the denial of food stamps did not infringe upon that right in any way. It was simply a refusal to subsidize strikes by feeding the strikers, a justifiable way of preserving government "neutrality" in labor disputes.[48]

The Court found no coercion, observing that it was "exceedingly unlikely" that the statute would in fact have any real impact on the strikers' right of association because the strikers in all probability would not desert their picket lines for food stamps.[49] In the absence of an impact on the fundamental right of association, no heightened scrutiny was necessary, and it was enough that the food stamp restriction had some rational relationship to the goal of preserving government neutrality.

I seriously question whether the Court would have reached the same result if the statute had placed an explicit burden on the right of association. If, for example, the statute had placed a ten-dollar penalty on the exercise of the right, would the Court even have asked whether the ten-dollar penalty was likely to have a "substantial impact" on the right of association? Our intuition and even the opinion itself suggest that it would not.[50] It was the Court's initial characterization of the government action as the mere denial of a government benefit—or, if you will, mere inaction—that allowed the Court to make its evaluation, on a dubious empirical basis, that no burden on the right of association was involved and so to avoid the heightened equal protection scrutiny that I believe is required whenever government benefits are conditioned on the exercise of a constitutional right. Justice Marshall's dissent in *Lyng* pointed out that the norm in this country is that one who is out of work is entitled to receive food stamps, even one who leaves his job voluntarily for "good cause."[51]

In determining whether the government has penalized the right of association, or has simply denied strikers a subsidy, the relevant question is not whether the state has taken money from the striker's pocket, but whether striking workers are being treated equally with regard to nonstriking workers and, if not, how this different treatment relates to the aims of the food stamp program. On any basis of comparison, it would seem that striking workers are penalized by being treated worse than workers who leave their jobs for any other reason. The Court was able to conclude that no penalty was involved only by resorting implicitly to the right-privilege distinction: food stamps are, in effect, a gratuitous benefit; their withdrawal from individuals who engage in certain kinds of conduct therefore amounts to no more than a refusal to subsidize that conduct.

The little-noticed case of *Selective Service v. Minnesota Public Interest Research Group*[52] provides another example. In *Selective Service*, the Court upheld a federal statute which required applicants for financial assistance under Title IV of the Higher Education Act of 1965[53] to certify either that they had registered for the draft or that they were not legally required to do so. The Court first rejected the assertion that the Act imposed a punishment on nonregistrants (or, more precisely, on those who failed to complete the required form). The Court reasoned that "[n]o affirmative disability or restraint is imposed" because "the sanction is the mere denial of a noncontractual governmental benefit."[54] The Court then held that the statute did not violate the applicants' fifth amendment rights. Since no one was compelled to apply for Title IV assistance, no one was required to incriminate himself in a completed form and no coercion on the exercise of fifth amendment rights had taken place.

In the eyes of most Americans, it might seem hypocritical—certainly unsympathetic—for an individual to claim federal financial benefits while refusing to undertake even the minimal reciprocal gesture involved in draft registration. The case nevertheless has some disturbing implications. The fifth amendment bars the government from requiring a person, on pain of penalty, to state whether he has registered for the draft. The condition on student aid at issue in *Selective Service* can be distinguished from such a scheme only by its attachment to a request for "privileges." For a needy college student, however, denial of the federal aid otherwise available is in every meaningful sense a penalty.

Grave danger lies in the state's use of its power to grant or withhold public benefits as a means of coercing behavior which the state could not compel directly and which is logically unrelated to the benefit itself. The Court in *Selective Service* made an effort to establish such a nexus, but could only suggest tepidly that Congress did not wish federal money to be spent on lawbreakers. If that link were sufficient, then plainly the state could condition any public benefit on an individual's willingness to submit to interrogation about any unlawful activity, certainly a disturbing thought to those of us who hold a driver's license, use the postal service, or have children in the public schools. An equal protection analysis, on the other hand, would have focused the Court's attention on whether there was a substantial justification for conditioning student loans on the surrender of the fifth amendment privilege. Perhaps the answer would have come out the same—perhaps not—but almost certainly the Court would have had to go through a more intellectually satisfying process than insisting that denial of a student loan did not penalize the exercise of a right.

I conclude, then, that a denial of government benefits based on the exercise of a constitutional right should be recognized as the penalty it is, triggering heightened scrutiny to assure relevance to the aims of the program that provides the benefits. Unfortunately, the right-privilege/burden-benefit distinction that has steadily crept back into our law since the 1970s avoids any such test. Consequently, I fear its potential to extinguish, or at least seriously undermine, important constitutional rights through the irresistible powers of the government presence and the government purse.

II. Procedural Due Process

Let me turn briefly to the other area of the law where perhaps an even sharper line between rights and privileges has been drawn. This is in the Supreme Court's effort to define the range of government actions giving rise to procedural protections under the due process clause. The fourteenth amendment provides that "[n]o State [may] deprive any person of life, liberty, or property, without due process of law."[55] Until recent years, as Dean John Hart Ely has written, the law was "pretty clear and uncontroversial. The phrase 'life, liberty or property' was read as a unit and given an open-ended, functional interpretation, which meant that the government could-n't seriously hurt you without due process of law."[56] Recently, however, the Court has taken a far less generous approach, one anchored in state law. Though the fourteenth amendment due process cases explicitly repudiate the vocabulary of rights and privileges, the Court nevertheless implicitly holds that procedural protections are triggered only when the state deprives an individual of a constitutional or statutory right, but not when the state simply denies or withdraws a privilege.

Thus, in *Board of Regents v. Roth*,[57] the Court considered the claim of an untenured state university professor who was informed that his contract would not be extended. The plaintiff contended that the fourteenth amend-ment required the university to provide him with a hearing and with a no-tice of the reasons for his nonrenewal. The Court demurred. "'Liberty' and 'property,'" it said, "are broad and majestic terms. . . . For that reason, the Court has fully and finally rejected the wooden distinction between 'rights' and 'privileges' that once seemed to govern the applicability of procedural due process rights."[58] The plaintiff, the Court held, had no constitutionally protected property interest in continued employment. "To have a property interest in a benefit," the Court said, "a person clearly must have more than an abstract need or desire for it. He must have more than a unilateral ex-pectation of it. He must, instead, have a legitimate claim of entitlement to it."[59] Since under state law the professor did not have a contractual right to continued employment, no deprivation of liberty or property had occurred and the due process clause was inapplicable.

The Court's decision was hardly a renunciation of the right-privilege dis-tinction. It simply redefined the boundary between the two. It discarded the old notion that public employment was by its nature a privilege, substitut-ing the view that tenured public employment was a right and untenured public employment was a privilege. As an Article III judge, I would be the last person to assert the irrelevance of tenure. It seems strange to me, how-ever, that state contract law should define the scope of federal due process rights. The fourteenth amendment, after all, was intended as a limitation on the state's authority over individual citizens.

The Court's implicit use of the right-privilege distinction in resolving procedural due process claims has since been extended beyond the realm of employment decisions. The focus of the Court's inquiry has been on whether state law creates an "entitlement" to the benefit the individual de-sires. This inquiry, in turn, hinges on whether state law compels the benefit to be granted under specified conditions.

Thus, the Court has held that, since a state need not establish a parole system, due process protections obtain only if a state's parole laws say that a prisoner must be granted parole under certain circumstances, and not if the state's laws give the parole board discretion.[60] Similarly, due process does not protect prisoners from arbitrary decisions by state officials as to whether they can receive visitors, so long as the applicable regulations lack "explicitly mandatory language" stating that visitors must be admitted under stated conditions.[61]

This approach to procedural due process, it seems to me, is anomalous in several respects. First, as I have noted, it is odd to allow the state to decide which of its decisions will be subject to constitutional scrutiny. Second, the current focus on "explicitly mandatory language" creates perverse incentives: a state can avoid unwanted procedural obligations by phrasing its substantive criteria in vague or uncertain terms. Logic, however, suggests a contrary imperative: that procedural protections are especially important when the substantive standards for decision making are fuzzy.

Finally, there is something almost surreal about the notion that an individual's "liberty" is not implicated when the government decides whether he is to remain in jail. And the intuition is by no means quieted by Chief Justice Burger's observation in *Greenholtz v. Nebraska Penal Inmates* that a state need not establish a parole system at all.[62] While no one yet has articulated a comprehensive theory of the scope of "life, liberty, and property," neither text, history, nor logic compels the hypertechnical reading that the Court has in fact adopted. I would hope some day to see the Court redefine "life, liberty, and property" in more functional terms, so that the applicability of due process guarantees will hinge on the substantiality of the individual interest, not on whether a particular government benefit is denominated "a legitimate claim of entitlement" (that is, a right) or a "privilege under state law."

III. Ross *and* Deshaney *Redivivus*

So I come full circle to *Ross* and *DeShaney*, with which I started this essay. In these two cases, the Court first established that a particular class of benefits—protective services in *DeShaney*, peremptory challenges in *Ross*—was constitutionally gratuitous, and then concluded that the state's failure to provide the benefit to a particular individual on a particular occasion did not create a constitutional violation. The crucial step, in each case, was to define the state's action as a mere failure to provide assistance—a sin of omission perhaps, but not of constitutional dimension.

I have serious difficulty with the Court's choice of a starting point in *Ross*. It believed the neutral baseline to be zero peremptory challenges and so was not distressed by the defendant's failure to receive his full complement of nine. But even if we ignore the fact that Ross's prosecutor had the full use of nine peremptory challenges, and that the case therefore has the unique and highly troubling effect of allowing the prosecution more peremptories than the defense, I think the proper starting point was the defendant's normal entitlement under Oklahoma law to nine peremptory challenges. Unlike the ordinary defendant who was not faced with an erroneous refusal to disqualify a biased juror, Ross was forced to give up a peremptory challenge in order to exercise his constitutional right not to have a prejudiced juror sit on his jury. Within the context of Oklahoma's criminal justice system, Ross had a right to nine peremptory challenges. The elimination of even one such challenge was therefore a denial of equal protection. The Court never undertook such an analysis, however, because its classification of peremptory challenges as gratuities concluded its inquiry. The Court never looked at how those gratuities were being dispensed.

Similarly, in *DeShaney*, Winnebago County had no obligation to provide child protection services. But, as Justice Brennan's dissent pointed out, the county's relationship to Joshua cannot accurately be described as "inaction": the Department of Social Services plainly held itself out as the government agency responsible for investigating complaints of child abuse. Individuals who otherwise might have sought to protect Joshua, including officials in other government departments as well as concerned citizens, were encouraged to direct their concerns to the Department instead. Having taken on this responsibility, and having thereby preempted sources of aid that otherwise might have been available, the Department should not have been allowed to withdraw at the crucial moment and then portray its behavior as a mere failure to act.

In *DeShaney*, the Court asked the right question—had the state contributed in any way to Joshua's peril?—but, in my view, it gave the wrong answer. The Court stated that "[t]he most that can be said of the state functionaries in this case is that they stood by and did nothing when suspicious circumstances dictated a more active role for them."[63] The argument, in short, was that the county officials were guilty only of inaction. But, as I noted earlier, the state had not simply stayed out of the child-protection field; its affirmative acts appear to have increased Joshua's vulnerability. The

Court could conclude that this was a case of inaction only by focusing on a narrowly defined slice of time—the moment at which Joshua's father struck the crippling blows—and by ignoring the broader context produced by the sum of the state's actions.

Thus, the decisions in those two cases are grounded in the notion that government inaction is always neutral, hence constitutionally innocuous. In many instances, however, government inaction vis-à-vis a particular individual may be highly unneutral. The state may, as in *DeShaney,* purport to act neutrally when it declines to protect its citizens from dangers that its own deeds have exacerbated, but in reality it does not. Nor does it act neutrally when it denies one citizen benefits which others receive, as in *Ross.*

And so, to my conclusion. Despite repeated interment by courts and commentators, the right-privilege distinction continues powerfully to influence constitutional law in a variety of ways. The doctrine's seductive appeal, it seems to me, has its roots in two legendary national traits.

The first is the American veneration of self-sufficiency and rugged individualism. In America, the resolute need rely only on their own initiative. In this view, there is something faintly disreputable about reliance on government; and it is ungrateful, even mean-spirited, to seek government assistance and then complain about the terms.

The second, I think, is the desire to set limits on judicial intervention in the nation's affairs. To those who fear judicial overreaching, there is something frightening about the notion that the courts may hold the state liable for its failure to provide benefits. Such a concept, some fear, could invite judges to create their own versions of a utopian society, and then hold the state accountable if reality falls short of their ideal.

On the first point: at a time when the role of the state was highly restricted, there may have been some justification for treating a public benefit as a pure windfall, to be granted or denied on whatever terms the government chose. Today, however, no such view is plausible. The neediest of our citizens are most conspicuously dependent on government largesse for the satisfaction of their most basic needs. But even those of us who are comparatively self-sufficient could hardly function in the modern world without relying on services and institutions provided by government. Most of these services may be gratuitous in a literal sense, but if their allocation were truly unconstrained by constitutional norms, there would be very little left of our liberties.

To say that public benefits are no longer windfalls because we all depend upon them is, however, to tell only half the story. It should also be said that public benefits are not windfalls because we have earned them; we support the state with our taxes. Our contributions to government do not, of course, give any of us an entitlement to whatever services we might deem desirable. These contributions do, however, give us the right to insist that public benefits be distributed in a manner consonant with constitutional principles.

When an individual contends that he has improperly been denied benefits which others receive, his claim cannot accurately be characterized as a challenge to government inaction. The old view was that the state's "greater" power to abolish a program entirely must necessarily include the "lesser" power to set any kind of condition for participation. A more illuminating perspective, however, was suggested by Justice Jackson's statement that "there is no more effective practical guaranty against arbitrary and unreasonable government than to require that the principles of law which officials would impose upon a minority must be imposed generally."[64] Justice Jackson's insight was that the greater—the more complete and the more dangerous—power is the power to grant benefits selectively, to favor some individuals and not others. Courts quite properly may place constitutional limits on this power without questioning the state's authority to refuse or even eliminate benefit programs entirely.

The Supreme Court is a busy place; it is not always clear, as one surveys its output of a hundred and fifty cases per year, that its members have had real opportunity to see beyond the case at hand to its effects upon the doctrine or body of national law. Some, I think, do write for the future, or perhaps more accurately to reverse the past, in selective areas. Others appear to react more to the equities of the case before them. Judges of lower courts like mine not only follow Supreme Court precedent as best we can, but rule on the basis of our predictions as to how the Supreme Court will act in a particular situation. That, I believe, puts upon the academics of our nation a heavy burden that judges cannot always share: to step back and take the long look, risk the odious taunt of digging up old and lost causes rather than launching brilliant new theories, retrace steps that should not have been taken in the first place.

NOTES

1. W. Shakespeare, *Hamlet*, Act III, sc. i, lines 80–81 (Riverside ed. 1974).
2. 109 S.Ct. 998 (1989).
3. 42 U.S.C. § 1983 (1988).

4. See *DeShaney*, 109 S.Ct. at 1001–2.

5. See Mansnerus, "Limits to the Duty to Rescue," N.Y. Times, Feb. 26, 1989, § 4, at 24.

6. See *DeShaney*, 109 S.Ct. at 1007.

7. Id. at 1003.

8. See id.

9. 108 S.Ct. 2273 (1988).

10. See id. at 2276.

11. See id. at 2280.

12. Id. at 2279 (citation omitted).

13. Id. at 2279–80.

14. 109 S.Ct. at 1006. The Court held that failure by the state to provide care and protection would rise to the level of constitutional harm only where the state imposed limitations on an individual's freedom to act and then failed to provide for the individual's needs. See id.

15. See, e.g., *Barsky v. Board of Regents*, 347 U.S. 442, 451 (1954).

16. See, e.g., *Flemming v. Nestor*, 363 U.S. 603, 617 (1960).

17. See, e.g., *Sherbert v. Verner*, 374 U.S. 398, 404 (1963).

18. See, e.g., *Youngberg v. Romeo*, 457 U.S. 307, 317 (1982) ("As a general matter, a State is under no constitutional duty to provide substantive services for those within its border."); *Harris v. McRae*, 448 U.S. 297, 317–18 (1980) (state need not provide such funds as may be necessary to exercise constitutionally protected freedoms).

19. 155 Mass. 216, 29 N.E. 517 (1892).

20. See id. at 220, 29 N.E. at 517–18.

21. Id., 29 N.E. at 517.

22. 293 U.S. 245 (1934).

23. Id. at 262.

24. 357 U.S. 513 (1958).

25. Id. at 518.

26. 374 U.S. 398 (1963).

27. Id. at 404.

28. See *Flemming v. Nestor*, 363 U.S. 603 (1960). In *Flemming*, the Court upheld a federal statute withdrawing Social Security benefits because of the claimant's prior membership in the Communist Party. "Here the sanction is the mere denial of a noncontractual governmental benefit," the Court held. "No affirmative disability or restraint is imposed." Id. at 617.

29. 81 Harv. L. Rev. 1439 (1968).

30. 403 U.S. 365 (1971) (per curiam).

31. Id. at 374.

32. 424 U.S. 1 (1976).

33. Id. at 57 (footnote omitted).

34. Id. at 57 n.65.

35. 432 U.S. 464 (1977).

36. Id. at 474.

37. 448 U.S. 297 (1980).

38. Id. at 317 n.19.

39. 109 S.Ct. 3040 (1989).

40. 468 U.S. 841 (1984).

41. See id. at 852–53.

42. 483 U.S. 203 (1987).

43. See id. at 211–12.

44. Id. at 209.

45. See *Lyng v. International Union, UAW*, 109 S.Ct., 1184, 1191 n.7 (1988). Indeed, while this article was in proofs, the Court suggested strongly that even in the context of religion clause claims, *Sherbert* has no application outside the specific field of unemployment compensation and perhaps other programs that "len[d themselves] to individualized governmental assessment of the reasons for the relevant conduct." *Employment Div., Dep't of Human Resources v. Smith*, 58 U.S.L.W. 4433, 4436 (U.S. 1990).

46. See Kathleen Sullivan, "Unconstitutional Conditions," 102 Harv. L. Rev. 1413 (1988).

47. 108 S.Ct. 1184 (1988).

48. Id. at 1191–93.

49. Id. at 1189.

50. See id. at 1190 n.5.

51. Id. at 1196–97.

52. 468 U.S. 841 (1984).

53. 20 U.S.C. § § 1070–1101 (1988).

54. 468 U.S. at 853 (quoting *Flemming v. Nestor*, 363 U.S. 603, 617 (1960)).

55. U.S. Const. amend. XIV, § 1.

56. J. Ely, *Democracy and Distrust* 19 (1980) (footnote omitted).

57. 408 U.S. 564 (1972).

58. Id. at 571.

59. Id. at 577.

60. See *Greenholtz v. Nebraska Penal Inmates*, 442 U.S. 1, 11 (1979).

61. *Kentucky Dept. of Corrections v. Thompson*, 109 S.Ct. 1904, 1907–8 (1989).

62. See *Greenholtz*, 442 U.S. at 7.

63. See *DeShaney v. Winnebago County Dep't of Social Servs.*, 109 S.Ct. 998, 1007 (1989).

64. *Railway Express Agency v. New York*, 336 U.S. 106, 112 (1949) (Jackson, J., concurring).

Chapter 2

Racism in American and South African Courts

Similarities and Differences

A. Leon Higginbotham, Jr.

More than a century ago, William Goodell observed that: "No people . . . were ever yet found who were better than their laws, though many have been known to be worse."[1] Similarly, I submit that in the United States and in South Africa, the justice that blacks, the powerless, and the near power-less encounter in the daily events of their lives is no better, and is probably worse, than the experiences they encounter in their courts.

In this article, I have chosen the issue of racism in the courts because the courts, in any society, should exemplify the nation's best and most just virtues. "Equal justice under the law" is what most civilized societies claim to offer their citizens. Yet if there is racism—patent or implicit—present in the very courts that dispense justice, the probability is that the entire soci-ety is far more oppressive than the racism revealed in their adjudicatory processes. Courts enforce racism in two different factual contexts: (1) those in which the judge chooses to act in a racist fashion in making discretionary decisions in areas that have not been preempted by any command of statute or precedent; and (2) those instances where the judge is applying substan-tive law that requires the court to treat a person in a racially adverse fashion, that is, in areas where even a nonracist judge is imposing racial oppression mandated by the state. While analytically each of these contexts is some-

This lecture was delivered on March 11, 1986, and appeared in 65 N.Y.U.L. Rev. 479 (1990).

what different, the consequence to the victim is just as pernicious whether the racism is that of the judge, the legislature, or binding precedent.

In this article, I will focus primarily on racism in the South African and American courts in order to consider how the two judicial systems reflect or reject the ideologies of apartheid and Jim Crow, respectively. My study also aims to assess the importance of the Bill of Rights and of constitutional supremacy as mechanisms for combating racism.

My analysis of both the South African and U.S. courts will reveal numerous cases where trial judges have practiced or tolerated racist behavior in their courtrooms. After discussing how these specific instances of judicial racism are symbols, symptoms, and signals of racism in the broader context of South African and American society, I consider how these decisions reveal both the virtues and the inadequacies of a Bill of Rights as a means of eradicating some forms of racism in courts. Unlike in South Africa, with its doctrine of parliamentary supremacy, blacks could appeal to the Constitution when racism appeared in the American courts. On occasion, these appeals have been successful, even at a time when the Southern states, where these cases generally arose, were not willing to give up any other portions of the reign of Jim Crow. However, I conclude that constitutional protections are ultimately of limited efficacy. The courts can serve as the vanguard for social change and as a beacon in dark times, but used as the sole tool, they cannot eradicate societal racism.[6]

I. The Difficulty in Comparing the Racial Histories of the United States and South Africa

Apartheid is a system of racial segregation, discrimination, or oppression in housing, employment, public accommodation, health care, freedom of association, freedom of speech, and education. As in the United States before *Brown v. Board of Education*[12] and its attendant changes, these forms of segregation serve, among other functions, as ways to stigmatize black people as less than fully human.

In addition, apartheid involves the systematic deprivation of political power and the economic opportunity that forms its basis. In South Africa, blacks are deprived of the right to vote, and, until [1990], many black political parties and organizations were either banned outright or had their activities severely restricted.[16] Furthermore, the existence of a government-imposed state of emergency from June 1986 to June 1990, marked by mass detentions and police beatings of demonstrators and detainees, prevented grassroots political action.

Apartheid also severely limits blacks' economic opportunities, further constricting their political power. Widespread job discrimination, in addition to residence laws, substantially restricts the work options of blacks. The provision of substandard education to nonwhites further ensures continued economic deprivation in a technological society.

[T]here is a high risk of superficiality in comparing two separate countries during different eras. Although there are similarities in the racial experiences of the two countries, these similarities must be viewed in light of the differences between the populations, demographics, economics, religions, cultures, and histories of the United States and South Africa.

Most significantly, in the United States whites have always been dominant in number as well as in economic and political power; blacks have constituted a minority of generally less than 15 percent in number and substantially less than that in power. In his famous dissent denouncing the "separate but equal" doctrine set forth in *Plessy v. Ferguson*, Justice Harlan stressed the fact that blacks were no threat to whites. He asserted: "Sixty millions of whites are in no danger from the presence here of eight millions of blacks."[36]

In contrast, whites in South Africa have always been a distinct numerical minority, constituting only 16 percent of the population, whereas Africans[38] constitute approximately 74 percent of the population.[39] Nevertheless, with the current turmoil in South Africa, whites retain political, military, and economic control of the country: whites run the government, establish social policy, and dominate business as well as the economy as a whole.

The variations in government policies concerning race relations over the past two centuries present another major difficulty in comparing the United States and South Africa. Unlike South Africa, where the government has a uniform policy of apartheid, the United States has not had a national policy on race relations. It is impossible to speak of a monolithic policy applied in all the states because of the different degrees of oppression that have existed in the fifty states. [Nevertheless,] valid and instructive comparisons [exist] between the South African courts of the past sixty years and American courts prior to the 1970s. The forces that have enforced the systemic oppression of blacks in both countries at these different time periods have been similar enough to make for a useful cross-cultural, cross-temporal comparison.

Such an analysis also reminds us that the legal process reflects both the human penchant of some members of a society to dominate others and the desire of others to use the law as a powerful vehicle on the "road to freedom" for all. The history of the effort to eradicate discrimination and injustice in the United States is replete with examples of how the law can be used both to perpetuate and eliminate racial injustice. Such examples will be instructive for those in both America and South Africa who seek to create more just societies.

II. Racism in the Courts: The South African and American Experiences

Before one word of evidence is presented in a trial and before one case is cited in an argument, several symbolic processes within a court deliver messages to those present. Architecturally, the judge sits in a higher position than the spectators—suggesting that the seat from which the judge presides is somewhat like an altar for one anointed with a special status and placed at a higher level to dispense justice adequately to the litigants "below." The command that "all rise for the court," as the robed figure enters, suggests again that the judge is entitled to celebratory recognition and thus the spectators cannot continue sitting as if some mere mortal has arrived. A judicially enforced racial segregation or denigration within the courtroom is another powerful symbol demonstrating which groups are viewed as dominant and which as inferior in the eyes of the law.

[The remainder of section II has been summarized for reasons of space. In this section, Judge Higginbotham provides a detailed comparative review of racist incidents and practices in South African and American courtrooms. In his discussion of South Africa, Higginbotham cites the segregation of lawyers and spectators as one of the most visible intrusions of apartheid into the courtroom. He focuses on the case of Godfrey Pitje, a young black lawyer who was charged with contempt for not sitting at the table for nonwhite practitioners. Pitje challenged the validity of the order, but the contempt conviction was eventually sustained as a matter "largely within [the] discretion of the judge"(see *R. v. Pitje*, 1960 (4) S.A. 709 (A.D.)). For Higginbotham, the case represents not only a clear case of racial stigmatization, but an example of how courts use seemingly neutral legal language and code words such as "discretion" as a mask for racism. Higginbotham also discusses the indignities faced by black witnesses, who unlike white witnesses, are routinely addressed by first name only, as if they were servants.

[In a series of examples with pernicious consequences, Higginbotham also shows how evidence given by blacks is discounted or disbelieved, with judges in bench trials characterizing blacks as foolish and prone to lie. Other racist judicial practices Higginbotham cites include the endorsement by the bench of racially derogatory myths, such as blacks having a greater propensity for violence, or the belief that black women submit more easily to rape than their white counterparts. A final example of discriminatory treatment involves the measurement of damages, and the higher value given to white life than to black life, which in Higginbotham's words "wreaks injustice in individual cases and publicly legitimizes the racist mythology that underlies these devaluations."

[Higginbotham finds that the experience of blacks in American courtrooms, particularly in the pre-civil rights period, has many parallels with South Africa. Examples of overt discrimination included segregated spectator seating, whites-only courthouse cafeterias, and segregated bathrooms. As in South Africa, black witnesses in the United States were not accorded the same civilities as whites, often being addressed by first name only. All these practices functioned as public statements of the inferiority of African Americans. Although Higginbotham cites examples of the Supreme Court striking down these practices as violations of equal protection, he points out that lower courts frequently used doctrines of standing or other legal devices to refuse to give these constitutional victories practical effect. Other insidious courtroom practices included attacks by counsel on the credibility of blacks as witnesses and defendants, and prosecutorial appeals to racial stereotypes, such as blacks' purported greater propensity to violence and black hatred of whites—examples of prosecutorial misconduct that often went unchecked by judges.]

III. Racism and Society: Racism in the Courts as Symptoms, Signals, and Symbols of Racism in the Broader Society

These instances of racism are more than mere aberrations or isolated blemishes that occasionally crop up and mar the normally effective dispensation of justice. Rather, they are symptoms, signals, and symbols of racism in the broader society.[341] When racism occurs in the courts, it is symptomatic of racist attitudes, myths, and assumptions that constitute the ideology of societal racism. Such instances of courtroom racism also act as signals, in that they trigger and mobilize those racist attitudes and stereotypes in the minds of all the courtroom participants, and may affect the judgment and actions of the judge, jury, and attorneys at this and other junctures in the case. Finally, racist occurrences in the courts are particularly powerful symbols, acting to reinforce, legitimate, and perpetuate racism in the broader society.

Reflecting on the American experience, Professor Charles Lawrence III has developed a theory of racism as the systemic imputation of stigma onto African Americans through the courts and through extralegal actions.[342] As he explains, racism is part of the common cultural heritage of all Americans. According to Lawrence, racism is a group of assumptions about the world and its inhabitants that are expressed, often unconsciously, in a "mutually reinforcing and pervasive pattern of stigmatizing actions that cumulate to compose an injurious whole that is greater than the sum of its parts." These assumptions are based on notions, explicit or implicit, of African Americans as dirty, lazy, oversexed, in poor control of their ids, and otherwise less than fully human. Indeed, such assumptions give rise to behavior, such as the establishment of race-segregated housing and bathrooms that dramatize white stereotypes of African Americans as impure, contaminating, or untouchable. Similarly, the use of devices that reduce the number of black policemen, or that challenge the competency of black professors or managers, reinforces a cultural message that whites should be in positions of authority over blacks. While, as Lawrence's article demonstrates, these cultural messages can be decoded, they are often tacit, or even unconscious.

Although Lawrence analyzed cultural racism in the United States, his theoretical framework can be applied just as productively to an analysis of cultural racism in South Africa.

A. Racism in the Courtroom as a Symptom of Societal Racism

Courts do not dispense justice in sterile isolation, unaffected by the prevailing political, social, and moral attitudes and currents of the broader society in which they operate. Judges, prosecutors, and other lawyers in South Africa and the United States are not immune to the unconscious influence of—and may even consciously subscribe to—the group of negative stigmatizing assumptions that Lawrence describes as characteristic of the ideology of racism. Thus, the broader societal racism may, consciously or unconsciously, infect the attitudes and behavior of judges and lawyers in the courtroom.[350]

For instance, the South African judges who took judicial notice of the "fact" that black women submit to rape more readily than white women were reflecting the racist cultural myth that black women are more submissive than white women. Similarly, the practice of prosecutors to prey on white fears of black rapists in the United States is symptomatic of the racist cultural stereotype, identified by Lawrence, that, compared to whites, blacks are more violent, less self-controlled, and more prone to rape women (particularly white women).

The comment by Judge Rumpff, while Chief Justice of the South African Supreme Court, that black males often stab people for no reason, "except for an apparent lust for stabbing,"[353] is symptomatic of a societal assumption that black males are inherently violent, a cornerstone of the racist ideology underlying the policies of apartheid consistently used to oppose reform or any form of power-sharing with blacks. Likewise, U.S. prosecutors' appeals to white fears of violence by blacks reflect racist stereotypes of blacks as being prisoners of their urges and therefore more violent than whites.

In describing courtroom racism as a symbol, my point is not simply that on particular occasions judges and lawyers have participated in the racism of their society. By seeing these discrete actions as symptomatic, one recognizes that an underlying racist ideology is present and likely to affect the judgment and behavior of the judge or lawyer in other instances. By presuming that all black alibi witnesses are liars and declaring that all blacks have an "inherent[ly] foolish . . . character," the South African judge in *S. v. Xhego*[354] is reflecting broad-based racist assumptions about blacks. Those assumptions, most certainly, extend beyond the issue of the reliability of black witnesses in this trial: They will affect the manner in which the judge treats black criminal defendants, civil litigants, and lawyers in every case for which he sits, although he may not always make obvious the effects of this racism in so blatant a declaration. Likewise, when counsel in American courts attack the credibility of black witnesses and defendants by appealing to racist stereotypes and assumptions that blacks are inherently more untrustworthy, and more prone to lie for their own race than are whites, broader cultural racism is likely infecting their perceptions and actions beyond issues of credibility.

B. Racism in the Courtroom as a Signal of Societal Racism

A second important effect of the fact that instances of racism in the courtroom are symptomatic of broader societal racism is the indication that racial bias affects other courtroom participants besides the judge or lawyer who makes a racist declaration. Instances of racism in the courtroom tap into the ideology of societal racism. A racist remark or insinuation by a judge or prosecutor acts as a signal, triggering and mobilizing a host of attitudes and assumptions that may be consciously held, or unconsciously harbored, by the judge, jury, and lawyers in the courtroom. The effect of the racist act or statement can permeate beyond its immediate context by tripping other racist assumptions at other junctures in the proceeding.

The actions of the judge in the *Pitje* case, Magistrate Dormehl, exemplify this effect. By requiring Mr. Pitje to utilize a separate counsel table reserved for "non-Europeans," he sent a signal to all in the courtroom that, in his mind, blacks and colored people are fundamentally different than and inferior to all other human beings, and ought to be accorded disfavorable treatment.[355]

In the United States, segregated courthouse restrooms, cafeterias, and spectator seating also acted as signals. In these cases, all participants, particularly juries in criminal or civil trials involving a black defendant or litigant, were constantly reminded that blacks were to be accorded inferior status in this society. Every time they walked into a courtroom, jurors and spectators were presented with a ringing affirmation of the assumptions, myths, and attitudes that compose the ideology of racism in the United States.

C. Racism in the Courtroom as Cultural Symbolism

In addition to acting as signals for those participants in the courtroom, instances of racism in the courts also send signals beyond the confines of any particular courtroom and affect society at large. The judicial system is charged with interpreting, upholding, and enforcing the law. Since most societies claim to offer their citizens equal justice under the law, the courts are the presumed repositories of equality and the solemn fora for the just adjudication of the law without regard to race, creed, color, appearance, or any other categorical distinction. Because of this role, instances of racism in the courtroom are particularly powerful symbols that act to legitimate, reinforce, and perpetuate the culture of racism operating in society as a whole.

By holding that it was "reasonable" for Magistrate Dormehl to require Mr. Pitje to be seated at a separate counsel table reserved for "non-Europeans," the South African Appellate Division was sending a powerful signal that the judicial system, a body which theoretically dispenses equal treatment to all those before it, views blacks as fundamentally different, inferior creatures, such that it is "reasonable" to accord them disparate treatment within the court's solemn walls. As a symbol, this form of segregation acts to legitimate, reinforce, and perpetuate the system and structures of apartheid.

Similarly, when courthouses in the southern United States maintained segregated restrooms, cafeterias, and spectator sections in courtrooms, the solemn fora of equality before the law and equal protection by the law, they sent a symbolic message that legitimated, reinforced, and perpetuated the segregation that was a way of life in the post-*Plessy* South and helped to justify the ideology of racism underlying its existence and enforcement.

When judges in South Africa discounted the evidence of black defendants and witnesses and took judicial notice of "facts" based upon racist myths, they indicated that the ideology of racism at the heart of the system of apartheid is so obviously true as to extend beyond judicial inquiry. By announcing that the courts ought to refrain from dispensing equal justice, these judges led their own legal system, and their own people, away from the idea of the rule of law.

Likewise, in the United States, when judges overruled defense objections to prosecutors' racist actions, the courts symbolically were affirming the racist myths and stereotypes of black untrustworthiness, dishonesty, lack of control, and proclivity to violence and rape (especially toward whites). By so doing, the courts helped to perpetuate the racist ideology of which these attitudes were a part.

IV. Racism and the Systemic Differences between the American and South African Judicial Systems

A. Differences in Civil Rights for Blacks in the United States and South Africa: The Importance of the Bill of Rights and the Civil War Amendments

The major difference between the judicial systems of the United States and South Africa is the stark difference in the substantive civil rights accorded to blacks in South Africa, with its laws of apartheid and concomitant lack of bill of rights, and those accorded to blacks in the United States, with its Bill of Rights, thirteenth, fourteenth, and fifteenth amendments, and related civil rights legislation.

The South African constitution contains no bill of rights, and the South African Parliament is supreme and free to establish any act that encroaches on the life, liberty, or property of any individual. Indeed, the result of this legislative supremacy is the intricate structure of apartheid: laws that systematically achieve racial segregation, discrimination, and oppression in nearly all realms of life, including political and economic rights, education, housing, employment, freedom of association, and freedom of speech. Blacks in contemporary South Africa have few, if any, rights that the apartheid regime respects.

Prior to the passage of the thirteenth, fourteenth, and fifteenth amendments, blacks in the United States had, as Chief Justice Taney described, "no rights which the white man was bound to respect."[365] The indispensable importance of the thirteenth, fourteenth, and fifteenth amendments for establishing equal rights for blacks is illustrated by the inability of civil rights-minded judges to promote racial justice in the U.S. judiciary prior to the passage of these amendments. Particularly instructive are decisions in fugitive slave cases where antislavery judges felt compelled to enforce the fugitive slave clause of the Constitution[366] and the Fugitive Slave Acts.[367]

However, after the passage of the thirteenth, fourteenth, and fifteenth amendments, and the related civil rights acts, significant differences emerged in the legal processes of the two countries, in that blacks in the United States were provided many de jure rights that blacks in South Africa are still denied.

B. The Importance of Judicial Review in the United States for the Promotion of Racial Social Justice

1. The United States

A. THE ROLE OF JUDICIAL REVIEW IN PROMOTING
RACIAL JUSTICE

Unlike in South Africa, where the judiciary is subordinate to Parliament, in the United States the Constitution is the supreme law of the land and the U.S. Supreme Court has the ultimate authority, and the duty, to interpret the Constitution, to nullify acts of Congress and state legislatures, and to reverse state court decisions that conflict with the Constitution.

The supremacy of the Constitution and the Supreme Court's power of judicial review have allowed the federal courts in the United States to play a key role in establishing and vindicating the rights of blacks and other minority and powerless groups. During the twentieth century in particular, the power to invalidate federal and state legislation and other governmental actions became one of the most important legal resources for black

Americans seeking to eradicate racial discrimination and to obtain true equality.

The Supreme Court has reversed some of the most racist decisions issued by state courts.[379] Recall, for example, that despite the hostility of the Alabama and Virginia state courts, the Supreme Court rulings in *Hamilton v. Alabama*[380] and *Johnson v. Virginia*[381] demonstrate that the Constitution can be, and often has been, a bulwark of liberty for blacks when fairly construed by the Supreme Court. Moreover, when state appellate courts have reversed lower courts' racist judgments, their holdings of law have been predicated on the federal Constitution rather than on that of the state. Thus, to the extent that we have experienced racial justice, the catalyst most often has been the U.S. Constitution, as construed by the Supreme Court.

B. THE LIMITS OF THE JUDICIAL SYSTEM IN PROMOTING SOCIAL CHANGE FOR RACIAL JUSTICE

While it had the same constitutional tools at its disposal as did the *Brown* Court decades later, the Supreme Court chose to limit the effect of the fourteenth amendment in the *Slaughter-House Cases*[386] and *Civil Rights Cases*.[387] In addition, the Court sanctioned the "separate but equal" doctrine in *Plessy v. Ferguson*,[388] which bolstered and legitimated the near-apartheid conditions in the American South during Reconstruction and provided the foundation for segregation statutes in the United States for more than fifty years.

The Supreme Court's decisions in the *Civil Rights Cases* and *Plessy* were symptomatic and symbolic of the broader social and political climate of the post-Reconstruction era. As Derrick Bell comments:

> In the final decades of the nineteenth century, American courts had become first the espousers and then the creators and propagators of a conservative ideology that permeated all aspects of American life. . . .
>
> Within this framework, racial law became an important conduit for the preservation and legitimation of the established order. Shaken by fears of a powerful coalition of white Populists and blacks, white conservatives in the South turned to disenfranchisement as well as legal separation in social and economic spheres. Race distinction, an instrument of popular suppression in other eras of American history, was once more brought forth by an elite wishing to maintain power. Here too, the courts were the espousers of conservative sentiment. Though eager to countermand state regulation in the economic realm, the justices were satisfied to leave state regulation of race relations untrammeled during these years.[390]

It would be decades before the political and social environment was ripe for the separate but equal doctrine of *Plessy* to be abandoned. As Lewis Steel noted in 1968,[391] there were many factors in the post-World War II United States that created a climate conducive to a reinterpretation of the four-teenth amendment. First, blacks in the armed services often had experienced integrated military units, and returned from World War II ready to fight for equal rights at home. Second, the expectations of blacks who had stayed at home during the war had been raised by the skilled jobs for which many had been trained because of wartime labor shortages. Further, the war against Nazi Germany had heightened sensitivity to the full implications of racism. In addition, the United States wanted to raise its image with third world countries from whom the United States was seeking loyalty and trade arrangements as a consequence of the emerging Cold War. Finally, many re-alized that the South could not be industrialized, modernized, and fully transformed from a rural, agrarian society if rigid, state-sponsored segrega-tion was maintained.

While the promotion of racial justice by the courts normally reflects currents of social change already afoot in the broader society, the impor-tance of the courts as a medium for affecting social change in the United States, as opposed to South Africa, should not be underestimated. While there were a number of political and social factors that provided a favor-able climate for overturning *Plessy* in 1954, its doctrine of "separate but equal" may never have been overturned had it not been for the concerted litigation strategy undertaken by the NAACP. Even before the social and political climate was ripe for the *Brown* decision, the NAACP obtained a series of decisions in the "graduate school cases"[397] which laid the foun-dation for *Brown* without addressing the constitutionality of *Plessy*'s "separate but equal" doctrine. The stage was finally set when the four state public school cases brought by the NAACP were consolidated in *Brown v. Board of Education.*

While the *Brown* Court did not expressly overturn *Plessy*, holding only "that in the field of public education, the doctrine of 'separate but equal' has no place," the Court subsequently cited *Brown*, often in per curiam or-ders, when holding segregation in a wide variety of public facilities uncon-stitutional. Of course, *Brown* did not reach the great bulk of privately owned segregated facilities in the South. In fact, only after a protracted campaign of litigation, civil disobedience, boycotts, and sustained agitation conducted by the NAACP, the Student Non-Violent Coordinating Com-mittee, the Southern Christian Leadership Conference, and charismatic leaders including Martin Luther King, Jr., Malcolm X and others,[401] did Congress enact the landmark civil rights legislation of the 1960s.

In 1969, I served on the President's Commission on the Causes and Prevention of Violence, convened to report on the racial unrest and violence experienced throughout the nation's urban centers during the 1960s. Seven of the Commission's thirteen members could not accept that nonviolent civil disobedience had a role to play in the struggle for racial justice and social change, concluding instead that litigants should initiate test cases to make constitutional challenges and "all other dissenters should abide by the law involved until it is declared unconstitutional."[403] I issued the following statement as part of the Commission's minority:

> Recent advances in the field of civil rights have not come about—and could never have come about—solely through judicial tests made "by one individual" while all others in the silent black majority waited for the ultimate constitutional determination.
>
> Rather, the major impetus for the Civil Rights Acts of 1957, 1960, 1964 and 1965, which promised more equal access to the opportunities of our society, resulted from the determination, the spirit, and the nonviolent commitment of the many who continually challenged the constitutionality of racial discrimination and awakened the national conscience.[404]

2. South Africa

A. THE ROLE OF PARLIAMENTARY SUPREMACY

Despite the South African government's insistence that its judiciary is independent,[407] the South African courts are fundamentally different institutions from their American counterparts. The South African judiciary, rather than providing a possible mechanism for loosening the strangling grip of apartheid and moving the country toward a democratic and racially just future, is instead a major part of the problem. In contrast to the U.S. system of constitutional rule, a parliamentary system rules South Africa. The constitution of the Republic of South Africa of 1983 is itself an act of Parliament, and therefore subject to parliamentary repeal or modification.[409] Similarly, it contains no bill of rights, and specifically provides, in Section 34B, that "no court of law shall be competent to inquire into or to pronounce upon the validity of an Act of Parliament."[410]

Although the doctrine of parliamentary supremacy prevents any South African court from declaring invalid an act of Parliament, the courts are still permitted to set aside laws enacted by subordinate legislatures where they are "unreasonable."[411] This doctrine allows a South African court to strike down proclamations issued by the state president, regulations issued by a cabinet minister, or municipal bylaws.[412] In this context, arguably, the concept of unreasonableness could be read to include discrimination on the basis of race.[413] Given that many of the discriminatory laws in South Africa are enacted by subordinate legislatures, South African judges are not as powerless as sometimes is suggested.[414]

Justified or not, this perception of powerlessness has led the judiciary to believe that "[p]arliament may make any encroachment it chooses upon the life, liberty or property of any individual subject to its sway, and . . . it is the function of courts to enforce its will."[417] Although most, if not all, of the guarantees of fundamental freedoms and equality contained in the Bill of Rights form part of the common law of South Africa, parliamentary supremacy renders them meaningless. As a result, South African Indians, coloreds, and especially blacks do not enjoy even minimal decencies of unsegregated facilities, equal treatment, due process, or equal protection of the laws. Unequal and generally separate is the sanctioned policy and law of the land in most areas of life for South African blacks,[418] and it is law which often receives the rubber stamp of a judiciary that feels itself powerless to intervene to prevent legal racism.

The ineffectiveness of the South African judiciary is not solely a function of the courts' inability to invalidate acts of Parliament. Without a bill of rights in the South African constitution, the judiciary lacks textual standards and, equally important, a body of jurisprudence interpreting those textual standards by which to evaluate alleged violations of civil liberties.[419]

However, even the adoption of a bill of rights, without other measures, would amount to no more than an empty promise to the black majority. A bill of rights will have currency only if it is part of a negotiated settlement that includes a new constitution, the enfranchisement of blacks, the sharing of political power, and the dismantling of apartheid.

B. THE BASIC IRRELEVANCY OF A JUDGE'S FAIR AND UNBIASED NATURE WHEN CALLED UPON TO ENFORCE A SYSTEM THAT HAS NO "MORAL, LEGAL, AND POLITICAL LEGITIMACY"

One effect of South Africa's parliamentary supremacy is that even fair-minded and unbiased judges are sworn to uphold the injustices of apartheid. Just as American antislavery judges, such as Joseph Story, were constrained by the fugitive slave clause of the Constitution and the Fugitive

Slave Acts, South African judges with anti-apartheid values are severely constrained by their duty to enforce the parliamentary system of apartheid.

Just as it took the visitor Alexis de Tocqueville to give fresh perspective on America's qualities in the 1830s, it likewise takes a wise outside observer to put the South African judiciary in proper perspective today. Judge Nathaniel R. Jones, after his visit to South Africa, was able to offer such insights.[433]

In 1985, at the request of the U.S. Lawyer's Committee for Civil Rights under Law, he went to observe the proceedings of *S. v. Ramgobin*.[434] After observing the trial for several weeks, he complimented the presiding judge, a Justice Milne, and said, "he deservedly enjoys an extremely high reputation among those who handle human rights/political cases." He noted that the judge "was patient and unhurried, courteous, incisive in his questioning, well informed on the papers in the case, and the relevant law. The defendants' [sic] were treated with dignity in the courtroom." By any standard, Justice Milne exemplified the qualities desired in any trial judge.

The milieu of *Pitje*, where a racially hostile judge presided, was not present in *Ramgobin*. But Judge Jones went on to stress that, despite his favorable "observations of the courtroom proceedings, the fairness and demeanor of the judge, . . . and the demonstrated skill of those counsel, [the fundamental issue] was whether justice [would] prevail. This is so because the fairness of the underlying laws themselves [is] at issue."

He noted that the South African court has no equivalents to provisions in America's Constitution and Bill of Rights that protect freedoms of speech and assembly or the right to counsel while incarcerated. In addition, the court had no way to assure due process and the equal protection of the laws in ways similar to the guarantees of the American Constitution. He also noted the impotence of the judiciary because of the "express prohibition on judicial intervention in cases involving sections of the Internal Security Act."

Judge Jones concluded with his customary civility that the South African "courts are under a serious handicap." But behind this polite assessment lay the facts he had described so well—impossible barriers that pervasively deny South African blacks any semblance of equal justice under the law. Indeed, Judge Jones stressed that the underlying apartheid laws raise "serious questions as to the moral, legal and political legitimacy" of the South African government.[442]

Even though Justice Milne was a fair judge and presided in a nonracist fashion, his personal demeanor is irrelevant to the thousands of blacks who are detained daily in South Africa without due process of law. The well-meaning spirit of one good South African judge, while commendable, is nevertheless a tragic irony so long as the judge is enforcing the unjust laws of apartheid that unfairly imprison thousands, and oppress millions, of blacks daily. Having some good judges is about as helpful as offering a few aspirins to cure a plague killing millions. The South African plague is the "detentions and disappearances, beatings and torture [imposed on thousands of blacks] carried out by the government of South Africa and its agents." In reality, even the nonracist judges in South Africa are enforcing, as Judge Jones said, "laws that render black racial groups legally and politically impotent."

At their core, present South African laws of apartheid give no hope to the 26 million black South Africans who "yearn to breathe free." The fair judges of South Africa are not dissimilar from the abolitionist judges who abhorred American slavery, yet nonetheless enforced the Fugitive Slave Acts that sent thousands of blacks back to a lifetime of cruelty and enslavement. They enforced a system of law that declared that blacks "had no rights which the white man was bound to respect."[447]

C. THE LIMITS OF EFFECTING SOCIAL CHANGE THROUGH THE SOUTH AFRICAN JUDICIARY AND THE PROGRESSIVE RADICALIZATION OF BLACK LAWYERS IN SOUTH AFRICA

Litigation strategies used in the United States have had limited success in affecting social change for racial justice, and largely have been effective only when social and political conditions were ripe for such change. This was true especially when those conditions were spurred by massive activist campaigns and spontaneous outpourings of civil disobedience. If working from within the judicial system has met with only limited success in the United States, with the promise and potential of the Constitution and its amendments, it is no wonder that black lawyers and activists in South Africa gave up attempts to dismantle apartheid by working within the judicial system.

If one wonders why responsible black lawyers became so radicalized in South Africa, one must recognize the extent to which the courts contributed to the process. If the country's highest appellate court says to the Mandelas, Tambos, and Pitjes that they are so inferior that, as a matter of law, it is reasonable for judges to treat both them and their clients differently from all others even in court, then it should come as no surprise that these lawyers would lose confidence in South African law as an instrument of justice and constructive change.[452]

The segregation of counsel in the South African courts is what most white South Africans would call "petty apartheid," involving symbolic rather than substantive deprivations. Nevertheless, the racism in South African courts constitutes daily catalysts for future revolution.[453] In many circumstances, courts[454] promote evolutionary, albeit limited, improvement in the rights of all people, whether by treating them with equal civility and according their testimony—and their injuries—equal weight, or by enforcing great constitutional principles. Courts in South Africa *could* not choose the latter route. But many also *did* not choose the former. In not availing themselves of the powers they possess, the South African courts of justice thus have been part of the problem when they could have been part of the solution.[456]

C. The Role of Political Leadership in the Judiciary, in Fostering Racism in the Courts, and in Achieving Broader Social Change for Racial Justice

There are at least two reasons to analyze the similarities and differences between the roles that political leadership plays in the judiciary, in fostering racism in the courts, and in achieving broader social change for racial justice in the United States and South Africa. First, judges are appointed by governments that are controlled by the leadership of various political parties and factions, or elected in campaigns affected by partisan politics. Therefore, the racial attitudes and policies of the prevailing political parties and leading political figures directly affect the racial practices of the courts. Racially insensitive or outright racist political leaders may refuse to appoint black judges and instead appoint or support only those judges who are racially indifferent or insensitive, or blatantly racist.

Second, just as the stigmatization of blacks that results from racist treatment in the courtroom is a particularly powerful symbol that legitimates and reinforces the general societal perceptions of blacks as inferior, the racial attitudes and behavior of political leaders, ranging from indifference to outright racist behavior, sends a clear signal that validates societal perceptions of the inferiority of blacks. Conversely, political leaders who advocate racial tolerance and the elimination of racial discrimination hasten the pace of social change for racial justice through appointments, policy pronouncements, and the establishment of a moral tone of harmonious racial attitudes. When leaders advocate these values, it often is irrelevant whether they are acting from enlightened visions for the future or pure political pragmatism.

1. The American Experience

Part of the problem of racism in the American courts has been that American political leaders have not provided a personal example of dedication against the forces of racism. Instead, they too often have reflected the worst aspects of the racist "moral tone" of contemporary society.[460]

Until the 1940s, blacks in the United States were restricted to the most menial jobs. Only in the rarest cases were the professional, managerial, secretarial, and other "white collar" jobs attainable for even the most talented and competent blacks.[462] From the presidency of Grover Cleveland (1885–89, 1893–97) through that of Herbert Hoover (1929–33), presidents were either patently hostile or generally unsympathetic to the muted and cautious requests by blacks for some slight improvement in their economic lot through government action.

Courts do not exist in a vacuum, but rather are an integral part of the society within which they operate. When American public culture was explicitly racist, it was no wonder that no blacks were appointed to the federal bench, and that many of the white judges who were appointed shared the prevailing racist ideology and therefore failed to interpret the Constitution to protect civil and human rights. It would take the election of more egalitarian presidents such as Truman, Kennedy, Johnson, Nixon, Ford, and Carter to give substance to the Constitution's expansive guarantees. Such presidents challenged racism both by their personal example and by their appointments. In turn, the aftermath of World War II and the sustained agitation of the NAACP, the Student Non-Violent Coordinating Committee, the Southern Christian Leadership Conference, and the charismatic leadership of Martin Luther King, Malcolm X, and others created a social climate supportive of major social change for racial justice. In this climate, many of the traditional habits of Southern courtrooms, from segregated spectator seating to the addressing of black (but not white) witnesses by their first names, were overturned. This series of victories for justice in turn established precedent that serves to check the more reactionary political forces that still exist in this day and age. Indeed, it is not clear whether, if there were no such favorable precedents on the books, yesterday's progressive decisions would be repeated in today's more conservative climate, by today's more conservative Supreme Court.

2. The South African Experience

The similarity between the racist rhetoric of American leaders and that of South African leaders of the twentieth century indicates one major similarity between the political practices of the two countries—one that supports the validity of comparing the race relations of the two countries. In both countries, a racist public culture would be reflected in discriminatory practices in the courts.

For brevity, it is sufficient simply to discuss John Jan Christian Smuts, a person who many generally describe as one of the more enlightened South African statesmen of his era.[484] A prodigy at Cambridge, Smuts became State Attorney of the Transvaal in 1898, a Minister in the Transvaal government in 1907, Prime Minister of South Africa from 1919 to 1924, Deputy Prime Minister from 1933 to 1939, and Prime Minister again from 1939 to 1948. Smuts eventually acquired a reputation "as the Pericles of the British Commonwealth, a visionary who foresaw the holistic evolution of a New World order."[487] He "parlayed his role in the Commonwealth into a position of eminence among the Allies when the world order collapsed, turning up with Winston Churchill at Cairo in 1942 and then at San Francisco in 1945 for the founding of the United Nations."[488] Ironically, he even wrote the concept of "fundamental human rights" into the preamble to the U.N. Charter. Surely, if the public remarks of so worldly a figure were racist, one should not expect more democratic views from the South African judiciary. Yet, in 1906, Smuts wrote:

> I sympathize entirely with the Native races of South Africa, but I don't believe in politics for them. . . . Perhaps at bottom, I do not believe in politics at all as a means for the attainment of the highest ends. . . . When I consider the future of the Natives in South Africa, I must say that I look into shadows and darkness and then I feel inclined to shift the intolerable burden of solving that sphinx problem to the ampler shoulders and stronger brains of the future.[490]

In the 1920s, Smuts articulated the theoretical basis that would subsequently form the paternalistic foundation of apartheid. When giving the Rhodes Memorial Lecture at Oxford in 1929, Smuts said: "The negro and the negroid Bantu form a distinct human type. It has largely remained a child type, with a child psychology and outlook. . . . A child-like human . . . cannot be a bad human, for are we not in spiritual matters bidden to be like unto children?"[492] Joseph L. Lelyveld argues convincingly in his insightful and classic book that the policies articulated by Smuts in 1929 "became in the 1980s the policy of P.W. Botha, who back in 1948 had been a young Nationalist firebrand for whom Jan Smuts and all his works were an anathema."[493]

The paternalistic concepts in Smuts's Oxford speech were transformed into oppressive policies by Hendrick Verwoerd, who was a member of Parliament for many years, and was also South Africa's Prime Minister from 1958 to 1966.

By June 1989, the National Party Government had returned to Smuts's rhetoric of conciliation and limited power sharing to take place at an indefinite future time. The importance of political leadership in fostering a climate conducive to social change for racial justice is demonstrated both by the recent shift in direction taken by the National Party Government upon F. W. de Klerk's ascension to the presidency in 1989, and by Nelson Mandela's release, his stature as an international political leader, and his articulation of the goal to transform South Africa into "a united, democratic and nonracial country."

3. Looking toward South Africa's Future

Just as numerous social, political, and moral forces created a milieu for overturning the doctrine of "separate but equal" in *Brown* and the subsequent enactment of the landmark Civil Rights Acts, numerous factors in South Africa have pushed President de Klerk to move toward negotiations with black leaders.

First of all, campaigns of civil disobedience, protest, and boycotts have effectively intensified the pressure on the National Party Government and raised the consciousness of liberal whites within South Africa, while also focusing worldwide attention on the injustices of apartheid. Similarly, civil disobedience played an important role in focusing the attention of our nation on racism and discrimination and in creating the social, political, and moral climate that led to our civil rights gains during the 1960s. Over the past decade in South Africa, internal black opposition has intensified and become more unified and effective. Rent strikes in the townships and consumer boycotts have become increasingly effective and well-orchestrated. Independent trade unions have carried out a record number of strikes over the past ten years. And students and teachers have boycotted classes to protest Bantu education.

A factor, noted by Derrick Bell, that helped bring about the abandonment of *Plessy*'s "separate but equal" doctrine was the recognition that the agrarian economy of the southern United States could not become industrialized and modernized if segregation were to continue. In South Africa, the policies of apartheid in large part have been responsible for more than ten years of economic downturn and ossification. Economic sanctions, such as bans or limits on investment, lending, and the import and export of goods to South Africa, enforced by governments and private entities around the globe, have become both increasingly common and increasingly effective in exacerbating South Africa's economic crisis.[507]

The damaging effect of economic sanctions and the realization that the South African economy can emerge from economic crisis only by mitigating the harsh economic consequences of apartheid have played a major role in de Klerk's calculated stance toward negotiations with black leaders.

In evaluating the recent negotiation process, Professor Thomas Irwin said that "in fact, South Africa today is closer to the United States of the 1850's than the 1950's. Like the North and South, South Africa's black majority and white minority are seeking a compromise from positions that are in many ways irreconcilable."[513] The current difficulties in the negotiating process demonstrate the wisdom in not attempting to predict their ultimate outcome. These difficulties also demonstrate that for the indefinite future, the judicial process will play a critical role in either perpetuating or restraining racism in South African society.

Conclusion

In the courtrooms of both the United States and South Africa, judges have practiced and tolerated racist behavior. Differences, of course, have emerged in our analysis of the instances of racism in the courtrooms of the United States and South Africa. These dissimilarities are attributable to the differences in the specific nature of the ideology of racism in the two countries and the different political, economic, moral, and legal traditions in the United States and South Africa.

The occurrences of racism in the South African and U.S. courts are symptomatic of those racist attitudes, myths, and assumptions which compose the ideology of racism in the broader American and South African societies. Racist occurrences in the courts are powerful symbols, acting to reinforce, legitimate, and perpetuate apartheid in South Africa and racism and racist institutions here in the United States.

One question raised by the similar instances of racism found in U.S. and South African courtrooms is whether a judicial system that treats blacks and whites differently is capable of administering justice to blacks. Did blacks receive fair treatment in those American courtrooms where judges practiced or tolerated segregation or racist behavior? When appellate courts held that such instances of racism constituted "harmless error," the assumption was that, regardless of the differential treatment meted out to blacks in those courtrooms, blacks were nevertheless able to receive a fair trial. This is precisely the same logic that the Appellate Division applied in *Pitje*—namely, that it was "reasonable" for Pitje to sit at a segregated counsel table since "a practitioner would in every way be as well seated at the one table as at the other."[515] As Professor Amsterdam notes, both the *Pitje* decision and the U.S. decisions that have held instances of racism in the courts to be "harmless error"

> steadfastly refuse even to contemplate the idea that a system which views blacks and whites as different in kind may be inherently incapable of administering justice to blacks. "'Harmless error'" and "'standing'" analyses atomize racial discrimination and thereby minimize it; they rest on the premise (which the courts neither justify nor seem to realize can be questioned) that a black man can get a fair trial in a forum that tolerates any kind of racial discrimination. The same questionable assumption . . . underlies *McClesky v. Kemp*.[516]

In the end, it is impossible to make precise calibrations that measure the actual amount of racism in either the South African or American courts. Nevertheless, I believe that, on the whole, the American courts were and are far less racist than the South African courts. The explanation lies in the systemic differences that I have summarized and which make bringing a legal challenge to racist acts both easier and more likely to succeed in American courts.

The differences exist not because, as a group, American judges are so much more virtuous and democratic than their South African counterparts. If South Africa had the legal equivalent to our Bill of Rights, and the fourteenth, fifteenth, and nineteenth amendments, South African judges such as John Didcott and Richard Goldstone would be as protective of the human rights of all citizens as have been Chief Justice Earl Warren and Justices William Brennan, Thurgood Marshall, Harry Blackmun, and John Paul Stevens. Indeed, if granted the same constitutional authority, some

South African judges would be more protective of human rights than are some contemporary American judges and justices. Another interesting difference is that, while there are many civil rights cases in America, in South Africa such cases are relatively rare. The rarity of reported South African cases reflects the following: (1) the lack of any clear precedent in South African jurisprudence holding that segregation or racial disparagement is a violation of South African statutory or constitutional law; (2) the feeling of many South African lawyers that, except in the most egregious circumstances, it would be futile to raise the argument of racism in the courts; (3) the shortage of black lawyers in the South African bar;[517] (4) the lack of a jury system in South Africa for the last few decades, which allows a more subtle and less detectable racist dialogue to take place between lawyers and judges; and (5) the disinclination of counsel and judges to admit on the record personal racism when the law is already racist and provides few rights and little protection to blacks.

While we have noted the differences between the American and South African courts, we must not forget that an analysis of American cases, even during the last three decades, reveals many instances of racial bigotry and hatred by American judges and lawyers.[520] Because racism in the courts constitutes a symptom, symbol, and signal of broader societal racism, our diminished degree of discrimination and racism should not constitute a basis for apathy at home.

While I have focused on laws and cases—areas where the American system is indisputably superior to South Africa—we still should be painfully aware of the gap between our egalitarian legal precepts and some of our nonegalitarian practices. There is still that broad wasteland where millions of Americans suffer from de facto racial discrimination, racial segregation, and the sequelae to racist practices that persisted for centuries in our country. Malcolm X "stressed that the United States differed from South Africa only in that they practiced what they preach, while we preach integration and deceitfully practice segregation."[522] While Malcolm X may have overstated and oversimplified the American dilemma, this article establishes that history has been filled with many instances of racial bigotry and hatred by American judges and lawyers, and that some of those instances are indistinguishable from the worst examples I have cited from South Africa.

Much has changed dramatically for the better and yet much remains to be done. I will be the first to concede that progress has been made in America. Through individual appointments by presidents and governors, through court decisions such as *Brown*, and through federal legislation such as the Civil Rights Acts of 1964, 1965, and 1968, substantial change has been effected and new standards of human and civil rights have been set. Change has also occurred within the private sector.

However, we cannot become smug and assume that the trend of recent decades toward eradicating racism will continue. It is obvious that the most effective way to weaken the fabric of human and civil rights for minorities would be to change the balance of the Supreme Court so that gradually, in a slow but determined process, the Court would repudiate its historic role in the protection of individual and minority rights.

Our review of American cases in the not too distant past sadly reveals that American judges and American lawyers often exemplified, in the words of William Goodell, that the treatment of black people was repeatedly worse than the promise of the American law.[527] For the future, both in the United States and South Africa, we should seek to eradicate the pernicious consequences of centuries of racism. We must seek to attain the ideal expressed by Justice Black a half-century ago:

> [C]ourts stand ... as havens of refuge for those who might otherwise suffer because they are helpless, weak, outnumbered, or ... [are] victims of prejudice and public excitement.... No higher duty, no more solemn responsibility, rests upon [a c]ourt, than that of translating into living law and maintaining this constitutional shield deliberately planned and inscribed for the benefit of every human being subject to our Constitution—of whatever race, creed or persuasion.[528]

NOTES

When the late Judge Leon Higginbotham delivered his James Madison Lecture, the system of racial apartheid was still solidly entrenched in South Africa, and enlightened jurists and others were preoccupied with discovering legal and other mechanisms to dislodge it. To this end, Judge Higginbotham devoted several years to preparing a comprehensive article, based on the lecture, on the similarities and differences in racism in American and South African courts. By the time the article was published in the New York University Law Review in mid-1990, it had grown to the length of a short book. Nelson Mandela had been freed and negotiations were under way between dissident political groups and the white government that was to lead, in a few years, to the end of the apartheid regime.

With the consent of his family, Judge Higginbotham's article has been edited to conform to the page limits for chapters in this book, but no attempt has been made to alter the article's structure or analysis. Those who are interested in the complete article, including its rich footnoting, should consult the law review version. Many footnotes have been dropped or shortened, but those retained have their original numbering; ellipses are generally not shown. Ed.

1. W. Goodell, *The American Slave Code in Theory and Practice* 17 (1853) (quoting Dr. Joseph Priestly).

6. See A. Leon Higginbotham, "A Dream Deferred," 18 Crime & Delinq. 30, 30–34 (1972).

12. 347 U.S. 483 (1954).

16. On February 2, 1990, President de Klerk legalized formerly outlawed political parties and organizations, including the African National Congress (ANC), the Pan-Africanist Congress (PAC), the South African Communist Party (SACP), and a host of subsidiary or affiliated organizations. In addition, severe restrictions upon thirty-three other political organizations, including the United Democratic Front (UDF), were lifted. See Address by the State President, Mr. F. W. de Klerk, Feb. 2, 1990 [hereinafter de Klerk Address] (on file at New York University Law Review).

36. 163 U.S. 537, 560 (Harlan, J., dissenting).

38. The race classification system is based upon the three broad categories of white, colored, and Bantu. See Act 30 of 1950 § 5. As Professor Dugard has noted, "[t]he legislature has had considerable difficulty in finding a definition that will defy all attempts to cross the color line and the definitions of 'white,' 'colored,' and 'Bantu' have frequently been amended." J. Dugard, *Human Rights and the South African Legal Order* 61 (1978). The "colored" group includes Indians, Chinese, other Asiatics, and still other groups. See id. at 60–61.

South Africa, with a total population of approximately 35,206,898, is divided demographically as follows: 913,000 are officially classified as "Asian," 26,313,898 as African, 3,069,000 as coloreds, and 4,911,000 as "whites." See South African Inst. of Race Relations, Race Relations Survey 1987–88, at 11 (1988) [hereinafter South Africa Inst. of Race Relations]. The black people of South Africa are then further divided into ten main ethnic groups, and the whites usually fall into two distinct groups, the Afrikaans-speaking and the English-speaking, although the influence of the different immigrant origins of the descendants can be discerned. See Report of the Study Comm'n on U.S. Policy toward South Africa: Time Running Out 42–47 (1981) [hereinafter Study Commission].

39. In 1980, Africans constituted 71.5 percent of the population, coloreds 9.4 percent, and Asians 2.9 percent. See Study Commission, supra note 38, at 42.

341. At this juncture, I wish to gratefully acknowledge the insightful and invaluable commentary of Professor Anthony Amsterdam of New York University School of Law on an earlier draft of this article. Professor Amsterdam's comments focused my analysis on racism in the courts as symptoms, signals, and symbols of

broader societal racism. Letter from Prof. Anthony Amsterdam to A. Leon Higginbotham (Oct. 10, 1989).

342. See C. Lawrence, "The Id, the Ego, and Equal Protection: Reckoning with Unconscious Racism," 39 Stan. L. Rev. 317, 322 (1987); see also S. Arons & C. Lawrence, "The Manipulation of Consciousness: A First Amendment Critique of Schooling," 15 Harv. C.R.-C.L. L. Rev. 309, 339 (1980) (American schools' value systems stigmatize ghetto minority children); C. Lawrence, "'Justice' or 'Just Us': Racism and the Role of Ideology," 35 Stan. L. Rev. 831, 841–45 (1983).

350. Because racism is pervasive and often unconscious, judges—who nearly always in South Africa, and most often in the United States, are members of a white, male, privileged elite—are often unaware that they are failing to notice an affront to a black person that they would have noticed as an affront to another white, privileged male. Thus, even racially sensitive and fair-minded judges unconsciously may fail to accord black witnesses or defendants the same civilities as whites, or fail to comprehend the consequences of segregating black spectators in the courtroom or maintaining segregated restroom facilities in the courthouse. See *Johnson v. Virginia*, 373 U.S. 61 (1963); *Dawley v. Norfolk*, 159 F. Supp. 642 (E.D. Va.), aff'd 260 F.2d 647 (4th Cir. 1958); *Plummer v. Casey*, 148 F. Supp. 326 (S.D. Tex. 1955), aff'd, 240 F.2d 922 (5th Cir. 1956), cert. denied, 353 U.S. 924 (1957).

353. *S. v. Augustine*, 1980 (1) S.A. 503, 506 (A.D.).

354. 1964 (1) P.H., H. 76 (E) at 197.

355. *R. v. Pitje*, 1960 (4) S.A. 709 (A.D.).

365. *Dred Scott v. Sandford*, 60 U.S. (19 How.) 393, 407 (1856).

366. Article IV provides:

No Person held to Service or Labour in one State, under the laws thereof, escaping into another, shall, in Consequence of any Law or Regulation therein, be discharged from such Service or Labour, but shall be delivered up on Claim of the Party to whom such Service or Labour may be due.

U.S. Const. art. IV, § 2, cl. 3.

367. Fugitive Slave Act of 1850, 9 Stat. 462 (1850); An Act Respecting Fugitives from Justice, and Persons Escaping from the Service of their Masters (Fugitive Slave Act of 1793), ch. 7, 2 Stat. 302 (1793).

379. See, e.g., *Loving v. Virginia*, 388 U.S. 1, 12 (1967) (holding state statute which prevented interracial marriage unconstitutional); *Johnson v. Virginia*, 373 U.S. 61, 62 (1963) (holding state may not require racial segregation in courtroom and reversing petitioner's contempt conviction); *Brown v. Mississippi*, 297 U.S. 278, 287 (1936) (reversing murder convictions based upon confessions by black defendants obtained by physical torture); *Buchanan v. Warley*, 245 U.S. 60, 82 (1917) (holding unconstitutional city ordinance forbidding blacks from occupying houses or places of public assembly in any block in which greater number of houses or

places of public assembly were occupied by whites—and vice versa); *Strauder v. West Virginia*, 100 U.S. 303, 312 (1879) (reversing murder conviction of black defendant by all-white jury where state statute excluded black people from grand and petit juries).

380. 376 U.S. 650 (1964).

381. 373 U.S. 61 (1963).

386. 83 U.S. (16 Wall.) 36, 74–82 (1873) (narrowly construing privileges and immunities clause to forbid infringement of rights of national citizenship, but not those of state citizenship).

387. 109 U.S. 3, 13, 17, 23 (1883) (invalidating public accommodations provisions of Civil Rights Act of 1875, holding that due process and equal protection clauses apply only to cases involving state action and that thirteenth amendment is inapplicable to statute, through narrow interpretation of what constitutes "a badge and incident slavery").

388. 163 U.S. 537, 551 (1896) ("underlying fallacy of the plaintiff's argument . . . consist[s] in the assumption that the enforced separation of the two races stamps the colored race with a badge of inferiority").

390. D. Bell, *Race, Racism, and American Law* 35, 37 (2d ed. 1980).

391. L. Steel, "Nine Men in Black Who Think White," N.Y. Times, Oct. 13, 1968, § 6 (Magazine), at 56. Steel, a staff attorney with the NAACP, created quite a controversy with his article, which was published without prior approval by the NAACP. See D. Bell, *Race, Racism, and American Law* 94 (1st ed. 1972).

397. See, e.g., *McLaurin v. Oklahoma State Regents*, 339 U.S. 637, 642 (1950) (holding that separation and isolation of black student admitted to graduate program in cafeteria, library, and classroom violated equal protection clause); *Sweatt v. Painter*, 339 U.S. 629, 636 (1950) (holding that admitting black student to three-room law school hastily established by state, rather than to state school, violated equal protection clause); *Sipuel v. Board of Regents*, 332 U.S. 631, 632–33 (1948) (equal protection clause requires state to provide legal education for blacks as soon as it does for applicants of any other group).

401. See generally C. Carson, *In Struggle: The Student Non-Violence Coordinating Committee and the Black Awakening of the 1960s* (1981); D. Morris, *The Origins of the Civil Rights Movement: Black Communities Organizing for Change* (1984); H. Sitkoff, *The Struggle for Black Equality, 1954–1980* (1981); *The Civil Rights Movement in America* (C. Eagles ed. 1986).

403. Nat'l Comm'n on the Causes and Prevention of Violence, to Establish Justice, to Insure Domestic Tranquility 91 (1969) (Commission Statement on Civil Disobedience).

404. Id. at 115 (Additional Statement of Judge Higginbotham) (footnote omitted).

407. Although the preamble to the Republic of South Africa Constitution Act No. 110 of 1983 promises to uphold, inter alia, the independence of the judiciary,

it precludes judicial review as to the constitutional validity of parliamentary statutes.

409. Republic of South Africa Constitution Act No. 110 of 1983, § 99.

410. Id. § 34B.

411. See J. Dugard, supra note 38, at 3–49.

412. See id.

413. See *Kruse v. Johnson*, 2 Q.B. 91, 99, 100 (1898) (bylaws found to be partial and unequal in operation between different classes may be unreasonable and ultra vires).

414. See *R. v. Lusu*, 1953 (2) S.A. 484, 490–91 (A.D.) (section of act of Parliament may be construed to have nondiscriminatory effect); R. v. Abdurahman, 1950 (3) S.A. 136, 144 (A.D.) (possible to read enabling legislation as aimed at impartiality and equality which, read literally, could be applied to affect partiality and inequality).

417. *Sachs v. Minister of Justice*, 1934 (A.D.) 11, 37.

418. The Reservation of Separate Amenities Act, Act 49 of 1953, was repealed by the South African Parliament on June 19, 1990. See N.Y. Times, June 20, 1990, at A5. In its thirty-seven-year existence, the Separate Amenities Act "allow[ed] any person in control of public premises to reserve separate but unequal facilities for different races and ousts the power of the courts to declare such reservations invalid." J. Dugard, supra note 38, at 65. The repeal of the Separate Amenities Act fulfilled President F. W. de Klerk's pledge, made in his February 2, 1990, address to Parliament, that the Act would "be repealed during this Session of Parliament." De Klerk Address, supra note 16, at 8.

419. The problem of the absence of jurisprudential precedent against racism was particularly obvious in the *Pitje* case, one of the few cases where the South African courts did rule on the "reasonableness" of a discriminatory practice. Unfortunately, the courts' interpretation of "reasonableness" depended entirely on the discretion of the judges involved in the case. Instead, the South African judges demonstrated that their constitution, laws, and judicial processes would disregard—as a matter of law—Godfrey Pitje's poignant plea that he should be treated with no less respect than was granted to the white members of the bar. See *Pitje*, 1960 (4) S.A. 709 (A.D.).

433. See N. Jones, *Yearning to Breathe Free, Trial Observer's Report in the Case of State v. Mawalal Ramgobin and 15 Others, Supreme Court of South Africa* (Natal Provincial Division) and Observations of the South African Legal System (Lawyer's Committee for Civil Rights under Law 1985) (on file at New York University Law Review).

434. 1986 (1) S.A. 68 (N) (trial court decision is unreported). The sixteen defendants, members of the United Democratic Front, were charged with treason, resulting from their nonviolent, organized boycott of the tricameral parliamentary election in August 1984. See N. Jones, supra note 433, at 6. While the indictments

did not allege that the defendants had engaged in any specific acts of violence, nor that they were members of the outlawed African National Congress, the government charged that the defendants' nonviolent tactics were calculated to further the objectives of the ANC and South African Communist Party and created a climate favorable to the violent revolutionary overthrow of the government. See id. at 6, 10–14. All sixteen defendants were ultimately acquitted. N.Y. Times, June 24, 1986, at A12. For a similar case involving political protesters, see *S. v. Malinde*, 1990 (1) S.A. 57 (A.D.).

442. Id. In fact, it is impossible to justify the morality or political legitimacy of the South African laws. Judge Jones concluded that the actions of the South African government seemed to be in direct conflict with the Universal Declaration of Human Rights and the International Covenant on Civil and Political Rights. See N. Jones, supra note 433, at 58; see also A. Leon Higginbotham, "International Law, the Use of Force in Self-Defense, and the Southern African Conflict," 25 Colum. J. Transnat'l L. 529, 582–86 (1987).

447. *Dred Scott v. Sandford*, 60 U.S. (19 How.) 393, 407 (1856); see also R. Cover, *Justice Accused* 159–93 (1975).

452. In October 1962, Nelson Mandela challenged the jurisdiction of a white magistrate to preside over his trial at which he was charged with inciting people to strike and with living in the country without a valid passport. His challenge was based on two grounds: first, that he was not going to be given a fair and proper trial, and second, that he was neither morally nor legally obliged to obey the laws made by a Parliament in which he was not represented. N. Mandela, *No Easy Walk to Freedom* 125–26 (1965). With regard to the first argument, he asked:

> How can I be expected to believe that this same race discrimination, which has been the cause of so much injustice and suffering right through the years, should now operate here to give me a fair and a proper trial? Is there no danger that an African may regard these courts, not as impartial tribunals dispensing justice without fear or favour, but as instruments used by the White man to punish those among us who clamor for deliverance from the fiery furnace of White rule?
>
> I have grave fears that this system of justice may enable the guilty to drag the innocent before the courts. It enables the unjust to prosecute and demand vengeance against the just.

Id. at 128.

The presiding magistrate nevertheless dismissed the application; thereafter the matter proceeded to trial, and Mandela was found guilty of both offenses. See id. at 131–45.

Oliver Tambo, a former partner of Nelson Mandela, preferred to go into exile rather than practice law in South Africa. Others, like Ntobeko Maqubela, are serving twenty-year prison terms in South African jails for convictions of "high treason, terrorism, sabotage and other offenses." See *Litha Jolobe v. State*, No. 75/83, at 2, 4 (1984)(unreported decision)(on file at New York University Law Review). The case against Maqubela can be found in the unreported decision *Maqubela v. State*, No. 118–82 (1982).

453. From my discussions with South African jurists and attorneys, I understand that segregation of counsel in South African courts no longer is practiced.

454. See R. Cover, "The Supreme Court, 1982 Term-Foreword: Nomos and Narrative," 97 Harv. L. Rev. 4, 59 n.164 (1983) (citing example of Ghana Supreme Court members being executed for standing on principle).

456. See "Pursuing Justice in an Unjust Society: The Centre for Applied Legal Studies in South Africa," 29 Carnegie Q. 1, 6 (1981) ("conventional perception by judges that their function is to apply the law, not to comment on its moral content, hinders the judiciary from using the powers it has to modify the inequities in the South African system").

460. To some extent, a president's vision on racial issues is reflected in the pluralism that he makes possible—or precludes—by his judicial appointments. Writing in July 1988, Elaine R. Jones and Janice King-Robinson stated:

> In the selection of federal judges and the provision of diversity on the federal bench, our most recent national experience is not one of greatness, of vision, of heroism or of soaring spirits; instead, that experience is one of short-sightedness, of near-total racial exclusion, of clubbiness and, yes, even of meanness.
>
> Yet, this experience is not accidental. It is one of choice.
>
> The appalling statistics reveal that the Reagan administration has seen fit to appoint only six blacks to the federal bench in the more than seven years that he has been in office. Moreover, by the six appointments, he has increased the number of black federal judges by only five. One of Reagan's judicial appointees was already serving on the federal district court prior to his elevation to the court of appeals.

E. R. Jones & J. King-Robinson, "Choices: Appointing Blacks to the Federal Judiciary," Nat'l Bar A. Mag., July 1988, at 17, 18.

462. See G. Myrdal, *An American Dilemma* 304–5 (1944). Myrdal details the low economic position of upper- and middle-class blacks as follows:

> In 1930 there were only 254,000 Negro workers in white collar and higher occupations. . . . This [statistic] means that only one out of fifteen Negro workers in nonagricultural pursuits had a status higher than that of wage earner. In the white nonfarm population as many as two out of every five workers were in business, managerial, professional, and white-collar jobs.

484. See, e.g., B. Lapping, *Apartheid: A History* 60–62 (1989); J. Lelyveld, *Move Your Shadow: South Africa Black and White* 350 (1985).

487. Lelyveld at 350.

488. Id.

490. Id. at 348–49.

492. Id. at 63.

493. Id. at 350.

507. It has been estimated that economic sanctions are costing South Africa roughly two billion dollars per year in real gross domestic product. See S. Lewis, "After Apartheid: Why South Africa Can Expect an Economic Boom," Wash. Post, Feb. 18, 1990, at B1, B2.

Sanctions imposed by the United States include bans on new lending and investment and on the import and export of certain products. See N.Y. Times, Feb. 12, 1990, at A17. Many congressional leaders and some administration officials recognize that sanctions have been effective in prodding South Africa toward dismantling apartheid. See id.

513. T. Irwin, "Mandela Cannot Be a Dr. King," N.Y. Times, Apr. 15, 1990, § IV, at 13.

515. Pitje, 1960 (4) S.A. at 710.

516. Amsterdam comments, supra note 341, at 3 (citing *McClesky v. Kemp*, 481 U.S. 279 (1987) (statistical evidence that petit juries recommend death penalty more often for blacks who murder whites than for blacks who murder blacks or for white murderers does not establish equal protection violation)). [For a full discussion of the "harmless error" rule, see Jon O. Newman, "Beyond Reasonable Doubt," in this volume. Ed.]

517. See D. D. Mokgatle, "The Exclusion of Blacks from the South African Judicial System," 3 S. Afr. J. Hum. Rts. 44, 44–51 (1987). It has been my observation in America and South Africa that, despite some notable exceptions, as a group the black lawyers have been the most critical and the most offended by the racist procedures in the courts. The relative shortage of black lawyers in South Africa decreases the probability of racist issues being raised by counsel in court.

520. See generally J. Bass, *Unlikely Heroes: The Dramatic Story of the Southern Judges of the Fifth Circuit Who Translated the Supreme Court's* Brown *Decision into a Revolution for Equality* (1981).

522. J. A. Kushner, "Apartheid in America: An Historical and Legal Analysis of Contemporary Racial Segregation in the United States" 5 n.8 (1965) (quoting *Malcolm X Speaks* 75 (G. Breitman ed. 1965)).

527. See note 1, supra.

528. *Chambers v. Florida*, 309 U.S. 227, 241 (1940).

Chapter 3

Portia's Progress

Sandra Day O'Connor

I am very happy to be celebrating with you the One Hundredth Anniversary of Women Graduates from New York University School of Law. New York University showed great foresight by admitting women law students before the turn of the century. It was one of the first major law schools to do so. Columbia Law School did not admit women until 1927; Harvard Law School did not admit women until 1950. In fact, New York University flouted the wishes of Columbia Law School committee member George Templeton Strong, who had written in his diary: "Application from three infatuated Young Women to the [Columbia] Law School. No woman shall degrade herself by practicing law in New York especially if I can save her."[1]

New York women wouldn't be saved, however. The first woman to sit on the federal bench was a New Yorker,[2] as was the first woman admitted to practice before the Supreme Court.[3] A New York woman wrote the state's first workmen's compensation law,[4] and a New York woman wrote the "Little Wagner" act that permitted New York City employees to bargain collectively without violating antitrust laws.[5] And a New York woman worked on every major civil rights case that came before the U.S. Supreme Court in the 1950s and 1960s. You all can be very proud of this tradition. But being an early woman lawyer was not an easy accomplishment, even for New Yorkers.

Most of the women legal pioneers faced a profession and a society that espoused what has been called "the Cult of Domesticity,"[6] a view that

This lecture was delivered on October 29, 1991, and appeared in 66 N.Y.U.L. Rev. 1546 (1991).

women were by nature different from men. Women were said to be fitted for motherhood and home life, compassionate, selfless, gentle, moral, and pure. Their minds were attuned to art and religion, not logic. Men, on the other hand, were fitted by nature for competition and intellectual discovery in the world, battle-hardened, shrewd, authoritative, and tough-minded.

Women were thought to be ill-qualified for adversarial litigation because it required sharp logic and shrewd negotiation, as well as exposure to the unjust and immoral. In 1875, the Wisconsin Supreme Court told Lavinia Goodell that she could not be admitted to the state bar.[7] The Chief Justice declared that the practice of law was unfit for the female character.[8] To expose women to the brutal, repulsive, and obscene events of courtroom life, he said, would shock man's reverence for womanhood and relax the public's sense of decency.[9]

In a similar case, Myra Bradwell of Chicago, who had studied law under her husband, applied to the Illinois Bar in 1869 and was refused admission[10] because as a married woman her contracts were not binding, and contracts were the essence of an attorney-client relationship.[11] The Court also proclaimed that "God designed the sexes to occupy different spheres of action, and that it belonged to men to make, apply, and execute the laws."[12]

The U.S. Supreme Court, I blush to admit, agreed with the Illinois court.[13] Justice Bradley, concurring in the Court's opinion, cited the natural differences between men and women as the reason Myra Bradwell could not be admitted. He wrote, "Man is, or should be, woman's protector and defender. The natural and proper timidity and delicacy which belongs to the female sex evidently unfits it for many of the occupations of civil life."[14]

Even Clarence Darrow, one of the most famous champions of unpopular causes, had this to say to a group of women lawyers: "You can't be shining lights at the bar because you are too kind. You can never be corporation lawyers because you are not cold-blooded. You have not a high grade of intellect. I doubt you can ever make a living."[15] Another male attorney of the period commented, " A woman can't keep a secret, and for that reason if no other, I doubt if anybody will ever consult a woman lawyer."[16]

Luckily for us women lawyers today, our female predecessors had far more spunk, spirit, and wit than they were given credit for. Clara Shortridge Foltz, the first woman lawyer in California and the first woman deputy district attorney in America, displayed the characteristic mettle of these early women lawyers. When an opposing attorney once suggested in open court that she had better be at home raising children, Foltz retorted: "A woman had better be in almost any business than raising such men as you."[17]

A New York woman lawyer pioneer, Belva Lockwood, was in 1879 the first woman admitted to practice before the U.S. Supreme Court.[18] To receive that honor, however, she had to try three times to get a special bill passed in the Senate to change the admission requirements.[19] Inexhaustible, she rode her three-wheeler all over Washington, lobbying senators and explaining to the press that she was going to "get up a fight all along the line."[20] In 1884, the redoubtable Mrs. Lockwood even ran for President, reasoning that even though women could not vote, there was nothing to stop them from running for office.[21] Even without women voters, she garnered 4,149 votes in that election.[22]

In my own time and in my own life, I have witnessed the revolution in the legal profession that has resulted in women representing nearly 30 percent of attorneys in this country and 40 percent of law school graduates.[23] Projections based on data from the Census Bureau and Department of Labor indicate that by 2031 half the country's attorneys will be women.[24] I myself, after graduating near the top of my class at Stanford Law School, was unable to obtain a position at any national law firm, except as a legal secretary. Yet I have since had the privilege of serving as a state senator, a state judge, and a Supreme Court Justice.

Women today are not only well represented in law firms, but are gradually attaining other positions of legal power, representing 7.4 percent of federal judges,[25] 25 percent of U.S. attorneys,[26] 14 percent of state attorneys,[27] 18 percent of state legislators,[28] 17 percent of state and local executives,[29] 9 percent of county governing boards,[30] 14 percent of mayors and city council members,[31] 6 percent of U.S. congresspersons,[32] and of course, just over 11 percent of U.S. Supreme Court Justices.[33] Until the percentages come closer to 50 percent, however, we cannot say we have succeeded. Still, the progress in my own time has been astounding.

That progress is due in large part to the explosion of the myth of the "True Woman" through the efforts of real women and the insights of real men. Released from these prejudices, women have proved they can do a "man's" job.

This change in perspective has been reflected, as most social change eventually is, in the Supreme Court's jurisprudence. I would like to sketch briefly how the Justices' comments about gender differences have changed in direct response to the change in the position of women in our society.

The ratification of the Bill of Rights in 1791 had little immediate effect on the legal status or rights of women. Its strictures were limited initially to the federal government; the states were free to continue as before in fashioning the political and legal rights of their citizens. State legislation affecting women was drawn primarily from the British common law, which gave women few property or contractual rights. Only in the case of unmarried women were the laws in this country somewhat more generous than in England, at least insofar as property ownership and management were concerned.

As you know, it was not until after the Civil War and the resultant adoption of the thirteenth, fourteenth, and fifteenth amendments to our Constitution that there were national guarantees for certain individual liberties which the states could not abridge. But even these additions to our Constitution did not easily translate into concepts that benefited women as a group until the last half of the twentieth century. Until that time, despite the efforts of women such as Elizabeth Cady Stanton, Susan B. Anthony, and Sojourner Truth, society as a whole, including the Court, generally accepted the separate and unequal status of women.

The fourteenth amendment prohibits states from "denying to any person ... the equal protection of the laws."[34] There is little evidence to suggest that at the time of its adoption in 1868 this amendment was seen as a vehicle of women's equality under law. In fact, the fourteenth amendment for the first time introduced sex-specific language into the Constitution. Section 2 of the amendment, which deals with legislative representation and voting, says that if the right to vote is "denied to any of the male inhabitants" of a state aged twenty-one or over then the proportional representation in that state shall be reduced accordingly.[35] Moreover, the Supreme Court determined in 1873 in the *Slaughter-House Cases*[36] that the equal protection clause should be narrowly interpreted to apply only to state laws that discriminated against blacks.[37]

The same Court on the very next day handed down the *Bradwell* decision, mentioned earlier,[38] denying Myra Bradwell's claim that the state of Illinois had denied her the privileges and immunities of U.S. citizenship when it refused, because of her sex, to give her a license to practice law.[39]

For the first half of the twentieth century the Court continued to defer to legislative judgments regarding the differences between the sexes. In 1948, Valentine Goesaert and three other women challenged the constitutionality of a Michigan statute forbidding a woman from being a bartender unless she was "the wife or daughter of the male owner" of the bar.[40] The Court, in an opinion by Justice Frankfurter, rejected the claim that the statute violated the equal protection clause, saying that "despite the vast changes in the social and legal position of women," the state un-questionably could forbid all women from working as bartenders.[41]

Even as late as 1961, the Court reaffirmed Florida's practice of restricting jury service to men, unless women registered separately.[42] The Court said, "Despite the enlightened emancipation of women from the restrictions and protections of bygone years, and their entry into many parts of community life formerly considered to be reserved to men, woman is still regarded as the center of the home and family life."[43]

The Supreme Court began to look more closely at legislation providing dissimilar treatment for similarly situated women and men in the early 1970s. The first case in which the Court found a state law discriminating against women to be unconstitutional was *Reed v. Reed*.[44] In *Reed*, the Court struck down an Idaho law giving men an automatic preference in appoint-ments as administrators of estates.[45] *Reed* signaled a dramatic change in the Court's approach to the myth of the "True Woman."

In subsequent cases, the Court made clear that it would no longer swal-low unquestioningly the story that women are different from men. In 1972, striking down a federal statute which made it easier for men to claim their wives as dependents than it was for women to claim their husbands as de-pendents, Justice Brennan wrote: "There can be no doubt that our nation has had a long and unfortunate history of sex discrimination. Traditionally, such discrimination was rationalized by an attitude of 'romantic paternal-ism' which, in practical effect, put women, not on a pedestal, but in a cage."[46]

Two years later, the Court struck down a Utah statute providing that child support was required for girls only until their legal majority at eigh-teen, while child support for boys was required until they reached the age of twenty-one.[47] The state had justified the difference by arguing that women matured faster, married earlier, and tended not to require continu-ing support through higher education, while men usually did require this additional support.[48] The Court took a hard look at these justifications, concluding:

A child, male or female, is still a child. No longer is the female destined solely for the home and the rearing of the family, and only the male for the marketplace and the world of ideas. . . . Women's activities and responsibil-ities are increasing and expanding. Coeducation is a fact, not a rarity. The presence of women in business, in the professions, in government and, in-deed, in all walks of life where education is a desirable, if not always a nec-essary, antecedent is apparent and a proper subject of judicial notice.[49]

In 1976, the Court made its more careful standard of review explicit, ruling that sex-based classifications would be upheld only if they served important governmental objectives and were substantially related to the achievement of those objectives.[50]

Through the next two decades, the Court invalidated, on equal protection grounds, a broad range of statutes that discriminated against women. The laws struck down included a Social Security Act provision allowing widows but not widowers to collect survivor's benefits;[51] a state law permitting the sale of beer to women at age eighteen but not to men until age twenty-one;[52] a state law requiring men but not women to pay alimony after divorce;[53] a Social Security Act provision allowing benefits for families with dependent children only when the father was unemployed, not when the mother was unemployed;[54] and a state statute granting only husbands the right to manage and dispose of jointly owned property without spousal consent.[55]

The volume of cases in the Supreme Court dealing with sex discrimination declined somewhat in the 1980s. Several of the more recent cases brought before the Court have involved interpretations of statutes such as Title VII rather than of the equal protection clause. In *Hishon v. King & Spalding*,[56] for example, the Court held that once a law firm makes partnership consideration a privilege of employment, the firm may not discriminate on the basis of sex in its selection of partners.[57]

In all these cases, the Court has looked with a somewhat jaundiced eye at the loose-fitting generalizations, myths, and archaic stereotypes that previously kept women at home. Instead, the Court has often asked employers to look to whether the particular person involved, male or female, is capable of doing the job, not whether women in general are more or less capable than men.[58]

Just when the Court and Congress have adopted a less sanguine view of gender-based classifications, however, the new presence of women in the law has prompted many feminist commentators to ask whether women have made a difference to the profession, whether women have different styles, aptitudes, or liabilities.[59] Ironically, the recent move to ask the question whether women are different merely by virtue of being women recalls the old myths we have struggled to put behind us. Undaunted by the historical resonances, however, more and more writers have suggested that women practice law differently than men. One author has even concluded that my opinions differ in a peculiarly feminine way from those of my colleagues.[60]

The gender differences currently cited are surprisingly similar to stereotypes from years past. Women attorneys are more likely to seek to mediate disputes than litigate them. Women attorneys are more likely to focus on resolving a client's problem than on vindicating a position. Women attorneys are more likely to sacrifice career advancement for family obligations. Women attorneys are more concerned with public service or fostering community than with individual achievement. Women judges are more likely to emphasize context and deemphasize general principles. Women judges are more compassionate. And so forth.

This "New Feminism" is interesting, but troubling, precisely because it so nearly echoes the Victorian myth of the "True Woman" that kept women out of law for so long. It is a little chilling to compare these suggestions to Clarence Darrow's assertion that women are too kind and warm-hearted to be shining lights at the bar.[61]

One difference between men and women lawyers certainly remains, however. Women professionals still have primary responsibility for children and housekeeping, spending roughly twice as much time on these cares as do their professional husbands.[62] As a result, women lawyers have special difficulties managing both a household and a career.

These concerns of how to blend law and family we share with women lawyers of over one hundred years ago, who, like us, debated whether a woman could have both a family and a profession. The prevailing view then, as Mrs. Marion Todd put it in an 1888 letter to the Women Lawyers' Equity Club, was that a husband was simply "too great a responsibility."[63]

Today, while many women juggle both profession and home admirably, it is nonetheless true that time spent at home is time that cannot be billed to clients or used to make contacts at social or professional organizations. As a result, women still may face what has been called a "mommy track" or a "glass ceiling" in the legal profession—a delayed or blocked ascent to partnership or management status due to family responsibilities.[64] Women who do not wish to be left behind sometimes are faced with a hard choice. Some give up family life in order to attain their career aspirations. Many talented young women lawyers decide that the demands of a career require delaying family responsibilities at the very time in their lives when bearing children is physically easiest. I myself chose to try to have and enjoy my family and to resume my career path somewhat later.

The choices that women must make in this respect are different from the choices that men must make. Men need not take time off from work to have a family—not even the bare minimum amount of time needed to deliver a child. It is in recognizing and responding to this fundamental difference that the Court has had its most difficult challenges. The dilemma is this: If society does not recognize the fact that only women can bear children, then "equal treatment" ends up being unequal. On the other hand, if society recognizes pregnancy as requiring special solicitude, it is a slippery slope back to the "protectionist" legislation that historically barred women from the workplace.

Again, the Court's decisions in the area of pregnancy discrimination reflect the social trends and illustrate the remaining ambivalences. In 1908, the Court in *Muller v. Oregon*[65] upheld regulations prescribing maximum working hours for women, but not men, because "maternal functions," "the burdens of motherhood," and society's concern for "vigorous offspring" justified treating women differently.[66]

After the Court began to look at gender classification more carefully in the 1970s, it struggled with the question of when it was appropriate to treat pregnancy differently. The Court ruled in *Cleveland Board of Education v. LaFleur*[67] that the school board violated due process when it placed schoolteachers on forced leave at an arbitrarily fixed stage in pregnancy well in advance of the expected delivery date.[68] The case was decided on due process grounds, not equal protection grounds. It nonetheless took the view that ability to work had to be evaluated individually, not stereotypically.[69]

At the same time, however, the Court held that excluding "pregnancy" from a disability policy did not amount to an equal protection violation.[70] Pregnancy, the Court said, was a disabling condition like any other; it was not a gender-based classification subject to more careful scrutiny.[71] A state disability insurance program was free to include or exclude pregnancy on any rational basis, as it could any other physical condition.[72]

In a similar case two years later, the Court reaffirmed its position on pregnancy by rejecting a similar challenge under Title VII,[73] a federal statute prohibiting employment discrimination based on race, color, religion, sex, or national origin. The Court held that an exclusion from disability benefits for pregnancy was "not a gender-based discrimination at all."[74]

These two cases took the view that equality required treating women and men precisely the same. Pregnancy had to be "degendered" in order to be treated fairly. Consequently, pregnancy was characterized as a disability that happened to occur in women, not men. As such, it was no different from a disability that occurred only in men. Hence, the Court reasoned, it should be treated the same as any other disability and could reasonably be excluded from disability insurance policies for reasons of cost.

Congress, however, disagreed with the Court's interpretation of Title VII and passed the Pregnancy Discrimination Act, which prohibits discrimination on the basis of pregnancy, childbirth, or related medical conditions, requiring pregnant women to be treated the same as other persons similar in their ability or inability to work.[75] In so doing, Congress declared that discrimination on the basis of pregnancy was discrimination against women,[76] instead of disavowing the connection between pregnancy and women as the Court had done. Senator Williams, a sponsor of the Act, made this change of heart explicit: "The entire thrust . . . behind this legislation is to guarantee women the basic right to participate fully and equally in the workforce, without denying them the fundamental right to full participation in family life."[77]

In 1987, the Court heard a reverse discrimination suit under the Pregnancy Discrimination Act.[78] An employer claimed that a state law requiring employers to provide four months of unpaid pregnancy leave improperly favored pregnant women over temporarily disabled men, in violation of the Pregnancy Discrimination Act's mandate that pregnant women be treated the same as other workers equally able to work.[79] The Court upheld the state statute, reasoning that Congress had established a floor for providing pregnancy benefits, not a ceiling.[80] Tellingly, the Court recognized that true equality between women and men was best achieved by taking pregnancy into account, so that "women, as well as men, could have families without losing their jobs."[81]

Nonetheless, the Court was concerned that the legislation not be overtly protectionist and suggested that the pendulum would not be allowed to swing too far toward treating women differently. It emphasized that "unlike the protective labor legislation prevalent earlier in this century, [the California statute] does not reflect archaic or stereotypical notions about pregnancy and the abilities of pregnant workers. A statute based on such stereotypical assumptions would, of course, be inconsistent with Title VII's goal of equal employment opportunity."[82] Obviously, *Muller v. Oregon's* patronizing concerns about the "burdens of motherhood"[83] continued to ring warning bells in the Justices' minds.

In the 1991 Term, the Court, again interpreting the Pregnancy Discrimination Act, held that fertile women could not be excluded from work at a battery plant on the ground that they were capable of becoming pregnant and would risk birth defects from lead exposure if they chose to bear children.[84] As in *Muller*, the employer had contended that society's concern for "vigorous offspring" was the benign reason for the employer's exclusion of fertile women.[85] The Court disagreed, holding instead that the employer could only justify excluding women from these jobs if they could not do the work safely and efficiently.[86] The Court held that the categorical exclusion of fertile women was not justified because "fertile women . . . participate in the manufacture of batteries as efficiently as anyone else."[87] The Court reaffirmed its rejection of traditional categories, stating that "women as capable of doing their jobs as their male counterparts may not be forced to choose between having a child and having a job."[88]

The question of when equality requires accommodating differences is one with which the Court will continue to struggle. I think in recent cases the Court has acknowledged, along with the "New Feminism," that sometimes to treat men and women exactly the same is to treat them differently, at least with respect to pregnancy. Women do have the gift of bearing children, a gift that needs to be accommodated in the working world. However, in allowing for this difference, we must always remember that we risk a return to the myth of the "True Woman" that blocked the career paths of many generations of women.

I would hope that your generation of attorneys will find new ways to balance family and professional responsibilities between men and women, recognizing gender differences in a way that promotes equality and frees both women and men from traditional role limitations. You must reopen the velvet curtain between work and home that was drawn closed in the Victorian era. Not only women, but men too, have missed out through the division of work and home. As more women enjoy the challenges of a legal career, more men have blessings to garner from taking extra time to nurture and teach their children.

If we are to continue to find ways to repair the existing difference between professional women and men with regard to family responsibilities, however, we must not allow the "New Feminism" complete sway. For example, asking whether women attorneys speak with a "different voice"[89] than men do is a question that is both dangerous and unanswerable. It again sets up the polarity between the feminine virtues of homemaking and the masculine virtues of breadwinning. It threatens, indeed, to establish new categories of "women's work" to which women are confined and from which men are excluded.

Instead, my sense is that as women continue to take on a full role in the professions, learning from those professional experiences, as from their experiences as homemakers, the virtues derived from both kinds of learning will meld. The "different voices" will teach each other. I myself have been thankful for the opportunity to experience a rich and fulfilling career as well as a close and supportive family life. I know the lessons I have learned in each have aided me in the other. As a result, I can revel both in the growth of my granddaughter and in the legal subtleties of the free exercise clause.

Do women judges decide cases differently by virtue of being women? I would echo the answer of my colleague, Justice Jeanne Coyne of the Supreme Court of Oklahoma, who responded that "a wise old man and a wise old woman reach the same conclusion."[90] This should be our aspiration: that, whatever our gender or background, we all may become wise— wise through our different struggles and different victories, wise through work and play, profession and family.

NOTES

1. K. Morello, *The Invisible Bar* 76 (1986) (quoting *The Diary of George Templeton Strong* 256 (A. Nevins & M. Thomas eds. 1952)).

2. Florence Ellinwood Allen was appointed to the U.S. Court of Appeals for the Sixth Circuit in 1934 by President Roosevelt. Id. at 234.

3. See text accompanying notes 18–22 infra (discussing Belva A. Lockwood).

4. See Morello, supra note 1, at 131 (discussing Crystal Eastman).

5. K. Morello, "Bar Admission Was Rough for 19th Century Women," N.Y.L.J., May 13, 1983, at 19.

6. See, e.g., R. Bloch, "American Feminine Ideals in Transition, the Rise of the Moral Mothers, 1785–1815," *Feminist Studies,* June 1978, at 101; B. Welter, "The Cult of True Womanhood: 1820–1860," 18 Am. Q. 151 (1966).

7. *In re Goodell*, 39 Wis. 232, 244 (1875).

8. Id. at 245 ("The peculiar qualities of womanhood . . . its purity, its delicacy, its emotional impulses . . . are surely not qualifications for forensic strife.").

9. Id. at 245–46.

10. *In re Bradwell,* 55 Ill. 535, 535 (1869).

11. See id. at 535–36.

12. Id. at 539.

13. See *Bradwell v. Illinois,* 83 U.S. (16 Wall.) 130, 139 (1872).

14. Id. at 141 (Bradley, J., concurring).

15. Morello, supra note 1, at x.

16. V. Elwood-Akers, "Clara Shortridge Foltz, California's First Woman Lawyer," 28 Pac. Historian 23, 25 (1984).

17. N. Polos, "San Diego's 'Portia of the Pacific': California's First Woman Lawyer," 26 J. San Diego Hist. 185, 188–89 (1980).

18. J. Davis, "Belva Ann Lockwood: Remover of Mountains," 65 A.B.A.J. 924, 927 (1979).

19. Id.

20. Id.

21. See id.

22. See id. at 928.

23. See *Feminist Majority, The Feminization of Power: Women in the Law* 1, 7 (1990) [hereinafter *Feminization of Power*].

24. See id. at 1 (the Feminist Majority projects that by the year 2000 one-third of the country's attorneys will be women).

25. Id. at 7.

26. Id.

27. Id. at 10.

28. S. J. Carroll, "Taking the Lead," 64 J. State Gov't 43, 43 (1991).

29. Id.

30. Id.

31. Annals Am. Acad. Pol. & Soc. Sci., May 1991, at 67.

32. Carroll, supra note 28, at 43.

33. *Feminization of Power*, supra note 23, at 3.

34. U.S. Const. amend. XIV, § 1.

35. Id. § 2.

36. 83 U.S. (16 Wall.) 36 (1873).

37. See id. at 81.

38. See text accompanying notes 10–12 supra.

39. See *Bradwell v. Illinois*, 83 U.S. (16 Wall.) 130, 138–39 (1872).

40. See *Goesaert v. Cleary*, 335 U.S. 464, 465 (1948).

41. See id. at 465–66.

42. See *Hoyt v. Florida*, 368 U.S. 57, 69 (1961). *Hoyt* was overturned on sixth amendment grounds in *Taylor v. Louisiana*, 419 U.S. 522, 534 (1975).

43. *Hoyt*, 368 U.S. at 61–62.

44. 404 U.S. 71 (1971).

45. See id. at 77.

46. *Frontiero v. Richardson*, 411 U.S. 677, 684 (1973) (plurality opinion).

47. See *Stanton v. Stanton*, 421 U.S. 7, 13–17 (1975).

48. See id. at 10.

49. Id. at 14–15.

50. See *Craig v. Boren*, 429 U.S. 190, 197 (1976).

51. See *Califano v. Goldfarb*, 430 U.S. 199, 212–17 (1977).

52. See *Craig*, 429 U.S. at 199–204.

53. See *Orr v. Orr*, 440 U.S. 268, 278–83 (1979).

54. See *Califano v. Westcott*, 443 U.S. 76, 83–89 (1979).

55. See *Kirchberg v. Feenstra*, 450 U.S. 455, 459–61 (1981).

56. 467 U.S. 69 (1984).

57. See id. at 73–76.

58. See, e.g., *Califano*, 443 U.S. at 89 (disallowing withholding of Social Security benefits when mother, not father was unemployed).

59. See, e.g., S. Sherry, "Civil Virtue and the Feminine Voice in Constitutional Adjudication," 72 Va. L. Rev. 543, 580–84 (1986).

60. See id. at 613.

61. See text accompanying note 15 supra.

62. R. Barnett & G. Baruch, "Determinants of Fathers' Participation in Family Work," 49 J. Marriage & Family 29, 33 (1987) (husbands of working women performed average of 30 percent of child-care tasks, and 19 percent of household chores).

63. V. Drachman, "My 'Partner' in Law and Life: Marriage in the Lives of Women Lawyers in Late 19th- and Early 20th-Century America," 14 Law & Soc. Inquiry 221, 231 (1989).

64. See, e.g., J. Kaye, "Women Lawyers in Big Firms: A Study of Progress toward Gender Equality," 57 Fordham L. Rev. 111 (1988); L. LaMothe, "Endangered Species," Stanford Law., Spring/Summer 1989, at 14; J. Kingson, "Women in Law Say Path Is Limited by 'Mommy Track,'" N.Y. Times, Aug. 8, 1988, at A1.

65. 208 U.S. 412 (1908).

66. See id. at 421.

67. 414 U.S. 632 (1974).

68. See id. at 651.

69. See id. at 644, 647–48.

70. See *Geduldig v. Aiello*, 417 U.S. 484, 492–97 (1974).

71. See id. at 496 n.20.

72. See id. at 497 n.20.

73. See *General Elec. v. Gilbert*, 429 U.S. 125, 133–36 (1976).

74. Id. at 136.

75. See 42 U.S.C. § 2000e(k) (1989).

76. H.R. Rep. No. 948, 95th Cong., 2d Sess. 3, reprinted in 1978 U.S.C.C.A.N. 4749, 4752 ("Pregnancy-based distinctions will be subject to the same scrutiny on the same terms as other acts of sex discrimination proscribed in the existing statute.").

77. 123 Cong. Rec. 29, 658 (1977).

78. See *Califano Fed. Sav. & Loan Ass'n v. Guerra*, 479 U.S. 272 (1987).

79. Id. at 278–79.

80. See id. at 285.

81. Id. at 289.

82. Id. at 290.

83. See text accompanying note 66 supra.

84. See *International Union v. Johnson Controls*, 111 S. Ct. 1196, 1207–8 (1991).

85. Id. at 1209–10.

86. See id. at 1207.

87. Id.

88. See id. at 1206.

89. See text accompanying notes 59–61 supra.

90. D. Margolick, "Women's Milestone: Majority on Minnesota Court," N.Y. Times, Feb. 22, 1991, at B16.

Chapter 4

Speaking in a Judicial Voice

Ruth Bader Ginsburg

The Madison Lecture series has exposed and developed two main themes: human rights and the administration of justice, particularly in our nation's federal courts.[1] My remarks touch on both themes; I will speak first about collegiality in style, and next about moderation in the substance of appellate decision making. My views on these matters reflect experiences over a span of three decades. They have been shaped by my years as a law teacher beginning in the 1960s, through the 1970s when I helped to launch the American Civil Liberties Union's Women's Rights Project, and most recently during the nearly thirteen years I have had the good fortune to serve on the U.S. Court of Appeals for the District of Columbia Circuit. What I hope to convey about courts, I believe, is in line with the founders'—Madison's and Hamilton's—expectation. As a preface, I will comment on that expectation.

James Madison's forecast still brightens the spirit of federal judges. In his June 1789 speech introducing to Congress the amendments that led to the Bill of Rights, Madison urged:

> If [a Bill of Rights is] incorporated into the Constitution, independent tribunals of justice will consider themselves in a peculiar manner the guardians of those rights; they will be an impenetrable bulwark . . . naturally led to resist every encroachment upon rights . . . stipulated for in the Constitution by the declaration of rights.[2]

Today's independent tribunals of justice are faithful to that "original understanding" when they adhere to traditional ways in which courts have realized the expectation Madison expressed.

This lecture was delivered on March 9, 1992, and appeared in 67 N.Y.U.L. Rev. 1185 (1992).

In *The Federalist No. 78*, Alexander Hamilton said that federal judges, in order to preserve the people's rights and privileges, must have authority to check legislation and acts of the executive for constitutionality.[3] But he qualified his recognition of that awesome authority. The judiciary, Hamilton wrote, from the very nature of its functions will always be "the least dangerous" branch of government, for judges hold neither the sword nor the purse of the community; ultimately, they must depend upon the political branches to effectuate their judgments.[4] Mindful of that reality, the effective judge, I believe and will explain why in these remarks, strives to persuade, and not to pontificate. She speaks in "a moderate and restrained" voice,[5] engaging in a dialogue with, not a diatribe against, coequal departments of government, state authorities, and even her own colleagues.

I spoke of the founders' "original understanding" a moment ago, and that expression, as I comprehend it, bears clarification in this preface. In his 1987 Foreword to *The Evolving Constitution,* the second collection of Madison Lectures, Norman Dorsen stressed, as Chief Justice John Marshall did in 1819, that our fundamental instrument of government is an evolving document, "an instrument 'intended to endure for ages to come.'"[6] Professor Dorsen quoted Chief Justice Charles Evans Hughes's 1934 rejection of the notion that "the great clauses of the Constitution must be confined to the interpretation which the framers, with the conditions and outlook of their time, would have placed upon them."[7] That understanding, as Professor Dorsen commented, has been and should remain common ground.[8]

In the recent decade and more of bicentennial celebrations, Supreme Court Justice Thurgood Marshall reminded us that while the Constitution's endurance is indeed something to celebrate, the framers had a distinctly limited vision of those who counted among "We the People."[9] Qualified voters when the nation was new bore more than a passing resemblance to the framers: The franchise was confined to property-owning adult white males, people free from dependence on others, and therefore considered trustworthy citizens, not susceptible to influence or control by masters, overlords, or supervisors.[10] In 1787, only five of the thirteen states had abolished slavery, women did not count as part of the franchise-holding, politically active community in any state, and wealth qualifications severely limited voter eligibility even among white males.[11] In correspondence with a friend about the qualifications for voting in his home state of Massachusetts, patriot and second president John Adams elaborated:

[I]t is dangerous to open so fruitful a source of controversy and altercation as would be opened by attempting to alter the qualifications of voters; there will be no end of it. New claims will arise; women will demand a vote; lads from twelve to twenty-one will think their rights not enough attended to; and every man who has not a farthing, will demand an equal voice with any other, in all acts of state. It tends to confound and destroy all distinctions, and prostrate all ranks to one common level.[12]

Our second president notwithstanding, equalizing voices and destroying rank distinctions have been dominant concerns in recent generations and, as one would expect, the focus of several Madison Lectures.[13] Although the word "equal," or "equality," in relation to individual rights does not even appear in the original U.S. Constitution or in the first ten amendments that compose the Bill of Rights,[14] the ideal of the equal dignity of individuals is part of our constitutional legacy, even of the pre–Civil War original understanding, in this vital sense. The founding fathers rebelled against the patriarchal power of kings and the idea that political authority may legitimately rest on birth status. Their culture held them back from fully perceiving or acting upon ideals of human equality and dignity. Thomas Jefferson, for example, when president, told his secretary of the treasury: "The appointment of a woman to public office is an innovation for which the public is not prepared, nor am I."[15] But the founders stated a commitment in the Declaration of Independence to equality and in the Declaration and the Bill of Rights to individual liberty. Those commitments had growth potential. As historian Richard Morris has written, a prime portion of the history of the U.S. Constitution is the story of the extension (through amendment, judicial interpretation, and practice) of constitutional rights and protections to once-excluded groups: to people who were once held in bondage, to men without property, to Native Americans, and to women.[16]

I. Collegiality in Appellate Decision Making

I turn now to the first of the two topics this lecture addresses—the style of judging appropriate for appellate judges whose mission it is, in Hamilton's words, "to secure a steady, upright, and impartial administration of the laws."[17] Integrity, knowledge, and, most essentially, judgment are the qualities Hamilton ascribed to the judiciary.[18] How is that essential quality, judgment, conveyed in the opinions appellate judges write? What role should moderation, restraint, and collegiality play in the formulation of judicial decisions? As background, I will describe three distinct patterns of appellate opinion casting: individual, institutional, and in between.[19]

The individual judging pattern has been characteristic of the Law Lords, who serve as Great Britain's Supreme Court. The Lords sit in panels of five and traditionally have delivered their opinions seriatim, each panel member in turn announcing his individual judgment and the reasons for it.[20]

In contrast to the British tradition of opinions separately rendered by each judge as an individual, the continental or civil law traditions typified and spread abroad by France and Germany call for collective, corporate judgments. In dispositions of that genre, disagreement is not disclosed. Neither dissent nor separate concurrence is published. Cases are decided with a single, per curiam opinion generally following a uniform, anonymous style.[21]

Our Supreme Court, when John Marshall became Chief Justice, made a start in the institutional opinion direction. Marshall is credited with establishing the practice of announcing judgments in a single opinion for the Court.[22] The Marshall Court, and certainly its leader, had a strong sense of institutional mission, a mission well served by unanimity. Marshall was criticized, in those early days, for suppressing dissent. Thomas Jefferson complained: "An opinion is huddled up in conclave, perhaps by a majority of one, delivered as if unanimous, and with the silent acquiescence of lazy or timid associates, by a crafty chief judge, who sophisticates the law to his own mind, by the turn of his own reasoning."[23]

But even Marshall, during his long tenure as Chief Justice, ultimately dissented on several occasions and once concurred with a separate opinion.[24] We continue in that middle way today. Our appellate courts generally produce a judgment or opinion for the court. In that respect, we bear some resemblance to the highly institution-minded civil law judges, although our judges individually claim authorship of most of the opinions they publish. In tune with the British or common law tradition, however, we place no formal limit on the prerogative of each judge to speak out separately.

To point up the difference between individual and institutional modes of judging, I have drawn upon a 1989 letter from a civilian jurist.[25] The letter came from a member of the Conseil d'Etat, the illustrious body created by Napoleon that still serves, among other functions, as Supreme Administrative Court for France. The conseiller who wrote to me had observed, together with several of his colleagues, an appellate argument in the District of Columbia Circuit. The appeal was from a criminal conviction; the prime issue concerned the fifth amendment's double jeopardy ban.[26] When the case was decided, I sent our French visitors copies of the slip sheet. It contained the panel's judgment, and three opinions, one per judge. I paraphrase the *conseiller*'s reaction:

> The way the decision is given is surprising for us according to our standards. The discussion of theory and of the meaning of precedents is remarkable. But the divided opinions seem to me very far from the way a judgment should issue, particularly in a criminal case. The judgment of a court should be precise and concise, not a discourse among professors, but the order of people charged to speak in the name of the law, and therefore written with simplicity and clarity, presenting short explanations. A judgment that is too long indicates uncertainty.
>
> At the same time, it is very impressive for me to see members of a court give to the litigants and to the readers the content of their hesitations and doubts, without diminishing the credibility of justice, in which the American is so confident.[27]

The *conseiller* seems at first distressed, even appalled, at our readiness to admit that legal judgments (including constitutional rulings) are not always clear and certain. In his second thought, however, the *conseiller* appears impressed, touched with envy or admiration that our system of justice is so secure that we can tolerate open displays of disagreement among judges about what the law is.[28]

But overindulgence in separate opinion writing may undermine both the reputation of the judiciary for judgment and the respect accorded court dispositions. The rule-of-law virtues of consistency, predictability, clarity, and stability may be slighted when a court routinely fails to act as a collegial body.[29] Dangers to the system are posed by two tendencies: too frequent a resort to separate opinions and the immoderate tone of statements diverging from the position of the court's majority.

Regarding the first danger, recall that "the Great Dissenter," Justice Oliver Wendell Holmes, in fact dissented less often than most of his colleagues.[30] Chief Justice Harlan F. Stone once wrote to Karl Llewellyn (both gentlemen were public defenders of the right to dissent): "You know, if I should write in every case where I do not agree with some of the views expressed in the opinions, you and all my other friends would stop reading my separate opinions."[31] In matters of statutory interpretation, Justice Louis D. Brandeis repeatedly cautioned: "It is more important that the applicable rule of law be settled than that it be settled right." "This is commonly true," Brandeis continued, "even where the error is a matter of serious concern, provided correction can be had by legislation."[32] Revered constitutional scholar Paul A. Freund, who clerked for Justice Brandeis, recalled Justice Cardozo's readiness to suppress his dissent in common law cases (the Supreme Court had more of those in pre-*Erie*[33] days), so that a unanimous opinion would come down.[34]

Separate concurrences and dissents characterize Supreme Court decisions to a much greater extent than they do court of appeals three-judge panel decisions. In the District of Columbia Circuit, for example, for the statistical year ending June 1992, the court rendered 405 judgments in cases not disposed of summarily; over 86 percent of those decisions were unanimous.[35] During that same period, the Supreme Court decided 114 cases with full opinions; only 21.9 percent of the decisions were unanimous.[36] A reality not highlighted by a press fond of separating Carter from Reagan-Bush appointees[37] accounts in considerable measure for this difference: The character of cases heard by courts of appeals combines with our modus operandi to tug us strongly toward the middle, toward moderation and away from notably creative or excessively rigid positions.[38] (The tug is not so strong, however, as to make a proposal I recently advanced acceptable. At a meeting of U.S. court of appeals judges in February 1993, I suggested that when panels are unanimous, the standard practice should be to issue the decision per curiam, without disclosing the opinion writer. That would encourage brevity, I thought, and might speed up dispositions. Few of the judges in attendance found the idea appealing.)

Concerning the character of federal cases, unlike the Supreme Court, courts of appeals deal far less frequently with grand constitutional questions than with less cosmic questions of statutory interpretation or the rationality of agency or district court decisions. In most matters of that variety, as Justice Brandeis indicated, it is best that the matter be definitively settled,[39] preferably with one opinion. Furthermore, lower court judges are bound more tightly by Supreme Court precedent than is the High Court itself.

Turning to the way we operate, I note first that no three-judge panel in a circuit is at liberty to depart from the published decision of a prior panel; the law of the circuit may be altered only by the court en banc.[40] To ensure that each panel knows what the others are doing, the District of Columbia Circuit, and several other federal circuit courts of appeals, circulate opinions to the full court, once approved by a panel, at least a week in advance of release.[41]

Second, in contrast to district judges, who are the real power holders in the federal court system—lords of their individual fiefdoms from case filing to first instance final judgment—no single court of appeals judge can carry the day in any case. To attract a second vote and establish durable law for the circuit, a judge may find it necessary to moderate her own position, sometimes to be less bold, other times to be less clear.[42] We can listen to and persuade each other in groups of three more effectively than can a larger panel.

On the few occasions each year when we sit en banc—in the District of Columbia Circuit, all twelve of us when we are full strength—I can appreciate why unanimity is so much harder to achieve in Supreme Court judgments. Not only do the Justices deal much more often with constitutional questions, where, in many cases, only overruling or constitutional amendment can correct a mistake. In addition, one becomes weary after going round the table on a first ballot. It is ever so much easier to have a conversation—and an exchange of views on opinion drafts—among three than among nine or twelve.[43]

In writing for the court, one must be sensitive to the sensibilities and mind-sets of one's colleagues, which may mean avoiding certain arguments and authorities, even certain words.[44] Should institutional concerns affect the tone of separate opinions, when a judge finds it necessary to write one?

I emphasize first that dissents and separate concurrences are not consummations devoutly to be avoided. As Justice William J. Brennan said in thoughtful defense of dissents: "None of us, lawyer or layman, teacher or student, in our society must ever feel that to express a conviction, honestly and sincerely maintained, is to violate some unwritten law of manners or decorum."[45] I question, however, the resort to expressions in separate opinions that generate more heat than light. Consider this sample from an April 1991 District of Columbia Circuit decision. The dissenter led off: "Running headlong from the questions briefed and argued before us, my colleagues seek refuge in a theory as novel as it is questionable. Unsupported by precedent, undeveloped by the court, and unresponsive to the facts of this case, the . . . theory announced today has an inauspicious birth."[46] That spicy statement, by the way, opposed an en banc opinion in which all of the judges concurred, except the lone dissenter.

It is "not good for public respect for courts and law and the administration of justice," Roscoe Pound decades ago observed, for an appellate judge to burden an opinion with "intemperate denunciation of [the writer's] colleagues, violent invective, attributi[on]s of bad motives to the majority of the court, and insinuations of incompetence, negligence, prejudice, or obtuseness of [other judges]."[47] Yet one has only to thumb through the pages of current volumes of United States Reports and Federal Reporter Second to come upon condemnations by the score of a court or colleague's opinion or assertion, as, for example, "folly,"[48] "ludicrous,"[49] "outrageous,"[50] one that "cannot be taken seriously,"[51] "inexplicable,"[52] "the quintessence of inequity,"[53] a "blow against the People,"[54] "naked analytical bootstrapping,"[55] "reminiscent . . . of Sherman's march through Georgia,"[56] and "Orwellian."[57]

"[L]anguage impugning the motives of a colleague," Senior Third Circuit Judge Collins J. Seitz recently commented, may give momentary satisfaction to the separate opinion writer, but "does nothing to further cordial relationships on the court."[58] Judge Seitz counseled "waiting a day"—I would suggest even a week or two—"before deciding whether to send a biting response."[59]

The most effective dissent, I am convinced, "stand[s] on its own legal footing";[60] it spells out differences without jeopardizing collegiality or public respect for and confidence in the judiciary. I try to write my few separate opinions each year as I once did briefs for appellees—as affirmative statements of my reasons, drafted before receiving the court's opinion, and later adjusted, as needed, to meet the majority's presentation. Among path-marking models, one can look to Justice Curtis's classic dissent in the *Dred Scott* case,[61] and, closer to our time, separate opinions by the second Justice John Marshall Harlan.[62]

Taking a comparative side-glance, I find instructive the March 5, 1992, judgment of the Supreme Court of Ireland in the case of *Attorney General v. X.*[63] The case involved a fourteen-year-old girl who, it was alleged, had been raped by the father of a school friend and had become pregnant. She and her parents had gone to England to secure an abortion. But they promptly returned home when notified that the Attorney General had obtained an order from the High Court (the court of first instance) in Ireland enjoining their travel and its purpose. At issue was a clause of the Constitution of Ireland that read: "The State acknowledges the right to life of the unborn and, with due regard to the equal right to life of the mother, guarantees in its laws to respect, and, as far as practicable, by its laws to defend and vindicate that right."[64]

In fact, no implementing laws had been passed, so the courts were called upon to interpret the Constitution directly. The Supreme Court, composed of five judges, voted four to one to set aside the High Court's February 17,

1992, injunction.[65] Each judge spoke separately, but the majority agreed that, in view of the documented "real and substantial" risk that the girl would take her own life, termination of her pregnancy was permissible, even in Ireland itself. In so ruling, the Chief Justice referred to precedent calling upon judges to bring to bear on their judgments the instruction in the Constitution's preamble that the fundamental instrument of government was adopted by the People "to promote the common good, with due observance of prudence, justice and charity so that the dignity and freedom of the individual might be assured."[66] Those concepts and judicial interpretations of them, the Chief Justice said, "may gradually change or develop as society changes and develops."[67]

The dissenting Justice spent no energy characterizing his colleagues' opinions as "activist" or "imperial."[68] He simply stated affirmatively his view that the evidence did not justify overturning the injunction.[69] "Suicide threats," he reasoned, "can be contained."[70] "The choice," he said, was "between the certain death of the unborn life and a feared substantial danger ... but no degree of certainty of the mother's death by way of self-destruction."[71] The Constitution's "equal right" provision, he concluded, required the judiciary to prevent the certain death, not the one that could be guarded against.

I did not select this example as a springboard to comparison of positions on access to abortion under constitutional prescriptions and legal regimes here and abroad.[72] I chose *Attorney General v. X* only to demonstrate that even in the most emotion-laden, politically sensitive case, effective opinion writing does not require a judge to upbraid colleagues for failing to see the light or to get it right.[73]

Concerned about the erosion of civility in the legal profession, the Seventh Circuit, commencing in the fall of 1989, conducted a "study and investigation into litigation practices and the attending relationships among lawyers, among judges, and between lawyers and judges."[74] The Final Report of the committee in charge of the study, released in June 1992, urges judges to set a good example by staying on the high ground. Specifically, the Report calls on judges to avoid "disparaging personal remarks or criticisms, or sarcastic or demeaning comments about another judge," and instead to "be courteous, respectful, and civil in opinions, ever mindful that a position articulated by another judge generally is the result of that judge's earnest effort to interpret the law and the facts correctly."[75] To that good advice, one can say "amen."

II. Measured Motions in Third-Branch Decision Making

Moving from the style to the substance of third-branch decision making, I will stress in the remainder of these remarks that judges play an interdependent part in our democracy. They do not alone shape legal doctrine but, as I suggested at the outset, they participate in a dialogue with other organs of government, and with the people as well.[76] "Judges do and must legislate," Justice Holmes "recognized without hesitation," but "they can do so," he cautioned, "only interstitially; they are confined from molar to molecular motions."[77] Measured motions seem to me right, in the main, for constitutional as well as common law adjudication. Doctrinal limbs too swiftly shaped, experience teaches, may prove unstable.[78] The most prominent example in recent decades is *Roe v. Wade*.[79] To illustrate my point, I have contrasted that breathtaking 1973 decision with the Court's more cautious dispositions, contemporaneous with *Roe*, in cases involving explicitly sex-based classifications,[80] and will further develop that comparison here.

The seven-to-two judgment in *Roe v. Wade*[81] declared "violative of the Due Process Clause of the Fourteenth Amendment" a Texas criminal abortion statute that intolerably shackled a woman's autonomy; the Texas law "excepted from criminality only a *life-saving* procedure on behalf of the pregnant woman."[82] Suppose the Court had stopped there, rightly declaring unconstitutional the most extreme brand of law in the nation, and had not gone on, as the Court did in *Roe*, to fashion a regime blanketing the subject, a set of rules that displaced virtually every state law then in force.[83] Would there have been the twenty-year controversy we have witnessed, reflected most recently in the Supreme Court's splintered decision in *Planned Parenthood v. Casey*?[84] A less encompassing *Roe*, one that merely struck down the extreme Texas law and went no further on that day, I believe and will summarize why, might have served to reduce rather than to fuel controversy.

In the 1992 *Planned Parenthood* decision, the three controlling Justices accepted as constitutional several restrictions on access to abortion that could not have survived strict adherence to *Roe*.[85] While those Justices did not closely consider the plight of women without means to overcome the restrictions, they added an important strand to the Court's opinions on abortion—they acknowledged the intimate connection between a woman's "ability to control her reproductive life" and her "ability . . . to participate equally in the economic and social life of the Nation."[86] The idea of the woman in control of her destiny and her place in society[87] was less prominent in the *Roe* decision itself, which coupled the rights of the pregnant woman with the free exercise of her physician's medical judgment.[88] The *Roe* decision might have been less of a storm center[89] had it both homed in more precisely on the women's equality dimension of the issue and, correspondingly, attempted nothing more bold at that time than the mode of decision making the Court employed in the 1970s gender classification cases.

In fact, the very term *Roe* was decided, the Supreme Court had on its calendar a case that could have served as a bridge, linking reproductive choice to disadvantageous treatment of women on the basis of their sex. The case was *Struck v. Secretary of Defense*;[90] it involved a captain the Air Force sought to discharge in Vietnam War days. Perhaps it is indulgence in wishful thinking, but the *Struck* case, I believe, would have proved extraordinarily educational for the Court and had large potential for advancing public understanding. Captain Susan Struck was a career officer. According to her commanding officer, her performance as a manager and nurse was exemplary.[91] Captain Struck had avoided the drugs and the alcohol that hooked many service members in the late 1960s and early 1970s,[92] but she did become pregnant while stationed in Vietnam. She undertook to use, and in fact used, only her accumulated leave time for childbirth. She declared her intention to place, and in fact placed, her child for adoption immediately after birth. Her religious faith precluded recourse to abortion.[93]

Two features of Captain Struck's case are particularly noteworthy. First, the rule she challenged was unequivocal and typical of the time. It provided: "A woman officer will be discharged from the service with the least practicable delay when a determination is made by a medical officer that she is pregnant."[94] To cover any oversight, the Air Force had a backup rule: "The commission of any woman officer will be terminated with the least practicable delay when it is established that she . . . has given birth to a living child while in a commissioned officer status."[95]

A second striking element of Captain Struck's case was the escape route available to her, which she chose not to take. Air Force regulations current at the start of the 1970s provided: "The Air Force Medical Service is not subject to State laws in the performance of its functions. When medically indicated or for reasons involving medical health, pregnancies may be terminated in Air Force hospitals . . . ideally before 20 weeks gestation."[96]

Captain Struck argued that the unwanted discharge she faced unjustifiably restricted her personal autonomy and dignity; principally, however, she maintained that the regulation mandating her discharge violated the equal protection of the laws guarantee implicit in the fifth amendment's due process clause.[97] She urged that the Air Force regime differentiated invidiously by allowing males who became fathers, but not females who became mothers, to remain in service and by allowing women who had undergone abortions, but not women who delivered infants, to continue their military careers.[98] Her pleas were unsuccessful in the lower courts, but on October 24, 1972, less than three months before the *Roe* decision, the Supreme Court granted her petition for certiorari.[99]

At that point the Air Force decided it would rather switch than fight. At the end of November 1972, it granted Captain Struck a waiver of the once unwaivable regulation and permitted her to continue her service as an Air Force officer. The Solicitor General promptly and successfully suggested that the case had become moot.[100]

Given the parade of cases on the Court's full calendar, it is doubtful that the Justices trained further attention on the *Struck* scenario. With more time and space for reflection, however, and perhaps a female presence on the Court, might the Justices have gained at least these two insights? First, if even the military, an institution not known for avant-garde policy, had taken to providing facilities for abortion, then was not a decision of *Roe*'s muscularity unnecessary? Second, confronted with Captain Struck's unwanted discharge, might the Court have comprehended an argument, or at least glimpsed a reality, it later resisted—that disadvantageous treatment of a woman because of her pregnancy and reproductive choice is a paradigm case of discrimination on the basis of sex?[101] What was the assumption underlying the differential treatment to which Captain Struck was exposed? The regulations that mandated her discharge were not even thinly disguised. They declared, effectively, that responsibility for children disabled female parents, but not male parents, for other work—not for biological reasons, but because society had ordered things that way.[102]

Captain Struck had asked the Court first to apply the highest level of scrutiny to her case, to hold that the sex-based classification she encountered was a "suspect" category for legislative or administrative action.[103] As a fallback, she suggested to the Court an intermediate standard of review, one under which prescriptions that worked to women's disadvantage would gain review of at least heightened, if not the very highest, intensity.[104] In the course of the 1970s, the Supreme Court explicitly acknowledged that it was indeed applying an elevated, labeled "intermediate," level of review to classifications it recognized as sex-based.[105]

Justice O'Connor carefully traced that development in last year's Madison Lecture,[106] and I will recall it only summarily. Until 1971, women did not prevail before the Supreme Court in any case charging unconstitutional sex discrimination.[107] In the years from 1971 to 1982, however, the Court held unconstitutional, as violative of due process or equal protection constraints, a series of state and federal laws that differentiated explicitly on the basis of sex.[108]

The Court ruled in 1973, for example, that married women in the military were entitled to the housing allowance and family medical care benefits that Congress had provided solely for married men in the military.[109] Two years later, the Court held it unconstitutional for a state to allow a parent to stop supporting a daughter once she reached the age of eighteen, while requiring parental support for a son until he turned twenty-one.[110] In 1975, and again in 1979, the Court declared that state jury-selection systems could not exclude or exempt women as a class.[111] In decisions running from 1975 to 1980, the Court deleted the principal explicitly sex-based classifications in social insurance[112] and workers' compensation schemes.[113] In 1981, the Court said nevermore to a state law designating the husband "head and master" of the household.[114] And in 1982, in an opinion by Justice O'Connor, the Court held that a state could not limit admission to a state nursing college to women only.[115]

The backdrop for these rulings was the phenomenal expansion, in the years from 1961 to 1971, of women's employment outside the home,[116] the civil rights movement of the 1960s and the precedents set in that struggle,[117] and a revived feminist movement, fueled abroad and in the United States by Simone de Beauvoir's remarkable 1949 publication, *The Second Sex*.[118] In the main, the Court invalidated laws that had become obsolete, retained into the 1970s by only a few of the states.[119] In a core set of cases, however, those dealing with social insurance benefits for a worker's spouse or family,[120] the decisions did not utterly condemn the legislature's product. Instead, the Court, in effect, opened a dialogue with the political branches of government. In essence, the Court instructed Congress and state legislatures: Rethink ancient positions on these questions. Should you determine that special treatment for women is warranted, that is, compensatory legislation because of the sunken-in social and economic bias or disadvantage women encounter, we have left you a corridor in which to move.[121] But your classifications must be refined, adopted for remedial reasons, and not rooted in prejudice about "the way women (or men) are."[122] In the meantime, the Court's decrees removed no benefits; instead, they extended to a woman worker's husband, widower, or family benefits Congress had authorized only for members of a male worker's family.[123]

The ball, one might say, was tossed by the Justices back into the legislators' court, where the political forces of the day could operate. The Supreme Court wrote modestly, it put forward no grand philosophy;[124] but by requiring legislative reexamination of once customary sex-based classifications, the Court helped to ensure that laws and regulations would "catch up with a changed world."[125]

Roe v. Wade,[126] in contrast, invited no dialogue with legislators. Instead, it seemed entirely to remove the ball from the legislators' court. In 1973, when *Roe* issued, abortion law was in a state of change across the nation. As the Supreme Court itself noted, there was a marked trend in state legislatures "toward liberalization of abortion statutes."[127] That movement for legislative change ran parallel to another law revision effort then under way— the change from fault to no-fault divorce regimes, a reform that swept through the state legislatures and captured all of them by the mid-1980s.[128]

No measured motion, the *Roe* decision left virtually no state with laws fully conforming to the Court's delineation of abortion regulation still permissible.[129] Around that extraordinary decision, a well-organized and vocal right-to-life movement rallied and succeeded, for a considerable time, in turning the legislative tide in the opposite direction.

Constitutional review by courts is an institution that has been for some two centuries our nation's hallmark and pride.[130] Two extreme modes of court intervention in social change processes, however, have placed stress on the institution. At one extreme, the Supreme Court steps boldly in front of the political process, as some believe it did in *Roe*.[131] At the opposite extreme, the Court in the early part of the twentieth century found—or thrust—itself into the rearguard opposing change, striking down, as unconstitutional, laws embodying a new philosophy of economic regulation at odds with the nineteenth century's laissez-faire approach.[132] Decisions at both of these poles yielded outcries against the judiciary in certain quarters. The Supreme Court, particularly, was labeled "activist" or "imperial," and its precarious position as final arbiter of constitutional questions was exposed.[133]

I do not suggest that the Court should never step ahead of the political branches in pursuit of a constitutional precept. *Brown v. Board of Education*,[134] the 1954 decision declaring racial segregation in public schools offensive to the equal protection principle, is the case that best fits the bill. Past the midpoint of the twentieth century, apartheid remained the law-enforced system in several states, shielded by a constitutional interpretation the Court itself had advanced at the turn of the century—the "separate but equal" doctrine.[135]

In contrast to the legislative reform movement in the states, contemporaneous with *Roe*, widening access to abortion, prospects in 1954 for state legislation dismantling racially segregated schools were bleak. That was so, I believe, for a reason that distances race discrimination from discrimination based on sex. Most women are life partners of men; women bear and raise both sons and daughters. Once women's own consciousness was awakened to the unfairness of allocating opportunity and responsibility on the basis of sex, the education of others—of fathers, husbands, sons as well as daughters—could begin, or be reinforced, at home.[136] When blacks were confined by law to a separate sector, there was no similar prospect for educating the white majority.[137]

It bears emphasis, however, that *Brown* was not an altogether bold decision. First, Thurgood Marshall and those who worked with him in the campaign against racial injustice, carefully set the stepping stones leading up to the landmark ruling.[138] Pathmarkers of the same kind had not been installed prior to the Court's decision in *Roe*.[139] Second, *Brown* launched no broadside attack on the Jim Crow system in all its institutional manifestations. Instead, the Court concentrated on segregated schools;[140] it left the follow-up for other days and future cases. A burgeoning civil rights movement—which *Brown* helped to propel—culminating in the Civil Rights Act of 1964,[141] set the stage for the Court's ultimate total rejection of Jim Crow legislation.

Significantly, in relation to the point I just made about women and men living together, the end of the Jim Crow era came in 1967, thirteen years after *Brown*: The case was *Loving v. Virginia*,[142] the law under attack, a state prohibition on interracial marriage. In holding that law unconstitutional, the Court effectively ruled that, with regard to racial classifications, the doctrine of "separate but equal" was dead—everywhere and anywhere within the governance of the United States.[143]

The framers of the Constitution allowed to rest in the Court's hands large authority to rule on the Constitution's meaning; but the framers, as I noted at the outset, armed the Court with no swords to carry out its pronouncements. President Andrew Jackson in 1832, according to an often-told legend, said of a Supreme Court decision he did not like: "The Chief Justice has made his decision, now let him enforce it."[144] With prestige to persuade, but not physical power to enforce, with a will for self-preservation and the knowledge that they are not "a bevy of Platonic Guardians,"[145] the Justices generally follow, they do not lead, changes taking place elsewhere in society.[146] But without taking giant strides and thereby risking a backlash too forceful to contain, the Court, through constitutional adjudication, can reinforce or signal a green light for social change. In most of the post-1970 gender-classification cases, unlike *Roe*, the Court functioned in just that way. It approved the direction of change through a temperate brand of decision making, one that was not extravagant or divisive. *Roe*, on the other hand, halted a political process that was moving in a reform direction and thereby, I believe, prolonged divisiveness and deferred stable settlement of the issue. The most recent *Planned Parenthood* decision[147] notably retreats from *Roe*[148] and further excludes from the High Court's protection women lacking the means or the sophistication to surmount burdensome legislation.[149] The latest decision may have had the sanguine effect, however, of contributing to the ongoing revitalization in the 1980s and 1990s of the political movement in progress in the early 1970s, a movement that addressed not simply or dominantly the courts but primarily the people's representatives and the people themselves. That renewed force, one may hope, will—within a relatively short span—yield an enduring resolution of this vital matter in a way that affirms the dignity and equality of women.[150]

Conclusion

To sum up what I have tried to convey in this lecture, I will recall the counsel my teacher and friend, Professor Gerald Gunther, offered when I was installed as a judge. Professor Gunther had in mind a great jurist, Judge Learned Hand, whose biography Professor Gunther is just now completing. The good judge, Professor Gunther said, is "openminded and detached, . . . heedful of limitations stemming from the judge's own competence and, above all, from the presuppositions of our constitutional scheme; th[at] judge . . . recognizes that a felt need to act only interstitially does not mean relegation of judges to a trivial or mechanical role, but rather affords the most responsible room for creative, important judicial contributions."[151]

NOTES

1. See Norman Dorsen, Foreword to *The Evolving Constitution*, at x (Norman Dorsen ed., 1987).

2. 1 Annals of Congress 457 (Joseph Gales ed., 1789), quoted in *Chapman v. California*, 386 U.S. 18, 21 n.4 (1967). While Madison originally doubted the effi-

cacy of bills of rights, he eventually joined Jefferson in recognizing the value of "the legal check [a declaration of rights] puts into the hands of the judiciary." Letter from Thomas Jefferson to James Madison (Mar. 15, 1789), in 14 *The Papers of Thomas Jefferson* 659 (Julian P. Boyd ed., 1958); see also Maeva Marcus, "The Adoption of the Bill of Rights," 1 Wm. & Mary Bill of Rts. J. 115, 117–19 (1992).

3. See The Federalist No. 78, at 466 (Alexander Hamilton) (Clinton Rossiter ed., 1961).

4. Id. at 465.

5. I borrow language here from Professor Brainerd Currie's guide to analysis of choice-of-law cases in which the policies of two states are in apparent conflict. See Brainerd Currie, "The Disinterested Third State," 28 Law & Contemp. Probs. 754, 757 (1963) ("[T]he conception should be re-examined, with a view to a more moderate and restrained interpretation both of the policy and of the circumstances in which it must be applied to effectuate the forum's legitimate purpose."); see also Herma Hill Kay, "A Defense of Currie's Governmental Interest Analysis," 215 Recueil des Cours 10, 68–73 (1989–III).

6. Dorsen, supra note 1, at xii (quoting *McCulloch v. Maryland*, 17 U.S. (4 Wheat.) 316, 415 (1819)).

7. Id. (quoting *Home Bldg. & Loan Ass'n v. Blaisdell*, 290 U.S. 398, 443 (1934)).

8. See id.

9. See Thurgood Marshall, "Reflections on the Bicentennial of the United States Constitution," 101 Harv. L. Rev. 1, 2 (1987).

10. See Richard B. Morris, *The Forging of the Union, 1781–1789*, at 162–93 (1987); Linda K. Kerber, "Ourselves and Our Daughters Forever: Women and the Constitution, 1787–1876," This Constitution: A Bicentennial Chron., Spring 1985, at 25.

11. See Deborah Jones Merritt, "What's Missing from the Bill of Rights?" 1991 U. Ill. L. Rev. 765, 766–69.

12. Letter from John Adams to James Sullivan (May 26, 1776), in 9 *The Works of John Adams* 378 (Charles Francis Adams ed., 1854).

13. See, e.g., Arthur Goldberg, "Equality and Governmental Action," in *The Evolving Constitution* 24 (Norman Dorsen ed., 1987); J. Skelly Wright, "Public School Desegregation," in id. at 44; Abe Fortas, "Equal Rights—for Whom?" in id. at 85; Thurgood Marshall, "Group Action in the Pursuit of Justice," in id. at 97.

14. See Merritt, supra note 11, at 765; Morris, supra note 10, at 162–63.

15. Letter from Thomas Jefferson to Albert Gallatin (Jan. 13, 1807), in 1 *The Writings of Albert Gallatin* 328 (Henry Adams ed., 1960). Jefferson, who declared it self-evident "that all men are created equal," also expressed this once prevailing view: "Were our State a pure democracy. . . there would yet be excluded from our deliberations. . . women, who, to prevent depravation of morals and ambiguity of issues, should not mix promiscuously in the public meetings of men." Letter from Thomas Jefferson to Samuel Kercheval (Sept. 5, 1816), in 10 *The Writings of Thomas Jefferson* 46 n.1 (Paul L. Ford ed., 1899).

16. Morris, supra note 10, at 193.

17. The Federalist No. 78, supra note 3, at 465.

18. See id. at 465, 471.

19. I have earlier addressed this topic in Ruth Bader Ginsburg, "Remarks on Writing Separately," 65 Wash. L. Rev. 133 (1990). See also Ruth Bader Ginsburg, "Styles of Collegial Judging," 39 Fed. Bar News & J. 199 (1992). These remarks borrow from, revise, and build upon my prior lectures.

20. See Louis Blom-Cooper & Gavin Drewry, *Final Appeal: A Study of the House of Lords in Its Judicial Capacity* 81–82, 523 (1972); see also Alan Paterson, *The Law Lords* 109–10 (1982) (noting that the Lords no longer routinely deliver five separate opinions).

21. It has been said of the French tradition that the ideal judgment is "considered all the more perfect for its concise and concentrated style, so that only experienced jurists are able to understand and admire it." Rene David & John E. C. Brierley, *Major Legal Systems in the World Today* 129 (2d ed. 1978).

22. See Karl M. ZoBell, "Division of Opinion in the Supreme Court: A History of Judicial Disintegration," 44 Cornell L.Q. 186, 193 (1959); see also G. Edward White, "The Working Life of the Marshall Court, 1815–1835," 70 Va. L. Rev. 1, 36–47 (1984).

23. Letter from Thomas Jefferson to Thomas Ritchie (Dec. 25, 1820), in 10 *The Writings of Thomas Jefferson* 169, 171 (Paul L. Ford ed., 1899).

24. See ZoBell, supra note 22, at 196 & n.57.

25. I first used this illustration in Ruth Bader Ginsburg, "On Muteness, Confidence, and Collegiality: A Response to Professor Nagel," 61 Colo. L. Rev. 715, 718 (1990).

26. *United States v. Rosenberg,* 888 F.2d 1406 (D.C. Cir. 1989).

27. Letter from B. Ducamin, President, Section of Finances, Conseil d'Etat, to Judge Ruth Bader Ginsburg (Dec. 15, 1989) (on file with the New York University Law Review).

28. But cf. Blom-Cooper & Drewry, supra note 20, at 81 (observing that, as an exception to the individual opinion tradition, separate opinions in English criminal appeals are disfavored and may be presented only when the presiding judge so authorizes).

29. See Robert W. Bennett, "A Dissent on Dissent," 74 Judicature 255, 258–59 (1991).

30. See ZoBell, supra note 22, at 202.

31. Walter F. Murphy, *Elements of Judicial Strategy* 62 (1964) (quoting letter from then Justice Stone to Karl Llewellyn (Feb. 4, 1935)).

32. *Burnet v. Coronado Oil & Gas Co.,* 285 U.S. 393, 406 (1932) (Brandeis, J., dissenting) (citation omitted); see also *Di Santo v. Pennsylvania,* 273 U.S. 34, 42 (1927) (Brandeis, J., dissenting).

33. *Erie R.R. Co. v. Tompkins,* 304 U.S. 64 (1938) (holding that federal courts

must apply state law except in matters governed by the federal Constitution or by Acts of Congress).

34. Colloquy, Proceedings of the Forty-Ninth Judicial Conference of the District of Columbia Circuit (May 24, 1988) (comment of Paul A. Freund), reprinted in 124 F.R.D. 241, 336, 347 (1989).

35. See Summary of Annual Report of D.C. Circuit Opinions for Statistical Year July 1, 1991–June 30, 1992 (the 405 figure includes 291 opinions published in the Federal Reporter series and 114 unpublished opinions issued in cases resolved after oral argument; separate concurrences and dissents numbered 55).

36. See "The Supreme Court, 1991 Term—The Statistics," 106 Harv. L. Rev. 378, 380 (1992). For the 68 memorandum orders, however, the unanimity rate was 91.2 percent. See id.

37. See, e.g., George Archibald, "Free Hill Mailings to Future Districts Banned by Court," Wash. Times, July 31, 1992, at A3 ("A three-judge panel of the U.S. Court of Appeals for the District of Columbia split 2–1. . . . Judges Laurence H. Silberman, a Reagan appointee, and A. Raymond Randolph, appointed by President Bush, voted to overturn" the district court's ruling; "Judge Patricia M. Wald, a Carter appointee, voted [to] affirm."); Philip J. Hilts, "Judge Overturns Federal Seizure of Abortion Pill," N.Y. Times, July 15, 1992, at A1 ("In the increasingly political battle over [the] RU486 [abortion pill], the decision favoring the woman, who brought the drug into the country to test the ban, came from a judge who had been appointed by President Jimmy Carter. Later, his order was stopped by a panel of three judges . . . : John M. Walker, President Bush's cousin and a Bush appointee, and Frank X. Altimari and Daniel J. Mahoney, both appointed by President Ronald Reagan."); Karen Riley, "Mayor to Flout Court Ruling," Wash. Times, May 9, 1992, at A1 ("[Mayor Sharon Pratt Kelly] said the Bush and Reagan administrations had packed the federal bench with judges who are in 'retreat' on civil rights issues"; she "threatened to defy" a unanimous federal appeals court decision "by two Carter-appointed judges and a judge appointed by President Bush" striking down the District's minority contracting program.); Cindy Rugeley, "Abortion Fight Now Heads to Legislature," Houston Chron., June 30, 1992, at A11 ("'President Bush has changed his opinion on abortion and so it's not surprising to see the Supreme Court—a majority of whom have been appointed by President Bush or Reagan—ignoring its own precedent and changing its opinion on a woman's right to choose.'") (quoting Texas Lieutenant Governor Bob Bullock); "Will DeKalb Students Win?" Atlanta J. & Const., April 2, 1992, at A18 (editorial) (People seeking "to end the last vestiges of segregation in American schools" face "a federal judiciary dominated by conservatives appointed by Presidents Reagan and Bush"; "[t]hose judges are likely to be more sympathetic to school officials arguing for a return of local control than to minority students seeking remedies to the lingering effects of segregation."). But see, e.g., Mary Deibel, "Supreme Surprises," Star Trib. (Minneapolis), July 5, 1992, at 14A ("Of the three dozen cases in which the administration advocated a position, it lost

20 times, often because of the votes of the five justices appointed by Bush and his predecessor, Ronald Reagan.").

38. See J. Woodford Howard, Jr., *Courts of Appeals in the Federal Judicial System* 189–221 (1981); Ruth Bader Ginsburg, "The Obligation to Reason Why," 37 U. Fla. L. Rev. 205, 212, 216 (1985).

39. See note 32 and accompanying text supra.

40. See Ginsburg, supra note 38, at 215 & n.47. If a panel opinion plainly has not stood the test of time, the court can abbreviate the en banc process. See id. at 215 n.48.

41. Under current District of Columbia Circuit practice, judgments that will not be published in the Federal Reporter series, as well as decisions scheduled for publication, are circulated to the full court before release to the public. See D.C. Cir. R. 36(a)(2), (c).

42. On the check exerted by colleagues, Chief Justice William H. Rehnquist has described the practice of one of his predecessors, Chief Justice Charles Evans Hughes, thus:

> He approached his own decisions with his usual meticulous care, turning out innumerable drafts in order to be certain of the most correct and precise language. But he had no particular pride of authorship, and if in order to secure a vote he was forced to put in some disconnected or disjointed thoughts or sentences, in they went and let the law schools concern themselves with what they meant.

William H. Rehnquist, "Chief Justices I Never Knew," 3 Hastings Const. L.Q. 637, 643 (1976) (quoting Edwin McElwain, "The Business of the Supreme Court as Conducted by Chief Justice Hughes," 63 Harv. L. Rev. 5, 19 (1949)).

43. Cf. Jon O. Newman, "The Second Circuit Review, 1987–1988 Term Foreword: In Banc Practice in the Second Circuit, 1984–1988," 55 Brook. L. Rev. 355, 369–70 (1989) ("[I]f we were confronting one another frequently each year as members of an in banc court, I believe there would be at least some risk to the extremely high level of civility that now pervades our relationships both in the decision-making and opinion-writing phases of our work.").

44. See Frank M. Coffin, *The Ways of a Judge: Reflections from the Federal Appellate Bench* 181–88 (1980).

45. William J. Brennan, Jr., "In Defense of Dissents," 37 Hastings L.J. 427, 437 (1986).

46. *Coalition for the Preservation of Hispanic Broadcasting v. FCC*, 931 F.2d 73, 80 (D.C. Cir. 1991) (Mikva, C.J., dissenting); see also id. at 84 (court's decision is "driven more by evasion than logic"; "nonsensical results will flow from [it]").

47. Roscoe Pound, "Cacoethes Dissentiendi: The Heated Judicial Dissent," 39 A.B.A. J. 794, 795 (1953). For more recent commentary, see Brenda Jones Quick, "Whatever Happened to Respectful Dissent?" A.B.A. J., June 1991, at 62.

48. *R.A.V. v. St. Paul,* 112 S. Ct. 2538, 2560 (1992) (White, J., concurring in the judgment) ("I join the judgment, but not the folly of the opinion.").

49. *Lee v. Weisman,* 112 S. Ct. 2649, 2679, 2681, 2685 (1992) (Scalia, J., dissenting) (describing Court's opinion as "oblivious to our history," "incoherent," "nothing short of ludicrous," and "a jurisprudential disaster").

50. *Planned Parenthood v. Casey,* 112 S. Ct. 2791, 2875 (1992) (Scalia, J., concurring in the judgment in part and dissenting in part) ("I must ... respond to a few of the more outrageous arguments in today's opinion, which it is beyond human nature to leave unanswered.").

51. *Webster v. Reproductive Health Servs.,* 492 U.S. 490, 532 (1989) (Scalia, J., concurring in part and concurring in the judgment) ("Justice O'Connor's assertion ... that a 'fundamental rule of judicial restraint' requires us to avoid reconsidering Roe, cannot be taken seriously."); cf. *Payne v. Tennessee,* 111 S. Ct. 2597, 2622 (1991) (Marshall, J., dissenting) ("majority cannot sincerely expect anyone to believe [its assertion]"); *McCleskey v. Zant,* 111 S. Ct. 1454, 1481 (1991) (Marshall, J., dissenting) ("It is difficult to take [the majority's] reasoning seriously."); *Maislin Indus., U.S., Inc. v. Primary Steel, Inc.,* 497 U.S. 116, 139 (1990) (Stevens, J., dissenting) ("Even wearing his famous blinders, old Dobbin would see through the tired arguments the Court accepts today.").

52. *Coleman v. Thompson,* 111 S. Ct. 2546, 2574 (1991) (Blackmun, J., dissenting) (describing majority's distinction as "inexplicable" and its conception as "entirely unprecedented").

53. Id. at 2578.

54. *Morgan v. Illinois,* 112 S. Ct. 2222, 2242 (1992) (Scalia, J., dissenting) ("Today ... the Court strikes a further blow against the People in its campaign against the death penalty.").

55. *Central States Motor Freight Bureau v. ICC,* 924 F.2d 1099, 1112 (D.C. Cir. 1991) (Silberman, J., dissenting) (majority's suggestion "is naked analytical bootstrapping").

56. *Synovus Fin. Corp. v. Board of Governors of the Fed. Reserve Sys.,* 952 F.2d 426, 437 (D.C. Cir. 1991) (Silberman, J., dissenting) ("The majority's opinion ... is reminiscent for Civil War buffs of Sherman's march through Georgia. Principles of administrative law are brushed aside like Johnston and Hood's army. Our precedents are overturned like Georgia plantations."). For a restrained and moderate reply from a South Carolinian, see id. at 437 n.8 (Henderson, J.) ("With all respect to our colleague in dissent, to equate the legal issues in this case with a Civil War campaign manifests not only a misunderstanding of those issues but also a lack of appreciation for a wrenching event in our country's history.").

57. *Planned Parenthood v. Casey,* 112 S. Ct. 2791, 2882 (1992) (Scalia, J., concurring in the judgment in part and dissenting in part) ("[T]o portray Roe as the statesmanlike 'settlement' of a divisive issue, a jurisprudential Peace of Westphalia that is worth preserving, is nothing less than Orwellian."); *County of Allegheny v.*

ACLU, 492 U.S. 573, 678 (1989) (Kennedy, J., concurring in the judgment in part and dissenting in part) ("Court lends its assistance to an Orwellian rewriting of history"); *FCC v. League of Women Voters,* 468 U.S. 364, 417 n.10 (1984) (Stevens, J., dissenting) (majority's argument "would be laughable were it not so Orwellian"); *United Steelworkers v. Weber,* 443 U.S. 193, 219–21 (1979) (Rehnquist, J., dissenting) (Court has behaved like "Orwellian speaker" who, in mid-sentence, "'switched from one line to the other'") (quoting George Orwell, *1984,* 181–82 (1949)).

58. Collins J. Seitz, "Collegiality and the Court of Appeals," 75 Judicature 26, 27 (1991).

59. Id.

60. Id.

61. *Dred Scott v. Sandford,* 60 U.S. (19 How.) 393 (1856), cited as a model of "reasoned discussion" in Pound, supra note 47, at 797.

62. See, e.g., *Welsh v. United States,* 398 U.S. 333, 344 (1970) (Harlan, J., concurring).

63. The various High Court and Supreme Court opinions in this case are reprinted in *The Attorney General v. X and Others* (Sunniva McDonagh ed., 1992).

64. Ireland Const. art. 40.3.3 (inserted following enactment of the Eighth Amendment of the Constitution Act, 1983). Following a referendum on November 25, 1992, two sentences were added to Article 40.3.3: "This subsection shall not limit freedom to travel between the State and another state"; "This subsection shall not limit freedom to obtain or make available, in the State, subject to such conditions as may be laid down by law, information relating to services lawfully available in another state."

65. See Opinion of Costello, J. (Ir. H. Ct.) (Feb. 17, 1992), reprinted in *The Attorney General v. X and Others,* supra note 63, at 9.

66. Opinion of Finlay, C.J. (Ir. S.C.) (Mar. 5, 1992) (quoting *McGee v. Attorney General,* 1974 I.R. 284, 318 (Walsh, J.)), reprinted in *The Attorney General v. X and Others,* supra note 63, at 47, 59.

67. Id. (quoting *State (Healy) v. Donoghue,* 1976 I.R. 326, 347 (O'Higgins, C.J.)); cf. text accompanying notes 6–8 supra.

68. Cf., e.g., *Planned Parenthood v. Casey,* 112 S. Ct. 2791, 2882 (1992) (Scalia, J., concurring in the judgment in part and dissenting in part) ("The Imperial Judiciary lives.").

69. See Opinion of Hederman, J. (Ir. S.C.) (Mar. 5, 1992), reprinted in *The Attorney General v. X and Others,* supra note 63, at 69, 83.

70. Id.

71. Id.

72. See generally Mary Ann Glendon, *Abortion and Divorce in Western Law* (1987); Donald P. Kommers, "Abortion and Constitution: United States and West Germany," 25 Am. J. Comp. L. 255 (1977).

73. Dissents might concede, for example, more often than they do, that "[t]he

majority's argument is by no means implausible." *Hubbard v. EPA,* 949 F.2d 453, 469 (D.C. Cir. 1991) (Wald, J., concurring in part and dissenting in part).

74. Final Report of the Committee on Civility of the Seventh Federal Judicial Circuit 3 (1992).

75. Id. at 7A; see also Interim Report of the Committee on Civility of the Seventh Federal Judicial Circuit 3, 13, 39–42 (1991).

76. See generally Louis Fisher, *Constitutional Dialogues: Interpretation as Political Process* (1988). Recent commentary on court-legislature communication includes Shirley S. Abrahamson & Robert L. Hughes, "Shall We Dance? Steps for Legislators and Judges in Statutory Interpretation," 75 Minn. L. Rev. 1045 (1991); Robert A. Katzmann, "Bridging the Statutory Gulf between Courts and Congress: A Challenge for Positive Political Theory," 80 Geo. L.J. 653 (1992); Deanell Reece Tacha, "Judges and Legislators: Renewing the Relationship," 52 Ohio St. L.J. 279 (1991).

77. *Southern Pac. Co. v. Jensen,* 244 U.S. 205, 221 (1917) (Holmes, J., dissenting).

78. The Supreme Court's post-1970 decisions on alienage as a "suspect" category are illustrative. Compare *Graham v. Richardson,* 403 U.S. 365, 372 (1971) (invalidating state legislation denying public assistance benefits to resident aliens, Court declared that "classifications based on alienage, like those based on nationality or race, are inherently suspect [under equal protection principles] and subject to close judicial scrutiny") (footnotes omitted) with *Cabell v. Chavez-Salido,* 454 U.S. 432, 436 (1982) (upholding citizenship requirement for a state's probation officers, Court commented that alienage cases "illustrate a not unusual characteristic of legal development: broad principles are articulated, narrowed when applied to new contexts, and finally replaced when the distinctions they rely upon are no longer tenable").

79. 410 U.S. 113 (1973).

80. Ruth Bader Ginsburg, "Some Thoughts on Autonomy and Equality in Relation to *Roe v. Wade,*" 63 N.C. L. Rev. 375 (1985).

81. Justices White and Rehnquist dissented.

82. *Roe,* 410 U.S. at 164 (emphasis in original).

83. In a companion case, *Doe v. Bolton,* 410 U.S. 179 (1973), the Court, again 7–2, held unconstitutional several provisions of Georgia's abortion law. The Georgia statute, enacted in 1968, had moved a considerable distance from the Texas extreme. It was based on the American Law Institute's Model Penal Code formulation, and resembled reformed laws then in force in about one-fourth of the states. The Court might have deferred consideration of *Doe v. Bolton* pending its disposition of *Roe;* indeed, the Court might have awaited the Fifth Circuit's resolution of an appeal taken by Georgia to the intermediate appellate court instead of ruling immediately on plaintiffs' direct appeal from a three-judge district court decision holding in substantial part for plaintiffs. See *Doe,* 410 U.S. at 187 & n.8.

84. 112 S. Ct. 2791 (1992).

85. See id. at 2841–43 (Stevens, J., concurring in part and dissenting in part) (maintaining that twenty-four-hour delay requirement and counseling provisions conflicted with Court precedent); id. at 2846, 2850–52 (Blackmun, J., concurring in the judgment in part, and dissenting in part) (maintaining that counseling, twenty-four-hour delay, and parental consent provisions conflicted with Court precedent).

86. Id. at 2809. On this point, the controlling Justices—Justices O'Connor, Kennedy, and Souter—spoke for the Court.

87. See generally Rachel N. Pine & Sylvia A. Law, "Envisioning a Future for Reproductive Liberty: Strategies for Making the Rights Real," 27 Harv. C.R.-C.L. L. Rev. 407 (1992).

88. See Roe v. Wade, 410 U.S. 113, 164–65 (1973) ("abortion decision . . . must be left to the medical judgment of the pregnant woman's attending physician"; "decision [in Roe] vindicates the right of the physician to administer medical treatment according to his professional judgment").

89. See Paul A. Freund, "Storms over the Supreme Court," 69 A.B.A. J. 1474, 1480 (1983).

90. 409 U.S. 947 (granting certiorari in 460 F.2d 1372 (9th Cir. 1971)), remanded for consideration of mootness, 409 U.S. 1071 (1972); see also Note, "Pregnancy Discharges in the Military: The Air Force Experience," 86 Harv. L. Rev. 568 (1973).

91. See Appendix to Brief for Petitioner at 34a, Struck (No. 72–178) (Memorandum of Colonel Max B. Bralliar, May 14, 1971, recommending waiver of discharge for Captain Struck).

92. See Brief for Petitioner at 67–69 & n.70, Struck (No. 72–178).

93. See id. at 3–5, 56.

94. Air Force Regulation 36-12(40), set out in relevant part in Brief for Petitioner at 2–3, Struck (No. 72–178); see also Struck, 460 F.2d at 1374.

95. Struck, 460 F.2d at 1374.

96. Appendix to Brief for Petitioner at 22a, Struck (No. 72–178) (quoting Air Force policy on therapeutic abortion, contained in Air Force Regulation 169–12(C2) (Sept. 23, 1970)). On his second full day in office, President Clinton ended a total ban on abortions at U.S. military facilities, imposed during the 1980s, and ordered that abortions be permitted at such facilities if paid for with non-Department of Defense funds. See Memorandum on Abortions in Military Hospitals, Jan. 22, 1993, 29 Weekly Comp. Pres. Doc. 88 (Jan. 25, 1993).

97. As earlier observed, see text accompanying note 14 supra, the original Constitution and the Bill of Rights contain no equality guarantee. Since 1954, however, the Supreme Court has attributed to the fifth amendment's due process clause an equal protection principle regarding federal action corresponding to the fourteenth amendment's equal protection clause controlling state action. See Bolling v. Sharpe, 347 U.S. 497, 499 (1954) (initial recognition); cf. Weinberger v. Wiesenfeld, 420 U.S. 636, 638 n.2 (1975) ("Court's approach to Fifth Amendment equal protection

claims has always been precisely the same as to equal protection claims under the Fourteenth Amendment").

98. See *Struck*, 460 F.2d at 1380 (Duniway, J., dissenting); Brief for Petitioner at 8, 54–55, Struck (No. 72–178). The Air Force had asserted that the purpose of its pregnancy discharge regulation was to "encourage" birth control. Brief for Respondents in Opposition to Certiorari at 11, Struck (No. 72–178). In response, Captain Struck observed, inter alia, that the "'encouragement' [was] directed at females only": "A man serves in the Air Force with no unwarranted governmental intrusion into the matter of his sexual privacy or his decision whether to beget a child. The woman serves subject to 'regulation'; her pursuit of an Air Force career requires that she decide not to bear a child." Brief for Petitioner at 54, 55, Struck (No. 72–178).

99. *Struck*, 409 U.S. 947, 947 (1972).

100. See Memorandum for the Respondents Suggesting Mootness (Dec. 1972), Struck (No. 72–178); *Struck*, 409 U.S. at 1071 (remanding for consideration of mootness).

101. See Reva Siegel, "Reasoning from the Body: A Historical Perspective on Abortion Regulation and Questions of Equal Protection," 44 Stan. L. Rev. 261 (1992).

102. Cf. *Weinberger v. Wiesenfeld*, 420 U.S. 636, 653 (1975) (holding unconstitutional, as a violation of the equal protection principle, the denial to a widowed father of child-in-care social security benefits Congress had provided solely for widowed mothers).

103. See Brief for Petitioner at 26, Struck (No. 72–178) ("The regulation applied to petitioner establishes a suspect classification for which no compelling justification can be shown.").

104. Id. (citing *Bullock v. Carter*, 405 U.S. 134, 144 (1972), as precedent for "an intermediate standard" under which the challenged classification would be "'closely scrutinized'").

105. See *Craig v. Boren*, 429 U.S. 190, 197 (1976) (sex-based classification would not be sustained if merely rationally related to a permissible government objective; defender of classification would be required to show a substantial relationship to an important objective); see also *Mississippi Univ. for Women v. Hogan*, 458 U.S. 718, 724 (1982).

106. Sandra Day O'Connor, "Portia's Progress," 66 N.Y.U. L. Rev. 1546 (1991).

107. The turning-point case was *Reed v. Reed*, 404 U.S. 71 (1971). *Reed* involved a youth from Idaho who had committed suicide while in his father's custody, the "mother's preference" regarding custody having endured only while the boy was "of tender years." The boy's mother and father, long separated, had each applied to be the administrator of their son's property. The Idaho court appointed the father under a state statute that provided: as between persons "equally entitled to administer, males must be preferred to females." Id. at 73 (quoting Idaho Code § 15–314 (1948)). The Court unanimously ruled that the

statute denied to the mother the equal protection of the laws guaranteed by the fourteenth amendment.

108. See Wendy W. Williams, "Sex Discrimination: Closing the Law's Gender Gap," in *The Burger Years: Rights and Wrongs in the Supreme Court 1969–1986*, at 109 (Herman Schwartz ed., 1987); see also Ruth Bader Ginsburg, "The Burger Court's Grapplings with Sex Discrimination," in *The Burger Court: The Counter-Revolution That Wasn't* 132 (Vincent Blasi ed., 1983).

109. *Frontiero v. Richardson*, 411 U.S. 677, 688 (1973).

110. *Stanton v. Stanton*, 421 U.S. 7, 17 (1975).

111. *Taylor v. Louisiana*, 419 U.S. 522, 525 (1975) (invalidating law restricting service by women to volunteers); *Duren v. Missouri*, 439 U.S. 357, 360 (1979) (invalidating law allowing "any woman" to opt out of jury duty).

112. *Weinberger v. Wiesenfeld*, 420 U.S. 636, 639 (1975) (extending to widowers social security benefits Congress had provided for widows); *Califano v. Goldfarb*, 430 U.S. 199, 201–2 (1977) (same); *Califano v. Westcott*, 443 U.S. 76, 85 (1979) (extending to unemployed mothers public assistance benefits Congress had provided solely for unemployed fathers).

113. *Wengler v. Druggists Mut. Ins. Co.*, 446 U.S. 142, 147 (1980).

114. *Kirchberg v. Feenstra*, 450 U.S. 455, 461 (1981).

115. *Mississippi Univ. for Women v. Hogan*, 458 U.S. 718, 723 (1982).

116. This expansion reflected a new reality: in the 1970s, for the first time in the nation's history, the "average" woman in the United States was experiencing most of her adult years in a household not dominated by childcare requirements. That development, Columbia University professor of economics Eli Ginzberg observed, may be "the single most outstanding phenomenon of our century." Jean A. Briggs, "How You Going to Get 'Em Back in the Kitchen? (You Aren't)," Forbes, Nov. 15, 1977, at 177 (quoting comment by Eli Ginzberg).

117. See, e.g., Brief for Appellant at 12–13, *Reed v. Reed*, 404 U.S. 71 (1971) (No. 70–4) (urging Court not to repeat "the mistake" of *Plessy v. Ferguson*, 163 U.S. 537 (1896—which had upheld a state statute requiring railway companies to provide, inter alia, separate, but equal, accommodations for blacks and whites—and to rank sex-based classifications with the recognized suspect classifications).

118. Simone de Beauvoir, *The Second Sex* (1949).

119. For example, the male preference at issue in *Reed v. Reed*, described at note 107 supra, had been repealed, but not retroactively, before the Supreme Court heard the case; the categorical exemption of women from jury service had been largely abandoned in state systems by the time the Court heard *Duren v. Missouri*, described at note 111 supra.

120. See the *Wiesenfeld* and *Goldfarb* cases cited in note 112 supra.

121. See *Califano v. Webster*, 430 U.S. 313 (1977) (upholding classification, effective from 1956 to 1972, establishing more favorable social security benefit calculation for retired female workers than for retired male workers).

122. Ruth Bader Ginsburg, "Some Thoughts on Benign Classification in the Context of Sex," 10 Conn. L. Rev. 813, 823 (1978).

123. See Ruth Bader Ginsburg, "Some Thoughts on Judicial Authority to Repair Unconstitutional Legislation," 28 Clev. St. L. Rev. 301, 310–12 (1979).

124. Notably too, the equal rights or sex equality advocates of the 1970s urged no elaborate theory. They did argue that by enshrining and promoting the woman's "natural" role as selfless homemaker, and correspondingly emphasizing the man's role as provider, the state impeded both men and women from pursuit of the opportunities and styles of life that could enable them to break away from familiar stereotypes. The objective, however, was not "assimilationist" in the sense of accepting a "man's world" and asking only that self-regarding, economically advantaged women be allowed to enter that world and play by men's rules. The endeavor was, instead, to remove artificial barriers to women's aspiration and achievement; if women became political actors in numbers, it was thought, they could then exercise their will and their judgment to help make the world and the rules fit for all humankind. See Ruth Bader Ginsburg & Barbara Flagg, "Some Reflections on the Feminist Legal Thought of the 1970s," 1989 U. Chi. Legal F. 9, 17–18; cf. Herma Hill Kay, "The Future of Women Law Professors," 77 Iowa L. Rev. 5, 18 (1991) ("The future of women law professors is not to adapt to legal education by being 'one of the boys,' but to transform the enterprise so that all of its participants are equal members of the same team.").

125. Williams, supra note 108, at 123. This brand of review has been aptly called "judicial enforcement of constitutional accountability." Guido Calabresi, "The Supreme Court, 1990 Term—Foreword: Antidiscrimination and Constitutional Accountability (What the Bork-Brennan Debate Ignores)," 105 Harv. L. Rev. 80, 103–8 (1991).

126. 410 U.S. 113 (1973).

127. Id. at 140; see also Ginsburg, supra note 80, at 385 & n.81.

128. See Herma Hill Kay, "Equality and Difference: A Perspective on No-Fault Divorce and Its Aftermath," 56 U. Cin. L. Rev. 1, 4–14, 26–55 (1987); see also Ginsburg, supra note 80, at 380 & n.36.

129. See Vincent Blasi, "The Rootless Activism of the Burger Court," in *The Burger Court: The Counter-Revolution That Wasn't* 198, 212 (Vincent Blasi ed., 1983) (Roe "burst upon the constitutional scene with very little in the way of foreshadowing or preparation."); Geoffrey C. Hazard, Jr., "Rising above Principle," 135 U. Pa. L. Rev. 153, 166 (1986) ("By making such an extensive change, the Court [in *Roe*] foreclosed the usual opportunities for assimilation [and] feedback . . . that are afforded in a decisional process involving shorter and more cautious doctrinal steps.").

130. See generally Louis Henkin, *The Age of Rights* 141–80 (1990).

131. Cf. Archibald Cox, "Direct Action, Civil Disobedience, and the Constitution," in *Civil Rights, the Constitution, and the Court* 2, 22–23 (1967) ("[S]harp changes in the law depend partly upon the stimulus of protest.").

132. See, e.g., *Lochner v. New York*, 198 U.S. 45 (1905) (state maximum hours regulation for bakery employees, covering men and women alike, held unconstitutional). But cf. *Muller v. Oregon*, 208 U.S. 412 (1908) (upholding maximum hours legislation for women only).

133. Cf. Calabresi, supra note 125, at 86 (labeling bold court intervention as the "judicial supremacy" model of constitutional review).

134. 347 U.S. 483 (1954).

135. See *Plessy v. Ferguson*, 163 U.S. 537, 540 (1896).

136. See Ginsburg & Flagg, supra note 124, at 18.

137. See *United States v. Carolene Products Co.*, 304 U.S. 144, 152 n.4 (1938) (suggesting heightened judicial scrutiny of legislation disadvantageous to "discrete and insular minorities," that is, classifications tending "seriously to curtail the operation of those political processes ordinarily to be relied upon to protect minorities"); cf. Owen M. Fiss, "Groups and the Equal Protection Clause," 5 Phil. & Pub. Aff. 107, 152 (1976) (stressing situation of blacks as "a numerical minority" and "their economic status, their position as the perpetual underclass").

138. See Richard Kluger, *Simple Justice* 256–84 (1976) (chronicling the efforts of Marshall and others in connection with *Sipuel v. Board of Regents of the Univ. of Oklahoma*, 332 U.S. 631 (1948); *Shelley v. Kraemer*, 334 U.S. 1 (1948); *Sweatt v. Painter*, 339 U.S. 629 (1950); and *McLaurin v. Oklahoma St. Regents for Higher Educ.*, 339 U.S. 637 (1950)); Jack Greenberg, "Litigation for Social Change: Methods, Limits and Role in Democracy," 29 The Record of the Ass'n of the Bar of the City of New York 320, 327–34 (1974) (discussing the "litigation campaign" preceding *Brown*).

139. Compare The Orison S. Marden Lecture in Honor of Justice Thurgood Marshall, 47 The Record of the Ass'n of the Bar of the City of New York 227, 254 (1992) (comments of Constance Baker Motley) ("[N]o civil action was ever initiated under [Marshall's] leadership unless it was part of an overall strategy. . . . No major legal thrust was made without months if not years of careful legal research and planning such as occurred in the early voting cases, teacher salary cases, restrictive covenant cases, interstate travel cases as well as the school desegregation cases.") with Blasi, supra note 129, at 212 (*Roe* "could not plausibly [be] justif[ied]. . . as the working out of a theme implicit in several previous decisions.").

140. The Court relied on the psychological harm, empirically documented, that segregated schools caused black children. See 347 U.S. at 493–94 & 494 n.11.

141. Pub. L. No. 88–352, 78 Stat. 241 (codified as amended at 28 U.S.C. § 1447, 42 U.S.C. § § 1971, 2000a–2000h–6 (1988 & Supp. II 1990)).

142. 388 U.S. 1 (1967).

143. The legislative reapportionment cases of the early 1960s present a second notable instance of the Court confronting blocked political processes. Be-

fore the 1960s, many state legislatures arranged their districts in ways that diluted the voting power of urban voters. Under precedent then in place, legal objections to these malapportioned schemes were not justiciable in federal court. See *Colegrove v. Green*, 328 U.S. 549 (1946). In *Baker v. Carr*, 369 U.S. 186 (1962), this changed: The Supreme Court declared challenges to malapportioned schemes justiciable and thereby opened the way for their invalidation by federal court decree. As one leading commentator on the reapportionment cases observed:

> The ultimate rationale to be given for *Baker v. Carr* and its numerous progeny is that when political avenues for redressing political problems become dead-end streets, some judicial intervention in the politics of the people may be essential in order to have any effective politics. In Tennessee, [for example,] at the time its legislative composition was challenged in *Baker*, there was a history of several years of unsuccessful state court litigation and unsuccessful efforts for corrective legislation.

Robert G. Dixon, Jr., *Democratic Representation: Reapportionment in Law and Politics* 8 (1968).

144. The decision in the legend is *Worcester v. Georgia*, 31 U.S. (6 Pet.) 515 (1832).

145. Learned Hand, *The Bill of Rights* 73 (1958).

146. Cf. Archibald Cox, "The Role of the Supreme Court: Judicial Activism or Self-Restraint?" 47 Md. L. Rev. 118, 124–25 (1987) (though the "style of interpretation" of Chief Justice Marshall's Court "was active and creative," that Court, "[I]n expanding national power[,] . . . was moving in step with the dominant trend in the political branches").

147. *Planned Parenthood v. Casey*, 112 S. Ct. 2791 (1992).

148. Three years before its *Planned Parenthood* decision, the Court had come close to overruling *Roe*. See *Webster v. Reproductive Health Servs.*, 492 U.S. 490 (1989), discussed in Sylvia A. Law, "Abortion Compromise—Inevitable and Impossible," 1992 U. Ill. L. Rev. 921, 923–26.

149. The hostile reaction to *Roe* has particularly hit women who are most vulnerable—"the poor, the unsophisticated, the young, and women who live in rural areas." Law, supra note 148, at 931; see also Ginsburg, supra note 80, at 383–85.

150. Indicative of the changed political climate, President Clinton, on his second full day in office, January 22, 1993, signed five Memoranda terminating abortion-related restraints imposed in the 1980s. See 29 Weekly Comp. Pres. Doc. 87–89 (Jan. 25, 1993) (Memorandum for the Secretary of Health and Human Services, on Federal Funding of Fetal Tissue Transplantation Research; Memorandum for the Secretary of Health and Human Services, on the Title X [of the Public Health Services Act] "Gag Rule"; Memorandum for the Acting Administrator of the Agency for International Development, on AID Family Planning

Grants/Mexico City Policy; Memorandum for the Secretary of Defense, on Privately Funded Abortions at Military Hospitals; Memorandum for the Secretary of Health and Human Services, on Importation of RU-486). Cf. Law, supra note 148, at 931–32 (setting out opposing assessments and commenting that "[o]nly time will tell").

151. "Professor Gerald Gunther Speaks at Investiture of Judge Ruth Ginsburg in Washington, D.C.," Colum. Law Alumni Observer, Dec. 31, 1980, at 8.

Chapter 5

Beyond "Reasonable Doubt"

Jon O. Newman

The James Madison Lectures were inaugurated "to enhance the appreciation of civil liberty and strengthen the national purpose."[1] A lecture named for the principal architect of the Bill of Rights could aspire to no lesser goal. I hope I do not stray outside the lofty objective of this distinguished series by focusing on a right that is not mentioned in Madison's handiwork and was not given formal recognition as comprehended within the general language of the Bill of Rights until 1970,[2] although assumed by the Supreme Court to be a requirement, at least in the federal courts, as early as 1881.[3] My focus is the implicit component of the due process clause that guarantees every person the right not to be convicted of a crime unless the evidence establishes guilt beyond a reasonable doubt.

My thesis may be stated quite simply. I believe that the constitutional jurisprudence of this nation has accepted the "reasonable doubt" standard as a verbal formulation to be conveyed to juries in jury charges but has failed to take the standard seriously as a rule of law against which the validity of convictions is to be judged. The consequences of this deficiency are, in my view, twofold: We are convicting some people who are not guilty beyond a reasonable doubt, a few of whom may in fact be innocent, and at the same time, quite paradoxically, we are acquitting some people who could be proven to be guilty beyond a reasonable doubt, most of whom are in fact guilty. Thus, the proposition I wish to discuss is that the time has come for American courts, especially federal courts, to move beyond "reasonable

This lecture was delivered on November 9, 1993, and appeared in 68 N.Y.U.L. Rev. 979 (1993).

doubt" as a mere incantation, to give renewed consideration to what reasonable doubt means and how it should be applied as a rule of law, so that the standard might serve as a more precise divider of the guilty from the innocent.

I say "more precise" because all must recognize that fact finders are fallible and that any system of adjudicating guilt will inevitably run some risk of both convicting the innocent and acquitting the guilty. The inevitability of both types of mistakes usually leads us to say that it is better to acquit some number of guilty persons than to convict one innocent person.[4] What we would not readily agree on is the appropriate ratio of guilty persons acquitted to innocent persons convicted. The cases have frequently mentioned a ratio of ten to one,[5] though ratios of twenty to one[6] and even ninety-nine to one have been mentioned in earlier literature.[7]

Whatever ratio we find acceptable, one of the major variables in achieving that ratio is the degree of certainty we impose on fact finders. If you would tolerate as many as one hundred guilty persons going free in preference to convicting one innocent person, then you will insist that no one be convicted unless the fact finder is sure of guilt to a degree approaching absolute certainty. If your ratio is ten to one, then you will likely impose a somewhat less rigorous standard upon the fact finder but still require a high degree of certainty. I believe that the "reasonable doubt" standard should express our society's view that criminal convictions require, at the least, a high degree of certainty of guilt. But first, let me review the current application of the "reasonable doubt" standard in our trial and appellate courts.

I. The Theory and Practice of Reasonable Doubt

A. The "Reasonable Doubt" Standard as a Jury Charge

The Anglo-American tradition has chosen a standard of certainty usually captured by the phrase "beyond a reasonable doubt." I think it unlikely that this phrase was selected to implement a particular ratio of the sort I have been discussing. Yet, in some imprecise way, it probably was arrived at on the assumption that it would achieve an error ratio that fell within an acceptable range. So let us examine the standard, keeping in mind that the rigor of its enforcement has a significant bearing on the mistake rate of our criminal trials.

Like most traditions we have observed for a long time, there are at least two versions as to how this one began. Most believe that the "reasonable doubt" standard was first urged upon courts in the *Irish Treason Cases*[8] in 1798 by defense lawyers who were endeavoring to raise the prosecution's burden of persuasion.[9] But there is a competing view that the standard was urged by prosecutors who were trying to lower their burden of persuasion from an often unattainable task of having to persuade the jury beyond all doubt.[10]

Whichever group deserves the credit, the standard became an accepted formulation in this country of the principle, widely shared throughout the world's legal systems, that an adjudication of guilt in criminal matters requires a high degree of certainty. For example, the British also use the "reasonable doubt" formulation but on occasion tell jurors not to convict unless they "feel sure" of the defendant's guilt,[11] or sometimes, "feel sure and satisfied."[12] The French Code of Criminal Procedure instructs the Cour d'Assise to read to a mixed panel of three judges and nine lay jurors a charge that includes the following: "The law asks judges only the single question, which encompasses the full measure of their duties: 'Are you thoroughly convinced?'"[13]

Having come to embrace the verbal formulation "beyond a reasonable doubt," American courts have flirted with efforts to elaborate on the meaning of these familiar words. The most widely used explanation, especially favored in most federal courts, is the brief advice that a reasonable doubt is "a doubt which would cause a reasonable person to hesitate to act in a matter of importance in his or her personal life."[14] Although, as a district judge, I dutifully repeated that bit of "guidance" to juries in scores of criminal trials, I was always bemused by its ambiguity. If the jurors encounter a doubt that would cause them to "hesitate to act in a matter of importance," what are they to do then? Should they decline to convict because they have reached a point of hesitation, or should they simply hesitate, then ask themselves whether, in their own private matters, they would resolve the doubt in favor of action, and, if so, go on to convict?[15]

Some courts have used additional phrasings that seem to make the standard more rigorous. One formulation, especially favored by defense attorneys, is that the evidence must persuade the jurors of guilt "to a moral certainty." Federal courts have explicitly rejected this formulation.[16] Many courts add the thought that a reasonable doubt is "a doubt based on reason."[17] A juror hearing the "doubt based on reason" formulation might think that a generalized unease or skepticism about the prosecution's evidence is not a valid basis upon which to resist entreaties to vote for conviction. That is probably a distortion of the concept that courts are seeking to implement. The "reasonable doubt" standard serves to prevent a finding of guilt unless the evidence dispels those doubts that would be entertained by that most useful construct of the law—the reasonable person—in this instance a group of twelve reasonable persons who form a reasonable jury. The standard ought not to mean that a doubt is reasonable only if the juror can articulate to himself or herself some particular reason for it.[18] The Supreme Court has wisely observed that the standard serves to impress "upon the factfinder the need to reach a subjective state of near certitude of the guilt of the accused."[19] The Court should have stayed with only a requirement of "near certitude," instead of also embracing the dubious explanation of "reasonable doubt" as a doubt "based upon 'reason.'"[20]

A somewhat curious aspect of the "reasonable doubt" standard is the reluctance of most trial courts to offer the jury any explanation as to what the standard means. Indeed, some federal courts have in recent years sternly admonished trial judges not to attempt any amplification of the standard whatsoever.[21] I find it rather unsettling that we are using a formulation that we believe will become less clear the more we explain it.[22]

The assumption underlying these various formulations is that any statement of the burden more rigorous than the "preponderance of the evidence" standard reduces the likelihood of conviction in close cases. Whether that assumption is true is difficult to measure. Academic exercises have provided some clues. In one study, groups of judges and jurors were asked to quantify as a percentage of certainty what the "preponderance" and "reasonable doubt" standards meant to them.[23] Both groups reported a higher percentage for the "reasonable doubt" standard than for the "preponderance" standard, although the jurors put the "reasonable doubt" percentage closer to the "preponderance" percentage than did the judges.[24] Another study tried a case before twenty-two mock juries, giving them three different instructions on the burden of persuasion.[25] The conviction rate for the jurors who heard the "reasonable doubt" standard was slightly lower than the vote for the group hearing the "preponderance" standard and fell significantly among the jurors hearing the "feel sure and certain" formulation.[26] These studies suggest that the traditional charge might be producing some unwarranted convictions. At the very least, the conclusion one draws from such studies is that the charge currently in use is ambiguous and open to widely disparate interpretation by jurors.

B. "Reasonable Doubt" and Sufficiency of Evidence

After deciding that American fact finders, whether jury or judge, would have to be persuaded "beyond a reasonable doubt" before they could convict, our courts then encountered the crucial legal issue that determines whether the "reasonable doubt" standard is merely a verbal formulation or a rule of law. Courts had to decide whether the "reasonable doubt" standard entered into the decision judges make in determining whether the evidence in each case is legally sufficient to permit a finding of guilt. For many years, many federal courts, likely influenced by the 1944 opinion of Learned Hand in *United States v. Feinberg*,[27] took the position that the judicial role in determining whether the evidence sufficed to permit a finding of guilt beyond a reasonable doubt was extremely limited. Judge Hand thought that the "reasonable doubt" standard was solely a matter to be included in a jury instruction and that a judge should require no more convincing evidence in a criminal case than in a civil one before ruling the evidence sufficient for a jury.[28] He refused to distinguish between "the evidence which should satisfy reasonable men, and the evidence which should satisfy reasonable men beyond a reasonable doubt."[29] In Hand's view, "the line between them is too thin for day to day use."[30]

That view was challenged as early as 1947 by the District of Columbia Circuit,[31] and by the 1970s every circuit except the Second came to accept the position that the "reasonable doubt" standard was to affect, in some way, the judge's determination of sufficiency.[32] I am chagrined to acknowledge that the Second Circuit did not formally abandon Hand's position until 1972, finally declaring that the "battle has now been irretrievably lost."[33] In rejecting Judge Hand's opinion in *Feinberg*, Judge Friendly referred to it as one of Learned Hand's "rare ill-advised opinions"[34] and ruled that more "facts in evidence" are needed to persuade a fact finder beyond a reasonable doubt than to persuade by a preponderance.[35] I prefer to think of the heightened burden as requiring evidence of greater persuasive force, not necessarily of greater quantity.

C. "Reasonable Doubt" as a Constitutional Requirement

While the courts of appeals were moving to incorporate the "reasonable doubt" standard into the legal assessment of the sufficiency of evidence, the Supreme Court was grappling with the extent to which the "reasonable doubt" standard was constitutionally required. In 1970, the Court decided in *In re Winship*[36] that the "reasonable doubt" standard was an implicit component of due process, required to be applied by fact finders in criminal cases in both federal and state courts.[37] Having made that decision, the Court did not consider the critically related issue of whether the Constitution set some standard for assessing the sufficiency of evidence that would permit a valid conviction under the "reasonable doubt" standard. At that time, the only constitutional ruling on sufficiency of evidence in a criminal case had been the unremarkable pronouncement in 1960 in the so-called "Shuffling Sam" case, more properly known as *Thompson v. City of Louisville*,[38] that due process was denied when there was no evidence whatsoever of a required element in a criminal offense.

Then, in the 1979 case of *Jackson v. Virginia*,[39] the Court agreed for the first time to consider whether and how the "reasonable doubt" standard affected the constitutional sufficiency of evidence in a criminal case.[40] Writing for a surprisingly narrow majority of five, Justice Stewart ruled that merely instructing a jury to observe the "reasonable doubt" standard did not ensure compliance with constitutional requirements. "The *Winship* doctrine," he wrote, "requires more than simply a trial ritual."[41] Due process, the Court continued, requires some consideration of the standard to be used in assessing the sufficiency of the evidence. The Court made clear that a reviewing court need not "'ask itself whether it believes that the evidence at the trial established guilt beyond a reasonable doubt.'"[42]

The Court was less clear in stating what was required. Justice Stewart's opinion used two key sentences, which might or might not have different meanings. First, the Court said that "[a]fter *Winship* the critical inquiry . . . must be . . . whether the record evidence could reasonably support a finding of guilt beyond a reasonable doubt."[43] Then, on the next page, the Court said that "the relevant question is whether . . . any rational trier of fact could have found the essential elements of the crime beyond a reasonable doubt."[44] The Court underscored the word "any."

I think the two sentences convey quite different thoughts. The first sentence, correctly in my view, applies the traditional test for determining sufficiency of evidence—namely, whether the law's ubiquitous reasonable person, in this case a reasonable jury, could find the matter proven by the requisite degree of persuasion, in this case beyond a reasonable doubt. The second sentence, however, shifts the emphasis away from the law's construct of the reasonable jury and conjures up the image of a vast random distribution of reasonable juries, with the risk of creating the misleading impression that just one of them need be persuaded beyond a reasonable doubt.

Though the opinion in *Jackson* articulates both the traditional standard of whether the evidence "could reasonably support a finding of guilt beyond a reasonable doubt" and the novel "any rational trier" standard, the Court gave no indication that it even realized it was setting out two different standards. Thus, I cannot be certain that the "any rational trier" standard was intended to authorize a less demanding form of review than the "reasonable jury" standard. Interestingly, the concurrence, written by Justice Stevens, and joined by Chief Justice Burger and then-Justice Rehnquist, seized on the distinction between the two standards and rejoiced that the Court had chosen the less demanding formulation.[45] Still more interestingly, the majority made no response to the concurrence, neither acknowledging nor disclaiming a preference for the less demanding standard.[46]

Regrettably, it is only the second formulation that most appellate opinions have extracted from *Jackson*. In countless decisions, federal courts of appeals have quoted the "any rational trier" sentence, without ever acknowledging the earlier sentence that uses a more traditional and more rigorous standard.[47]

D. The "Reasonable Doubt" Standard as a Rule of Law

With the "reasonable doubt" standard thus having entered the constitutional jurisprudence of our nation, the question arises as to what significance the standard has had as a rule of law governing the outcome of criminal trials. The answer, for the most part, is very little. Thus, in the federal courts, the primary expositors of federal requirements, we have insisted that juries be instructed that they must be persuaded beyond a reasonable doubt, but we have not insisted on meaningful observance of this standard as a rule of law for testing the sufficiency of the evidence.

I do not mean to suggest that federal courts never conclude that evidence in a criminal case is insufficient. Occasionally they do, usually to overturn a conviction on a particular count of a multicount indictment, rather than to exonerate a defendant entirely. Rather, my factual point is that they do so very rarely, and my legal point is that they almost never do so by applying, in explicit terms, the "reasonable doubt" standard. On those rare occasions when a federal appellate court accepts a claim that a case should not have gone to a jury, it typically says simply that the evidence is "insufficient."[48] In some cases, the court is doing no more than applying the baseline rule of the "Shuffling Sam" case, concluding that there is no evidence at all to support a necessary element.[49]

Though the analogy is not exact, it is interesting to compare how differently federal appellate courts review "reasonable doubt" rulings when the context shifts from whether the evidence is sufficient to support a conviction to whether a constitutional error is harmless. Appellate courts rarely reverse a trial court's ruling that the evidence is sufficient to permit a finding of guilt beyond a reasonable doubt. However, when trial courts apply the harmless error doctrine to constitutional violations and rule that the prosecution has not sustained its burden of showing that a constitutional error was harmless beyond a reasonable doubt,[50] they are frequently reversed.[51]

If appellate courts were taking seriously the legal standard of proof that persuades beyond a reasonable doubt, we should expect to see at least a modest number of cases in which a reviewing court says, "The evidence perhaps suffices to persuade a reasonable trier by the 'preponderance' standard but it does not suffice to persuade beyond a reasonable doubt." It is astonishing how rarely we see a federal appellate court using anything like that language. A Westlaw search of all federal court opinions disclosed only two opinions in which a federal court of appeals explicitly stated that the evidence might be sufficient to satisfy the "preponderance" standard but was insufficient to satisfy the higher "reasonable doubt" standard.[52] Both were rendered before the decision in *Jackson*.

II. Moving beyond "Reasonable Doubt"

My argument is that the time has come for American courts to move beyond "reasonable doubt," to take this standard seriously and apply it conscientiously as a rule of law. By "moving beyond 'reasonable doubt'" I do not mean discarding the "reasonable doubt" standard in favor of some higher degree of certainty. I am entirely content to stay with "reasonable doubt" as the standard to which the jury must be persuaded of guilt. Nor do I mean to challenge the doctrine that, on appeal from convictions, appellate courts should view the evidence "in the light most favorable to the prosecution."[53] Rather, my point is that courts must do more than verbalize the "reasonable doubt" standard in jury instructions; they must make that standard an enforceable rule of law. There are several ways in which courts could move beyond the current approach to reasonable doubt.

A. Taking "Reasonable Doubt" Seriously

1. Clarifying the "Reasonable Doubt" Jury Instruction

First, we could make the "reasonable doubt" instruction clearer to jurors by focusing their attention solely on the need to be sure of guilt to a high degree. A model charge, prepared in 1987 by a subcommittee of the Judicial Conference's Committee on the Operation of the Jury System, contains very useful language. Its key sentence reads: "Proof beyond a reasonable doubt is proof that leaves you firmly convinced of the defendant's guilt."[54] Notably absent from the subcommittee's model charge is the misleading phrase about a doubt "based on reason" and the ambiguous language about "hesitating on important matters."[55] For reasons not clear to me, this authoritatively formulated model instruction has not been widely adopted.

2. Redefining the Appellate Standard

Second, we could return to the genesis of the constitutional standard for assessing sufficiency in *Jackson* and discard the novel "any rational trier" standard for the more traditional "reasonable jury" standard. The adoption of this novel standard was flawed at the outset. The Court enlisted dubious authority for its "any rational trier" formulation, citing only the marginally relevant opinion in *Johnson v. Louisiana*.[56] That case held that the due process rights of a defendant were not violated by a guilty verdict subscribed to, as permitted under Louisiana law, by only nine of the twelve jurors.[57] The case had little if anything to do with appellate review of sufficiency. At the page of *Johnson* cited in *Jackson*, the Court said only that "verdicts finding guilt beyond a reasonable doubt are regularly sustained even though the evidence was such that a jury would have been justified in having a reasonable doubt."[58] There is no hint in *Johnson* that the standard of review is whether the evidence would have sufficed for "any rational trier," a phrase nowhere to be found in *Johnson* or in any prior opinion of the Supreme Court. Indeed, prior to *Jackson*, no federal court had ever used the phrase "any rational trier" or "any rational jury" in determining whether the evidence in a criminal case was sufficient.[59]

My concern is not with the word "rational." That word is often used interchangeably with "reasonable," though I prefer the word "reasonable" in this context. Rather, what distresses me is the word "any" and the wholly gratuitous and potentially misleading underscoring of that word, which I fear can subtly shift an appellate court's attention from the correct construct of the reasonable jury to the quite incorrect construct of just one out of a distribution of reasonable juries.

In the civil context, the "reasonable person" construct has never been thought to require persuasion of just one out of a random distribution of many. When we ask whether the evidence in a negligence case is sufficient to permit a jury to find in the plaintiff's favor, we ask whether a reasonable jury could have concluded that negligence was proved;[60] we do not permit a plaintiff's verdict to stand just because it could be said that any one of a thousand reasonable juries could have found in the plaintiff's favor.

So my second plea is that we should abandon the "any rational trier" formulation and review sufficiency determinations in criminal cases by the more traditional "reasonable jury" test, which is also set forth in *Jackson*, a test that asks only whether a reasonable jury could find guilt beyond a reasonable doubt. Courts use the "reasonable jury" standard to assess the sufficiency of evidence in civil cases, where claims must be proved only by the modest burden of a preponderance of the evidence. Surely, then, it makes no sense to permit a less rigorous standard of review to test the sufficiency of evidence in criminal cases, where claims must be proved by the more rigorous burden of proof beyond a reasonable doubt. At a minimum, if we cannot discard the "any rational trier" formulation entirely, we should at least confine it to the context in which it was first articulated—habeas corpus review of state convictions—and apply the "reasonable jury" standard to all direct reviews of federal convictions.

I recognize that the distinction between "any rational trier" and the "reasonable jury" might be largely semantic. But words guide action, especially words uttered repeatedly in appellate opinions. The repetition of the "any rational trier" formulation in countless appellate opinions persuades me that it has influenced appellate courts to regard a successful claim of insufficiency as an occurrence to be encountered only a bit more frequently than the seventeen-year locusts.

3. Reinvigorating Appellate Review

If, for the foreseeable future, we must accept the "any rational trier" formulation for testing sufficiency of evidence in a criminal case, my third and most urgent plea is that we at least take seriously our obligation to apply even this deferential standard of review. My concern is that federal appellate courts, including my own, examine a record to satisfy themselves only that there is some evidence of guilt and do not conscientiously assess whether the evidence suffices to permit a finding by the high degree of persuasion required by the "reasonable doubt" standard. The irony is that ever since winning the battle to discard Learned Hand's "civil sufficiency" approach, we have been losing the war to achieve meaningful appellate review of insufficiency claims in criminal cases.

Federal courts have signaled their retreat with the language they use in reviewing insufficiency claims. They rarely say that the issue is whether the prosecution has presented evidence from which a reasonable jury could be persuaded by the constitutionally required high standard of proof beyond a reasonable doubt. Instead, they often begin by saying that the defendant "bears a very heavy burden"[61] or "faces a formidable burden"[62] to persuade the appellate court that the constitutional standard of proof has not been met.

Not surprisingly, rhetoric of this sort has led to highly restrictive substantive rulings. Let me illustrate my point with an example from the law of criminal conspiracy. Preliminarily, I must briefly digress to note my longstanding doubts as to whether a conspiracy prosecution is ever warranted in a completed crime. A conspiracy is an agreement to commit a crime.[63] Certainly punishment should be available for those who make such an agreement and demonstrate their seriousness by taking at least one overt act toward its accomplishment. But when the substantive crime that was agreed to has been committed, the government should prosecute only for the substantive offense, with those at the fringes of the venture culpable either for causing, or aiding and abetting, the offense whenever the elements for those specific crimes are established.[64] When a substantive offense has been completed, permitting a jury that acquits on the substantive offense to convict for conspiracy is too dangerous. It is a dragnet approach to criminal law, inviting the jurors to resolve doubtful cases by pronouncing guilt for an offense that may seem to them less serious than the substantive offense. I think many jurors who have acquitted a fringe defendant of a substantive drug offense but convicted of conspiracy would be astounded to learn that the sentences for these offenses are identical.

Whatever my reservations on this score, I recognize the established law that a conspiracy conviction is permissible even where the substantive offense has been completed. My concern is how seriously we take the obligation to insist on proof beyond a reasonable doubt when we permit conviction for this most amorphous of crimes. Consider the pervasive rule as to review of the sufficiency of evidence to support the crucial element that a defendant joined the conspiracy. Many circuits, including my own, hold that once the existence of a conspiracy has been established, it takes only "slight" evidence to connect a defendant to it.[65] How can that possibly be correct? How can "slight" evidence suffice to permit a finding beyond a reasonable doubt? Since the conspiracy count itself is a crutch available for the prosecutor to lean on when proof of the substantive offense is thin, we should at least discard the "slight evidence" test for linking a defendant to a conspiracy, and seriously insist that the evidence of participation be substantial enough to permit a reasonable jury to find this element, like all other elements, established beyond a reasonable doubt.

The "slight evidence" test seems to have entered our jurisprudence quite unobtrusively in 1930 in a decision of the Fifth Circuit in *Tomplain v. United States*.[66] It was later embraced by several other circuits.[67] The test gained acceptance because of a confusion between the correct rule that only a slight connection between a defendant and a conspiracy need be shown and the incorrect rule that only slight evidence is needed to prove that connection.[68] A few circuits have properly rejected the "slight evidence" test to varying degrees.[69] It is time to recognize that this test is inconsistent with serious enforcement of the "reasonable doubt" standard.

The "slight evidence" test for participation in a conspiracy is not the only example of the tendency of appellate courts to accept thin evidence as sufficient to establish guilt beyond a reasonable doubt. Some courts have permitted a witness's prior inconsistent statements to provide substantial support for conviction, even though they were nominally offered only for impeachment.[70] My quarrel is not with the admissibility of such statements; it is with the courts' failure to assess the sufficiency of such evidence against a rigorous application of the "reasonable doubt" standard.

Other examples are cases where thin proof of guilt was deemed sufficient to convict because it was bolstered by evidence showing consciousness of guilt[71] or an inference from the defendant's demeanor on the witness stand.[72] Again, I do not question the relevance of such evidence, only the heavy reliance on it to carry a case above the line of proof beyond a reasonable doubt. The fact that evidence is relevant does not automatically make it sufficient to support a criminal conviction. That point should be obvious, yet it is rarely mentioned in the appellate reports.[73]

All these examples illustrate my basic point—that courts do not take seriously their obligation to assess sufficiency of evidence in light of the "reasonable doubt" standard. They end their inquiry upon noticing the existence of "some" evidence of guilt. But the Supreme Court warned in *Jackson* against sustaining convictions supported by only a "modicum" of evidence. In a passage rarely mentioned by federal appellate courts, Justice Stewart wrote:

> Any evidence that is relevant—that has any tendency to make the existence of an element of a crime slightly more probable than it would be without the evidence, cf. Fed. Rule Evid. 401—could be deemed a "mere modicum." But it could not seriously be argued that such a "modicum" of evidence could by itself rationally support a conviction beyond a reasonable doubt.[74]

If the constitutional standard of proof in criminal cases is to have meaning, courts must heed this caution and ask themselves in every case whether a reasonable jury could have found guilt proven beyond a reasonable doubt.

If an appellate court is unwilling to say that the evidence is insufficient to permit a finding of guilt beyond a reasonable doubt, it should at least be willing to say, in some marginal cases of doubtful sufficiency, that the verdict is against the weight of the evidence and, on that ground, order a new trial. Trial courts have the authority to set aside convictions as being against the weight of the evidence,[75] and some circuits have accorded them authority to reweigh evidence and even consider the credibility of witnesses.[76] The Supreme Court has recognized that, at least in a state judicial system, even appellate courts may exercise such authority, sitting, in effect, as a thirteenth juror.[77] However, federal appellate courts generally take a restrictive view of "weight of the evidence" challenges, routinely affirming district court denials of such motions[78] and usually reversing the rare district court rulings that grant such motions.[79]

A notable recent exception is *United States v. Morales*.[80] A trial judge had denied a motion to set aside a conviction as contrary to the weight of the evidence. The Seventh Circuit reversed. In Judge Posner's words: "If the complete record, testimonial and physical, leaves a strong doubt as to the defendant's guilt, even though not so strong a doubt as to require a judgment of acquittal, the district judge may be obliged to grant a new trial."[81] Those words could be written only by a judge who takes the "reasonable doubt" standard seriously.

4. Examining Credibility

My fourth plea is that, in taking seriously our obligation to determine whether the evidence suffices to permit a finding of guilt beyond a reasonable doubt, we make some modest adjustment in our absolute rejection of any inquiry as to the credibility of witnesses. Here, I acknowledge, I am moving past the provocative to the heretical. It has been an article of faith among judges steeped in the Anglo-American jury tradition that the credibility of witnesses is for the jury and not for the appellate court to judge.[82] So when the Supreme Court formulated its standards for testing sufficiency in civil and criminal cases, it naturally directed reviewing judges not to weigh the credibility of witnesses.[83]

Should this always be so? I think our confidence in the ability of juries to assess credibility is generally well placed. Deciding whether a witness speaks the truth is never easy, and judges are no better than jurors at looking inside the mind or heart of a witness and detecting mendacity. But it is a romantic notion that the jury should be an infallible determiner of credibility. It is one thing to permit the jury unfettered discretion in choosing between the conflicting accounts of two upstanding members of the community. But it is quite another to defer blindly to their acceptance of testimony from a seriously impeached witness. For example, if a witness is indisputably shown to have lied on prior occasions, perhaps under oath, and is currently in a position to save himself years of jail time by accusing the defendant, does it make sense to say that his testimony alone is sufficient to prove guilt beyond a reasonable doubt, simply because twelve jurors have decided to believe him? Again, I do not mean to suggest that such testimony should be inadmissible. We should permit the jury to consider it along with other evidence. But if the other evidence is slender or nonexistent, then, at least in some cases, the substantial impeachment of an accusing witness, based on objective facts, should prompt a court to say that a reasonable jury (even any rational jury) could not find guilt beyond a reasonable doubt.

At one time Judge Jerome Frank expressed the view that in a criminal case a judge could, on occasion, include the judge's own assessment of credibility in determining whether a case was sufficient to persuade a reasonable jury beyond a reasonable doubt.[84] He later receded from this view,[85] though maintaining at least the possibility that a judge in a criminal case should reject testimony deemed "patently false," even though precluded by the seventh amendment from doing so in a civil case.[86] I think Judge Frank was right the first time.

5. Heightened Scrutiny in Special Categories of Cases

My final plea is that we give serious thought to adjusting sufficiency review in special categories of cases. If we are not going to be rigorous in enforcing the "reasonable doubt" standard in all cases, at least we should do so in those cases where we know the risk of convicting the innocent is higher than ordinary. When Professor Borchard confronted us in 1932 with chilling examples of innocent persons found guilty by juries,[87] he reminded us that a major cause of such injustice is unwarranted reliance on eyewitness testimony.[88] Are the only safeguards a jury charge that cautions about the hazards of such testimony[89] and court rejection of unduly suggestive identifications?[90]

I believe that the "reasonable doubt" standard requires us to do more. Appellate courts must not end their sufficiency inquiry as soon as they notice that at least one eyewitness identified the defendant. If that witness did not previously know the accused and had only a brief opportunity to observe him, and if the remaining evidence is thin or nonexistent, courts should face up to their responsibilities and rule that, though there is some evidence of guilt, it is insufficient to persuade a reasonable jury by the high standard of proof beyond a reasonable doubt.

Another likely category for such an approach would be cases where a finding of guilt rests primarily, and sometimes entirely, on the uncorroborated testimony of an accomplice. In the federal courts, such testimony is sufficient.[91] I ask you: Is it sufficient to satisfy merely the civil standard, which is all Learned Hand required,[92] or can we honestly say, in every case, that it is sufficient to persuade a reasonable jury of guilt beyond a reasonable doubt? Rather than choose between the federal rule, which always permits a conviction on the uncorroborated testimony of an accomplice, and the New York rule, which never permits a conviction on such testimony alone,[93] I would prefer to see such testimony deemed sufficient only in those cases where, based on all the circumstances, we can confidently say that a reasonable jury could be persuaded of guilt beyond a reasonable doubt.

Other categories where we ought to be especially careful in determining whether a reasonable jury could have found guilt beyond a reasonable doubt are cases in which the jury might have been unduly swayed to convict by inflammatory, though relevant, evidence about the crime or the victim, and complex cases in which the jury might not have given individual consideration to each one of a large group of defendants.

In similar vein, we might consider applying the "reasonable doubt" standard more rigorously where the penalty is severe. Should not "reasonable doubt" be taken more seriously when a defendant's life is at stake?[94]

B. Risk of Undeserved Acquittals

The enhanced scrutiny I have in mind is not advocated simply to tilt the balance of criminal justice a shade more favorably toward defendants. As I said at the outset, I believe that our unwillingness to apply the "reasonable doubt" standard rigorously has resulted not only in some unjust convictions, but it has also precipitated some unwarranted acquittals. I cannot prove that paradoxical effect, but I can tell you why I believe it is occurring. It stems from the expectation of courts that jury verdicts of guilty are extremely unlikely to be upset on appeal for insufficient evidence. With this expectation firmly in mind, courts are reluctant to admit some evidence that is relevant to guilt but that also has some tendency to be prejudicial. I think that courts would be more receptive to relevant evidence, despite its somewhat prejudicial effects, if they were confident that when all the evidence was in, a guilty verdict resting on thin evidence would be rejected either by the trial judge or on appeal.

For example, courts do not permit juries to consider evidence that all the world regards as probative in ordinary dealings among people—the fact that the defendant has committed the same offense on prior occasions. We accept such evidence, somewhat hypocritically, for the "limited" purpose of impeaching the credibility of the occasional defendant who testifies. But when the defendant does not testify, we normally exclude such evidence, not because it is irrelevant, but because it is too relevant—that is, because it might too readily lead the jury to convict. We also exclude some forms of hearsay that people often rely on in ordinary matters.

I think we would be more willing to broaden the categories of evidence that juries are permitted to hear if we were more confident that appellate courts would scrutinize insufficiency claims with care. The lack of such evidence, I suspect, costs the prosecution some convictions that should be obtained.

C. The Approach of Foreign Courts

The reluctance of most American courts to take the "reasonable doubt" standard seriously stands in marked contrast to the approach of many foreign courts. Recently the world took note of the courageous decision of the Supreme Court of Israel in ruling that there was a reasonable doubt whether John Demjanjuk was guilty of war crimes.[95] That decision is not precisely analogous to the American cases I have been discussing, as it involves both a review of sufficiency of a completed trial record and an assessment of newly discovered evidence. But it was a decision rendered by a court that took the "reasonable doubt" standard seriously.

In England, the Court of Appeal is obliged to set aside a conviction that it regards as "unsafe or unsatisfactory."[96] British judges take that obligation seriously.[97] They ask themselves, in the words of a 1968 decision of the Court of Appeal, "whether there is not some lurking doubt in our minds which makes us wonder whether an injustice has been done."[98] The Court of Appeal frankly acknowledges that this inquiry poses "a subjective question,"[99] though it would seem that the court is not purporting to act as a thirteenth juror, deciding whether it is persuaded of guilt beyond a reasonable doubt. Instead, the court is making up its own mind as to whether the evidence, although perhaps sufficient to persuade a reasonable jury beyond a reasonable doubt, nevertheless leaves the appellate judges with a "lurking doubt causing concern that an injustice has been done."[100]

Until recently, the Canadian Supreme Court had articulated two standards for testing sufficiency, paralleling the dichotomy of the language our Supreme Court used in *Jackson*.[101] A restrictive test stated that a verdict should be vacated only if no twelve jurors "could possibly have reached it,"[102] while a broader test stated that a verdict is sustainable if a jury "could reasonably have rendered it."[103] In 1987, the Canadian Supreme Court repudiated the more restrictive formulation.[104]

Of particular current interest is the new statute of the Russian Federation that authorizes the resumption of jury trials in certain areas of Russia in the fall of 1993, a practice last seen there in 1917. Pertinent to my concern is the provision requiring the judge in a jury trial to order a new trial in any case in which "the defendant's participation in the commission of the crime has not been proved."[105] Though we do not yet know how this provision will be applied in practice, it appears to place the trial judge squarely in the role of a thirteenth juror, making the same subjective inquiry as to whether guilt has been proven beyond a reasonable doubt as was made by the Israeli Supreme Court in the *Demjanjuk* case.

Conclusion

I hope that all the proposals I have outlined have given some vision of what appellate review would look like if we took the "reasonable doubt" standard more seriously. Why have we not done so? Is it simply a pro-prosecution bias in appellate courts? I think not. My guess is that American courts have permitted their unbounded enthusiasm for the jury to dilute the rigor of their enforcement of the "reasonable doubt" standard as a rule of law. We say that we do not wish to invade the "province of the jury."[106] But that "province" is not a fortress that can never be entered, nor is it a black box into which we dare not look. It is simply a group of twelve people doing their level best. Generally we should accept their verdict. But our task as judges includes the enforcement of constitutional standards. And a vital component of those standards is the requirement of proof beyond a reasonable doubt.

The time has come to move beyond the mere incantation of the "reasonable doubt" standard in jury charges and to apply it faithfully as a rule of constitutional law in the course of appellate review of criminal convictions. I believe that is what James Madison would have expected us to do.

NOTES

1. Norman Dorsen, Foreword to *The Evolving Constitution*, at ix, ix (Norman Dorsen ed., 1987).

2. See *In re Winship*, 397 U.S. 358, 364 (1970) ("The Due Process Clause protects the accused against conviction except upon proof beyond a reasonable doubt of every fact necessary to constitute the crime with which he is charged.").

3. See *Miles v. United States*, 103 U.S. 304, 312 (1880) ("The evidence upon which a jury is justified in returning a verdict of guilty must be sufficient to produce a conviction of guilt, to the exclusion of all reasonable doubt.").

4. See *Winship*, 397 U.S. at 372 (Harlan, J., concurring) ("It is far worse to convict an innocent man than to let a guilty man go free.").

5. See *Furman v. Georgia*, 408 U.S. 238, 367 n.158 (1992) (Marshall, J., concurring) (quoting William O. Douglas, Foreword to Jerome Frank & Barbara Frank, *Not Guilty* 11–12 (1957)); *Goetz v. Crosson*, 967 F.2d 29, 39 (2d Cir. 1992) (Newman, J., concurring); *Bunnell v. Sullivan*, 947 F.2d 341, 352 (9th Cir. 1991) (en banc) (Kozinski, J., concurring); *United States v. Greer*, 538 F.2d 437, 441 (D.C. Cir. 1976); see also 4 William Blackstone, *Commentaries* 358.

6. See Sir John Fortescue, *De Laudibus Legum Angliae* 65 (Dr. Chrimes ed., Cambridge Univ. Press 1942) (1471) ("I should, indeed, prefer twenty guilty men to escape death through mercy, than one innocent to be condemned unjustly.").

7. See Thomas Starkie, *Evidence* 756 (1724), quoted in IX *Wigmore on Evidence* § 2497, at 409–10 (Chadbourn rev. 1991) ("The maxim of the law is . . . that it is better that ninety-nine . . . offenders shall escape than that that one innocent man be condemned.").

8. *Bond's Case*, 27 How. St. Tr. 523 (Ir. 1798); *Finney's Case*, 26 How. St. Tr. 1019 (Ir. 1798).

9. See Charles McCormick, *Law of Evidence* § 321, at 682 n.3 (lst ed. 1954) (quoting May, "Some Rules of Evidence: Reasonable Doubt in Civil and Criminal Cases," 10 Am. L. Rev. 642, 656–57 (1876)). The phrasing has also been traced even earlier to the "Boston Massacre Trials of 1770, *Rex v. Wemms*," in 3 *Legal Papers of John Adams* 98, 309 (L. Kinvin Wroth & Hiller Zobel eds., 1965).

10. See Anthony A. Morano, "A Reexamination of the Development of the Reasonable Doubt Rule," 55 B.U. L. Rev. 507, 508 (1975).

11. See, e.g., *Ferguson v. The Queen*, 1979 1 All E.R. 877, 878 (P.C. 1978) (appeal taken from Gren.).

12. See *Regina v. Allan*, 1969 1 All E.R. 91, 92 (1968); see also *Regina v. Holland* (C.A. Aug. 20, 1968), digested in 118 New L.J. 1004, 1004 (unreported case affirming instruction that jury feel "satisfied" because court was confident that "the jury were left in no doubt that, before they could convict, they had to be so satisfied as to be sure" of guilt).

13. C. Pr. Pzen. Art. 353 (Gerald L. Kock & Richard S. Frase, trans., 1988). The court must also post this instruction "in large letters in the most prominent place in the conference room." Id.

14. 1 Leonard B. Sand et al., *Modern Federal Jury Instructions* X 4.01, Instruction 4–2 (1993). But see *United States v. Noone*, 913 F.2d 20, 28–29 (1st Cir. 1990) (criticizing charges explaining "reasonable doubt" standard with reference to hesitating in personal affairs as "risking trivialization of the constitutional standard"), cert. denied, 111 S. Ct. 1686 (1991).

The "hesitate to act" formulation may have originated in *Posey v. State*, 93 So. 272, 273 (Ala. Ct. App. 1922). The formulation from *Posey* was cited in *Bishop v. United States*, 107 F.2d 297, 303 (D.C. Cir. 1939), which, in turn, was given an authoritative citation by the Supreme Court in *Holland v. United States*, 348 U.S. 121, 140 (1954). State courts often use this formulation. See, e.g., *State v. Gomez*, 622 A.2d 1014, 1017 n.8 (Conn. 1993); *People v. Jackson*, 421 N.W.2d 697, 699 (Mich. Ct. App. 1988); *Commonwealth v. Bowser*, 624 A.2d 125, 138 (Pa. Super. Ct. 1993); *Geesa v. State*, 820 S.W.2d 154, 162 (Tex. Crim. App. 1991).

15. A recommended pattern instruction advises jurors to convict only if sufficiently persuaded that they would not hesitate to act on important matters. See 1 Sand et al., supra note 14, X 4.02, Instruction 4–2 ("Proof beyond a reasonable doubt must, therefore, be proof of such a convincing character that a reasonable person would not hesitate to rely and act upon it in the most important of his own affairs.").

16. See, e.g., *United States v. Indorato*, 628 F.2d 711, 720–21 (1st Cir.), cert. denied, 449 U.S. 1016 (1980); *United States v. Byrd*, 352 F.2d 570, 575 (2d Cir. 1965). Some state courts, however, continue to endorse the "moral certainty" formulation. See, e.g., *People v. Sims*, 853 P.2d 992, 1024 (Cal. 1993); *People v. Dahlin*, 539 N.E.2d

1293, 1296 (Ill. App. Ct. 1989); *People v. Wong*, 619 N.E.2d 377, 381 (N.Y. 1993). But see *Victor v. Nebraska*, 62 U.S.L.W. 4179, 4185 (U.S. Mar. 22, 1994) (stating that although "we do not countenance its use, the inclusion of the moral certainty did not render the instruction" unconstitutional).

The "moral certainty" standard was originally introduced to lessen the prosecution's burden, since "moral certainty" was thought of as "reasonable certainty" as opposed to "absolute certainty." See Morano, supra note 10, at 513–14.

17. See, e.g., *United States v. Johnson*, 343 F.2d 5, 6 n.1 (2d Cir. 1965), cited with approval in *Johnson v. Louisiana*, 406 U.S. 356, 360 (1972); see also *Jackson v. Virginia*, 443 U.S. 307, 317 n.9 (1979); 1 Sand et al., supra note 14, X 4.01, Instruction 4–2 (noting that reasonable doubt "is a doubt based upon reason").

18. See *United States v. Farina*, 184 F.2d 18, 23–24 (2d Cir.) (Frank, J., dissenting), cert. denied, 340 U.S. 875 (1950); *Pettine v. Territory of New Mexico*, 201 F. 489, 495–97 (8th Cir. 1912).

19. *Jackson v. Virginia*, 443 U.S. 307, 315 (1979). This statement is a slightly less rigorous variation of the statement in *Winship*, where the Court said that the "reasonable doubt" standard "'impresses on the trier of fact the necessity of reaching a subjective state of certitude of the facts in issue.'" *In re Winship*, 397 U.S. 358, 364 (1970) (quoting Dorsen & Rezneck, "*In re Gault* and the Future of Juvenile Law" 1 Fam. L.Q. 1, 26 (1967)).

20. *Jackson*, 443 U.S. at 317. The Court had earlier endorsed both this "doubt based on 'reason'" explanation and the "subjective state of certitude" formulation in *Johnson v. Louisiana*, 406 U.S. 356, 360 (1972).

21. See, e.g., *United States v. Hall*, 854 F.2d 1036, 1037–39 (7th Cir. 1988); *Murphy v. Holland*, 776 F.2d 470, 478–79 (4th Cir. 1985), vacated on other grounds, 475 U.S. 1138 (1986). See generally "Note, Defining Reasonable Doubt: To Define, or Not to Define," 90 Colum. L. Rev. 1716, 1718–21 (1990).

22. See 1 Sand et al., supra note 14, X 4.01, Instruction 4–11 ("The better practice is to spend some moments with the jury discussing the government's burden of proof in order to clarify the meaning."); see also Note, supra note 21 (arguing that jury instructions defining reasonable doubt should always be given).

23. See generally Rita James Simon & Linda Mahan, "Quantifying Burdens of Proof," 5 Law & Soc'y Rev. 319 (1971); see also Rita James Simon, "'Beyond a Reasonable Doubt'—An Experimental Attempt at Quantification," 6 J. Applied Behavioral Sci. 203, 207 (1970) (estimating, as result of mock trial experiment, that student jurors voted to convict when they thought probability of guilt was at least 74 percent).

24. See Simon & Mahan, supra note 23, at 325.

25. See generally "London School of Economics Jury Project, Juries and the Rules of Evidence," 1973 Crim. L. Rev. 208.

26. See id. at 216–17.

27. 140 F.2d 592 (2d Cir.), cert. denied, 322 U.S. 726 (1944).

28. See id. at 594 ("But courts—at least federal courts—have generally declared that the standard of evidence necessary to send a case to the jury is the same in both civil and criminal cases.").

29. Id.

30. Id.

31. See *Curley v. United States*, 160 F.2d 229 (D.C. Cir.), cert. denied, 331 U.S. 837 (1947).

32. See Robert J. Gregory, "Whose Reasonable Doubt? Reconsidering the Appropriate Role of the Reviewing Court in the Criminal Decision Making Process," 24 Amer. Crim. L. Rev. 911, 927–28 (1987) (citing cases).

33. *United States v. Taylor*, 464 F.2d 240, 243 (2d Cir. 1972). Even before *Taylor*, the Second Circuit had begun to assess sufficiency by asking whether the evidence was sufficient to convince a jury beyond a reasonable doubt. See, e.g., *United States v. Glasser*, 443 F.2d 994, 1006 (2d Cir.), cert. denied, 404 U.S. 854 (1971); *United States v. Kahaner*, 317 F.2d 459, 467–68 (2d Cir.), cert. denied, 375 U.S. 835 (1963); *United States v. Robertson*, 298 F.2d 739, 741 (2d Cir. 1962); *United States v. Lefkowitz*, 284 F.2d 310, 315 (2d Cir. 1960). The assault upon *Feinberg* had been led by Judge Frank in his notable concurring opinions in *United States v. Masiello*, 235 F.2d 279, 285 (2d Cir.), cert. denied, 352 U.S. 882 (1956); *United States v. Gonzales Castro*, 228 F.2d 807, 809 (2d Cir.), cert. denied, 351 U.S. 940 (1956); *United States v. Costello*, 221 F.2d 668, 679–80 (2d Cir. 1955), aff'd, 350 U.S. 359 (1956).

34. *Taylor*, 464 F.2d at 242.

35. Id. (quoting *Bridges v. Railway Co.*, 1874 L.R. 7 H.L. 213, 233).

36. 397 U.S. 358 (1970).

37. The Court said that the standard "reduces the risk of convictions resting on factual error" and "provides concrete substance for the presumption of innocence." Id. at 363. Later, in *Jackson v. Virginia*, 443 U.S. 307 (1979), the Court divided that first rationale in two, stating that the standard operates "to ensure against unjust convictions, and to reduce the risk of factual error." Id. at 315.

38. 362 U.S. 199 (1960).

39. 443 U.S. 307 (1979).

40. Two years earlier, Justice Stewart had unsuccessfully urged the Court to decide whether due process is violated by a conviction "where the evidence cannot fairly be considered sufficient to establish guilt beyond a reasonable doubt." See *Freeman v. Zahradnick*, 429 U.S. 1111, 1116 (1977) (Stewart, J., dissenting from denial of certiorari).

41. *Jackson*, 443 U.S. at 316–17.

42. Id. at 318–19 (quoting *Woodby v. INS*, 385 U.S. 276, 282 (1966)).

43. Id. at 318 (footnote omitted).

44. Id. at 319.

45. "The Court does not require the reviewing court . . . to decide . . . whether, based on the entire record, rational triers of fact could be convinced of guilt beyond

a reasonable doubt. Instead . . . it chooses a still narrower standard that merely asks whether, 'after viewing the evidence in the light most favorable to the prosecution, any rational trier of fact could have found the essential elements of the crime beyond a reasonable doubt.'" Id. at 334 (Stevens, J., concurring).

The concurring Justices noted two distinctions between the two formulations in the majority's opinion. They emphasized not only the distinction between "rational triers of fact" and "any rational trier of fact," but also between review of "the entire record" and review of "the evidence in the light most favorable to the prosecution." Id. Possibly the second distinction was of more concern to these Justices.

46. See Joseph Goldstein, *The Intelligible Constitution* 81–91, 116–24 (1992) (criticizing Supreme Court majorities for not engaging in productive dialogues with dissenters who raise significant issues).

47. See, e.g., *United States v. Gordils*, 982 F.2d 64, 70 (2d Cir. 1992), cert. denied, 113 S. Ct. 1953 (1993); *United States v. Chaney*, 964 F.2d 437, 448 (5th Cir. 1992); *United States v. Beddow*, 957 F.2d 1330, 1334 (6th Cir. 1992); *United States v. Long*, 905 F.2d 1572, 1576 (D.C. Cir.), cert. denied, 498 U.S. 948 (1990); *United States v. Linn*, 880 F.2d 209, 215 (9th Cir. 1989).

State supreme courts reveal the same pattern. See, e.g., *People v. Clair*, 828 P.2d 705, 729 (Cal. 1992), cert. denied, 113 S. Ct. 1006 (1993); *People v. Wilson*, 614 N.E.2d 1227, 1229 (Ill. 1993); *Letica v. State*, 569 N.E.2d 952, 955 (Ind. 1991); *State v. Bourque*, 622 So. 2d 198, 242 (La. 1993); *Hebron v. State*, 627 A.2d 1029, 1035 (Md. 1993); *Commonwealth v. Montanez*, 571 N.E.2d 1372, 1382 (Mass. 1991); *State v. McLain*, 815 P.2d 147, 150 (Mont. 1991); *State v. Thomas*, 407 S.E.2d 141, 148 (N.C. 1991); *People v. Mattiace*, 568 N.E.2d 1189, 1191 (N.Y. 1990); *State v. Hawkins*, 612 N.E.2d 1227, 1231 (Ohio), cert. denied, 114 S. Ct. 486 (1993); *State v. Rogers*, 836 P.2d 1308, 1325 (Or. 1992), cert. denied, 113 S. Ct. 1420 (1993); *State v. Smith*, 857 S.W.2d 1, 9 (Tenn.), cert. denied, 114 S. Ct. 561 (1993); *Green v. State*, 840 S.W.2d 394, 401 (Tex. Crim. App. 1992), cert. denied, 113 S. Ct. 1819 (1993).

48. See, e.g., *United States v. Soto*, 716 F.2d 989, 993 (2d Cir. 1983).

49. See, e.g., *United States v. Lopez-Alvarez*, 970 F.2d 583, 593–94 (9th Cir.), cert. denied, 113 S. Ct. 504 (1992); *United States v. Casper*, 956 F.2d 416, 421–22 (3d Cir. 1992); *United States v. Long*, 905 F.2d 1572, 1576–79 (D.C. Cir.), cert. denied, 498 U.S. 948 (1990); *United States v. Bruun*, 809 F.2d 397, 404–5, 410–11 (7th Cir. 1987).

50. See *Chapman v. California*, 386 U.S. 18, 24 (1967).

51. See, e.g., *Tucker v. Borgert*, No. 91–1059, 1991 WL 255583, at *1 (6th Cir. Dec. 4, 1991), cert. denied, 112 S. Ct. 2311 (1992); *Logan v. Abshire*, 778 F.2d 283, 284 (6th Cir. 1985) (per curiam); see also *United States ex rel. Miller v. Greer*, 789 F.2d 438, 446–47 (7th Cir. 1986) (en banc) (reversing trial court's ruling that constitutional error was harmless under *Chapman* standard), rev'd sub nom. *Greer v. Miller*, 483 U.S. 756, 765–67 (1987) (upholding state supreme court's determination that error "was harmless beyond reasonable doubt"). But see *Clemons v. Mississippi*, 494 U.S. 738, 753–54 (1990) (vacating and remanding for clarification

state supreme court ruling that constitutional error was harmless under *Chapman* standard).

52. See *Stevens v. United States*, 319 F.2d 733, 735 (D.C. Cir. 1963); *Wolf v. United States*, 238 F. 902, 906 (4th Cir. 1916). *Winship* itself was a case where the fact finder might have reached different outcomes by using different burdens of persuasion. In that case, the New York Family Court Judge, who had based the determination of juvenile delinquency on a finding that a larceny had been proven by a preponderance of the evidence, indicated that the proof "might not establish guilt beyond a reasonable doubt." *In re Winship*, 397 U.S. 358, 360 (1970); see also *United States v. Masiello*, 235 F.2d 279, 285–86 (2d Cir.) (Frank, J., concurring) (noting in dictum that if one particular item of evidence were put aside, the remaining evidence would have been sufficient to satisfy the "preponderance" standard but not sufficient to satisfy the "reasonable doubt" standard), cert. denied, 352 U.S. 882 (1956); *United States v. Paglia*, 190 F.2d 445, 448 (2d Cir. 1951) (comparing civil and criminal standards for purposes of determining that resentencing was required), overruled on other grounds by *United States v. Taylor*, 217 F.2d 397, 399 (2d Cir. 1954); *United States v. Milken*, 759 F. Supp. 109, 122–23 (S.D.N.Y. 1990) (finding evidence that might have been sufficient for civil liability insufficient as basis for criminal sentencing).

53. See *Jackson v. Virginia*, 443 U.S. 307, 319 (1979). But see Gregory, supra note 32, at 980 (arguing that "reasonable doubt" standard cannot properly be infused into sufficiency review as long as all reasonable inferences are construed in favor of prosecution).

54. Federal Judicial Center, Pattern Criminal Jury Instructions 28, Instruction 21 (1987).

55. The complete instruction reads:

> As I have said many times, the government has the burden of proving the defendant guilty beyond a reasonable doubt. Some of you may have served as jurors in civil cases, where you were told that it is only necessary to prove that a fact is more likely true than not true. In criminal cases, the government's proof must be more powerful than that. It must be beyond a reasonable doubt.
>
> Proof beyond a reasonable doubt is proof that leaves you firmly convinced of the defendant's guilt. There are very few things in this world that we know with absolute certainty, and in criminal cases the law does not require proof that overcomes every possible doubt. If, based on your consideration of the evidence, you are firmly convinced that the defendant is guilty of the crime charged, you must find him guilty. If on the other hand, you think there is a real possibility that he is not guilty, you must give him the benefit of the doubt and find him not guilty.

Id.; see also *Victor v. Nebraska*, 62 U.S.L.W. 4179, 4186 (U.S. Mar. 22, 1994) (Ginsburg, J., concurring) ("This Model instruction surpasses others I have seen in stating the reasonable doubt standard succinctly and comprehensibly.").

56. See *Jackson*, 443 U.S. at 319 (citing *Johnson v. Louisiana*, 406 U.S. 356, 362 (1972)).

57. *Johnson*, 406 U.S. at 360.

58. Id. at 362.

59. A Westlaw search of the words "any rational" used within two words of "jury," "judge," "trier of fact," "fact finder," "factfinder," or "finder of fact" discloses only two uses of the phrase in any context before 1979. In *Johnson v. Estelle*, 506 F.2d 347 (5th Cir.), cert. denied, 422 U.S. 1024 (1975), the Court, endeavoring to show how preposterous it would have been to believe that the defendant could have changed his intent from robbery to rape as he crossed the victim's threshold, said it did not believe that "any rational jury" would have so concluded. Id. at 351. In *United States v. Schiller*, 187 F.2d 572 (2d Cir. 1951), the Court rejected a claim that the charge on conspiracy was flawed by omission of the word "alleged," a word the Court thought would have been regarded as implied by "any rational jury." Id. at 574.

60. See *Brady v. Southern Ry.*, 320 U.S. 476, 479–80 (1943) ("When the evidence is such that without weighing the credibility of the witnesses there can be but one reasonable conclusion as to the verdict, the court should determine the proceeding."); see also 5A James W. Moore & Jo D. Lucas, *Moore's Federal Practice* X 50.02) 1, at 50–25 to 50–26 (2d ed. 1993).

61. See, e.g., *United States v. Pitre*, 960 F.2d 1112, 1120 (2d Cir. 1992).

62. See, e.g., *United States v. Burrell*, 963 F.2d 976, 987 (7th Cir.), cert. denied, 113 S. Ct. 357 (1992).

63. See *United States v. Falcone*, 311 U.S. 205, 210 (1940).

64. See 18 U.S.C. s 2 (1988) (requiring punishment as a principal for persons culpable of causing, aiding, or abetting commission of a crime against the United States).

65. *United States v. Vaquero*, 997 F.2d 78, 82 (5th Cir.), cert. denied, 114 S. Ct. 614 (1993); *United States v. Smiley*, 997 F.2d 475, 479 (8th Cir. 1993); *United States v. Lee*, 991 F.2d 343, 348 (6th Cir. 1993); *United States v. Brooks*, 957 F.2d 1138, 1147 (4th Cir.), cert. denied, 112 S. Ct. 3051 (1992); *United States v. Tejada*, 956 F.2d 1256, 1265 (2d Cir.), cert. denied, 113 S. Ct. 124 (1992); *United States v. Sanchez-Mata*, 925 F.2d 1166, 1167 (9th Cir. 1991).

66. 42 F.2d 202, 203 (5th Cir.), cert. denied, 282 U.S. 886 (1930).

67. See, e.g., *United States v. Knight*, 416 F.2d 1181, 1184 (9th Cir. 1969); *Bradford v. United States*, 413 F.2d 467, 469 (5th Cir. 1969). *Bradford* and *Knight* were cited by the Second Circuit in *United States v. Marrapese*, 486 F.2d 918, 921 (2d Cir. 1973), cert. denied, 415 U.S. 994 (1974).

68. See *United States v. Marsh*, 747 F.2d 7, 12–13 & n.3 (1st Cir. 1984).

69. See, e.g., *United States v. Clavis*, 977 F.2d 538, 539 (11th Cir. 1992), cert. denied, 113 S. Ct. 1619 (1993); *United States v. Durrive*, 902 F.2d 1221, 1228–29 (7th Cir. 1990); *United States v. Coleman*, 811 F.2d 804, 807–8 (3d Cir. 1987); *United States v. Marsh*, 747 F.2d 7, 13 (1st Cir. 1984).

70. See, e.g., *Gibbons v. State*, 286 S.E.2d 717, 721 (Ga. 1982)(holding that prior inconsistent statement of witness may be used as substantive evidence, not just for impeachment, and that statement, together with other "limited" evidence, was sufficient to support conviction); see also *People v. Brown*, 198 Cal. Rptr. 260, 263 (Cal. App. 1 Dist. 1984) (holding, under California Evidence Code § 1235 which allows prior inconsistent statements to be used as substantive evidence, that prior inconsistent statements of defendant were sufficient to support conviction); *State v. Moore*, 424 So. 2d 920, 922 (Fla. Dist. Ct. App. 1983) (holding that because Florida Evidence Code § 801(2)(a) allows prior inconsistent statements to be admitted as substantive evidence, State could survive motion to dismiss based solely on witness's prior inconsistent statements). See generally Stanley A. Goldman, "Guilt by Intuition: The Insufficiency of Prior Inconsistent Statements to Convict," 65 N.C. L. Rev. 1 (1986).

71. See, e.g., *United States v. Morgan*, 914 F.2d 272, 276 (D.C. Cir. 1990) (holding consciousness of guilt and momentary possession sufficient to support conviction for possession of marijuana); *United States v. Nichols*, 820 F.2d 508, 512 (1st Cir. 1987) (holding that defendant's behavior allowed jury inference that defendant had "something to hide").

72. See, e.g., *United States v. Zafiro*, 945 F.2d 881, 888 (7th Cir. 1991) (holding that jury could conclude on basis of defendant's demeanor and expert evidence that defendant knew she was aiding a conspiracy), aff'd, 113 S. Ct. 933 (1993).

73. See *United States v. Young*, 745 F.2d 733, 766 (2d Cir. 1984)(Newman, J., concurring) ("It is one thing to permit a jury to weigh an expert's opinion that actions are criminal in considering an otherwise adequate case, it is quite another matter to let that opinion salvage an insufficient case."), cert. denied, 470 U.S. 1084 (1985); *United States v. Sette*, 334 F.2d 267, 269 (2d Cir. 1964) (holding that expert evidence of government agents that behavior was criminal is insufficient to establish prima facie case).

74. *Jackson v. Virginia*, 443 U.S. 307, 320 (1979).

75. See *Tibbs v. Florida*, 457 U.S. 31, 42 (1982) ("These policies underlying double jeopardy bar to retrial after insufficiency ruling do not have the same force when a judge disagrees with a jury's resolution of conflicting evidence and concludes that a guilty verdict is against the weight of the evidence."); Fed. R. Crim. P. 33 ("The court on motion of a defendant may grant a new trial to that defendant if required in the interest of justice."); 3 Charles A. Wright, *Federal Practice and Procedure* § 553, at 246 (1982) (noting that on motion for new trial, court can conclude "that the verdict is contrary to the weight of the evidence and that a miscarriage of justice may have resulted").

76. See, e.g., *United States v. Brown*, 956 F.2d 782, 786 (8th Cir. 1992); *United States v. Rothrock*, 806 F.2d 318, 321 (1st Cir. 1986); *United States v. Arrington*, 757 F.2d 1484, 1485 (4th Cir. 1985).

77. See *Tibbs*, 457 U.S. at 42 ("[T]he appellate court sits as a 'thirteenth juror' and disagrees with the jury's resolution of the conflicting testimony.").

78. See, e.g., *United States v. Pitner*, 979 F.2d 156, 161–62 (9th Cir. 1992); *United States v. Garcia*, 978 F.2d 746, 748–50 (1st Cir. 1992); *United States v. Ludwig*, 897 F.2d 875, 882–83 (7th Cir. 1990).

79. See, e.g., *United States v. Cox*, 995 F.2d 1041, 1044 (11th Cir. 1993); *United States v. Sanchez*, 969 F.2d 1409, 1414 (2d Cir. 1992).

80. 902 F.2d 604 (7th Cir.), amended, 910 F.2d 467 (7th Cir. 1990).

81. Id. at 468.

82. See, e.g., *United States v. Dunigan*, 884 F.2d 1010, 1013 (7th Cir. 1989); *United States v. Shulman*, 624 F.2d 384, 388 (2d Cir. 1980).

83. See *Jackson v. Virginia*, 443 U.S. 307, 318–19 (1979); *Brady v. Southern Ry.*, 320 U.S. 476, 479 (1943); see also *Burks v. United States*, 437 U.S. 1, 16–17 (1978) ("Even the trial court, which has heard the testimony of witnesses firsthand, is not to . . . assess the credibility of witnesses when it judges the merits of a motion for acquittal. . . . Obviously, a federal appellate court applies no higher a standard.").

84. See *United States v. Castro*, 228 F.2d 807, 809–10 (2d Cir.) (Frank, J., concurring), cert. denied, 351 U.S. 940 (1956).

85. See *United States v. Masiello*, 235 F.2d 279, 290 n.8 (2d Cir.) (Frank, J., concurring), cert. denied, 352 U.S. 882 (1956).

86. Id.

87. See generally Edwin M. Borchard, *Convicting the Innocent: Errors of Criminal Justice* (1932).

88. See id. at xiii–xv. More than half of the sixty-five cases reported by Borchard of innocent persons convicted resulted from misidentification by eyewitnesses. See id.; see also *Kampshoff v. Smith*, 698 F.2d 581, 585–86 (2d Cir. 1983) (reporting academic studies detailing empirical unreliability of eyewitnesses identification).

89. See 1 Edward J. Devitt et al., *Federal Jury Practice and Instructions* 14.10 (4th ed. 1992).

90. See *Gilbert v. California*, 388 U.S. 263, 272 (1967) (holding that absence of counsel at postindictment lineup violates sixth amendment right to counsel due to dangers of eyewitness identifications); see also *United States v. Wade*, 388 U.S. 218, 228–37 (1967) (same).

91. See, e.g., *Caminetti v. United States*, 242 U.S. 470, 495 (1917); *United States v. Gordon*, 987 F.2d 902, 906 (2d Cir. 1993).

92. See text accompanying notes 27–30 supra.

93. See N.Y. Crim. Proc. Law 60.22 (McKinney 1992).

94. A number of state courts require a somewhat greater showing of sufficiency of evidence in death penalty cases. See, e.g., *Kimbrough v. State*, 352 So. 2d 512, 516 (Ala. 1977); *West v. State*, 485 So. 2d 681, 688 (Miss. 1985), cert. denied, 479 U.S. 983 (1986); *State v. Ramseur*, 524 A.2d 188, 291 n. 84 (N.J. 1987), cert. denied, 113 S. Ct. 2433 (1993).

95. See *Supreme Court of Israel, sitting as a Court of Criminal Appeals, in the Matter of Ivan (John) Demjanjuk v. State of Israel* (Cr. A. 347/88).

96. See Criminal Appeal Act, 1968, ch.19 § 2(1)(a)(Eng).

97. See, e.g., *Daley v. Regina*, 1993 4 All E.R. 86 (P.C.) (appeal taken from Jam.) (overturning conviction supported by eyewitness identification because "the evidence even if taken to be honest has a base which is so slender that it is unreliable").

98. *Regina v. Cooper*, 1969 1 Q.B. 267, 271 (C.A. 1968).

99. Id.

100. Id.

101. See text accompanying notes 43–47 supra.

102. *Corbett v. Regina*, 1975 2 S.C.R. 275, 278–79.

103. Id. at 282.

104. See *Regina v. Yebes*, 1987 2 S.C.R. 168, 183–85; see also *Regina v. R.W.*, 1992 2 S.C.R. 122, 131–32 ("As a matter of law it remains open to an appellate court to overturn a verdict based on findings of credibility where, after considering all the evidence and having due regard to the advantages afforded to the trial judge, it concludes that the verdict is unreasonable.").

105. Criminal Procedure Code art. 459 (RSFSR), adopted in Law of the Russian Federation: On Making Changes to the RSFSR Law "On the Judicial System of the RSFSR," the Criminal Procedure Code RSFSR, the Criminal Code of the Russian Federation, and the RSFSR Code on Administrative Legal Violations 13 (July 16, 1993) (unpublished translation by Foreign Broadcast Information Service on file at the New York University Law Review).

106. See, e.g., *United States v. Garcia*, 995 F.2d 556, 561 (5th Cir. 1993); *United States v. Holland*, 992 F.2d 687, 690 (7th Cir. 1993).

Chapter 6

The Death Penalty in America
Can Justice Be Done?

Betty B. Fletcher

James Madison might be surprised to hear the topic I have chosen for the lecture that bears his name. Madison neither championed nor deplored the death penalty. He apparently gave it little thought, for there is almost no reference to it in his voluminous writings. It is not discussed in *The Federalist Papers*.[1] The Constitution mentions it only by implication in the Fifth Amendment, forbidding the deprivation of life without due process of law.[2]

Madison did promote Thomas Jefferson's legal reforms for Virginia, which included a provision to restrict capital crimes to murder and treason.[3] But Madison criticized this provision because he felt that it would unduly "tie the hands of Government."[4] Still, we cannot be sure that Madison's views, and the principles he espoused, are consistent with capital punishment as it exists today. In one of his few recorded statements on the subject, Madison—himself not a lawyer—suggested that juries could not impose capital punishment fairly, and that safeguards were needed to ensure that only the deserving were executed. Discussing a proposal to eliminate executive pardons for those sentenced to death, Madison wrote that such a change

> would have practical consequences which render it inadmissible. A single instance is a sufficient proof. The crime of treason is generally shared by a number, and often a very great number. It would be politically if not morally wrong to take away the lives of all even if every individual were

This lecture was delivered on November 15, 1994, and appeared in 70 N.Y.U.L. Rev. 811 (1995).

equally guilty. What name would be given to a severity which made no distinction between the legal and the moral offence—between the deluded multitude and their wicked leaders. A second trial would not avoid the difficulty; because the oaths of the jury would not permit them to hearken to any voice but the inexorable voice of the law.[5]

The characteristics of the jury and the executive are not necessarily the same today as Madison thought them to be. Madison contemplated the jury as an infallible instrument of legal will, inevitably "hearkening" to the "inexorable voice of the law"; today, we see a jury as sometimes susceptible to the call of prejudice and caprice. Madison saw the executive as an instrument of fairness and moral discrimination; today, we see the executive as a political actor, often pressured by the electorate to deny clemency in all but the cases of blatantly obvious injustice. But the general problem Madison identified—finding a reliable means of distinguishing those who deserve the death penalty from those who do not—remains the central dilemma of capital punishment in our time, as it was in Madison's.

Justice Blackmun was a supporter of capital punishment for twenty years on the Supreme Court. Near the end of his long and distinguished career, he announced that "I no longer shall tinker with the machinery of death."[6] He saw an irreconcilable conflict between the exercise of individual judgment and discretion, on the one hand, and the application of legal rules designed to ensure fairness and uniformity, on the other.[7] "It seems," he wrote, "that the decision whether a human being should live or die is so inherently subjective—rife with all of life's understandings, experiences, prejudices and passions—that it inevitably defies the rationality and consistency required by the Constitution."[8]

Justice Blackmun's experience and conclusion after twenty years are troubling, but I will not revisit the arguments for and against the existence of capital punishment. I accept the political judgment of the electorate and the constitutional judgment of the Supreme Court that capital punishment is permissible. My concern is more practical. I sit as an appellate judge on the U.S. Court of Appeals for the Ninth Circuit, which has one of the heaviest death penalty caseloads in the country. I want to address how judges on the lower courts, trial and appellate, are to fulfill the obligation of ensuring that the death penalty is imposed in a constitutional manner. Specifically, I want to speak about the obligation to provide habeas corpus review in capital cases, to ensure that the death penalty is imposed in as fair a manner as possible, and to prevent the execution of innocent people.

I. The Evolution of Capital Punishment in America

Before discussing habeas corpus in detail, it may be useful to review briefly the history of capital punishment in the United States. We inherited capital punishment from England.[9] In eighteenth-century England, capital punishment was imposed for more than two hundred crimes, most of them crimes against property and crimes that today we would consider petty.[10] For those guilty of capital crimes but spared the death penalty, the alternative was usually exile,[11] first (and to a limited extent) to the American colonies, and later (to a much greater extent) to Australia. In the American colonies, people could be executed for many offenses, some that are not even considered crimes today, including adultery, idolatry, witchcraft, and blasphemy.[12]

An execution was a major public event in both England and America.[13] It was announced in London by the ringing of church bells and was accompanied by hawkers selling execution ballads and copies of "last dying speeches."[14] Execution day was sometimes called a "hanging match."[15] The crowds behaved like spectators at today's soccer matches, drinking and carousing to such an extent that executions were finally moved inside the prison walls in the mid-nineteenth century to preserve public order.[16]

Pain was not a concern in early executions. In fact, it was the primary goal of some punishments imposed for noncapital crimes and included pillorying, branding, and cropping and nailing of the ears.[17] In the United States, prisoners were usually executed by hanging until the late 1800s, when the electric chair was invented.[18] The gas chamber followed in the 1920s,[19] and lethal injection, now the mechanism of choice in most states,[20] in the 1970s.[21]

Since colonial times, there have been sporadic efforts to abolish the death penalty in the United States, and many individual states have repealed capital statutes.[22] Many European countries abandoned capital punishment after World War II,[23] but abolition has never taken hold on a national scale here as it did in Europe. The United States is now the only Western industrialized country that retains the death penalty.[24]

There was a brief period of de facto abolition, and a still briefer period of de jure abolition. The number of executions plummeted from a high of 199 in 1935 to zero in the five years between 1967 and 1972.[25] There were many reasons for the drop in executions. Habeas corpus petitions for state prisoners, rare before World War II, had become more common as the federal courts became more concerned with the federal rights of state criminal defendants.[26] The Civil Rights movement focused attention on capital trials in the South.[27] In 1972, when the Supreme Court declared capital punishment unconstitutional in *Furman v. Georgia*,[28] there were about six hundred people on death row around the country[29] and about two hundred fifty capital punishment statutes on the books for crimes such as murder, rape, bombing, burglary, arson, and treason.[30] But only about half the public supported capital punishment.[31]

Things are far different today. Capital punishment is imposed in thirty-eight states.[32] Two more states are actively considering restoring it.[33] A majority of the Supreme Court believes it to be constitutional, and opinion polls show that a huge percentage of the public favors it.[34] Roughly 295 people have been executed in the eighteen years since the Court reinstated the death penalty in *Gregg v. Georgia*[35] in 1976.[36] In 1995 over three thousand people were on death row awaiting execution.[37]

The death penalty is still imposed very selectively, if selectivity means imposing it only on a small portion of those eligible to receive it. No one has been executed for a crime other than murder or felony murder since capital punishment for rape was held unconstitutional in 1977 in *Coker v. Georgia*.[38] The twenty thousand homicides committed each year in the United States result in only about two hundred fifty death sentences.[39] Almost half the death sentences that receive habeas review are eventually overturned,[40] and a few more lucky prisoners receive executive clemency.[41]

The procedures of executions have been dramatically altered. No longer public rituals, modern executions are generally conducted in the middle of the night inside a prison before a small number of official witnesses. We insist that executions be neither disfiguring, nor, within limits, painful. These are very recent developments. Justice Brennan argued that inhumane punishments "are unconstitutional because they are inconsistent with the fundamental premise of the Eighth Amendment that 'even the vilest criminal remains a human being possessed of common human dignity.'"[42] No one would have made such a statement in the eighteenth century, when more than a dozen American slaves were burned at the stake,[43] and heads were placed on pikes and paraded through the streets of Paris.[44] As late as 1849, suggestions that the condemned be chloroformed before hanging were rejected with little debate.[45]

In 1994 a federal district judge held the gas chamber unconstitutional because California could not prove that there were not several minutes of pain before death.[46] Another district judge refused to allow an obese man to be hanged because of the possibility of decapitation.[47] Soon, the only acceptable method of execution may be lethal injection.

While these developments have made methods of execution more humane, we must be clear that these are still executions. The Fifth and Fourteenth Amendments forbid the federal and state governments from taking a life without due process of law. The Eighth Amendment, as interpreted by the Court in *Furman*, tells us that the death penalty is prohibited as cruel and unusual punishment if the process of selecting those who must die is not fair and reliable.[48]

While the imposition of the death penalty in the states is initially controlled by local police, prosecutors, and judges, operating under state law, the federal courts are ultimately responsible for ensuring compliance with the federal Constitution. Direct review of state court convictions by the Supreme Court on certiorari is available theoretically, but in practice is almost nonexistent. The Court is not equipped to deal with justice at retail. The case-by-case supervision of the imposition of the death penalty by federal courts must be accomplished, if at all, by the lower federal courts on habeas corpus review. Preserving the reliability and integrity of habeas review should be a priority for all federal judges. As Justice Frankfurter wrote: "Perfection may not be demanded of law, but the capacity to correct errors of inevitable frailty is the mark of a civilized legal mechanism."[49]

Inadequacies of habeas review are not only a problem for criminal defendants. They also threaten the credibility of the federal courts as an institution. While some may view the courts as obstructions when appeals drag on for years, the federal courts are surely not doing their duty if they fail to protect the constitutional rights of capital defendants and if they tolerate the execution of innocent people. The task of the federal courts has become increasingly difficult as the pace of capital convictions has increased, focusing attention both on the dispatch with which we make our decisions and on the ultimate decisions on the merits.

II. Limiting the Availability of Habeas Review

The restrictions imposed by the Supreme Court on the availability of review by habeas corpus during the past twenty years contribute to the difficulty. First, the Supreme Court has altogether exempted from habeas review certain categories of state court judgments. Fourth Amendment claims of unlawful search and seizure are not cognizable in habeas, so long as there was an opportunity for full and fair litigation of the claim in state court.[50] Further, under a well-established principle of federalism, state court judgments that rest on clearly stated, independent, and adequate state grounds are immune from federal review.[51] Furthermore, in 1991 the Court held in *Coleman v. Thompson*[52] that ambiguous state decisions are presumed to be based on state rather than federal law and that the federal court must ferret out any plausible state ground.

Second, since its 1977 decision in *Wainwright v. Sykes*,[53] the Court has barred from federal review the claims of petitioners who have defaulted under state procedural rules, unless both adequate cause for the default can be shown and actual prejudice demonstrated. Similarly, a defendant seeking to bring new exculpatory evidence before a habeas court must show cause and prejudice before he is entitled to an evidentiary hearing.[54]

The test for determining whether adequate cause and actual prejudice have been shown is formidable, tightened in the vice grip of *Murray v. Carrier*[55] on one side and *Strickland v. Washington*[56] on the other. *Murray* requires the cause for the default to emanate from external circumstances, unless counsel's performance is unconstitutionally deficient,[57] and *Strickland* defines constitutionally ineffective assistance of counsel as professional performance so poor that it can be demonstrated that the result probably would have been different but for the lawyer's mistakes.[58]

The one important exception to the cause and prejudice standard of *Wainwright*, significantly tempering its harshness, was that a claim of innocence was thought always to be available.[59] But that exception has, for practical purposes, almost disappeared. Miscarriage of justice since *Kuhlmann v. Wilson*[60] can be shown only by a demonstration of actual innocence and, since *Herrera v. Collins*,[61] even actual innocence, by itself, is probably not enough. Under *Herrera* a claim of actual innocence of the crime must be accompanied by a violation of an independent constitutional right, such as a biased jury or a violation of the Confrontation Clause, that resulted in the failure to establish innocence at trial.[62] Further, for habeas review of the sentencing phase of a death penalty case, *Sawyer v. Whitley*[63] requires that no aggravating circumstances exist. The omission of mitigating evidence, even evidence so strong that it would likely capture any jury's sympathies, is not enough to lift the bar.[64]

The third bar to review by federal habeas, the handmaiden to the bar of cause and prejudice, is the exhaustion requirement of *Rose v. Lundy*.[65] No habeas petition containing an unexhausted claim may be entertained in federal court, but a petitioner at his peril dismisses unexhausted claims in order to proceed on exhausted claims if he has any thought that he may wish to raise the unexhausted claims in a subsequent petition in federal court.[66] *McCleskey v. Zant*[67] acts as a form of claim preclusion in habeas, holding that a second petition is, in almost all circumstances, an abuse of the writ.[68]

The final bars to habeas review that I will note here are those imposed by the "old rule" rule and the "new rule" rule. The Supreme Court in *Wainwright* established that a habeas petitioner could not have the benefit of an existing rule of law at the time of his trial if the claim had not been properly raised to the trial court.[69] But since *Teague v. Lane*,[70] new rules announced after a petitioner's trial generally cannot be applied retroactively to benefit a habeas petitioner. Only in the unusual circumstance in which the new rule finds a "bedrock procedural" element wanting, or where it places the criminal penalty beyond the constitutional power of the lawmaking authority to impose, will the new rule be applied retroactively.[71]

The petitioner who has successfully negotiated these formidable barriers faces review that is exceedingly deferential to the state courts. Not only is the state court's fact finding presumptively correct, but under *Brecht v. Abrahamson*,[72] conceded constitutional errors—for example, even coerced confessions or the prosecution's failure to turn over exculpatory evidence—also require a showing of actual prejudice before relief will be granted. The court in *Brecht* found that the traditional harmless error standard applicable on direct appeal is too burdensome to the state on habeas review and held that a habeas petitioner must show that an error had "substantial and injurious effect or influence" on the jury's verdict.[73]

III. The Challenge Facing Modern Habeas Courts

For lower federal courts, performing habeas review within these restrictions is an awesome task. We cannot allow ourselves to be lulled into the belief that the crimes for which the death penalty is imposed are uniformly heinous and that the chance of actual innocence in any given case is virtually nonexistent. Unfortunately, that belief is false. The danger of executing innocent people is real, and any clear-eyed assessment of the death penalty must recognize this.

Judge Hand wrote: "Our procedure has been always haunted by the ghost of the innocent man convicted."[74] And so it is today. A book entitled *In Spite of Innocence*, by Radelet, Bedau, and Putnam,[75] catalogs the real-life cases of one hundred thirty people whom the authors claim were wrongly convicted and sentenced to death in America in the twentieth century because of such things as false testimony, mistaken eyewitness testimony, racism, or police error.

Two unsettling facts emerge from the book. First, our legal system does not prevent innocent people from being wrongly sentenced to death. This is particularly so when law enforcement officers are under great pressure to solve brutal, highly publicized crimes.[76] Second, it is often a chance event, rather than the safeguards of the justice system, that brings one of these terrible errors to light.[77] Given the apparent inability of the justice system systematically and uniformly to detect such errors, and given that the discovery of an erroneous conviction often is truly chancy, it necessarily follows that at least some defendants who are innocent will be executed.

The most famous case of mistaken capital sentencing is probably that of the *Scottsboro Boys*.[78] They were nine black teenagers condemned to death in 1931 for the rape of two white women on a train in Alabama, a crime later shown never to have occurred. Current examples strike us even more forcibly. In 1994, Joe Burrows was released after five years on death row in Illinois when both main prosecution witnesses recanted, and one confessed to the murder.[79] One of the recanting witnesses claimed that prosecutors had pressured him to implicate Burrows, and according to Burrows, the prosecution withheld evidence favorable to him.[80]

In 1988, Randall Adams was saved by a documentary film.[81] Adams had been sentenced to death eleven years earlier for the murder of a Dallas policeman. The Supreme Court had already upheld Adams's conviction when the documentary *The Thin Blue Line* was released.[82] The film revealed so many holes in the evidence used to convict Adams—perjured testimony, mistakes in eyewitness identification, the use of hypnotism to refresh a key witness's memory—that Adams was granted a hearing at which his chief accuser confessed to the murder Perry Mason-style.[83]

Clarence Brandley was freed in 1990 after ten years on death row.[84] Six days after the 1980 rape and murder of a white high school student in Texas, Brandley, a black janitor at the school, was arrested by an investigator who had taken the case just that afternoon. Brandley was convicted on the basis of circumstantial evidence and sentenced to death by an all-white jury. Six years later, a woman asserted that her former husband, a white janitor, had confessed to the crime; others then came forward to offer incriminating evidence against him and another white janitor. A state judge reviewing the unfolding information ordered a new trial, accusing prosecutors of ignoring evidence implicating anyone other than Brandley, and declaring that he had never seen a case in his thirty years on the bench that presented "a more shocking scenario of the effects of racial prejudice."[85]

The Innocence Project, a group of attorneys and law students in New York, recently won the release of a mentally retarded man serving a life sentence in Virginia by showing that his DNA did not match evidence from the crime scene.[86] It is inevitable that some death row inmates will be freed in the same manner.[87]

These cases are just a sample.[88] A root cause of the failures of our system to protect the innocent is inadequacy of representation at trial. There is ample evidence that many defendants are badly represented. A 1990 study by the American Bar Association reached the disturbing conclusion that "[e]ven in cases in which the performances of counsel have passed constitutional muster under the test of *Strickland v. Washington* and executions have been carried out, the representation provided has nevertheless been of very poor quality."[89] This is not the voice of an outside critic. It is the legal profession's evaluation of its own work.

Stephen Bright of the Southern Center for Human Rights described many shocking examples of inadequate capital representation in a recent article in the *Yale Law Journal*:[90] a woman whose court-appointed attorney was so drunk that the trial was delayed for a day while the lawyer was jailed for contempt;[91] a man whose attorney failed to introduce evidence that his client had an IQ of forty-nine and the intellectual capacity of a seven-year-old;[92] another whose attorney submitted, on state supreme court appeal, a single page of argument citing one case and failed even to show up for oral argument;[93] another whose attorney called him a "nigger" in court.[94]

It should be no surprise that there are too few talented, experienced attorneys willing to represent capital defendants. Capital cases are exceptionally technical, time-consuming, and emotionally draining. A lawyer must know how to investigate and try a murder case, and must know well a sizable and continually evolving body of constitutional law and specialized procedures.[95] Further, capital trials are typically bifurcated, with a sentencing phase that requires additional extensive investigation into a defendant's personal history and is governed by different rules of evidence.[96]

Compensation is generally inadequate, and is shockingly low in many states. Mississippi pays lawyers no more than $1,000 to defend a death penalty case,[97] and Texas has paid attorneys as little as $800 to handle capital trials.[98] On an hourly basis, fees paid to a conscientious death penalty lawyer in such states drop below the minimum wage. Funds for investigation are sometimes entirely wanting.[99]

IV. Improving the Process

Within the framework I have described, how can the lower federal courts prevent the execution of innocent people? How can they ensure that from among the guilty only the death-worthy are chosen for capital punishment? How can they safeguard constitutional rights that do not go directly to the question of guilt or innocence?

Fortunately, at the federal level, Congress has recognized the importance of adequate representation in death penalty cases. Federal law requires the appointment of counsel and provision of funds for investigation and experts for indigent capital defendants in federal habeas proceedings.[100] These court-appointed attorneys must have at least five years of experience, including three years of trying felonies.[101]

Although the Supreme Court has restricted mandatory evidentiary hearings,[102] district courts still have the discretionary authority to hold such hearings.[103] Hearings often prove critical in capital cases. Allowing full development of the facts may establish cause and prejudice, or, in some dramatic cases, allow the defendant to offer significant new evidence from witnesses whom trial counsel neglected to interview or exculpatory evidence that the prosecution withheld. Hearings are particularly significant to determine the adequacy of the sentencing hearing in capital cases,[104] and they can be critically important in cases where the competence of counsel is at issue.[105]

In the many cases in which there is no preclusion or bar to review, the federal courts, both district and appellate, review for adherence to the whole panoply of constitutional rights, albeit subject to the Brecht requirement of proof of "'substantial and injurious effect.'"[106] We review for proof of guilt beyond a reasonable doubt.[107] And we review for the observance of the rights to confrontation;[108] to compulsory process;[109] to assistance of counsel;[110] to effective assistance of counsel;[111] to jury trial;[112] to disclosure of exculpatory evidence;[113] to an unbiased jury;[114] and to instruction free of error.[115]

Our scrutiny requires review in minute detail of the entire state court record—of the trial and the appeals and the subsequent habeas proceedings. This invariably includes volumes and volumes of material. At the federal appellate level, we have to review, in addition, the overlay of federal district court proceedings. Sometimes a case makes more than one journey through the state and federal courts. The review we do must be scrupulously thorough. Not only is it time-consuming, but it is also a stressful and anxious process.

To the rational mind, it is surely apparent that the system has it backward. The intense effort and resources are concentrated at the wrong end. We have inadequate representation at the trial level, which erodes the capacity of judges and juries to acquit the innocent and to save from death those who deserve less severe punishment; we have prolonged review processes that more often than not deflect attention from the real issues of fair trial and possible innocence to arcane examinations of technical bars.

The system incurs huge costs in time and money. The toll upon the judges individually and the courts institutionally is immense. In my own already overburdened circuit, the press of death penalty review is increasing steadily as the state courts process these cases. It soon will be crushing. One of my colleagues, a senior judge of a decidedly conservative bent, states flatly that, merit and morality aside, institutionally the death penalty is one punishment we simply cannot afford.

The review process in the federal courts begins long after the critical events, usually after the defendant has spent many, many years on death row, sometimes waiting years for the appointment of counsel to represent him in his state habeas, and then waiting more years for a hearing first before the state courts and then before the federal courts. How much better would everyone be served had there been competent counsel, provided with adequate resources, in the first instance, for the state court trial?

One wonders what benefit those involved—the families of victims, the courts, the penal institutions, and the condemned—receive from delay that ultimately ends in execution. The delay is costly, sapping the confidence of all concerned in the capacity of the system to do justice. I have seen no studies on the views of death row inmates or the psychological cost of uncertainty and prolonged delay. But I suggest that existence on death row is hardly life at all. Few would seek to justify the current system as one that has merit simply because it prolongs life.

What can be done? Congress had before it at one time proposals for statutory reform of federal habeas review linked to the states' obligation to devote adequate resources to providing competent counsel and adequate investigation for trial.[116] That approach appears to have substantial merit. If we, as federal judges, were able to accord or withhold deference to state court determinations depending upon the adequacy of state provision of representation, I suggest that some of the vices of the present system could be eliminated. Not only the federal review, but also the states' appellate and collateral proceedings, could be more confident, competent, and effective. I suggest also that considerable delay would be avoided.

Conclusion

I close by circling back to other more intractable problems for which, unfortunately, I have no answers. Perhaps there are none. The death penalty is unconstitutional if imposed arbitrarily, capriciously, unreasonably, discriminatorily, freakishly, or wantonly. *Furman* tells us this.[117] Yet every capital defendant has an absolute right to present mitigating evidence arising from the circumstances of his life, the motivation for the crime, or whatever else might sway the sympathies of the jury.[118] Although we can determine objectively whether a person has committed the acts that make him eligible for the death penalty, whether actually to impose it is a subjective decision.[119] Prosecutor to prosecutor, jury to jury, state to state, judge to judge, caprice is an inevitable ingredient of death sentences. Justice Blackmun who, ironically, was a dissenter in *Furman*,[120] ultimately concluded that the decision of life or death "defies the rationality and consistency required by the Constitution."[121]

Although *Furman* pronounced discriminatory sentences unconstitutional, to date the Court has been unwilling to look at discrimination beyond specific discrimination in a particular case. Justice Powell now publicly regrets his deciding vote in *McCleskey v. Kemp*,[122] in which the majority refused to consider evidence of generalized discrimination in capital cases.[123]

Even the most ardent supporters of the death penalty cannot but subscribe to the view that it should be administered evenhandedly and without bias. Yet a majority of those executed today are society's most disfavored: Forty-five percent are people of color,[124] and virtually all are too poor to hire a lawyer.[125] This may accurately reflect the population of the most violent criminals, but how can we be sure?

We are a civilized nation. We are a caring people. We value human life. We prize human dignity. The decision deliberately to take a human life is an awesome responsibility. I close with a question: Can justice be done?

NOTES

1. See The Federalist Nos. 1–85 (Alexander Hamilton, John Jay, James Madison).

2. U.S. Const. amend. V.

3. Louis P. Masur, *Rites of Execution: Capital Punishment and the Transformation of American Culture, 1776–1865*, at 62 (1989); see James Madison, Observations on

the "Draught of a Constitution for Virginia," in 5 *The Writings of James Madison, 1787–1790*, at 284, 288–89 (Gaillard Hunt ed., 1904) (commenting on Jefferson's draft constitution for Virginia).

4. Madison, supra note 3, at 288.

5. Id.

6. *Callins v. Collins*, 114 S. Ct. 1127, 1130 (1994) (Blackmun, J., dissenting) (denial of certiorari).

7. Id. at 1132.

8. Id. at 1134–35.

9. *The Death Penalty in America* 6 (Hugo A. Bedau ed., 3d ed. 1982)(1964).

10. William J. Bowers, *Legal Homicide: Death as Punishment in America, 1864–1982*, at 136 (1984); Douglas Hay, "Property, Authority, and the Criminal Law," in Douglas Hay et al., *Albion's Fatal Tree: Crime and Society in Eighteenth-Century England* 17, 17–18, 20–21 (1975).

11. Hay, supra note 10, at 22.

12. Bowers, supra note 10, at 133–34; *The Death Penalty in America*, supra note 9, at 7. Only some of these sentences were actually invoked. For example, while nineteen people were executed as a result of the Salem Witch Trials in the late seventeenth century, no one was executed under a Massachusetts law permitting capital punishment for a "stubborn or rebellious son" aged sixteen or older "which will not obey the voice of his Father, or the Voice of his Mother" and committed "sundry notorious crimes." Lawrence M. Friedman, *Crime and Punishment in American History* 41, 46 (1993).

13. Bowers, supra note 10, at 4, 43 (noting large and unruly crowds at early American executions); Masur, supra note 3, at 25–39 (describing execution as important civil and religious ceremony in early American republic).

14. Peter Linebaugh, "The Tyburn Riot against the Surgeons," in *Albion's Fatal Tree*, supra note 10, at 65, 67.

15. Id. at 66.

16. Bowers, supra note 10, at 8, 43 (describing reasons that states ended public executions); Masur, supra note 3, at 5, 93–116 (detailing origins of private executions in America); Linebaugh, supra note 14, at 67 (citing seizure of bodies of executed for medical research and training as a cause of disorder at public executions). The last public execution in America occurred in Galena, Missouri, on May 21, 1937. *The Death Penalty in America*, supra note 9, at 13.

17. *Furman v. Georgia*, 408 U.S. 238, 430 (1972) (Powell, J., dissenting) (noting evolution of cruel and unusual punishment concept). As late as the eighteenth century, criminals were executed in England and America by being pressed, drawn, and quartered, or burned at the stake. *The Death Penalty in America*, supra note 9, at 14.

18. Bowers, supra note 10, at 12.

19. Id.

20. Harriet Chiang, "Gas Chamber's Effects Debated," S.F. Chron., Jan. 27, 1994, at A13.

21. *The Death Penalty in America*, supra note 9, at 15.

22. Bowers, supra note 10, at 6–24; *The Death Penalty in America*, supra note 9, at 21; Masur, supra note 3, at 50–70.

23. Bowers, supra note 10, at 145, 146 tbl. 5–3.

24. Amnesty International, "The Death Penalty: List of Abolitionist and Retentionist Countries" (Jan. 1994) (reporting that United States is only Western industrialized country that retains and uses death penalty for ordinary crimes, i.e., crimes not committed under military law or in exceptional circumstances such as wartime). South Africa eliminated capital punishment in 1995. Howard W. French, "South Africa's Supreme Court Abolishes Death Penalty," N.Y. Times, June 7, 1995, at A3.

25. Bowers, supra note 10, at 25–26 tbl. 1–4.

26. See id. at 15 (stating "this was the time when the United States Supreme Court became sensitive to defendants' rights in capital cases and responsive to appeals under the 'due process' clause of the Fourteenth Amendment").

27. See id. at 16, 31 (discussing efforts of NAACP Legal Defense and Educational Fund and ACLU).

28. 408 U.S. 238, 239–40 (1972).

29. John C. Jeffries, Jr., Justice Lewis F. Powell, Jr. 407 (1994).

30. Bowers, supra note 10, at 33 tbl. 1–7, 36–37 tbl. 1–8, 39.

31. See *The Death Penalty in America*, supra note 9, at 65 (describing the mid-1960s as "the high point of abolition sentiment, when the pros and cons [in the public debate] were about equally divided"); Jeffries, supra note 29, at 406 (Gallup polls showing about 50 percent support).

32. "Crime: Executions in America," L.A. Times, May 11, 1994, at A5.

33. See "Elections and Electric Chairs," Wash. Post, Nov. 25, 1994, at A30 (stating that Iowa and Wisconsin are considering enacting death penalty legislation).

34. See Yale Kamisar, "This Judge Was Not for Hanging," N.Y. Times, July 17, 1994, s 7, at 12, 17 ("more than four out of five Americans are in favor of the death penalty").

35. 428 U.S. 153 (1976).

36. *Death Row, U.S.A.* (NAACP Legal Defense & Educ. Fund, Inc., New York, N.Y.), Summer 1995, at 3.

37. Id. at 1 (setting figure at 3,028 as of August 31, 1995).

38. 433 U.S. 584, 592 (1977).

39. Stephen B. Bright, "Counsel for the Poor: The Death Sentence Not for the Worst Crime but for the Worst Lawyer," 103 Yale L.J. 1835, 1841 (1994). In the early part of the twentieth century, the murder to execution ratio was estimated as 70:1 and 85:1. By the 1960s, the ratio fell to 504:1. *The Death Penalty in America*, supra note 9, at 31.

40. See William J. Brennan, Jr., "Foreword: Neither Victims nor Executioners," 8 Notre Dame J.L. Ethics & Pub. Pol'y 1, 3–4 & nn.18–20 (1994) ("Even conservative estimates place the total reversal rate at an astounding 45%; some commentators believe the figure may be as high as 60% or more."); see also Terry Pristin, "More in New York Bar Avoid Capital Appeals," N.Y. Times, Dec. 30, 1994, at B6 (citing 1992 study showing 42 percent of federal habeas corpus petitions filed in state capital cases between 1976 and 1991 resulted in reversal).

41. Executive clemency can be quite rare. In Florida, for example, no death row inmate has received clemency in twelve years. Rick Barry, "Go Slow Legal Processes Create Jam on Death Row," Tampa Trib., Apr. 10, 1995, at 1.

42. William J. Brennan, Jr., "Constitutional Adjudication and the Death Penalty: A View from the Court," 100 Harv. L. Rev. 313, 329–30 (1986) (quoting *Furman v. Georgia*, 408 U.S. 238, 273 (1971)).

43. Thirteen slaves were burned at the stake in New York in 1741 for their role in an alleged plot to rise up, pillage, and burn. Friedman, supra note 12, at 46. Perhaps the most gruesome American punishment was peine forte et dure, or pressing to death under rocks, a punishment imposed upon a man who refused to plead or testify at the Salem Witch Trials. Id. at 46.

44. See Simon Schama, *Citizens: A Chronicle of the French Revolution* 405 (1989) ("[t]he heads were stuck on pikes that bobbed and dipped above cheering, laughing and singing crowds that filled the streets").

45. Masur, supra note 3, at 20–22. Nor was there any analog to our modern animal rights movement. Professor Lawrence Friedman notes that both perpetrators and victims of bestiality were often executed in the seventeenth century. After Thomas Granger of Plymouth, Massachusetts, was required to identify a sheep that he victimized, both he and the sheep were executed. Friedman, supra note 12, at 34–35. Another Massachusetts man, Benjamin Goad, who committed bestiality on a mare, was forced to watch that mare "be knockt on the head" before his execution. Id. at 35.

46. See *Fierro v. Gomez*, 865 F. Supp. 1387, 1415 (N.D. Cal. 1994) ("[t]he evidence presented concerning California's method of execution by administration of lethal gas strongly suggests that the pain experienced by those executed is unconstitutionally cruel and unusual").

47. See *Rupe v. Wood*, 863 F. Supp. 1307, 1314 (W.D. Wash. 1994) ("A hanging that is likely to result in decapitation is contrary to 'public perceptions of standards of decency.'" (quoting *Gregg v. Georgia*, 428 U.S. 153, 173 (1976))).

48. *Furman v. Georgia*, 408 U.S. 238, 310 (1972) (Stewart, J., concurring) (concluding "the Eighth and Fourteenth Amendments cannot tolerate the infliction of a sentence of death under legal systems that permit this unique penalty to be so wantonly and so freakishly imposed").

49. Felix Frankfurter, *The Case of Sacco and Vanzetti* 108 (1927).

50. *Stone v. Powell*, 428 U.S. 465, 482 (1976).

51. *Wainwright v. Sykes*, 433 U.S. 72, 81 (1977).

52. 501 U.S. 722, 733 (1991).

53. 433 U.S. at 86–87.

54. *Keeney v. Tamayo-Reyes*, 112 S. Ct. 1715, 1720–21 (1992).

55. 477 U.S. 478 (1986).

56. 466 U.S. 668 (1984).

57. *Murray*, 477 U.S. at 488.

58. *Strickland*, 466 U.S. at 694.

59. *Wainwright v. Sykes*, 433 U.S. 72, 90–91 (1977) (recognizing exception to avoid miscarriage of justice).

60. 477 U.S. 436, 454 (1986).

61. 113 S. Ct. 853 (1993).

62. Id. at 862.

63. 505 U.S. 333 (1992) (holding that "actual innocence" showing requires demonstration by petitioner of clear and convincing evidence that but for constitutional error, no reasonable juror would have found petitioner eligible for death penalty under state law).

64. Id. at 346–49.

65. 455 U.S. 509, 520–21 (1982) (concluding that district court must dismiss habeas petitions containing both unexhausted and exhausted claims).

66. Id. at 520–21.

67. 499 U.S. 467 (1991).

68. Id. at 493–97, 503 (observing, however, that later petition can be made under appropriate circumstances).

69. *Wainwright v. Sykes*, 433 U.S. 72, 87–91 (1977).

70. 489 U.S. 288, 295–96 (1989) (depriving petitioner benefit of new equal protection rule announced two and a half years after petitioner's conviction became final).

71. Id. at 307, 311 (quoting *Mackey v. United States*, 401 U.S. 667, 693 (1971) (Harlan, J., concurring and dissenting)).

72. 113 S. Ct. 1710 (1993).

73. Id. at 1720–22 (holding that state's improper references to petitioner's post-*Miranda* silence did not "substantially influence" jury).

74. *United States v. Garsson*, 291 F. 646, 649 (S.D.N.Y. 1923).

75. Michael L. Radelet et al., *In Spite of Innocence: Erroneous Convictions in Capital Cases* (1992).

76. See, e.g., case discussed infra at text accompanying notes 84–85 (when popular high school student was raped and murdered, parents threatened to keep their children home unless murderer was arrested by the time school registration was complete).

77. See, e.g., Radelet et al., supra note 75, at 33–39 (describing how death row inmate was set free after career criminal, angry at former partner in crime, notified

defense lawyers that his former partner was real murderer, eventually leading to full confession by that partner).

78. Id. at 116–18.

79. Dirk Johnson, "Back to Family from Life on Death Row," N.Y. Times, Sept. 25, 1994, at A22.

80. Id.

81. Radelet et al., supra note 75, at 60–73.

82. *The Thin Blue Line* (Miramax 1988).

83. Radelet et al., supra note 75, at 68–70.

84. Id. at 119–36.

85. Id. at 134.

86. "DNA Testing Frees a Long-Jailed Man," N.Y. Times, Oct. 22, 1994, at A4.

87. Many of the three hundred cases being investigated by the Innocence Project are capital cases. Telephone Interview with Mira Gur-Arie, Professor, Benjamin N. Cardozo School of Law, Yeshiva University (Jan. 3, 1994).

88. It is disquieting that we tend to hear about only those mistaken convictions that attract media attention. For example, *60 Minutes* publicized the case of Walter McMillan, who was freed after his attorney discovered a tape recording of police instructing witnesses on how to fabricate their testimony. Martha Ezzard, "Hoopla Won't Harm Simpson Trial," Atlanta J. & Const., Sept. 25, 1994, at D1.

89. American Bar Ass'n, "Toward a More Just and Effective System of Review in State Death Penalty Cases" 53 (Ira P. Robbins Project Reporter, Aug. 1990).

90. Bright, supra note 39.

91. Id. at 1835. The death penalty was imposed a few days after resuming the trial. Id.

92. Id. at 1837 (noting that jury could thus not perform its constitutional obligation to impose sentence after considering defendant's background, character, and crime).

93. Id. at 1860–61 (although counsel's performance was determined to be deficient, Court of Appeals did not find that deficient performance prejudiced conviction).

94. Id. at 1843 n.51 (specifically, defense counsel called client "little old nigger boy" in closing argument).

95. American Bar Ass'n, supra note 89, at 50.

96. Id.

97. Id. at 61; Bright, supra note 39, at 1867.

98. Bright, supra note 39, at 1846 ("Courts often refuse to authorize funds for investigation and experts by requiring an extensive showing of need that frequently cannot be made without the very expert assistance that is sought.").

99. American Bar Ass'n, supra note 89, at 65; Bright, supra note 39, at 1846–47.

100. 21 U.S.C. s 848(q)(4), (9) (1988).

101. 21 U.S.C. s 848(q)(5) (1988).

102. See *Keeney v. Tamayo-Reyes*, 112 S. Ct. 1715, 1721 (1992) (holding that "[r]espondent . . . is entitled to an evidentiary hearing if he can show cause for his failure to develop the facts in state-court proceedings and actual prejudice resulting from the failure" and adopting "the narrow exception to the cause-and-prejudice requirement: A . . . hearing [will be] mandated if he can show that a fundamental miscarriage of justice would result from failure to hold an evidentiary hearing").

103. See id. at 1727 (O'Connor, J., dissenting) ("[D]istrict courts . . . still possess the discretion . . . to hold hearings even when they are not mandatory.").

104. See, e.g., *Mak v. Blodgett*, 970 F.2d 614, 616 (9th Cir. 1992) (overturning death sentence after district court evidentiary hearing uncovered significant mitigating evidence not offered in sentencing phase).

105. See, e.g., *Harris v. Blodgett*, 853 F. Supp. 1239 (W.D. Wash. 1994) (overturning death sentence, following evidentiary hearing, on grounds including ineffective assistance of counsel).

106. See *Brecht v. Abrahamson*, 113 S. Ct. 1710, 1714 (1993) (quoting *Kotteakos v. United States*, 328 U.S. 750, 776 (1946)).

107. See *In re Winship*, 397 U.S. 358, 368 (1970) (holding proof beyond reasonable doubt is constitutionally required in juvenile delinquency adjudications).

108. See *Coy v. Iowa*, 487 U.S. 1012, 1020–22 (1988) (holding constitutional right to face-to-face confrontation was violated when complaining witnesses testified from behind screen).

109. See *Taylor v. Illinois*, 484 U.S. 400, 401–2 (1988) (holding Sixth Amendment right to compulsory process not violated when trial judge refused to allow defense witness to testify as sanction for failure to disclose that witness's identity during discovery).

110. See *Gideon v. Wainwright*, 372 U.S. 335, 344 (1963) (establishing right to counsel in criminal trials).

111. See *Strickland v. Washington*, 466 U.S. 668, 698–700 (1984) (establishing test for ineffective assistance of counsel).

112. See *Duncan v. Louisiana*, 391 U.S. 145, 162 (1968) (holding appellant entitled to jury trial when charged with crime punishable by two years in prison).

113. See *Brady v. Maryland*, 373 U.S. 83, 87 (1963) (holding that "suppression by the prosecution of evidence favorable to an accused upon request violates due process where the evidence is material either to guilt or to punishment, irrespective of the good faith or bad faith of the prosecution").

114. See *In re Murchison*, 349 U.S. 133, 136 (1955) ("A fair trial in a fair tribunal is a basic requirement of due process. Fairness of course requires an absence of actual bias in the trial of cases.").

115. See *Beck v. Alabama*, 447 U.S. 625, 638 (1980) ("If the unavailability of a lesser included offense instruction enhances the risk of an unwarranted conviction, Alabama is constitutionally prohibited from withdrawing that option from the jury in a capital case.").

116. See, e.g., Habeas Corpus Reform Act of 1993, S. 1441, 103rd Cong., 1st Sess. ss 8–9 (1993) (introduced by Sen. Biden at 139 Cong. Rec. S10925–27 (daily ed. Aug. 6, 1993)).

117. See *Furman v. Georgia*, 408 U.S. 238, 310 (1972) (Stewart, J., concurring) (concluding "the Eighth and Fourteenth Amendments cannot tolerate the infliction of a sentence of death under legal systems that permit this unique penalty to be so wantonly and so freakishly imposed").

118. See *Lockett v. Ohio*, 438 U.S. 586, 604 (1978) ("[T]he Eighth and Fourteenth Amendments require that the sentencer, in all but the rarest kind of capital case, not be precluded from considering, as a mitigating factor, any aspect of a defendant's character or record and any of the circumstances of the offense that the defendant proffers as a basis for a sentence less than death." (footnotes and emphasis omitted)).

119. "This Court has previously recognized that '[f]or the determination of sentences, justice generally requires consideration of more than the particular acts by which the crime was committed and that there be taken into account the circumstances of the offense together with the character and propensities of the offender.'" *Woodson v. North Carolina*, 428 U.S. 280, 304 (1976) (quoting *Pennsylvania ex rel. Sullivan v. Ash*, 302 U.S. 51, 55 (1937)).

120. *Furman*, 408 U.S. at 375 (Burger, C.J., Blackmun, J., Powell, J., and Rehnquist, J., dissenting).

121. *Callins v. Collins*, 114 S. Ct. 1127, 1135 (1994) (Blackmun, J., dissenting).

122. 481 U.S. 279, 319 (1987) ("Despite *McCleskey*'s wide ranging arguments that basically challenge the validity of capital punishment in our multiracial society, the only question before us is whether in this case the law of Georgia was properly applied." (citation omitted)).

123. See Jeffries, supra note 29, at 451–52 (1994) (describing conversation in which Powell told Jeffries he had "come to think that capital punishment should be abolished" and would change his vote in *McCleskey v. Kemp*).

124. As of August 31, 1995, of the 295 persons executed since the death penalty was restored in 1976, 39.66 percent were African American, 5.42 percent were Hispanic, and 0.34 percent were Native American. *Death Row, U.S.A.*, supra note 36, at 3.

125. In California, all 384 men and women awaiting execution as of July 1, 1994, qualified for appointed counsel. Bob Egelko, "The Rich Don't Live on Death Row," *Seattle Times*, Sept. 6, 1994, at A3.

Chapter 7

To Err Is Human, but Not Always Harmless
When Should Legal Error Be Tolerated?*

Harry T. Edwards

Assume an appellate judge must decide the following case:

Joe Didit, who is six feet five inches tall, about two hundred and seventy pounds, Caucasian, and bald-headed, was recently tried for the murder of a convenience-store proprietor. The indictment charged that, sometime near midnight on the evening in question, Didit entered the convenience store with a loaded gun, intending to rob the proprietor. It was further charged that, when he faced resistance from his victim, Didit purposefully shot the proprietor in the head and face six times, and then fled the store. Two customers, who were in the store at the time of the murder, called the police and identified Didit, a well-known neighborhood thug, as the murderer. Following this lead, the police located Didit at his girlfriend's apartment, arrested him, and took him to police headquarters for interrogation. After being given his Miranda warning, Didit refused to say anything. His refusal agitated one of the police officers, who then proceeded to slap and punch Didit repeatedly. The officers then left Didit in an isolated room, telling him, "you'll stay here unless you talk to us." Two hours later, Didit summoned the officers and asked for a sandwich and coffee, which he was given. After eating, he told the officers that he wanted to talk. Then, without giving any further Miranda warning, the officers took a confession from Didit.

---

* See Roger J. Traynor, *The Riddle of Harmless Error* 3 (1970) ("To err is human, as a judge well knows, but to err is not always harmless.").

This lecture was delivered on October 18, 1995, and appeared in 70 N.Y.U.L. Rev. 1167 (1995).

At trial, one of the customers testified that he was about thirty feet from the place of the murder, but could "clearly" see Didit shoot the proprietor. The other customer testified that she did not have a clear view of Didit, but she was "sure" that she recognized the defendant's voice when he threatened to kill the store owner. A third witness testified that he had seen Didit at about midnight on the night in question, running down a street about a block away from the convenience store. A fourth witness testified that he had seen Didit with what he thought was a .45-caliber pistol two days before the shooting. No gun was ever found, but police experts testified that the bullets that killed the murder victim came from a .45-caliber. All four witnesses claimed that they personally knew Didit from the neighborhood. The prosecutor also introduced a videotape recording of the murder, showing a view of the murderer from the rear; the recorded view of the murderer strongly resembled the defendant. Finally, over strong objection, the trial judge allowed Didit's confession to be introduced in evidence, along with evidence indicating that the defendant had been beaten several hours before he confessed. For the defense, Didit's girlfriend testified that he had been with her all evening; on cross-examination, however, she admitted that she was "unsure" whether he may have left the apartment once during the evening to buy some cigarettes. The jury returned a verdict of guilty within two hours after commencing deliberations. The case is now on appeal, and the defendant seeks reversal on a claim that the trial judge committed error in admitting what amounted to a coerced confession. Government counsel responds that any error committed by the trial judge was harmless.

How should the court rule? If the conviction is reversed, the government and the trial court will be forced to undergo the time and expense of retrying a case in which there appears to be little doubt of the defendant's guilt. (And in many criminal cases, the expense and time involved are enormous.) A reversal, therefore, may run counter to "the 'principle that the central purpose of a criminal trial is to decide the factual question of the defendant's guilt or innocence, and [to promote] public respect for the criminal process by focusing on the underlying fairness of the trial rather than on the virtually inevitable presence of immaterial error.'"[1]

However, if the court decides against reversal, finding the error to be harmless, it will embrace the questionable assumption that appellate judges reliably may assess guilt on a cold record, and, in this case, on the basis of "eyewitness" testimony that is not infrequently mistaken. A failure to reverse will also diminish the constitutional proposition that a defendant in a criminal case is deprived of due process of law when his conviction is founded, in whole or in part, upon an involuntary confession. And this result will likely undermine the integrity of the criminal justice system by sending dubious messages to the police officer who brutalized the defendant and thereby gained the coerced confession, to the prosecutor who introduced the evidence at trial, and to the trial judge who erroneously admitted it.

The law can be an aggravating thing. It imposes duties and responsibilities, and it sometimes forces results that many people in society find unpalatable. For example, some might find it positively offensive to reverse Joe Didit's conviction in a case like this where there is ample evidence aside from the coerced confession to support a finding of guilt. The harmlesserror doctrine[2] offers us a way to deal with the aggravation. Under this doctrine, when an appellate court's review of trial proceedings uncovers a legal error that might produce a disfavored result (such as the retrial of a defendant who appears to be guilty), the court may simply call the error "harmless," and the potential aggravation is removed. This approach seems to work like magic. Appellate judges merely apply a "drop" of harmless error, and the coerced confession, warrantless search, erroneous jury instruction, faulty exclusion of evidence, unfair restriction on cross-examination, and a host of other errors simply vanish as though they never had occurred. And, most important, the defendant remains in prison to suffer the punishment that he or she appears to deserve.

The problem, of course, is that the solution offered by this harmlesserror "tonic" can be illusory, for, although it resolves the immediate dilemma created by an error that may free a guilty defendant, it creates its own set of aggravations. And, like the sorcerer's apprentice, we have discovered that the "magic" formula we invoke creates problems that are arguably more momentous than the difficulties we sought to resolve. Put simply, each time we employ the imaginary tonic of harmless error, we erode an important legal principle. When we hold errors harmless, the rights of individuals, both constitutional and otherwise, go unenforced. Moreover, the deterrent force of a reversal remains unfelt by those who caused the error. In his seminal book on harmless error, entitled *The Riddle of Harmless Error*,[3] the late Justice Roger Traynor aptly observed that "[i]n the long run there would be a closer guard against error at the trial, if appellate courts were alert to reverse, in case of doubt, for error that could have contaminated the judgment."[4]

This is not to say that harmless error has no place in our jurisprudence. Indeed, countless cases present errors that truly are harmless under any interpretation of the standard, and my colleagues and I have engaged in extensive use of the harmless-error doctrine where we have concluded that an error failed to affect the substantial rights of a defendant. The problem with harmless error arises when we as appellate judges conflate the harmlessness inquiry with our own assessment of a defendant's guilt. This approach is dangerously seductive, for our natural inclination is to view an error as harmless whenever a defendant's conviction appears well justified by the record evidence. However, the seductiveness of this approach is its chief defect, for, drawn in by its attractions, we have applied the harmlesserror rule to such an extent that it is my impression that my colleagues and I are inclined to invoke it almost automatically where the proof of a defendant's guilt seems strong.

In other words, I believe that, more often than not, we review the record to determine how we might have decided the case; the judgment as to whether an error is harmless is therefore dependent on our judgment about the factual guilt of the defendant. I call this application of harmless error the "guilt-based approach." Justice Traynor persuasively argues, however, that the role of an appellate judge should instead be limited to a determination of whether the error influenced the jury and hence contaminated the verdict; in such an event, the appellate court has a duty to find that the appellant did not get the jury trial to which he was entitled.[5] This alternative framework I will call the "effect-on-the-verdict approach."[6]

I have the same concerns about the guilt-based approach that Justice Traynor identified in 1970; indeed, the problems may be even worse now. As the guilt-based approach to harmless error has taken hold in our courts, the "plain-error" rule, which governs appellate review of errors to which counsel failed to object at trial, has been employed in such a way that findings of error are rare. As a result, defendants asserting violations of individual rights and liberties on appeal frequently receive a standard response: the errors to which they objected at trial were harmless; the errors to which they failed to object were not plain. One solution to this problem is to break the stranglehold of the guilt-based approach to harmless error and reconsider Traynor's alternative framework.

I enjoy thinking like a law teacher about what I do as a judge. When I do that, some of my judicial decisions look ridiculous; but then, in turn, when I try to apply some of my scholarly ideas to my work as a judge, those ideas sometimes appear inane. Judges must reach results based on legal prescriptions, and then explain their judgments to interested parties who have a lot at stake in the outcome of a case. Law teachers rarely face this pressure. Indeed, there are some in the academy who believe that a truly good law

adding few to (and, indeed, subtracting one from) the list of violations that are per se reversible. Errors that may be harmless under the *Chapman* standard now include violations of the Fourth Amendment right against unreasonable searches and seizures;[29] the Sixth Amendment rights against admission of the out-of-court statement of a nontestifying codefendant,[30] against interrogation by government agents after the right to counsel has attached,[31] and to cross-examination of a witness for bias;[32] and the due process right against a jury instruction that shifts the burden of proof to the defendant.[33] In 1991, the Court in *Arizona v. Fulminante*[34] held that even the admission of a coerced confession at trial may constitute harmless error, thereby reversing the position it appeared to have taken in *Chapman*.[35] In a statement that accurately describes the thrust of the Supreme Court's post-*Chapman* jurisprudence, the *Fulminante* Court said flatly that "most constitutional errors can be harmless."[36]

In addition to expanding the number of constitutional errors subject to *Chapman*-style harmless-error analysis, the Court in certain cases has gone so far *as to incorporate the harmlessness inquiry into the determination of whether an error has even occurred.* Thus, although application of the harmless-error rule normally presupposes the existence of a trial error, in these cases a defendant must make a showing of prejudice even to establish that there is a constitutional right to be asserted. For example, to prove a violation of the due process right to discovery of favorable evidence, the defendant must show that the evidence was "material either to guilt or to punishment."[37] Evidence is material under this standard "only if there is a reasonable probability that, had the evidence been disclosed to the defense, the result of the proceeding would have been different."[38] Thus, a defendant seeking to vindicate a constitutional right to discovery of exculpatory evidence generally must show that a challenged action was reasonably likely to have affected the actual verdict.[39] A similar showing is necessary to establish a violation of the Sixth Amendment right to effective assistance of counsel. A defendant asserting such a violation must establish not only that his or her counsel's work "fell below an objective standard of reasonableness,"[40] but also that the shortcomings in counsel's work prejudiced the defense, meaning "a reasonable probability that, but for counsel's unprofessional errors, the result of the proceeding would have been different."[41] What is significant about these cases is that, unlike those governed by the *Chapman* and *Kotteakos* standards, the burden of proof in such instances falls not upon the government, but upon the defendant.[42]

In another twist on the doctrine, the Court has held that the *Chapman* reasonable-doubt standard for constitutional errors does not apply to constitutional challenges to state-court convictions brought pursuant to the federal courts' habeas corpus jurisdiction. In the 1993 case of *Brecht v. Abrahamson*,[43] the Court, motivated by concerns with finality, comity, and federalism, held that, instead, the less stringent harmless-error rule articulated in *Kotteakos*—inquiring whether an error substantially influenced a jury's verdict—applies on collateral review of constitutional error in state-court criminal trials.[44] The Court reasoned that "[o]verturning final and presumptively correct convictions on collateral review because the State cannot prove that an error is harmless under Chapman undermines the States' interest in finality and infringes upon their sovereignty over criminal matters."[45]

By applying *Kotteakos* rather than *Chapman* in habeas review, the Court's decision in *Brecht* gives the appearance of being an important change in the law. However, if the truth be told, it is hard to discern any material differences in the two standards. As Justice Stevens notes in his concurring opinion in *Brecht*,

> [the *Kotteakos*] standard accords with the statutory rule for reviewing other trial errors that affect substantial rights; places the burden on prosecutors to explain why those errors were harmless; requires a . . . court to review the entire record de novo in determining whether the error influenced the jury's deliberations; and leaves considerable latitude for the exercise of judgment by federal courts. . . .
>
> The *Kotteakos* standard that will now apply on collateral review is less stringent than the *Chapman v. California* standard applied on direct review. Given the critical importance of the faculty of judgment in administering either standard, however, that difference is less significant than it might seem— a point well illustrated by the differing opinions expressed by THE CHIEF JUSTICE and by Justice KENNEDY in *Arizona v. Fulminante*. While THE CHIEF JUSTICE considered the admission of the defendant's confession harmless error under Chapman, Justice KENNEDY's cogent analysis demonstrated that the error could not reasonably have been viewed as harmless under a standard even more relaxed than the one we announce today. In the end, the way we phrase the governing standard is far less important than the quality of the judgment with which it is applied.[46]

Justice Stevens's comment, at least in retrospect, appears to mark a shift in the tone of the Court's decisions on harmless error, and it gives some content to what Justice Breyer said in the 1995 *O'Neal* decision. Nonetheless, the stated result in *Brecht* clearly is designed to broaden the harmless-error doctrine. Indeed, the opinion for the majority goes so far as to state that habeas petitioners "are not entitled to habeas relief based on trial error unless they can establish that it resulted in 'actual prejudice,'"[47] thereby appearing to relieve the government of its normal burden of showing the absence of prejudice when advancing a claim of harmless error. The *O'Neal* opinion overturns this suggestion[48] but the dictum in *Brecht* highlights just how far the Court had gone in expanding the harmless-error doctrine during the pre-*O'Neal* years.

In sum, the period since the Court's decision in *Kotteakos* in 1946 has seen a trend toward expansion of the scope of the harmless-error doctrine. The Court has applied harmless-error review to an ever-expanding list of constitutional violations, incorporated a harmfulness requirement into the standards for proving a violation of certain constitutional rights, and has eased the harmful constitutional error standard in habeas cases. The result is that the doctrine now applies to errors far more serious than the "technicalities"[49] that prompted congressional action in the first place.

However, the application of harmless-error analysis to a larger set of violations accounts for only part of the expansion of the harmless-error doctrine. Accompanying this trend is another one involving the frequency with which the doctrine actually is invoked. Although meaningful statistics on the use of harmless error in the federal courts of appeals are hard to come by, research that I and others have conducted suggests that after the *Chapman* decision, applications of the harmless-error doctrine increased dramatically. In 1966, the year before the Supreme Court decided *Chapman*, only 30 of the 3,815 reported federal appellate court cases, or 0.79 percent, mentioned the words "harmless error."[50] By 1969, two years after *Chapman*, the percentage of such cases using the "harmless error" phrase had more than doubled, jumping to 2.09 percent of all cases reported.[51] The proportion of "harmless error" cases remained at approximately 2 percent of all cases reported until 1986, when the percentage dropped to 1.58 percent—a number around which it has hovered ever since.[52]

If anything, the 1.58 percent figure understates the actual use of the harmless-error doctrine, because the figure does not include unpublished case dispositions by the courts of appeals, which have increased substantially in recent years. I suspect that a large number of judgments and orders without opinions include dispositions based on findings of harmless error.

Another reason for the slight decrease in the statistic measuring the invocation of the harmless-error doctrine since 1985 may be that judges no longer need the doctrine in order to disregard errors as they did during the

1970s and 1980s. During the decade and a half between 1970 and 1985, the Supreme Court carved out numerous exceptions to criminal procedure rules mandated by the Constitution, particularly the exclusionary rule remedy for violations of the Fourth Amendment.[53] Thus, some of the post-1985 decline in use of the harmless-error rule may be attributable to the fact that such exceptions have reduced the likelihood of "error" in any given criminal case.

My own experience suggests that appellate panels confronted with allegations of error in criminal cases sometimes simply narrow the application of the rule the defendant seeks to invoke. This is a kind of backhanded use of the harmless-error rule, which allows a court to preserve a conviction without seeming to erode an important right by declaring a breach of it to be harmless. Propriety and common sense preclude me from venturing to verify this hypothesis. My main point is that it appears that there simply are not as many errors to hold harmless today as there were in the 1970s and early 1980s. In any event, what statistics we do have suggest that courts still are resorting to harmless-error analysis at least twice as frequently as they did before *Chapman* was decided.

Another troubling aspect of this trend is judicial use of the harmless-error rule to avoid reaching a difficult issue in a case. Courts sometimes openly decline to decide whether a defendant's rights have been violated, instead evading the issue by stating that any error that might have occurred was harmless.[54] This practice leaves unresolved the question of whether an error even occurred, thus offering no guidance to trial courts. What may be an important question of trial error is therefore sidestepped by the application of a doctrine that itself presupposes the existence of such an error. Nothing suggests that the harmless-error rule was meant to serve such a purpose.[55] The flip side of this practice is the needless use of harmless error, which occurs when, upon rejecting the merits of some claim of error in an action of the trial judge, the appellate court goes on to say that even if error had occurred, it would have been harmless.[56]

This tendency of harmless-error analysis to creep into federal case law even when it is unnecessary is hardly surprising, given the routine reliance on the harmless-error rule. It sometimes appears that harmless error has become the inevitable last resort of government lawyers arguing criminal cases. My colleagues and I occasionally joke that prosecutors defending criminal convictions on appeal never have seen an error that cannot somehow be rendered harmless. A 1995 case offers a notable example of the extremes to which the harmless-error doctrine may be taken. In the case I have in mind, the trial court erroneously rejected a defendant's guilty plea, and the defendant ultimately was convicted of three offenses in addition to those encompassed by the rejected plea agreement. The conviction also required the defendant to pay a criminal forfeiture of $3,500 that was not required under the rejected plea agreement. At oral argument in the case, the government's attorney contended that the defendant suffered no prejudice from the error because he was sentenced to serve the same prison term that the plea agreement would have required. When pressed by the court as to whether the $3,500 forfeiture, not to mention the collateral consequences of three additional criminal convictions, might not constitute sufficient prejudice to overcome the harmless-error rule, the government acknowledged that "rights are affected," but questioned whether such rights were "substantial enough to reverse."[57] The court did not share counsel's doubts, and remanded the case for a new guilty plea proceeding.[58] However, I harbor no illusions that our decision will prevent similar arguments in the future. And, given the frequency with which appellate courts have come to find errors harmless, one can hardly be surprised.

B. Plain Error

To complement the expansion of the harmless-error doctrine, since the mid-seventies federal criminal jurisprudence has also seen a general constriction of the doctrine governing appellate review of errors to which counsel failed to object during trial. Federal Rule of Criminal Procedure 52(b) provides that "[p]lain errors or defects affecting substantial rights may be noticed although they were not brought to the attention of the court."[59] As the Advisory Committee's note on the rule makes clear, its drafters intended it as "a restatement of existing law,"[60] which had provided that, "if a plain error was committed in a matter . . . absolutely vital to defendants, [the court is] at liberty to correct it."[61] The Supreme Court more fully described the doctrine now embodied in Rule 52(b) in its 1936 decision in *United States v. Atkinson*,[62] where it stated: "In exceptional circumstances, especially in criminal cases, appellate courts, in the public interest, may, of their own motion, notice errors to which no exception has been taken, if the errors are obvious, or if they otherwise seriously affect the fairness, integrity or public reputation of judicial proceedings."[63]

At about the same time that it began expanding the use of harmless error, the Supreme Court appeared to tighten the standard for a finding of plain error. Instead of focusing the rule upon obvious errors, or errors affecting the integrity of the judicial process, as it had done in *Atkinson*, the Court in the 1982 case of *United States v. Frady*[64] stated that "Rule 52(b) was intended to afford a means for the prompt redress of *miscarriages of justice*,"[65] and cited approvingly several appellate cases suggesting that "the power granted ... by Rule 52(b) is to be used sparingly."[66] Approximately three years later, the Court reiterated the new "miscarriage of justice" plain-error standard in *United States v. Young*.[67] Although that opinion also made reference to the need to correct errors impugning the integrity of the judicial process,[68] many lower courts have seized upon its "miscarriage of justice" language when applying the rule.[69]

In 1993, in *United States v. Olano*,[70] the Court set forth a more complete articulation of the plain-error test, explaining that Rule 52(b) encompasses unwaived legal error that "'seriously affect[s] the fairness, integrity or public reputation of judicial proceedings.'"[71] Notably, this formulation, although not expressly discarding the "miscarriage of justice" standard,[72] deemphasized that standard—a matter that I take up in the final part of this article. The point to be made here is that, from the early 1980s until *Olano*, many federal courts applied a plain-error test concerned not so much with the standards specifically stated in Rule 52(b)—that is, whether the error was "plain," or one "affecting substantial rights"[73]—but rather with a more demanding standard requiring an error to precipitate a miscarriage of justice before correction is warranted.

Thus, Supreme Court jurisprudence since the mid-sixties has encompassed both a tightening of the standard for finding plain error and a broadening of the applicability of the doctrine of harmless error. These two trends create an obvious effect: Fewer trial errors require reversal. Those errors to which counsel objected almost always face the possibility of being disregarded as harmless. Those to which counsel failed to object may not be reviewed unless they are so dramatic as to qualify under the stringent plain-error standard. These two trends share more than a common effect, however. They also share the same source: a guilt-based theory governing appellate review of trial error.

II. Underlying the Doctrine: A Guilt-Based Theory of Error

In 1969, two years after the Supreme Court decided *Chapman*, the Justices once again faced a case involving a question of harmless error. The petitioner in *Harrington v. California*[74] challenged his conviction on the ground that the trial judge had admitted the confessions of three code-fendants, only one of whom took the stand at their joint trial. In the previous term, the Court had made clear that admission of such a confession of a nontestifying codefendant violates a defendant's Sixth Amendment right to confront the witnesses against him.[75] In *Harrington*, however, the Court, in a terse four-page opinion by Justice Douglas, held the Sixth Amendment violation harmless beyond a reasonable doubt in light of what it described as "overwhelming" untainted evidence against the defendant.[76] While the majority stated that it was "reaffirm[ing]" *Chapman*,[77] three dissenters perceived in the Court's brief discussion nothing less than the overruling of *Chapman* itself.[78] Justice Brennan explained the dissenters' view:

> *Chapman* . . . meant no compromise with the proposition that a conviction cannot constitutionally be based to any extent on constitutional error. The Court today by shifting the inquiry from whether the constitutional error contributed to the conviction to whether the untainted evidence provided "overwhelming" support for the conviction puts aside the firm resolve of *Chapman* and makes that compromise. As a result, the deterrent effect of such cases as *Mapp v. Ohio*, 367 U.S. 643 (1961); *Griffin v. California*, 380 U.S. 609 (1965); *Miranda v. Arizona*, 384 U.S. 436 (1966); *United States v. Wade*, 388 U.S. 218 (1967); and *Bruton v. United States*, 391 U.S. 123 (1968), on the actions of both police and prosecutors, not to speak of trial courts, will be significantly undermined.[79]

Today, more than thirty years later, I am convinced that the *Harrington* dissenters correctly perceived the danger in the majority's approach. Their assertion that *Harrington* overruled *Chapman* was perhaps overstated, since *Chapman* had, in fact, ruled that a constitutional error may be harmless. But their observations about the dangerous ramifications of *Harrington* were entirely accurate. As I have shown, the Court's decision in *Chapman* heralded a major expansion in both the number of violations subject to harmless-error analysis and the frequency with which that analysis is employed.[80] Accompanying that expansion, and, I believe, underlying much of it, is the fact that the *Harrington* approach to harmless-error analysis—one of looking to whether the record evidence adequately demonstrates the appellant's guilt, rather than whether the error contributed to the verdict—has become standard practice for many appellate panels considering both constitutional and nonconstitutional error.[81] As matters now stand in 1995, in many criminal cases an error is harmless so long as the appellate court remains convinced of the defendant's guilt; an error warrants reversal only where it raises doubts about the defendant's culpability.[82]

Even a brief survey of harmless-error case law in the D.C. Circuit and elsewhere reveals the tendency of judges to apply the doctrine by assessing whether the evidence adduced at trial, or the untainted evidence in the case of an evidentiary error, appears sufficient to support a guilty verdict.[83] In some cases this is as it should be, for the presence of massive evidence of a defendant's guilt surely is one factor for a court to consider in ascertaining whether it can say with fair assurance that an error substantially affected the jury's verdict (or, in the case of constitutional error, whether the error was harmless beyond a reasonable doubt). Frequently, however, the weight of the evidence against a defendant is not just one factor playing into the harmless-error analysis, but rather the sole criterion by which harmlessness is gauged. As Justice Traynor aptly observed:

> All too often an appellate court confuses review by applying the substantial evidence test to determine whether an error is harmless. Such a court considers only the evidence in support of the judgment and ignores erroneous matter. It assumes that the trier of fact, having decided against the appellant, believed all properly admitted evidence against him and disbelieved all evidence in his favor. No wonder that under such a review most errors are found harmless.[84]

That appellate courts measure harmlessness according to their own assessments of guilt is hardly surprising, because the jurisprudence of the Supreme Court for a time embraced a guilt-based theory of harmless error. While some members of the Court, particularly Justice Stevens,[85] have been firm in the view that "[h]armless-error analysis is not an excuse for overlooking error because the reviewing court is itself convinced of the defendant's guilt,"[86] a guilt-based theory of harmless error focusing on the reliability of the trial outcome has found favor with the Court, at least until the 1990s. This theory, which first sprouted in *Harrington*, bloomed fully to life in the 1972 case of *Schneble v. Florida*,[87] in which a majority found a Confrontation Clause violation to be harmless upon finding "the independent evidence of guilt . . . overwhelming."[88] The Court's equation of guilt and harmlessness became more explicit in the ensuing years. Thus, in a 1986 opinion holding *Chapman*-style harmless-error analysis applicable to a denial of the Sixth Amendment right to cross-examine on the subject of bias, the Court commented that "[t]he harmless-error doctrine recognizes the principle that the central purpose of a criminal trial is to decide the factual question of the defendant's guilt or innocence."[89] Later during the same term, the Court went so far as to declare that "[w]here a reviewing court can find that the record developed at trial establishes guilt beyond a reasonable doubt, the interest in fairness has been satisfied and the judgment should be affirmed,"[90] notwithstanding the presence of constitutional error.

Arguably, the culmination of this line of reasoning was *Fulminante*. In one of two majority opinions for the Court, Chief Justice Rehnquist, for a five-Justice majority, sets forth an analytical framework for the assessment of all constitutional errors.[91] Such errors are divided into two classes: One consisting of "trial error," meaning "error which occurred during the presentation of the case to the jury, and which may therefore be quantitatively assessed in the context of other evidence presented in order to determine whether its admission was harmless beyond a reasonable doubt,"[92] and the other consisting of "structural defect[s] affecting the framework within which the trial proceeds," and, in the presence of which, "'a criminal trial cannot reliably serve its function as a vehicle for determination of guilt or innocence, and no criminal punishment may be regarded as fundamentally fair.'"[93] All trial errors are subject to harmless-error analysis; only structural errors require automatic reversal.[94] Under the view enunciated by Chief Justice Rehnquist, it is clear that most constitutional errors will be subject to harmless-error review, notwithstanding anything to the contrary that might be gleaned from *Chapman*.

Chief Justice Rehnquist's framework, which expanded the harmless-error doctrine further than ever before, is only one-half of the *Fulminante* decision, however. His opinion, after all, commanded a majority only on the question of whether a coerced confession should be subject to harmless-error review; on the merits, the Court ruled that the trial court's error in admitting a coerced confession was not harmless.[95] The majority opinion on this latter point, written by Justice White, does not embrace a guilt-based view of harmless error. Rather, the Court held that *Chapman v. California* made clear that "before a federal constitutional error can be held harmless, the court must be able to declare a belief that it was harmless beyond a reasonable doubt. . . . [I]t must be determined whether the State has met its burden of demonstrating that the admission of the confession . . . did not contribute to *Fulminante's* conviction. Five of us are of the view that the State has not carried its burden."[96]

Similarly, Justice Kennedy, who provided the swing vote in support of Justice White's position, looked to the likely impact of the error on the jury verdict in assessing the claim of harmless error:

I agree that harmless-error analysis should apply in the case of a coerced confession. That said, the court conducting a harmless-error inquiry must appreciate the indelible impact a full confession may have on the trier of fact, as distinguished, for instance, from the impact of an isolated statement that incriminates the defendant only when connected with other evidence. If the jury believes that a defendant has admitted the crime, it doubtless will be tempted to rest its decision on that evidence alone, without careful consideration of the other evidence in the case. Apart, perhaps, from a videotape of the crime, one would have difficulty finding evidence more damaging to a criminal defendant's plea of innocence.[97]

The opinions of Justice White and Justice Kennedy adhere to a view that is much like the one advanced by Justice Traynor, and seem far removed from the guilt-based version of harmless error found in *Harrington*. *Fulminante* may be seen as marking a high point in the expansion of the harmless-error doctrine, but it also may have been a critical turning point for the Court. The judicial application of the plain-error rule, although not as extensively developed as the harmless-error doctrine, also has been affected by the guilt-based approach. Numerous federal appellate court opinions applying the "miscarriage of justice" plain-error standard articulated in the Court's *Frady* and *Young* decisions[98] have stated that such a miscarriage of justice occurs only where the possibility exists that jurors have convicted an innocent defendant.[99] Typical of such decisions is the Seventh Circuit's opinion in *United States v. Whaley*,[100] where the court stated that "plain error is an error resulting in 'an actual miscarriage of justice, which implies the conviction of one who but for the error would have been acquitted.'"[101]

In some respects, the pre-*Fulminante* practice of the Supreme Court and appellate courts in applying the harmless- and plain-error standards could have been predicted. Numerous factors have driven and, indeed, continue to drive, judges to focus primarily on the factual guilt of the accused. For one, the nationwide problems of drug use and drug trafficking and the often-related scourge of random violence have generated intense pressure to convict defendants accused of such crimes. Many judges are undoubtedly influenced by the perceived exigencies of the government's "war on drugs" when they confront a defendant who clearly appears to be guilty of a drug-related crime, yet whose trial included a significant legal error. I have noted before the heavy toll that the war on drugs has taken upon our individual rights and liberties.[102] Suffice it to say that an expanded application of harmless-error analysis appears in many cases to be yet another effect of that war.

Adding to the pressures generated by such societal problems is the increasing burden of the judicial docket. With filings in the courts of appeals increasing by 218 percent between 1972 and 1992[103] it frequently may seem like nothing more than a wise use of judicial resources to affirm the conviction of a defendant who appears, from the record, to be guilty, despite the admission of a coerced confession, the denial of confrontation rights, the use of inadmissible evidence, or some other error. From the perspective of a judge considering a challenge to such a conviction, it often seems that little will be gained by retrial, for the conviction surely was justified. Moreover, appellate judges know that their colleagues on the district court, who also labor under a heavy caseload, do not want their cases returned for additional proceedings. Indeed, several district court judges have told me, only half jokingly, that they can tolerate our reversals, so long as we do not combine them with a remand.

Finally, judges are, of course, human, and I think the development of the case law proves, if anything, the constraints of human nature. Put simply, the *Kotteakos* and *Chapman* opinions ask a reviewing court to do something that frequently cannot be done without great discipline. It is one thing to state that the harmless-error analysis looks to the effect of the error on the verdict, rather than to the sufficiency of the evidence to support the verdict. It is yet another, more difficult thing for us as appellate judges to adhere to that analytical framework when confronted with the concrete facts of a particular case in which the defendant's guilt seems well established. In such circumstances, it is by far the simpler and more natural course to construct a jurisprudence that cares only for punishment of the guilty, and, accordingly, to discount all errors that fail to cast doubt upon our own perceptions of culpability. Only through a determined adherence to principle do we look beyond the weight of the evidence to the likely impact of an error. Often, pressed by the demands of the docket and mindful of a society wracked by crime, we simply lack such determination.

While I recognize the many temptations of a guilt-based approach to harmless error, however, I also believe that such an approach overlooks much in its myopic fixation on factual guilt. As an initial matter, this approach is inconsistent with the constitutional framework of our judicial system. The Supreme Court's many admonitions in *Kotteakos* and other early cases make clear that the question involved in harmless-error analysis is not whether the jury reached the correct verdict despite the error, but whether the verdict was substantially swayed by the error.[104] This rule rests on a sound premise, for our Constitution grants criminal defendants the right to have juries, not appellate courts, render judgments of guilt or innocence.[105] Justice Frankfurter's comments on this subject in 1946 hold equally true today:

> In view of the place of importance that trial by jury has in our Bill of Rights, it is not to be supposed that Congress intended to substitute the belief of appellate judges in the guilt of an accused, however justifiably engendered by the dead record, for ascertainment of guilt by a jury under appropriate judicial guidance, however cumbersome that process may be.[106]

It is for a similar reason that trial courts in our system are prohibited from directing verdicts of guilty against criminal defendants, no matter how weighty the evidence favoring such outcomes.[107] Put simply, "the error in such a case is that the wrong entity judged the defendant guilty."[108]

I recognize that the foregoing argument can be carried too far, because the mere existence of the harmless-error doctrine (embodied by statute) contemplates the fact that appellate judges will consider the evidence developed at trial. In fact, a complaining defendant may be well served when appellate judges consider the record of evidence on the question of guilt. For example, an appellate court may find that, absent some erroneously admitted evidence, the evidence is insufficient to support a finding of guilt—but this can only be done if the appellate judges carefully examine the entire record. In other words, those who glibly claim that appellate courts overstep their role in finding harmless error, overstate their case. As Justice Traynor pointed out:

> If the court is convinced upon review of the evidence that the error did not influence the jury, and hence sustains the verdict, a fortiori there is no invasion of the province of the jury. There is likewise no invasion should it appear instead that the error did influence the jury, and hence contaminated the verdict, for the appellant then did not get the jury trial to which he was entitled. In that event, the appellate court clearly acts within its own province when it affords the appellant a right to a new trial.[109]

Concern over the institutional competency of the appellate courts also strongly counsels against the practice of focusing solely on the question of factual guilt. The very nature of the appellate function leaves judges of the courts of appeals poorly equipped to make such guilt determinations. An appellate judge's view of the trial is limited to the record, and, as any observer of the judicial process is aware, many events of trial pass without casting so much as a shadow upon the printed transcript. The appellate judge cannot watch the demeanor of witnesses, listen to the intonations of their voices, or engage in any of the countless other observations that inhere in an assessment of credibility.[110] And, most importantly, an appellate panel cannot possibly know what a jury might have done if the case had been tried without error. Therefore, if there is any serious doubt on this score, the case ought to be returned to the jury.

The most serious flaw in the guilt-based approach, however, is its tendency to undermine our most important legal principles. As the *Harrington* dissenters warned, any analysis measuring the harmlessness of error according to the weight of the evidence that the prosecution stacks against a defendant erodes the individual rights and liberties that are presumed to elevate our system of justice.[111] A focus on guilt skews the judicial assessment of harmlessness. The values that underlie the individual rights guaranteed by the Constitution, federal statutes, and procedural rules are often general. Constitutional rights, in particular, often represent broad ideals of individual liberty and human dignity. By contrast, a criminal act appears vivid and almost tangible, so the need to punish the guilty is both immediate and strongly felt. A wrong, often a grievous wrong, has occurred, and the defendant, by all appearances, is responsible. It is, therefore, to be expected that the desire to punish the guilty will frequently prevail over the need to honor individual rights.[112]

When this happens, much is lost. Our system of justice stands above others only because it recognizes a sphere of personal liberty into which the government cannot intrude.[113] Marking the boundary of this sphere are the individual rights guaranteed by our Constitution, and, to a lesser extent, by our laws. These rights, however, do not remain vital merely because they are enshrined in our most revered documents. They remain vital only if an active and alert federal judiciary stands ready to enforce them, even when their enforcement yields unpalatable results. As Justice Frankfurter put it, "it is an abuse to deal too casually and too lightly with rights guaranteed by the Federal Constitution, even though they . . . may be invoked by those morally unworthy."[114] We commit just such an abuse when we hold errors harmless in a criminal case based solely on our own perceptions of a defendant's guilt. Such guilt-based application of the harmless-error doctrine dilutes the force of our laws and shrinks the boundaries of the sphere of individual autonomy. When evidence is not excluded, indictments are not quashed, and convictions are not overturned, we eviscerate the deterrent effect of these and other similar measures, and consequently infect the entire criminal process with an ambivalence toward our most fundamental liberties. We would do well to remind ourselves of what Justice Traynor described as the "cleansing effect on the trial process"[115] created by vigorous enforcement of legal rights. After all, we can hardly expect prosecutors to respect the rights of criminal defendants whom they believe to be guilty when we as judges are unwilling to do so.[116]

An obvious example of the loss we sustain by overreliance on the harmless-error doctrine arises from the admission of a coerced confession. Federal jurisprudence long has recognized that the extraction of a confession by physical or psychological pressure is inconsistent with the very nature of our criminal process. As the Supreme Court stated in the 1961 case of *Rogers v. Richmond*,[117] "ours is an accusatorial and not an inquisitorial system—a system in which the State must establish guilt by evidence independently and freely secured and may not by coercion prove its charge against an accused out of his own mouth."[118] Accordingly, our Constitution bars the use of coerced confessions at trial.[119] This rule reflects the "strongly felt attitude of our society that important human values are sacrificed where an agency of the government, in the course of securing a conviction, wrings a confession out of an accused against his will," as well as "the deep-rooted feeling that the police must obey the law while enforcing the law; that in the end life and liberty can be as much endangered from illegal methods used to convict those thought to be criminals as from the actual criminals themselves."[120]

When we enforce this rule, we honor these societal attitudes. Conversely, when we hold that use of a coerced confession is mere harmless error, we denigrate them.[121] Apparently Justice Kennedy had such a concern in mind when he provided the swing vote in *Fulminante*. Justice Kennedy did not even concur in the view that the confession in that case was coerced; but, respecting the view of the majority, he agreed that if the confession had been coerced, then the error could not have been harmless.[122]

An apt illustration of the danger posed by an overly expansive view of harmless error is the Sixth Circuit's decision in *United States v. Daniel*.[123] In that case, police executing a search warrant at a house in Michigan forced its occupants to lie face down on the floor, handcuffed them, and covered their heads with a sheet[124]—all without an arrest warrant or, apparently, probable cause to support such a seizure[125]—while they searched the premises for what the court described as "an hour or so."[126] Approximately twenty minutes into this period of detention, an officer asked the occupants whether they knew who owned a weapon found on the premises, and the defendant answered that he owned it.[127] After this statement was admitted at trial, the defendant appealed. Addressing his claim, the Sixth Circuit first assumed, without deciding, that the defendant's statement was coerced, then held that admission of the coerced statement was harmless because a later, more detailed, and voluntary confession provided the same information.[128]

I do not mean to question the Sixth Circuit's decision on the application of governing case law. What I do mean to question, however, is the impact that decisions such as *Daniel* may have upon our criminal justice system. The officers who executed a search warrant by handcuffing Daniel and his companions, forcing them to lie face down, and covering their heads with a sheet are not reminded of the importance of the privilege against self-incrimination when admission of the confession they extracted is deemed harmless error, and we can expect them to behave no differently in the future. We have come a long way from the brutal beating with whips and leather straps used to extract a confession in *Brown v. Mississippi*,[129] or the thirty-six uninterrupted hours of questioning under bright lights employed in *Ashcraft v. Tennessee*,[130] but we have done so only because the reversal of a conviction was the sure penalty for these actions. While I do not expect to see a resurrection of such tactics in the law-enforcement community, I do fear that unbridled judicial infatuation with harmless error could lead to more subtle, but equally dangerous, adverse effects on the integrity of our system of justice.[131]

Similar concerns arise with respect to the impact that excessive application of the harmless-error rule may have upon the deterrent force of the Fourth Amendment's exclusionary rule. Our case law long has recognized that the Fourth Amendment's prohibition on unwarranted searches and seizures is the Constitution's primary protection for "the sanctity of a man's home and the privacies of life."[132] Since 1914, federal courts have enforced the Fourth Amendment by applying a rule excluding from use at trial all evidence seized in violation of its requirements.[133] As Justice Holmes put it, this rule is necessary to prevent the Fourth Amendment's guarantee against unreasonable searches and seizures from becoming no more than "a form of words."[134] According to Holmes, "[t]he essence of a provision forbidding the acquisition of evidence in a certain way is that not merely evidence so acquired shall not be used before the Court but that it shall not be used at all."[135] By applying the harmless-error rule to Fourth Amendment violations every time we as appellate judges deem a defendant to be guilty, we threaten to reduce the Fourth Amendment to the "form of words" of which Justice Holmes warned.

The numerous exceptions to the exclusionary rule that the Supreme Court has developed since the Warren Court era only make this threat more immediate. Such exceptions include those allowing for admission at trial of evidence seized in violation of the Fourth Amendment if police officers who seized the evidence relied in good faith on a facially valid warrant later found to lack probable cause,[136] if the evidence also was discovered through an independent source,[137] and if the evidence inevitably would have been discovered through lawful means.[138] Given the presence of these and other exceptions, any general appellate court eagerness to invoke the harmless-error doctrine in the reduced number of cases that actually warrant application of the exclusionary rule is hard to comprehend.

What I mean to illustrate by these few examples is that we as appellate judges display a dangerous shortsightedness when, in pursuit of the goal of punishing the guilty, we trade away results in individual cases. We send a message through our criminal justice system each time we reverse or remand a conviction on the ground that the police or prosecutors have violated a defendant's individual rights. Upon receiving such a message, the criminal justice process corrects itself accordingly. Thus, when we shrink from our duty to overturn convictions in individual cases, we accomplish nothing less than a subversion of the rules that we have devised to protect our shared values.

In advancing my concerns over the expansion of the harmless-error doctrine, I am quick to concede that our system of justice will not work if appellate courts are one-sided in catering to the interests of defendants at the expense of police officers, prosecutors, and trial courts. Just as appellate judges are "only human" in their efforts to apply the law, so too are police officers, prosecutors, and trial judges in their efforts to enforce and administer the law. It is the rare case indeed that is prosecuted completely free of error, so we should not expect perfection. And appellate judges cannot be self-righteous in judging the efforts of police officers, prosecutors, and trial judges; the incredible demands of their work far exceed anything that we can glean from our own daily fare of activities. My concerns over the expansion of the harmless-error doctrine pertain only to the threatened loss of substantial rights.[139]

III. The Future: A Hopeful Direction from the Supreme Court?

As for the future, if it is possible to be cautiously optimistic and somewhat skeptical, that would be my view. I am optimistic because of a recent trend in the Supreme Court's case law toward a more constrained approach to harmless error. I am cautious, however, because it remains too early to tell whether this trend is a brief aberration or, instead, the inception of some new and meaningful development in the Court's jurisprudence. And I am skeptical, because I am not sure that in practical application we can ever solve the riddle of harmless error.

Although some judges, scholars, and practitioners may disagree with me on this, I think that any new trend in the case law began with the Court's decision in *Fulminante*. In that case, one of the two majority opinions—the one authored by Chief Justice Rehnquist—establishes a questionable dichotomy between "structural errors" affecting the trial framework (which can never be harmless), and "trial errors," which always are subject to a claim of harmless error.[140] The obvious design of the opinion is to limit sharply the number of "structural errors" so as to broaden the reach of the harmless-error doctrine. Nonetheless, the second majority opinion in *Fulminante*—the one written by Justice White—applies the harmless-error test in a way that avoids guilt-based decision making.[141] Indeed, Justice Kennedy's swing vote in *Fulminante* clearly focuses on the substantiality of the right of a criminal defendant not to have a coerced confession used against him, and on the powerful effect that such erroneously admitted evidence is likely to have on the verdict regardless of other evidence against the defendant.[142] In sum, the majority position on the merits of the harmless-error issue in *Fulminante* in no way relies on the guilt-based approach endorsed by the Court's *Harrington* decision.

Even if *Fulminante* is not viewed as a trend-setting decision, there can be no doubt about the importance of the Supreme Court's 1993 decision in *Sullivan v. Louisiana*.[143] Although addressed specifically to the question of whether a constitutionally deficient reasonable-doubt instruction may be harmless error, the Court's opinion includes a general discussion of harmless-error review that appears to reject the guilt-based approach. In this regard, Justice Scalia writes:

> Consistent with the jury-trial guarantee, the question [*Chapman*] instructs the reviewing court to consider is not what effect the constitutional error might generally be expected to have upon a reasonable jury, but rather what effect it had upon the guilty verdict in the case at hand. Harmless-error review looks, we have said, to the basis on which the jury actually rested its verdict. The inquiry, in other words, is not whether, in a trial that occurred without the error, a guilty verdict would surely have been rendered, but whether the guilty verdict actually rendered in this trial was surely unattributable to the error. That must be so, because to hypothesize

a guilty verdict that was never in fact rendered—no matter how in-
escapable the findings to support that verdict might be—would violate the
jury-trial guarantee.[144]

Later in the opinion, in noting that a constitutionally defective reasonable-
doubt instruction could not logically be deemed harmless, the Court even
more emphatically rejects the guilt-based approach to harmless error, stating:

> The most an appellate court can conclude is that a jury would surely have
> found petitioner guilty beyond a reasonable doubt—not that the jury's actual
> finding of guilty beyond a reasonable doubt would surely not have been dif-
> ferent absent the constitutional error. That is not enough. The Sixth Amend-
> ment requires more than appellate speculation about a hypothetical jury's ac-
> tion, or else directed verdicts for the State would be sustainable on appeal; it
> requires an actual jury finding of guilty.[145]

By expressly rejecting the idea that an appellate court may find harmless
error upon satisfying itself that a jury "would surely have found" the defendant guilty in the absence of error, *Sullivan* certainly casts doubt upon the
continuing vitality of the *Harrington* Court's approach, for the conclusion
that a jury "would surely have found" a defendant guilty appears to differ
little from a conclusion that "overwhelming" evidence of guilt rendered any
error harmless. And, in calling for an inquiry regarding "whether the guilty
verdict actually rendered in this trial was surely unattributable to the error,"
Sullivan seems to swing the focus of harmless-error analysis back where
Chapman and *Kotteakos* directed it: to the effect that an error may have had
upon the verdict actually rendered. Finally, in reaching its determination
that constitutionally defective reasonable-doubt instructions may never be
deemed harmless, the *Sullivan* Court treats the *Fulminante* structural de-
fect/trial error dichotomy, with its emphasis on trial accuracy, not as the
centerpiece of its analysis, but as an alternative method of evaluation to be
considered only after the application of simple logic has already yielded a
result.[146]

In sum, then, *Sullivan*, although limited in its holding, includes language
that can be read broadly to repudiate earlier cases embracing the idea that
the harmlessness of an error may be gauged simply through an appellate
court's own assessment of guilt. In a separate concurring opinion, Chief
Justice Rehnquist reiterates his strong view that "it is the rare case in which
a constitutional violation will not be subject to harmless-error analysis,"[147]
but he does not otherwise challenge the views of Justice Scalia. Indeed, Chief
Justice Rehnquist says that, in any harmless-error review, the role of the ap-

pellate court is to "determine whether it is possible to say beyond a reasonable doubt that the error did not contribute to the jury's verdict."[148]

In 1995, the Supreme Court offered up its decision in *O'Neal v. McAninch*,[149] the crown jewel in the decisions moving away from guilt-based applications of the harmless-error doctrine. In *O'Neal,* the Court considered what action a federal habeas court must take when, upon review of a state-court judgment from a criminal trial, it finds itself left in "grave doubt" as to whether a constitutional error was harmless.[150] The Court, in an opinion by Justice Breyer, held that the appellate judge in such a case should treat the error not as harmless, but rather as though it affected the verdict.[151] This conclusion, the Court stated, is consistent with the application of the *Kotteakos* standard, which applies even to constitutional errors in habeas proceedings,[152] and which admonishes that "'if [a reviewing court] is left in grave doubt [as to the harmlessness of an error], the conviction cannot stand.'"[153]

O'Neal is very important, in my view, because it cites and expressly endorses critical portions of Justice Traynor's position on the application of the harmless-error doctrine. Justice Breyer, like the majority in *Sullivan*, presents a commonsense view of harmless error, focused not on artificial categories of cases, but on notions of fundamental fairness. First, the Court makes it clear that, both under *Chapman* and *Kotteakos*, the government bears the burden of showing the absence of prejudice on any claim of harmless error.[154] Second, the Court holds that the "risk of doubt" always remains on the government, rejecting the statement to the contrary made only two years earlier, in 1993, in *Brecht v. Abrahamson*.[155] Third, the Court rules that the proper measure of harmlessness is whether the error "had substantial and injurious effect or influence in determining the jury's verdict,"[156] not whether the record evidence is sufficient absent the error to warrant a verdict of guilt. And finally, the Court makes an attempt to explain to appellate judges what they ought to be doing when considering claims of harmless error:

> When a federal judge . . . is in grave doubt about whether a trial error of federal law had "substantial and injurious effect or influence in determining the jury's verdict," that error is not harmless. And, the petitioner must win.
>
> As an initial matter, we note that we deliberately phrase the issue in this case in terms of a judge's grave doubt, instead of in terms of "burden of proof." . . . [W]e think it conceptually clearer for the judge to ask directly, "Do I, the judge, think that the error substantially influenced the jury's decision?" than for the judge to try to put the same question in terms of proof burdens.

... [W]here the record is so evenly balanced that a conscientious judge is in grave doubt as to the harmlessness of an error ... the [defendant] must win.

... [W]e are dealing here with an error of constitutional dimension—the sort that risks an unreliable trial outcome and the consequent conviction of an innocent person. We also are assuming that the judge's conscientious answer to the question, "But did that error have a 'substantial and injurious effect or influence' on the jury's decision?" is, "It is extremely difficult to say." In such circumstances, a legal rule requiring [reversal], will, at least often, avoid a grievous wrong. ... Such a rule thereby both protects individuals from unconstitutional convictions and helps to guarantee the integrity of the criminal process by assuring that trials are fundamentally fair. See Traynor 23[157] ("In the long run there would be a closer guard against error at trial, if ... courts were alert to reverse, in case of doubt, for error that could have contaminated the judgment").[158]

The majority opinion in *O'Neal* is an undeniably strong statement that serves to pull the harmless-error doctrine from its broadest reaches, particularly when considered alongside *Sullivan*. And it is of no moment that *O'Neal* arises in the context of a habeas petition, because the Court's decision rests on *Kotteakos* itself. Given the Court's holding in *O'Neal* (in a less-favored habeas case), it surely will require no less in more-favored cases, such as direct appeals of nonconstitutional trial errors involving the application of Rule 52(a),[159] and in the most-favored cases, direct appeals of constitutional trial errors involving an application of *Chapman*.[160]

With respect to the plain-error doctrine, the Supreme Court's 1993 decision in *United States v. Olano*[161] similarly provides some basis for optimism. In discussing the standard to guide an appellate court's discretionary decision to correct a plain error, the *Olano* Court acknowledged that prior decisions had stated that courts should exercise their authority under Rule 52(b) to prevent miscarriages of justice.[162] The Court then noted that, as used in its habeas corpus jurisprudence, the miscarriage-of-justice standard contemplates the conviction of an innocent defendant.[163] However, the Court stated that "we have never held that a Rule 52(b) remedy is only warranted in cases of actual innocence."[164] Under *Olano*, the correct standard to govern plain-error review is whether the error "seriously affects the fairness, integrity or public reputation of judicial proceedings,"[165] and the Court makes it clear that "[a]n error may seriously affect the fairness, integrity or public reputation of judicial proceedings independent of the defendant's innocence."[166] Just as *Sullivan* and *O'Neal* do with the harmless-error doctrine, *Olano* requires that the plain-error doctrine not be applied simply on the basis of the reviewing court's own assessment of the defendant's guilt.

Thus, *Fulminante, Sullivan, O'Neal,* and *Olano* may indicate a shift in the application of the harmless-error and plain-error doctrines to avoid the reaches of guilt-based decision making. And it should not be doubted for a minute that, if federal appellate judges adhere to these decisions, it will make a difference in appellate decision making. For example, in the hypothetical problem that I raised at the outset, an application of the *Sullivan/O'Neal* standard of harmless error will likely produce a reversal, while an application of a *Harrington*-type guilt-based test will likely result in a finding of harmless error. Most judges viewing the record in the hypothetical case will agree that, absent the erroneously admitted coerced confession, there is more than enough evidence to uphold a finding of the defendant's guilt. A judge who relies on a guilt-based theory of harmless error will, accordingly, vote to deny the appeal on grounds of harmless error. In contrast, a judge who follows *Sullivan/O'Neal* will reverse because, at the very least, a judge should have "grave doubts" as to the harmlessness of the error. If a judge believes what Justice Kennedy said in *Fulminante,* that almost nothing is more damaging to a defendant's plea of innocence than a confession,[167] then he or she could not reasonably find that the erroneous admission of the confession could not have contaminated the judgment.

In dealing with my hypothetical case, a judge following *Sullivan/O'Neal* will also realize that, given the possible effect of the confession on the verdict, it does not matter that the evidence against the defendant otherwise looks overwhelming. To indulge this reasoning is to usurp the function of the jury, for the judge would have to assume that the jury would have been persuaded by the remaining evidence, absent the confession. But that is not an assumption that an appellate judge can make. The "eyewitness" in my hypothetical looks great on a cold record, but (by virtue of his demeanor and tone of presentation) he may have been seen by the jury to be a liar. Likewise, the jury may have entirely discounted the video recording because it did not give a front view of the killer. And the remaining evidence offered by the prosecution may have been viewed by the jury as helpful, but hardly determinative. At bottom, the jury may have relied principally on the erroneous confession to reach its result. This is why it would be a hazardous business indeed for an appellate panel to assume that evidence against the defendant, absent the confession, was enough to support a finding of harmless error.

As I said at the outset, I am optimistic but skeptical about the future. My skepticism comes from a worry that appellate judges may fail to acknowledge the force of *O'Neal,* and continue to subscribe to guilt-based decision making. Indeed, in at least one post-*O'Neal* decision issued by the Fourth Circuit in August 1995,[168] the court cited *O'Neal* but still held that the admission of a coerced confession was harmless error primarily because the evidence against the defendant was viewed by the court to be "overwhelming."[169] The court was required to assess the weight of eyewitness testimony, without knowing how the jury might have assessed it absent the erroneous admission of the confession. This decision highlights the dilemma that appellate judges face: there is no way for a judge to consider the possible effect of an error on the verdict without also considering the entire record of evidence. And once the entire record has been considered, a judge faces the risk of being influenced by that evidence. In other words, it is hard for a judge to discount a strong feeling that the defendant is guilty.

There is another problem that my colleagues and I face in trying to apply the harmless-error doctrine. It is often a very hard assignment to distinguish between the effect of an error on the verdict and the effect of an error on one's intuition about factual guilt. In 1969, the dissenting Justices in *Harrington* tried to make this distinction when they said that "[t]he focus of appellate inquiry should be on the character and quality of the tainted evidence as it relates to the untainted evidence and not just on the amount of untainted evidence."[170] I think this is another way of formulating what Justice Breyer says in *O'Neal,* but it more starkly addresses the point that I have in mind. The *Harrington* dissent properly recognizes that, in considering a harmless-error claim, the error not only must be identified as one involving a substantial right, but it must also be assigned some weight in our overall scale of values and then considered in the context of the case at hand. This is no mean assignment.

For example, if my hypothetical is changed so that the error is a simple failure of the police to give a *Miranda* warning (rather than a coerced confession), most judges would be more inclined to find the error harmless. But how do we explain this result?[171] I think it is either because the *Miranda* violation would not be seen to be as significant an infringement as a coerced confession, or because it would be assumed that a coerced confession is more likely to have an influence on the verdict. Presumably, as the dissenters in *Harrington* argued, the way an appellate panel reaches a result is to consider how the "tainted evidence . . . relates to the untainted evidence." This inquiry requires a judge to ask: Did the error involve a central issue in the case? Did the error somehow significantly undermine the untainted evidence? Did the error provide a crucial link in the government's case? Did the error adversely affect the ability of the defendant to present his case? Did the error shift the burden of proof from the government to the defendant? These questions may seem straightforward, but they are not. In the end, it is much easier for a judge to rely on guilt-based decision making, and for that reason I believe the current trend will be difficult to reverse.

In an effort to test some of my thinking, I used my hypothetical problem to conduct a survey among my colleagues on the D.C. Circuit, and among federal prosecutors and public defenders who practice before my court.[172] The participants in the survey were asked to read the hypothetical and then, without conducting any research or conferring with anyone, vote either to "uphold the conviction, finding harmless error," or "reverse and remand for a new trial." Fifty-three persons participated in the survey: eleven judges, twenty-five appellate criminal attorneys from the U.S. Attorney's Office, six appellate criminal attorneys from the Federal Public Defender, and eleven appellate criminal attorneys from the Public Defender Service for the District of Columbia. The results were as follows: twenty-eight (53 percent) voted to uphold the conviction, and twenty-five (47 percent) voted to reverse and remand. Among the judges only two of eleven voted to reverse, equaling only 18 percent. In contrast, all but one of the seventeen public defenders (94 percent) voted to reverse, while seven of twenty-five U.S. Attorneys (28 percent) voted to reverse.

Interestingly, 55 percent of the attorneys surveyed, but only 18 percent of the judges, voted to reverse. In fact, a higher percentage of U.S. Attorneys (28 percent) than judges rejected the claim of harmless error. Probably the most interesting aspect of the survey is that, for the most part, people who voted to uphold the conviction were persuaded by the overwhelming evidence against the defendant, and people who voted to reverse tended to focus on the influence of a coerced confession on a verdict.

Obviously, because of the limitations of the survey, the results reflect nothing more than "first reactions" from a group of experts—judges, prosecutors, and defenders—who routinely deal with criminal appeals and applications of the harmless-error doctrine. Nonetheless, these "first reactions" do nothing to dispel my concerns about the dangerous effects of guilt-based decision making.

An easy way to avoid the problems that I perceive is to endorse a bright-line test, such as the one followed in *Sullivan*, where the Court declared that a constitutionally deficient reasonable-doubt instruction can never be harmless error. In other words, we could return to the pre-*Chapman* practice of assuming that most constitutional errors are not amenable to harmless-error review.[173] Under this test, even the *Miranda* violation becomes easy to resolve. Because a constitutional right is at stake, the error cannot be harmless. However, now that the Court has adopted the distinction between "structural" and "trial" errors[174]—a distinction that I find baffling and mostly unhelpful—we know that there will be no trend toward this bright-line rule. As Chief Justice Rehnquist has made clear (with no apparent disagreement from the rest of the Court), "it is the rare case in which a constitutional violation will not be subject to harmless-error analysis."[175]

Therefore, the question for appellate judges is: Given that constitutional errors will remain subject to a harmless-error analysis, how should judges actually apply *O'Neal's* "effect on the verdict" standard? One possibility, of course, is merely to import a different bright-line rule. Given Justice Breyer's pronouncements in *O'Neal* and the concerns I have articulated, it seems plausible to argue that most constitutional violations necessarily have an effect on the jury and therefore cannot ever be harmless. Such a rule would apply to Miranda violations no less than coerced confessions, and the weight of the incriminating evidence would be irrelevant. While this version of the harmless-error standard would certainly be simpler to apply, it does seem flatly at odds with the Chief Justice's opinion in *Fulminante*. Nevertheless, this approach may eventually find support if the Court continues down the path paved by *O'Neal*.

Absent such a bright-line approach, I think harmless error is best analyzed on a spectrum depending on the importance of the right that has been violated. For example, I consider the coerced confessions in *O'Neal* and in my hypothetical to be such egregious errors that I have no trouble finding that the confession must have had an effect on the verdict. Similarly, cases like *Kotteakos* and *Sullivan*, in which the jury may have been seriously confused by erroneous instructions that go to the heart of the case, seem relatively clear. After all, regardless of whether they are called "structural" or "trial" errors, it would be unfair for appellate judges to assume that the jurors were so well informed in the law that they could overcome erroneous instructions of such importance. Here again, the judge may believe that the result reached by the jury was ultimately correct, but it is hard to say that the error had no effect on the jury because the judge cannot know for sure what a jury might have done had it been instructed correctly.

A harder case is one like *Olano*, where the trial judge erroneously permitted alternate jurors to take part in deliberations. While the Court decided that case under its plain-error jurisprudence because there was no objection raised at trial, had an objection been raised the harmless-error inquiry would have been complicated. On the one hand, the presence of additional people in the jury room surely had an effect on the jury. However, a defendant would never be able to prove that he or she had suffered actual prejudice as a result of the inclusion of extra people. Thus, I suspect many appellate judges would be inclined to say the error was harmless, thereby leaving a clear violation of law unattended. Such a result seems to me to contradict *O'Neal*, which firmly places the burden of proof in the harmless-error analysis on the government. Under *O'Neal*, the defendant should not be required to prove prejudice. Yet, again, I believe it will be very difficult in practice for appellate judges to banish the question of prejudice from their minds when conducting the harmless-error inquiry.

In the end, it need not matter that very few errors are considered "structural," and therefore almost all trial defects will be subject to the harmless-error analysis. As the result in *Fulminante* shows, if the courts aim to be faithful to the approach outlined by Justice Breyer in *O'Neal*, justice will be served. Up until recently, the Court has wasted a lot of words on somewhat artificial distinctions—such as "structural" versus "trial" errors, and constitutional trial errors versus nonconstitutional trial errors, and habeas petitions versus direct appeals, and the test of *Chapman* versus the test of *Kotteakos*—none of which have usefully served to assist the lower appellate courts in their applications of harmless error. Indeed, I have always suspected that the many confusing lines that have been drawn by the Supreme Court have provided further excuses for appellate judges to opt in favor of guilt-based decision making. For this reason, *O'Neal* marks a refreshing change in the direction of the law.

The mission of the appellate courts in evaluating claims of harmless error should be to address significant errors and ensure fundamental fairness. This is what Justice Traynor calls for in his book on harmless error, and this is what the Court endorses in *O'Neal*. I am not sure whether Justice Breyer's prescription is more professorial than practical, but I am sure that what he means to say is important and right.

NOTES

1. *Arizona v. Fulminante*, 499 U.S. 279, 308 (1991) (quoting *Delaware v. Van Arsdall*, 475 U.S. 673, 681 (1986)).

2. The harmless-error doctrine has several sources. With respect to nonconstitutional error, Federal Rule of Criminal Procedure 52(a) states that "[a]ny error, defect, irregularity or variance which does not affect substantial rights shall be disregarded." Fed. R. Crim. P. 52(a). See also infra note 11. With respect to constitutional error, the Supreme Court has held that such error may be harmless if a court is "able to declare a belief that it was harmless beyond a reasonable doubt." *Chapman v. California,* 386 U.S. 18, 24 (1967).

3. Roger J. Traynor, *The Riddle of Harmless Error* (1970).

4. Id. at 23.

5. Id. at 13.

6. Traynor calls this approach the "effect on the judgment" test of harmless error. Id. at 22.

7. 115 S. Ct. 992 (1995).

8. Id. at 994.

9. Benjamin N. Cardozo, *The Nature of the Judicial Process* 51 (1921).

10. *Kotteakos v. United States,* 328 U.S. 750, 759 (1946) (citation omitted).

11. Fed. R. Crim. P. 52(a). A separate statutory provision, 28 U.S.C. s 2111 (1994), applies the harmless-error rule to the federal appellate courts, stating, "[o]n the hearing of any appeal or writ of certiorari in any case, the court shall give judgment after an examination of the record without regard to errors or defects which do not affect the substantial rights of the parties." Id. This statutory provision appears to be unnecessary, however, because Federal Rule of Criminal Procedure 54(a) makes clear that all the Federal Rules "apply to all criminal proceedings . . . in the United States Courts of Appeals." Fed. R. Crim. P. 54(a); see 3A Charles A. Wright, *Federal Practice and Procedure* s 852, at 296 (2d ed. 1982) (stating that s 2111 was enacted "apparently on the mistaken belief that [the criminal harmless-error rule and its civil counterpart] apply only to the district courts").

12. Act of Feb. 26, 1919, ch. 48, 40 Stat. 1181 (repealed 1948).

13. Id.

14. 328 U.S. 750 (1946).

15. Id. at 759.

16. Id. at 760 n.14.

17. 109 S.W. 706 (Mo. 1908).

18. Id. at 711–13.

19. *Kotteakos,* 328 U.S. at 760.

20. Id. at 764–65 (citation and footnote omitted).

21. See Philip J. Mause, "Harmless Constitutional Error: The Implications of Chapman v. California," 53 Minn. L. Rev. 519, 520 (1969) (noting that, until *Chapman,* "there was some suggestion that federal constitutional errors could never be held to be harmless, and that the automatic reversal of any criminal conviction based on such error was required").

22. See *Chapman v. California*, 386 U.S. 18, 42 (1967) (Stewart, J., concurring in the result) ("[I]n a long line of cases, involving a variety of constitutional claims in both state and federal prosecutions, this Court has steadfastly rejected any notion that constitutional violations might be disregarded on the ground that they were 'harmless.' Illustrations of the principle are legion.").

The sole case in which the Supreme Court even arguably applied the harmless-error rule to a constitutional violation prior to 1967 was *Motes v. United States*, 178 U.S. 458 (1900). In *Motes*, the Court held that a violation of the Sixth Amendment's Confrontation Clause was harmless where the defendant's own testimony provided conclusive proof of his guilt. Id. at 475–76. Although the Court did not explicitly phrase its holding in terms of harmless error, it stated that "[i]t would be trifling with the administration of the criminal law to award [Motes] a new trial because of a particular error committed by the trial court, when in effect he has stated under oath that he was guilty of the charge preferred against him." Id. at 476.

23. 386 U.S. 18 (1967).

24. Id. at 22.

25. Id. at 24.

26. 380 U.S. 609, 615 (1965).

27. See *Chapman*, 386 U.S. at 24–26.

28. Id. at 23.

29. See *Chambers v. Maroney*, 399 U.S. 42, 52–53 (1970); *Bumper v. North Carolina*, 391 U.S. 543, 550 (1968).

30. See *Brown v. United States*, 411 U.S. 223, 230–32 (1973); *Harrington v. California*, 395 U.S. 250, 254 (1969).

31. See *Milton v. Wainwright*, 407 U.S. 371, 377–78 (1972).

32. See *Delaware v. Van Arsdall*, 475 U.S. 673, 681–84 (1986).

33. See *Rose v. Clark*, 478 U.S. 570, 579–82 (1986). Violations of numerous other constitutional rights also are subject to harmless-error analysis. See, e.g., *Brecht v. Abrahamson*, 113 S. Ct. 1710, 1716–17 (1993) (violation of due process right against use at trial of defendant's silence after arrest and after receiving Miranda warnings); *Clemons v. Mississippi*, 494 U.S. 738, 752–54 (1990) (inclusion of constitutionally invalid aggravating circumstance in jury instruction at sentencing stage of capital case); *Carella v. California*, 491 U.S. 263, 266–67 (1989) (violation of due process by inclusion of mandatory conclusive presumption in jury instruction); *Coy v. Iowa*, 487 U.S. 1012, 1020–21 (1988) (violation of Sixth Amendment Confrontation Clause by denial of face-to-face confrontation).

34. 499 U.S. 279 (1991).

35. See id. at 309–12.

36. Id. at 306; accord *States v. Hasting*, 461 U.S. 499, 509 (1983) ("Since *Chapman*, the Court has consistently made clear that it is the duty of a reviewing court to consider the trial record as a whole and to ignore errors that are harmless, including most constitutional violations.").

Nevertheless, *Fulminante* makes clear that a few constitutional errors remain automatically reversible. See *Fulminante*, 499 U.S. at 309–10. These errors include the total deprivation of the right to counsel at trial, see *Gideon v. Wainwright*, 372 U.S. 335, 344 (1963), trial by a biased judge, see *Tumey v. Ohio*, 273 U.S. 510, 522 (1927), exclusion of members of the defendant's race from a grand jury, see *Vasquez v. Hillery*, 474 U.S. 254, 264 (1986), the right to self-representation at trial, see *McKaskle v. Wiggins*, 465 U.S. 168, 174 (1984), and the right to public trial, see *Waller v. Georgia*, 467 U.S. 39, 46–47 (1984). In 1993, the Court added another entry to this list, holding that a constitutionally deficient reasonable-doubt instruction never may be harmless error. See *Sullivan*, 113 S. Ct. at 2080–83.

37. *Brady v. Maryland*, 373 U.S. 83, 87 (1963).

38. *United States v. Bagley*, 473 U.S. 667, 682 (1985) (plurality opinion).

39. A defendant also must show prejudice to establish, inter alia, that the government has violated a defendant's due process and Sixth Amendment rights by deporting a favorable witness, see *United States v. Valenzuela-Bernal*, 458 U.S. 858, 873–74 (1982), or that the government's delay in bringing an indictment has violated the defendant's due process rights, see *United States v. Marion*, 404 U.S. 307, 324 (1971).

40. *Strickland v. Washington*, 466 U.S. 668, 688 (1984).

41. Id. at 694.

42. See *Chapman v. California*, 386 U.S. 18, 24 (1967) ("Certainly error, constitutional error, in illegally admitting highly prejudicial evidence or comments, casts on someone other than the person prejudiced by it a burden to show that it was harmless."); see also *United States v. Olano*, 113 S. Ct. 1770, 1776–78 (1993) (ruling that, where harmless-error review applies, burden of persuasion with regard to prejudice is on government); *O'Neal v. McAninch*, 115 S. Ct. 992, 995–96 (1995) (explaining why government bears burden of showing absence of prejudice).

43. 113 S. Ct. 1710 (1993).

44. Id. at 1718–22.

45. Id. at 1721. The *Brecht* majority left open "the possibility that in an unusual case, a deliberate and especially egregious error of the trial type, or one that is combined with a pattern of prosecutorial misconduct, might so infect the integrity of the proceeding as to warrant the grant of habeas relief, even if it did not substantially influence the jury's verdict." Id. at 1722 n.9. However, as Justice O'Connor noted in her dissent, this potential exception appears to be "exceedingly narrow." Id. at 1731 (O'Connor, J., dissenting).

46. Id. at 1723, 1724–25 (Stevens, J., concurring) (citations omitted).

47. Id. at 1722.

48. *O'Neal v. McAninch*, 115 S. Ct. 992, 995–96 (1995).

49. See supra text accompanying note 13.

50. Donald A. Winslow, Note, "Harmful Use of Harmless Error in Criminal Cases," 64 Cornell L. Rev. 538, 545 n.36 (1979).

Winslow surveyed the prevalence of harmless-error analysis in the federal courts of appeals by conducting a LEXIS computer search of all cases decided by such courts between January 1, 1960, and December 31, 1978, and then ascertaining how many of those cases employed the phrase "harmless error." Id. at 544 n.36. I have updated this survey by conducting an identical LEXIS search in the GENFED library and USAPP file for the period from January 1, 1979, to December 31, 1994. See infra note 52. As Winslow acknowledged,

> [t]his sampling technique is imprecise. It is overinclusive because it retrieves all cases discussing harmless error, not merely those that hold an error harmless. It is underinclusive because it does not identify cases that hold an error harmless without using the phrase "harmless error." Therefore, this study does not measure with exactness the use of the harmless error doctrine; it only suggests that this use is on the rise.

Winslow, supra, at 546 n.36.

The same flaws inhere in my own study. In addition, the study does not isolate the use of the phrase "harmless error" in criminal cases, which is the focus of my discussion here. Nonetheless, it provides a general benchmark by which to gauge the use of harmless-error analysis in the courts of appeals.

51. Winslow, supra note 50, at 545 n.36.

52. [A chart with statistics generated by Judge Edwards's LEXIS survey has been omitted for reasons of space—ED.]

53. See, e.g., *United States v. Leon*, 468 U.S. 897, 913 (1984) (holding exclusionary rule inapplicable to Fourth Amendment violations where police act in good faith reliance on facially valid search warrant); *Nix v. Williams*, 467 U.S. 431, 448 (1984) (holding exclusionary rule inapplicable to Fourth Amendment violations where evidence in question inevitably would have been discovered by independent, lawful means).

54. See, e.g., *United States v. Allen*, 960 F.2d 1055, 1059 (D.C. Cir.) (declining to reach question involving admission of alleged hearsay "because even if admission of the testimony ... constituted error, it was undoubtedly harmless"), cert. denied, 113 S. Ct. 231 (1992).

55. See *Winslow*, supra note 50, at 542 ("The purpose of the harmless error doctrine is to save the time and effort of retrial. It was not meant to shelter courts from difficult questions of law.").

56. See, e.g., *United States v. Williams*, 980 F.2d 1463, 1466 n.1 (D.C. Cir. 1992) (finding no error in admission of expert testimony, but stating that, "[e]ven if [the expert's] testimony had violated [Federal] Rule [of Evidence] 704(b), its admission would have been a harmless error").

57. Transcript of Oral Argument at 30, *United States v. Maddox*, 48 F.3d 555 (D.C. Cir. Jan. 19, 1995) (No. 93–3172).

58. *United States v. Maddox*, 48 F.3d 555, 560 (D.C. Cir. 1995) (finding that "the

collateral consequences of [the defendant's] additional convictions amply demonstrate the prejudice of the trial judge's error").

59. Fed. R. Crim. P. 52(b).

60. Id. advisory committee's note.

61. *Wiborg v. United States*, 163 U.S. 632, 658 (1896).

62. 297 U.S. 157 (1936).

63. Id. at 160.

64. 456 U.S. 152 (1982).

65. Id. at 163 (emphasis added).

66. Id. at 163 n.14.

67. 470 U.S. 1, 15 (1985) ("[T]he plain-error exception to the contemporaneous-objection rule is to be 'used sparingly, solely in those circumstances in which a miscarriage of justice would otherwise result.'" (quoting *Frady*, 456 U.S. at 163 n.14)).

68. See id.

69. See, e.g., *United States v. Neumann*, 887 F.2d 880, 882 (8th Cir. 1989), cert. denied, 495 U.S. 949 (1990); *United States v. Yamin*, 868 F.2d 130, 132 (5th Cir.), cert. denied, 492 U.S. 924 (1989); *United States v. Whaley*, 830 F.2d 1469, 1476 (7th Cir. 1987), cert. denied, 486 U.S. 1009 (1988).

70. 113 S. Ct. 1770 (1993).

71. Id. at 1779 (alteration in original) (quoting *Atkinson*, 297 U.S. 157, 160 (1936)).

72. See id. ("We previously have explained that the discretion conferred by Rule 52(b) should be employed in those circumstances in which a miscarriage of justice would otherwise result." (internal quotations omitted)).

73. Fed. R. Crim. P. 52(b).

74. 395 U.S. 250 (1969).

75. See *Bruton v. United States*, 391 U.S. 123, 137 (1968).

76. *Harrington*, 395 U.S. at 254.

77. Id.

78. Id. at 255 (Brennan, J., dissenting).

79. Id.

80. See supra notes 23–58 and accompanying text.

81. Indeed, a 1994 informal survey of post-1992 federal case law determined that federal courts are approximately twice as likely to use *Harrington*'s "overwhelming evidence" formulation of the constitutional harmless-error test as *Chapman*'s formulation, focusing on whether the error contributed to the conviction. See Gregory Mitchell, "Against 'Overwhelming' Appellate Activism: Constraining Harmless Error Review," 82 Cal. L. Rev. 1335, 1348 n.82 (1994). The same survey found that, of twenty cases in which courts employed the *Harrington* "overwhelming evidence" approach to harmless-error questions, all twenty resulted in a finding of harmless error. Id. at 1349. By contrast, only one of seventeen cases employing the *Chapman* approach resulted in a harmless error finding. Id.

82. The conflict between whether to emphasize the factual guilt of the defendant or the integrity of the procedure by which the defendant is prosecuted and tried is an example of the dichotomy between what Herbert Packer has called the Crime Control and Due Process models of the criminal process. See Herbert L. Packer, *The Limits of the Criminal Sanction* 149–73 (1968).

83. See, e.g., *United States v. Williams*, 980 F.2d 1463, 1466 n.1 (D.C. Cir. 1992) (stating that admission of expert testimony in violation of Federal Rule of Evidence 704(b) was harmless error due to "overwhelming evidence" of defendant's guilt); *United States v. Stock*, 948 F.2d 1299, 1302 (D.C. Cir. 1991) (stating that "core of the inquiry" in determining harmlessness of constitutional error in curtailment of cross-examination "is the strength of the government's residual case").

84. *Traynor*, supra note 3, at 28 (footnote omitted). Justice Marshall recognized this very problem in his dissent in *Schneble v. Florida*, 405 U.S. 427 (1972), where the majority found a violation of the *Bruton* doctrine to be harmless error based on overwhelming evidence of the petitioner's guilt, id. at 428. Marshall stated that "[t]he mistake the Court makes is in assuming that the jury accepted as true all of the other evidence." Id. at 436 (Marshall, J., dissenting).

85. See, e.g., *Brecht v. Abrahamson*, 113 S. Ct. 1710, 1724 (1993) (Stevens, J., concurring) ("The habeas court cannot ask only whether it thinks the petitioner would have been convicted even if the constitutional error had not taken place.").

86. *Lane*, 474 U.S. at 465 (Brennan, J., concurring in part and dissenting in part); see also *Rose v. Clark*, 478 U.S. 570, 593 (1986) (Blackmun, J., dissenting) ("The Constitution does not allow an appellate court to arrogate to itself a function that the defendant, under the Sixth Amendment, can demand be performed by a jury.").

87. 405 U.S. 427 (1972).

88. Id. at 431.

89. *Delaware v. Van Arsdall*, 475 U.S. 673, 681 (1986).

90. *Rose*, 478 U.S. at 579.

91. *Arizona v. Fulminante*, 499 U.S. 279, 306–12 (1991) (opinion of Rehnquist, C.J.).

92. Id. at 307–8.

93. Id. at 310 (quoting *Rose*, 478 U.S. at 577–78 (citation omitted)).

94. Id. at 309–10; see Charles J. Ogletree, Jr., "*Arizona v. Fulminante*: The Harm of Applying Harmless Error to Coerced Confessions," 105 Harv. L. Rev. 152, 162 (1991) ("To the *Fulminante* majority, a trial error seems to be one for which we can sometimes know for sure whether it has caused inaccuracy in a trial outcome, and a structural error seems to be one for which we can never know with any certainty.").

95. *Fulminante*, 499 U.S. at 297.

96. Id. at 295–96 (opinion of White, J.)(citations omitted).

97. Id. at 313 (Kennedy, J., concurring in the judgment).

98. See supra text accompanying notes 64–69.

99. See, e.g., *United States v. Stone*, 987 F.2d 469, 471 (7th Cir. 1993) ("[P]lain error must be of such a great magnitude that it probably changed the outcome of the trial." (internal quotation omitted)).

100. 830 F.2d 1469 (7th Cir. 1987), cert. denied, 486 U.S. 1009 (1988).

101. Id. at 1476 (citation omitted).

102. See *Hartness v. Bush*, 919 F.2d 170, 174–81 (D.C. Cir. 1990) (Edwards, J., dissenting), cert. denied, 501 U.S. 1251 (1991); *United States v. Tavolacci*, 895 F.2d 1423, 1430–31 (D.C. Cir. 1990) (Edwards, J., dissenting); Harry T. Edwards, "The Judicial Function and the Elusive Goal of Principled Decision-Making," 1991 Wis. L. Rev. 837, 839–41.

103. See Federal Judicial Ctr., Structural and Other Alternatives for the Federal Courts of Appeals 18 (1993). The number of filings rose from 13,694 in 1972 to 43,481 in 1992. Id.

104. See *Kotteakos v. United States*, 328 U.S. 750, 764 (1946) ("[T]he question is, not were [jurors] right in their judgment, regardless of the error or its effect upon the verdict. It is rather what effect the error had or reasonably may be taken to have had upon the jury's decision.").

105. U.S. Const. art. III, s 2, cl. 3 ("The Trial of all Crimes, except in Cases of Impeachment, shall be by Jury."); id. amend. VI ("In all criminal prosecutions, the accused shall enjoy the right to a speedy and public trial, by an impartial jury of the State and district wherein the crime shall have been committed.").

106. *Bollenbach v. United States*, 326 U.S. 607, 615 (1946).

107. *United States v. Martin Linen Supply Co.*, 430 U.S. 564, 572–73 (1977) (explaining that basis of prohibition is jury's function to stand between accused and the government).

108. *Rose v. Clark*, 478 U.S. 570, 578 (1986).

109. Traynor, supra note 3, at 13–14.

110. Justice Traynor has discussed in detail the defects presented by what he describes as "a quasi trial on appeal." Id. at 20–21 (footnote omitted).

111. See supra notes 78–79 and accompanying text.

112. For a discussion of how these two concerns compete throughout the criminal process, see generally Packer, supra note 82, at 149–246.

113. One notable example of this idea is the adage underlying much of our Fourth Amendment jurisprudence that "a man's house is his castle," *Miller v. United States*, 357 U.S. 301, 307 (1958).

114. *Brown v. Allen*, 344 U.S. 443, 498 (1953) (opinion of Frankfurter, J.).

115. Traynor, supra note 3, at 50 ("If appellate judges forthrightly opened the way to a new trial whenever a judgment was contaminated by error, there would be a cleansing effect on the trial process. A sharp appellate watch would in the long run deter error at the outset, thereby lessening the need of appeal and retrials.").

116. See *Rose v. Clark*, 478 U.S. 570, 588–89 (1986) (Stevens, J., concurring) ("An

automatic application of harmless-error review in case after case, and for error after error, can only encourage prosecutors to subordinate the interest in respecting the Constitution to the ever-present and always powerful interest in obtaining a conviction in a particular case."); see also *United States v. Jackson*, 429 F.2d 1368, 1373 (7th Cir. 1970) (Clark, J., sitting by designation) ("'Harmless error' is swarming around the 7th Circuit like bees. Before someone is stung, it is suggested that the prosecutors enforce Miranda to the letter and that the police obey it with like diligence; otherwise the courts may have to act to correct a presently alarming situation.").

117. 365 U.S. 534 (1961).

118. Id. at 541.

119. Id. at 540–41; see also *Bram v. United States*, 168 U.S. 532, 542–43 (1897).

120. *Arizona v. Fulminante*, 499 U.S. 279, 293 (1991) (White, J., dissenting) (quoting *Blackburn v. Alabama*, 361 U.S. 199, 206–7 (1960), and *Spano v. New York*, 360 U.S. 315, 320–21 (1959)).

121. Indeed, Justice White's *Fulminante* dissent criticized the majority for categorizing admission of a coerced confession as a "trial error" that may be weighed against other evidence to evaluate the reliability of the trial outcome. According to Justice White, the right against use of such a confession "'protect[s] important values that are unrelated to the truth-seeking function of the trial.'" 499 U.S. at 295 (quoting *Rose v. Clark*, 478 U.S. 570, 587 (1986) (Stevens, J., concurring)); see also Ogletree, supra note 94, at 162 (arguing that "the [*Fulminante*] Court's analysis . . . fail[s] by virtue of its insufficient recognition of other values in our criminal justice system").

122. *Fulminante*, 499 U.S. at 313 (Kennedy, J., concurring in the judgment).

123. 932 F.2d 517 (6th Cir.), cert. denied, 502 U.S. 890 (1991).

124. Id. at 518. The Sixth Circuit's opinion states that "[t]he police covered the suspects' heads with a sheet so that they would not see undercover agents who were among the officers searching the house." Id.

125. In this regard, the Sixth Circuit observed that "[i]t is not clear why the three persons in the house were placed in custody in this manner immediately after the police entered to execute the search warrant. The defendant, however, does not raise a false arrest claim or a claim that probable cause for restraint was missing." Id. at 518 n.2.

126. Id. at 518.

127. Id. at 518–19.

128. Id. at 521–22. Because the court assumed, but did not decide, that the statement was coerced, *Daniel* constitutes yet another example of judicial use of the harmless-error doctrine to avoid decision of a difficult issue. See supra notes 54–56 and accompanying text.

129. 297 U.S. 278, 281–83 (1936).

130. 322 U.S. 143, 149–50 (1944).

131. See *Spano v. New York*, 360 U.S. 315, 321 (1959) ("[A]s law enforcement officers become more responsible, and the methods used to extract confessions more sophisticated, our duty to enforce federal constitutional protections does not cease. It only becomes more difficult because of the more delicate judgments to be made.").

132. *Boyd v. United States*, 116 U.S. 616, 630 (1886).

133. See *Weeks v. United States*, 232 U.S. 383, 393 (1914) ("If letters and private documents can thus be seized and held and used in evidence against a citizen accused of an offense, the protection of the Fourth Amendment declaring his right to be secure against such searches and seizures is of no value, and, so far as those thus placed are concerned, might as well be stricken from the Constitution."); see also *Stone v. Powell*, 428 U.S. 465, 486 (1976) ("The primary justification for the exclusionary rule . . . is the deterrence of police conduct that violates Fourth Amendment rights.").

134. *Silverthorne Lumber Co. v. United States*, 251 U.S. 385, 392 (1920).

135. Id.

136. *United States v. Leon*, 468 U.S. 897, 913 (1984).

137. *Murray v. United States*, 487 U.S. 533, 537 (1988).

138. *Nix v. Williams*, 467 U.S. 431, 443–44 (1984).

139. Of course, which rights should qualify as substantial is often a very difficult question.

140. *Arizona v. Fulminante*, 499 U.S. 279, 306–12 (1991) (opinion of Rehnquist, C.J.).

141. See id. at 295–302 (opinion of White, J.).

142. Id. at 313–14 (Kennedy, J., concurring in the judgment).

143. 113 S. Ct. 2078 (1993).

144. Id. at 2081–82 (citations omitted).

145. Id. at 2082 (citations omitted).

146. See id. (describing *Fulminante* framework as "[a]nother mode of analysis" that "leads to the same conclusion that harmless-error analysis does not apply").

147. Id. at 2083 (Rehnquist, C.J., concurring).

148. Id. at 2084.

149. 115 S. Ct. 992 (1995).

150. Id. at 994.

151. Id.

152. See id. at 995–96.

153. Id. at 995 (quoting *Kotteakos v. United States*, 328 U.S. 750, 765 (1946)) (emphasis omitted).

154. Id. at 995.

155. Id. at 995–96; see supra notes 47–48 and accompanying text.

156. Id. at 994.

157. Traynor, supra note 3.

158. *O'Neal*, 115 S. Ct. at 994–95, 997 (citation omitted).

159. Fed. R. Crim. P. 52(a); see supra note 2.

160. Indeed, in a decision issued during the same term as *O'Neal*, the Court applied a similar analysis to a Brady violation. In *Kyles v. Whitley*, 115 S. Ct. 1555, 1566 (1995), the Court ruled that, in determining whether the defendant has been prejudiced by a violation of Brady, "[t]he question is not whether the defendant would more likely than not have received a different verdict with the evidence, but whether in its absence he received a fair trial, understood as a trial resulting in a verdict worthy of confidence." The Court then went on to reject a "sufficiency of the evidence" test for determining when the government's nondisclosure of evidence violates Brady. Id. at 1558.

161. 113 S. Ct. 1770 (1993).

162. Id. at 1779.

163. Id.

164. Id.

165. Id. (internal quotation and alteration omitted).

166. Id. (internal quotation omitted).

167. See supra text accompanying note 97.

168. *Correll v. Thompson*, 63 F.3d 1279 (4th Cir. 1995), cert. denied, 116 S. Ct. 688 (1996).

169. Id. at 1291–92. But see *Cooper v. Taylor*, 70 F.3d 1454, 1463–69 (4th Cir. 1995) (distinguishing *Correll* and following *O'Neal*'s harmless-error analysis).

170. *Harrington v. California*, 395 U.S. 250, 256 (1969) (Brennan, J., dissenting).

171. For an excellent discussion of "mere Miranda violations," see Yale Kamisar, "On the 'Fruits' of Miranda Violations, Coerced Confessions, and Compelled Testimony," 93 Mich. L. Rev. 929, 953, 968–75 (1995).

172. The full details of the survey appear in the Appendix to this article. [The Appendix has been omitted for reasons of space. For its results, see 70 N.Y.U.L. Rev. 1167 (1995)—ED.]

173. See supra notes 21–22 and accompanying text.

174. See supra notes 91–94 and accompanying text.

175. *Sullivan v. Louisiana*, 113 S. Ct. 2078, 2083 (1993) (Rehnquist, C.J., concurring).

Chapter 8

How James Madison Interpreted
the Constitution

Richard S. Arnold

The topic I have chosen is "How James Madison Interpreted the Constitution." As I sat down to write, I realized that this title is itself ambiguous. It could refer to the various substantive positions Madison took on constitutional questions throughout his life—whether the Bank of the United States was constitutional, whether Congress could build roads and canals, and the like. Or it could refer to methodology—did Madison believe in "original intent," to use that dread phrase so familiar in modern controversy, was he a textualist, and so forth. I intend the phrase to be understood primarily in the latter sense: what criteria, what sources did Madison use in arriving at his own opinion of the meaning of the Constitution? One of the things you learn very quickly when you begin trying to interpret the Constitution is that the words themselves are almost never without some ambiguity. So perhaps it is fitting that the title of a lecture on constitutional interpretation should itself be ambiguous, even though I didn't realize it when I first dreamed up the title.

You may also be wondering why anyone cares what James Madison thought about constitutional interpretation. I remember one occasion when a student asked Professor Paul Freund what Thomas Jefferson would think of a certain constitutional question if he were alive today. Professor Freund answered: "If Thomas Jefferson were alive today, he'd be too old to think." The question of the relevance of Madison's views is one you will have

This lecture was delivered on October 8, 1996, and appeared in 72 N.Y.U.L. Rev. 267 (1997).

to answer for yourselves. My own view is that history is important because it's intrinsically interesting, or, to put it in plain language, history is fun. It may also be of some use in the work we have to do in our own time, and I will suggest why at the end of this talk.

I.

So what about Mr. Madison? Let me begin by reminding you of a few facts about his life and work, facts we all learned at one time or another, but that it helps to recall.[1] James Madison was born in 1751 and died in his eighty-fifth year, in 1836.[2] He was often in poor health. In fact, in 1772, at the age of twenty-one, having recently graduated from the College of New Jersey, now called Princeton, he was sure he would die young. "[M]y sensations for many months past," he wrote to a friend, "have intimated to me not to expect a long or healthy life."[3] Almost sixty years later, in another letter, he seemed almost surprised to be still alive. "Having outlived so many of my co[n]temporaries," he said, "I ought not to forget that I may be thought to have outlived myself."[4] In 1831, when this letter was written, only Madison and Charles Carroll of Carrollton survived of the political leadership of the Revolution, and when Madison died five years later he was the last survivor.[5]

From 1774, when he became a member of the Committee of Safety in Orange County, Virginia, until 1817, when he completed his second term as President of the United States, Madison was almost continuously in public office.[6] He was a member of the Virginia General Assembly and a passionate defender there of liberty of conscience. He was a member of Congress both before and after the adoption of the Constitution, most notably in the first four Congresses of the new government, from 1789 to 1798. He drafted the Bill of Rights. He was, with Hamilton and Jay, the author of *The Federalist Papers* under the pen name "Publius."[7] He was Secretary of State for eight years under President Thomas Jefferson, and in that capacity was the winning party (but what a Pyrrhic victory it was) in the most famous lawsuit in American history, an original action in the Supreme Court styled *William Marbury v. James Madison, Secretary of State of the United States.*[8]

And, most importantly for present purposes, Mr. Madison was the prime mover in the drafting and adoption of the Constitution. He was the quintessential Founder, known for generations by the title "Father of the Constitution." He was a constitutional and political scholar and logician of the first rank, though not encumbered by membership in the Bar, having studied law only briefly and never practiced. He was the leading intellectual force in the Constitutional Convention at Philadelphia in 1787, and through his notes of the proceedings, he is our main source of knowledge about what went on there.[9] And, at the crucial Virginia State Convention of 1788, at which the Constitution was ratified by the narrow margin of eighty-nine to seventy-nine,[10] Madison triumphed in debate over none other than that glorious orator of the Revolution, Patrick Henry.[11] Still, in spite of all these achievements and contributions, he was, in company with other leaders of his own and other times, viciously attacked in the press. Madison was, as Ingersoll put it, "[e]xposed to that licentious abuse which leading men in free countries with an unshackled press cannot escape."[12]

II.

So how did the Father of the Constitution go about divining the meaning of his own creation? One would expect that he would appeal, above all, to the desires and intentions of the Framers at Philadelphia, in whose number he enjoyed such pride of place. One can imagine Mr. Madison, in the heat of argument over some point of interpretation, triumphantly carrying the day by quoting from his own notes. To our surprise, perhaps, this is not at all what happened. In fact, Madison ended up almost entirely negating the subjective intention of the delegates at Philadelphia as a consideration of any importance in constitutional interpretation. He was not, however, completely consistent in that respect, and the history of his inconsistency is of some interest.

Madison's first post in the new government was as a member of the House of Representatives from Virginia.[13] He was, that is, a successful politician. When he and the other Representatives and Senators finally assembled in sufficient numbers to make a quorum here in New York, the temporary capital, the Constitution, grand as it was, was just a piece of paper.[14] It had to be brought to life by practice in order to become a living plan of government.[15] So everything the First Congress did was of constitutional significance, in some sense. That body was "a sort of continuing constitutional convention."[16] In fact, eight Representatives and eleven U.S. Senators had been delegates to the Philadelphia Convention.[17] One of the first bills introduced was one proposed by Madison to create the Departments of Foreign Affairs (now called State), the Treasury, and War (now part of the Department of Defense). The bill provided, as indeed the Constitution itself did, that the secretaries of these departments would be appointed by the President, by and with the advice and consent of the Senate, but would be removable by the President alone.[18] Ultimately the House agreed with Madison that the removal power was necessarily, under the Constitution, a solely executive attribute, and that has been the prevailing view, more or less, ever since.

In the course of this debate several interesting kinds of arguments were made about how to interpret the Constitution. Elbridge Gerry of Massachusetts, for example, hardly the most stable of characters, declared himself opposed to any sort of interpretation at all. Mr. Gerry was "decidedly against putting any construction whatever" on the Constitution.[19] He thought that "all construction" was "dangerous, or unnatural."[20] The words alone are authoritative. Interpretation serves only to distort. This view, admirable enough in the abstract, breaks down immediately in practice, but it was a well-entrenched part of the intellectual culture of the times. Anglo-American Protestantism, taking its cue from Martin Luther's cry, "sola Scriptura," took the position that "the only authoritative, and indeed the only safe, interpreter of Scripture was Scripture itself."[21] This view lives on today whenever anyone says that our true allegiance should be to the Constitution itself, not to anyone's interpretation of it.

In this debate Madison argued from the Constitution's text and from what he saw as its overall plan, "spirit," or "intention," though the reference to "intention" seems to refer to the theme of the whole document rather than to what may have been in the minds of its drafters.[22] Madison also argued from practicality, from what he saw as the inconvenient consequences of requiring the consent of Congress or of the Senate for removal of one of the heads of the principal departments, but, in a bow to what we would now call originalism, he explained that such arguments "were intended only to throw light upon what was meant by the compilers of the constitution."[23] The term "compilers" is vague, maybe deliberately so. It could mean the Framers at Philadelphia; it could mean the delegates to the state-ratifying conventions; it could mean all of the above.

I digress briefly to mention what seems to me the most interesting, even hilarious, aspect of the debate over the removal power, though it did not directly concern Madison himself. I can do no better than quote at length from Jack Rakove's brand-new book, *Original Meanings*:[24]

One noteworthy effort to draw a leading inference from the records of ratification was made, however. After failing to prove that removal required impeachment, William L. Smith insisted that the consent of the Senate was constitutionally required to remove as well as appoint. This opinion was supported by "[a] publication of no inconsiderable eminence, in the class of political writings on the constitution," Smith told the House on June 16. He then read a passage from Federalist 77 affirming that "The consent of [the Senate] would be necessary to displace as well as appoint." But a rude shock awaited Smith. As he wrote to Edward Rutledge, the brother of the Framer, shortly thereafter:

> the next day [Egbert] Benson [of New York] sent me a note across the House to this effect: that Publius had informed him since the preceding day's debate, that upon mature reflection he had changed his opinion & was now convinced that the President alone should have the power of removal at pleasure; He is a Candidate for the office of Secretary of Finance!

The candidate was, of course, Hamilton; and Smith probably knew that Madison was the other of the "two gentlemen of great information" who had written as "Publius." Neither man felt obliged to stand by their joint work. So ended the first effort to use extrinsic evidence taken from the period of the adoption of the Constitution to interpret its meaning.[25]

In my mind's eye I can see Colonel Hamilton, as he was known at the time, quietly approaching Congressman Benson on some side street a few blocks south of here, and solemnly imparting the news that on mature reflection he had changed his published opinion of the year before and now stood foursquare in support of the power of the President, the officer whose favor he now wished to attract. It is hard to think of an intention more original than this.

Let's go forward a couple of years now to 1791, the Third and last Session of the First Congress. The debate this time was over the bill to create the First Bank of the United States, one of the defining issues that split city and country, East and West, North and South, strict constructionists and latitudinarians, over the first half century or so of our history as an independent nation.[26] Madison, in league with that great master of party politics, Thomas Jefferson, opposed the Bank on constitutional grounds. Secretary Hamilton and, in the end, President Washington supported it, and they prevailed. Briefly recall what the constitutional debate was about, though it seems passing strange at this remove of time. The Constitution says nothing about banks, or indeed about congressional power to create any kind of corporation. The Bank's proponents had to argue in favor of implied powers, powers appropriate to give full effect to other powers granted expressly.

In the case of the Bank, two express powers were relied upon, the power "[t]o regulate Commerce with foreign Nations, and among the several States, and with the Indian Tribes"[27] and the power "[t]o coin Money [and] regulate the value thereof."[28] It is not impossible to regulate commerce or coin money or to regulate its value without creating a national bank, but, advocates argued, a bank would help. The Bank would fall under another provision, the famous Necessary and Proper Clause, granting Congress the power "[t]o make all Laws which shall be necessary and proper for carrying into Execution the foregoing Powers, and all other Powers vested by this Constitution in the Government of the United States, or in any Department or Officer thereof."[29]

Madison's main basis for constitutional opposition to the Bank was his general conviction that the federal government was, and had been intended to be, a government of limited and enumerated powers.[30] If the argument based on the Necessary and Proper Clause were accepted, he thought—and history has largely proved him right—there would be few limits on the national legislative power. But he also made a more specific appeal to the proceedings at Philadelphia. He himself had proposed that Congress be given a general power to issue charters of incorporation. When the committee of detail did not include such a power in the draft it reported, Madison renewed his motion. It was not successful, and the Constitution as proposed and adopted contained no such express grant of authority. Madison thought this bit of history persuasive, and justified his position as follows: "In controverted cases, the meaning of the parties to the instrument, if to be collected by reasonable inference, is a proper guide. Contemporary and concurrent expositions are a reasonable evidence of the meaning of the parties."[31]

Madison lost this argument and later, as we shall see, caved in entirely on the question of the constitutionality of the Bank, but the passage is interesting because it takes a rather different approach to constitutional interpretation from the one Madison adopted in later life. Here, by referring to "the meaning of the parties"[32] to the Constitution, Madison may be saying that the document is to be construed like a contract. But if the Constitution is a contract, who are the parties? Surely not the Framers. They are more like drafters. The parties are the whole "People of the United States"[33] or perhaps the (not yet created) federal government on the one hand and the sovereign states on the other or, perhaps better, the people of the several states as represented in the ratifying conventions.[34] Indeed, Madison referred to some general passages about limited powers in the ratifying-convention debates.[35] The difficulty is that the delegates to those conventions did not and could not know in any comprehensive way what the deliberations at Philadelphia had been like. The Convention itself was held in secret; Madison's notes, the fullest of any, were not published until 1840, and no notes at all were published until 1820.[36]

The next great constitutional debate in Congress that is relevant for our purposes occurred in 1796.[37] The Senate had ratified the Jay Treaty with Great Britain, negotiated by John Jay while serving concurrently as Minister to Great Britain and Chief Justice of the United States. The text of the Treaty was not made public until it had been ratified. (In fact, all proceedings in the Senate were secret until 1795.)[38] It became instantly controversial. The Republicans, who in general were more pro-French and anti-British than the Federalists, saw a way of making the issue of the Treaty concrete. They tried to assert a sort of constitutional authority of the House of Representatives in treaty making, and, indeed, if public funds need to be appropriated in order to execute a treaty, the House unquestionably has a legitimate say.

In March 1796, Washington asked the House to appropriate funds to implement the Treaty.[39] The Republicans then introduced a resolution asking the President to provide the House with the executive papers, reflecting the negotiating history, to enable it to place the Treaty in its proper light. Does any of this sound familiar? Federalists answered that the Treaty should be considered on the basis of its words alone. On March 10, Madison joined the fight on the side of the House. The resolution passed, sixty-two to thirty-seven.[40] Washington replied in a memorandum on March 30.[41] Hamilton had reminded him that the Convention had defeated a motion to involve the House in treaty making. Washington had deposited the Journal of the Convention with the Department of State. The Journal reflected that a motion to require that treaties be ratified by law had been explicitly rejected. The President refused to deliver the papers, claiming what we would now call executive privilege. Notice that Washington's appeal was not to the debates or anyone's notes of them, but to the Journal, the formal record of proceedings that the Convention had officially approved.

The House continued to pursue the issue. On April 6, 1796, Madison made another speech.[42] He affected to believe that Washington's appeal to the Journal of the Convention was improper, even though he had in 1791 reasoned in much the same way.[43] He had been stung by criticism from Representative William Vans Murray of Maryland. During a speech on March 23, Murray urged Madison, as a principal Framer, to give the House the benefit of his recollection of the drafting history.

If the Convention spoke mysterious phrases, and the gentleman helped to utter them, will not the gentleman aid the expounding of the mystery? If the gentleman was the Pythia in the temple, ought he not to explain the ambiguous language of the oracle? To no man's expositions would he listen with more deference.[44]

In his response, Madison disclaimed the ability to speak for the intention of the whole body of the Convention. The Framers had disagreed in their opinions. He also had a personal reason to avoid this kind of argument, because he had been criticized for using it during the Bank debate of 1791. He then said:

But, after all, whatever veneration might be entertained for the body of men who formed our Constitution, the sense of that body could never be regarded as the oracular guide in expounding the Constitution. As the instrument came from them, it was nothing more than the draft of a plan, nothing but a dead letter, until life and validity were breathed into it by the voice of the people, speaking through the several State Conventions. If we were to look, therefore, for the meaning of the instrument beyond the face of the instrument, we must look for it, not in the General Convention, which proposed, but in the State Conventions, which accepted and ratified the Constitution.[45]

Turning to the evidence, Madison was not able to find in the published records of the state conventions much that was useful. Even the Virginia debates, as published, "contained internal evidences in abundance of chasms, and misconceptions of what was said."[46] A better authority, he thought, was amendments proposed by the state conventions.[47] He speculated that the Framers of those amendments would have favored the construction now advanced by the Republican majority. It was not explained how proposals designed to remedy perceived defects in the Constitution could prevail over the explicit language of the Treaty Clause. It is hard to shake the suspicion— and I hope you will not think me disrespectful for voicing it—that Madison was simply using the arguments he thought best suited to his position of the moment.

III.

The position taken by Madison during the debates over the Jay Treaty in 1796, so far as I can tell, remained his firm opinion for the rest of his life.[48] He never again relied mainly on the subjective intentions of the delegates in

Philadelphia and, in fact, he took care that his notes of the Convention's de-liberations not even be published until after his death. But other people's notes began to leak out, and Madison's reaction to this development was in-teresting. In 1808, when Madison was running for President as, of course, a Jeffersonian Republican, a campaign pamphlet was published in support of his rival, George Clinton, Governor of New York and a strong Anti-Federal-ist.[49] The pamphlet was edited by Clinton's son-in-law, none other than Ed-mond Genet, known to history as Citizen Genet, the trouble-making Min-ister of France to the United States who had kicked up so much dust in the 1790s and then settled permanently in America. The pamphlet consisted of quotations from notes of the Convention taken by Robert Yates, a delegate from New York. Yates had been at the Convention for only seven of the six-teen weeks and had not signed the Constitution, but his notes were, at the time, the only first-hand source of the Convention's deliberations available to the public. (The official Journal of the Convention was not printed and published, by order of Congress, until 1820.)[50] The notes portrayed Madi-son as a strong nationalist. There was, of course, a great deal of truth in this portrayal; Madison had proposed to the Convention, unsuccessfully, to give the federal government a veto over state laws. One can imagine that this publication caused Madison a degree of political embarrassment, but he did not counter the pamphlet by publishing his own notes or even, so far as I have discovered, quoting from them in his own defense. Perhaps he thought such a tactic would be self-serving and unpersuasive.

In any case, the problem recurred in 1821, when Yates's notes were pub-lished in full.[51] Yates had died twenty years before. As I have noted, he was a fierce Anti-Federalist and had been at the Convention for only seven of the sixteen weeks it was in session. He had, however, become Chief Justice of the highest court of New York, and his account was something to be reckoned with. Madison's friends began urging him to publish his own notes, and, in-deed, the fact that he had taken such pains to make them in the first place—he later said the labor involved had endangered his health—and then pre-served them for so many years must mean that he considered them of great value. Madison had in fact begun as early as 1780, at the age of twenty-nine, to keep and compile various letters, notes, essays, and other papers contain-ing the record of his public life. Still, and even in the face of what he thought to be the distortions of the record made by Yates, he kept his own notes pri-vate. Critics, including Professor Crosskey, might say that Madison needed time to alter his notes to make them fit the states' rights, proslavery needs of the Southern politics of the time.[52] I leave that controversy to one side. I will say only that I start, in Madison's case as in that of others, with a presumption of rectitude and I am not convinced that it has been overcome in this instance.

Let's look at what Madison himself said about the notes at the time. For one thing, he continued to downplay their value as indicators of the meaning of the Constitution. "[W]hatever might have been the opinions entertained in forming the Constitution," he wrote to his brother-in-law, John G. Jackson, in 1821, "it was the duty of all to support it in its true meaning as understood by the nation at the time of its ratification."[53] It is in this same letter that Madison showed his strong conservative, even antiquarian, feelings by inveighing against "constructive innovations"[54] or, as we would phrase it today, novel constructions. The sentiment expressed here can be called "originalist" in the sense that it seemed to regard the Constitution's "true meaning" as having been fixed at the time of ratification. But this view is not a wholly accurate picture of Madison's approach, as we shall see when we examine Madison's concept of "precedent." The important point for now is that Madison consistently downplayed the significance of his own notes. I quote from one more letter:

> As a guide in expounding and applying the provisions of the Constitution, the debates and incidental decisions of the Convention can have no authoritative character. However desirable it be that they should be preserved as a gratification to the laudable curiosity felt by every people to trace the origin and progress of their political institutions, . . . the legitimate meaning of the Instrument must be derived from the text itself; or if a key is to be sought elsewhere, it must be, not in the opinions or intentions of the body which planned and proposed the Constitution, but in the sense attached to it by the people in their respective State Conventions, where it received all the authority which it possesses.[55]

Notice that in this formulation it is not "the nation" in general that is appealed to, surely a concept so amorphous as to be of little practical use, but the more particular group of "the people in their respective State Conventions."[56] But what about those points on which state conventions might disagree? What about the fact that the debates at those conventions were not published in any systematic form until 1836, the year of Madison's death, when Jonathan Elliot's five volumes of *Debates on the Federal Constitution* came out? It is small wonder, perhaps, that Madison himself consulted only his own recollections of the Virginia Convention of 1788, and then never cited any of the actual debates, not even his own speeches.[57] So one of the reasons Madison did not publish his notes during his lifetime was that the notes would, or at any rate, should be given no authoritative character in resolving issues of constitutional interpretation.

It is interesting to speculate about what some of the other reasons might have been. Madison may have had scruples about violating the Convention's rule of secrecy. This would be a reason, perhaps, for withholding publication, if not altogether, at least until all the delegates had died. On the other hand, all the delegates except Madison were dead by 1831, and yet he still did not publish the notes. He could have done so at that point and been safe from contradiction by anyone living. He feared the notes might be misused. But every public document is misused by somebody—the privilege of doing so is secured by the First Amendment—and misuse could more readily have been corrected had the author still been living when the notes were published. Madison did think that constitutional debates would become less partisan with the passage of time—he was wrong about that—and that the proceedings of the founding period would, over time, become more revered.

Another possible reason has to do with money. Madison may have thought the notes would be worth more after his death. One authority has rejected such a suggestion indignantly. "Anyone who has read Madison's writings and followed his political career . . . would find it impossible to believe that mercenary motives could influence him in such a case."[58] But one does not have to be exactly "mercenary" to be concerned about one's family's material well-being, and the record is clear that Madison was worried about how his wife, born Dolly Payne, would be able to support herself after his death. (Recall Dr. Johnson's famous dictum that "[n]o man but a blockhead ever wrote except for money.")[59] Mrs. Madison was quite a bit younger than he, and in fact lived for about another fifteen years.[60] Madison's will instructed his wife to have the manuscript published.[61] He left detailed instructions about the legacies to be paid out of the revenues anticipated, including $2,000 to the American Colonization Society. (Madison's solution to the issue of slavery, that peculiar and peculiarly evil institution, was to resettle the slaves in Africa—a wholly unworkable idea, not least because most of the slaves did not want to go.)

Unhappily, no commercial publisher willing to undertake the task without a substantial advance from the family could be found.[62] So recourse was had to the buyer of last resort, the government. (The United States had bought Washington's papers.) The family approached Congress with a suggested price of $100,000. This proved impossibly high. So Mrs. Madison came down, first to $50,000 and then to $30,000. The leaders of Congress agreed, but a major hurdle remained, getting Congress to pass a bill. I quote now from Professor McCoy's excellent book, *The Last of the Fathers*:[63]

> Senator Calhoun took the lead in opposing the bill, which he promptly branded unconstitutional. The *Register of Debates* recorded some of his sentiments:
>
>> The question now before the Senate, Mr. C. said, was whether Congress had the power to purchase the copy-right to Mr. Madison's papers, which, in the present state of political feelings, were regarded of little or no value in the money market. Mr. C. regarded it as truly deplorable, that these invaluable papers, which threw a light upon the constitution which had never been shed upon it before, should be deemed of no value by the public, absorbed with party politics and the low love of gain, so that such a work could not be published. But where, Mr. C. asked, was the special power in the constitution for Congress to publish such a work?

Certainly not in the "general welfare" clause, Calhoun maintained, and to make the point he read from Madison's famed Report of 1800, which denied the false interpretation of that notorious clause that supporters of the present bill would need to rely on. Indeed, Calhoun touted the Virginia Report as Madison's greatest constitutional testament and said that Congress would dishonor his name by assenting to an appropriation of money for which the Constitution gave no sanction. "Mr. C. felt that his position in opposition to this resolution was a painful one; but the opinions of Mr. Madison, which were the text book of Mr. C., and of those with whom he acted, demanded that he should not abandon it."[64]

Could Senator Calhoun have been recalling and repeating the very constitutional theories that Madison once used in opposing the Bank and, at the very end of his term as President, in vetoing the cherished internal improvements bill sponsored by none other than Congressman John C. Calhoun? However that may be, Calhoun lost the vote, the bill passed, and Madison's estate got the money.

So we see that most of the time at least, Madison deprecated not only his own notes, but also anyone else's recollections of the subjective intentions expressed by the Framers at the Convention in Philadelphia. The question why he nevertheless took such care to compile and publish his notes remains, in my mind anyway, without a definite answer. If the notes were of such little value in constitutional interpretation, why make them available to a public that, Madison surely must have known, would use them for that very purpose? If, as we learned in the first year of law school, it is reasonable to infer that one intends the natural and probable consequences of one's acts, we might even say that Madison intended his notes to be used for a purpose he himself disavowed. However that may be, it is clear that he was willing to cite public comments made at the time, either in speeches, as at the state-ratifying conventions, or in the newspapers. And the leading instance of such a public comment was, of course, *The Federalist*. Of this series of anonymous publications, today we would say columns, Madison warned that "it is fair to keep in mind that the authors might be sometimes influenced by the zeal of advocates."[65] He seems nevertheless to have thought highly of *The Federalist* as a legitimate means of constitutional interpretation. In a sketch prepared for Thomas Jefferson on the proposed curriculum for the University of Virginia, Madison described *The Federalist* as "an Authority to which appeal is habitually made by all & rarely declined or denied by any, as evidence of the general opinion of those who framed & those who accepted the Constitution of the U. States on questions as to its genuine meaning."[66] Perhaps it is a mistake to parse a one-time statement, drafted presumably for the eyes of Thomas Jefferson only, but I cannot resist pointing out that at least in this passage, the opinion of those who framed the Constitution (the delegates at Philadelphia) seems to be placed on an equal footing with that of "those who accepted" it. It is, however, only the "general" opinion that Madison mentions, so perhaps it would be wrong to cite this passage as evidence that Madison would countenance citing the views of the delegates on any particular issue of constitutional interpretation.

Another important aspect of Madison's approach is his emphasis on the document as a thing in itself, a creation, so to speak, with existence independent of its creators. If I remember my college course in English correctly, this is roughly what modern critics think about poetry. T. S. Eliot can try to help us by writing a commentary explaining what he meant in *The Waste Land*, but what he meant is not necessarily what the poem means.[67] The poem means what its readers, from time to time, find in it. If we transpose this maxim into the field of construction of legal documents, we might say that a legal document, other, perhaps, than a private contract, means whatever its readers from time to time reasonably think it means. Madison, I suspect, would eliminate the phrase "from time to time" from this formulation. He was tremendously cautious about language. He knew that the meaning of words changed over time.[68]

It was the original meaning, not some "constructive innovation," to which he would look.

We see this approach in some comments Madison made when President Andrew Jackson vetoed the renewal of the Second Bank of the United States in 1830. Jackson had cited in his support a veto message that Madison had sent to Congress in 1817.[69] Madison wrote the Secretary of State, Martin Van Buren, that Jackson had misunderstood what he, Madison, had meant. Madison conceded, however, that Jackson might have correctly interpreted the public meaning of the earlier veto message:

> On the subject of the discrepancy between the construction put by the Message of the President [Jackson] on the veto of 1817 and the intention of its author, the President will of course consult his own view of the case. For myself, I am aware that the document must speak for itself, and that that intention cannot be substituted for [the intention derived through] the established rules of interpretation.[70]

In this regard, it was important to Madison to take into account the kind of document that was being construed. The Constitution, he warned, should not be interpreted as if it were "an ordinary statute, and with the strictness almost of a penal one."[71] He had taken much the same position in an earlier letter to Judge Spencer Roane of Virginia, a correspondent who probably would have wanted to interpret the Constitution as if it were a penal statute.[72] At that time, Madison pointed out that there was "certainly a reasonable medium between expounding the Constitution with the strictness of a penal law, or other ordinary statute, and expounding it with a laxity which would vary its essential character."[73] One thinks immediately of Chief Justice Marshall's famous statement that "we must never forget that it is a constitution we are expounding,"[74] though Madison agreed with Marshall on little else.

IV.

The most distinctive aspect of Madison's approach to constitutional interpretation may be his concept of "precedent." When we use the word, we think instantly of judicial decisions. For many years, and perhaps this is still true, the law schools behaved as if the only law in existence were that contained in the opinions of appellate courts. We knew there were such things as statutes, of course, like the Statute of Uses, for example, but they were to be strictly construed if in derogation of the common law; that is, they were regarded with distrust and were to prevail over judicial opinions only in a clear case. I believe this attitude still obtains when we think of constitutional law. "Law is what judges do," Holmes said, and he was echoed by Chief Justice Hughes: "The Constitution . . . is finally what the Supreme Court determines it to mean."[75] There is a sense, no doubt, in which this is true, but when Madison spoke of "precedent" he was not primarily thinking of courts. He knew that courts are not the only organs of government that make constitutional law. Congress and the President make constitutional law whenever they enact a statute, in the sense that they necessarily decide that what they are about to do is within the powers granted by the Constitution. Their action, to be sure, can be tested in court at some point down the road, but even courts are often impressed by a settled course of legislation, especially one begun early in the history of the Republic. So Madison did agree, unlike his mentor Jefferson, that the Supreme Court of the United States had "definitive power" to settle constitutional questions.[76]

The Madisonian concept of precedent that I'm discussing here is legislative precedent. The acts of the first few Congresses, it seemed to him, were important in this regard. "[E]arly, deliberate & continued practice under the Constitution"[77] was of importance, though some statutes, apparently, were more equal than others. He complained that Congress would alternate between procrastination and precipitation, often producing a careless rush of legislation at the end of a session. Not much has changed in one hundred eighty years, has it? These "midnight precedents . . . ought to have little weight in any case," Madison said.[78] So it was not merely any statute that would establish a practice, but a statute that was enacted only after careful deliberation. This is hardly a bright-line standard, and judges would probably complain that it would be difficult to apply if it were a rule of judicial interpretation. But still it's hard to purge our minds entirely of the fact that some congressional enactments, even ones with far-reaching effect, appear to have received relatively little thought. Madison, in any case, thought that was important.

The most famous instance of Madison's use of the concept of precedent came when he changed his mind with respect to the Bank of the United States. You recall that in 1791, toward the end of the First Congress, Madison had unsuccessfully opposed the bill to create the First Bank.[79] He did so mainly on constitutional grounds.[80] The Bank—whether to renew it and, if so, on what terms and conditions—remained a defining issue in American politics for about the next fifty years. It divided the country. On the one hand, the commercial and financial interests of the North and East thought banks, and specifically a national bank, merely a natural tool of economic progress. On the other hand, the agricultural and frontier interests of the South and West thought of banks, and probably intangible property in general, as something sinister. The existence of wealth that cannot be touched, plowed, looked at, and lived on was an idea especially uncongenial to Jefferson and his followers. So, when the First Bank of the United States expired of its own terms in 1811, having been authorized for only twenty years, the country was sharply divided on whether to renew it. A bill to create the Second Bank of the United States failed in the Senate in 1811 by the casting vote of Madison's Vice President, Elbridge Gerry.[81] In 1815, a similar bill passed both houses and was presented to the President.[82] He vetoed the bill, but only on policy grounds.[83] (Later, in 1816, Madison signed a better bill, he said, creating the Second Bank of the United States.)[84] The veto message, and Madison's subsequent comments about it, are most interesting. The President expressly disclaimed the view, so tenaciously advocated by himself twenty-three years earlier, that the Bank was unconstitutional.[85] How to explain this seeming about-face?

The answer lay in the concept of precedent. Madison felt that the country had, so to speak, ratified the validity of the Bank. He insisted that his private opinion remained unchanged. If he had not been in public life, if he had been a law teacher, for example, I suppose he would have felt unconstrained by history. But he was a public man, and believed himself obligated to relinquish his private view. The Bank had been thoroughly discussed in Congress before it was established (who would know this better than Madison?), and it had operated for twenty years, with annual appropriations confirming its existence and validity each year. Madison thought that:

> [T]he question of the constitutional authority of the Legislature to establish an incorporated bank [had been] precluded in my judgment by repeated recognitions under varied circumstances of the validity of such an institution in acts of the legislative, executive, and judicial branches of the Government, accompanied by indications, in different modes, of a concurrence of the general will of the nation.[86]

The Bank had received "the entire acquiescence of all the local authorities, as well as of the nation at large to all of which may be added, a decreasing prospect of any change in the public opinion adverse to the constitutionality of such an institution."[87] To veto the bill under these circumstances would be "a defiance of all the obligations derived from a course of precedents amounting to the requisite evidence of the national judgment & intention."[88] For the same reasons, when Andrew Jackson later vetoed a bill to extend the Bank's existence, Madison disagreed.

Some of Madison's contemporaries suspected that his constitutional conversion was disingenuous. It seems clear that Madison had become convinced of the necessity of the Bank as a policy matter.[89] In addition, we must remember that Madison was a politician. Names like Washington, Jefferson, and Madison come down to us with an almost godlike aura, but they were not gods, they were people, and what's more, they were people who had to run for office. Well, maybe Washington didn't really have to run for it, but he did have to manage the country after he got in office, and that is certainly a political job. The fact that the country had accepted an institution, that most of the country seemed to want to keep it, and that it appeared to be working well could not fail to weigh with any elected official, especially one who, like Madison, had changed his mind during his first congressional campaign on a subject as important as the necessity of a Bill of Rights. We can sympathize with a remark, referring to the issue of the Bank, that was made to Madison late in his life: "It may be proper . . . to remark that your opinion is very strongly relied on on both sides of the question."[90]

Still, I think we have to accept Madison's genuine feeling that his own "abstract opinion of the text"[91] could not prevail against "a construction put on the Constitution by the nation, which, having made it, had the supreme right to declare its meaning."[92] "I did not feel myself, as a public man, at liberty to sacrifice all these public considerations to my private opinion."[93] "It could not but happen, and was foreseen at the birth of the Constitution, that difficulties and differences of opinion might occasionally arise in expounding terms and phrases necessarily used in such a charter . . . and that it might require a regular course of practice to liquidate and settle the meaning of some of them."[94]

Professor Powell has aptly summed the matter up:

> [H]owever strongly he might have fought constitutional error when it first appeared, for Madison there could be no return to the unadorned text from interpretations that had received the approbation of the people. The Constitution is a public document, and its interpretation, for Madison, was in the end a public process.[95]

One may be pardoned, I hope, for objecting that concepts like "the approbation of the people" and "the will of the nation" are rather formless.

They are what we call today "public opinion." But I am sure Madison did not have in mind daily tracking polls, and there is a distinction between what he was talking about and what now goes by the name of public opinion. Madison was talking about public opinion, all right, but about opinion manifested and solidified over decades of time. A shift by the general public from one opinion of the Constitution to another would, I believe, have had no influence whatever on Madison, unless the shift had proved itself permanent by remaining unchanged for years and years. This concept is, in a way at least, the opposite of original intent or original meaning of any kind: it appears to contemplate that the meaning of the document can change because of what people think about it years after its drafting and enactment. The idea, if taken literally and pushed to its logical conclusion, is dangerous in the extreme. It could justify almost any sort of excess, any sort of encroachment on the rights of minorities, for example, if enough of the public desired it for a long enough time. That is not the sort of thing, I think, that Madison had in mind.

Let's be clear, too, that Madison's idea of precedent, in the sense of consistent governmental practice, was not simply invented in 1816 for political purposes. Madison had consistently taken this same position. Indeed, in *Federalist No. 37*, he had this to say: "All new laws, though penned with the greatest technical skill and passed on the fullest and most mature deliberation, are considered as more or less obscure and equivocal, until their meaning be liquidated and ascertained by a series of particular discussions and adjudications."[96] This passage contains at least the germ of the Madisonian concept of precedent, and it was written long before any particular concrete issues of constitutional interpretation had arisen.

I could go on at some length, but you will be relieved to know that I won't. I shall content myself with just a few other references to Madison's position on constitutional questions of the day. One such question, hotly debated, was that of the protective tariff.[97] Madison thought that forty years of history had settled this question, if indeed it amounted to much in the first place. The First Congress had affirmed the power to enact tariff legislation for the purpose of protecting domestic manufactures, and a continuous course of legislation since that time had confirmed this decision. Madison therefore felt himself compelled to disagree strongly with Calhoun and others who insisted that the power to impose taxes on imports had to be exercised for the purpose of raising revenues only. In articulating his position, Madison again appealed to precedent, in the sense in which I have used that word. "No novel construction however ingeniously devised, or however respectable and patriotic its Patrons, can withstand the weight of such authorities, or the unbroken current of so prolonged & universal a practice."[98]

Madison also vigorously opposed Calhoun on the issue of nullification.[99] Such an idea, Madison thought, was a dangerous innovation and completely inconsistent with the history of the 1780s. He warned that we must go "back to times & scenes in which I was often an actor, always an observer; & which are too much overlooked in discussing the objects & meaning of our Constitution."[100] Nullification, Madison thought, would repeal the achievement of 1787. The Constitution should be understood in light of the evils it was designed to cure: commerce and navigation were in disarray, the states were passing retaliatory legislation against each other, and the nation, if it was a nation, was being given no respect abroad. To countenance the possibility of nullification, Madison said, would turn the country into "a mere league of independent sovereigns,"[101] a concept completely at war with what the nation had decided to do when it ratified the Constitution in the first place.

Less than six years before his death, Madison himself summed up his approach to constitutional interpretation in a letter. The most pertinent considerations, he said, were the following three:

1. The evils & defects for curing which the Constitution was called for & introduced.
2. The comments prevailing at the time it was adopted.
3. The early, deliberate & continued practice under the Constitution, as preferable to constructions adapted on the spur of occasions, and subject to the vicissitudes of party or personal ascendencies.[102]

This formulation is deeply rooted in history. It does not, to be sure, mention the subjective intentions of the Framers at Philadelphia, or, for that matter, anybody else's subjective intentions. It focuses rather on the objective meaning that the nation must reasonably be understood to have given the words of the Constitution at the time of their adoption. Nor is there much comfort here for those who thought that the Constitution ought to be reinvented for each succeeding generation. Thomas Jefferson had a great deal of sympathy for this view, but Madison was markedly more cautious about new interpretations. He did lay stress on actual governmental practice under the Constitution, but, in his view, the practice must be "early, deliberate & continued."[103]

Conclusion

What can we learn from Madison that is of any use in present-day constitutional decision making? Maybe the answer is nothing. Perhaps the kinds of issues with which Madison dealt are so different that his interpretive criteria cannot easily be transposed into the present generation. Most of the great constitutional questions with which the courts grapple nowadays seem to be related to limitations on the power of government, limitations contained either in the original Bill of Rights or in the great Civil War Amendments. This was not what constitutional argument was mainly about in the first decades of our history. The argument then was about distribution of power between the federal government and the states, specifically whether certain powers asserted by Congress fell within the delegation made by Article I, Section 8. This kind of constitutional question has been largely unmentioned in this country for many years now, with the exception of the celebrated case of *United States v. Lopez*,[104] indicating that there are some limits on the commerce power. Nor did Madison have a great deal of confidence in the courts. The federal judges, after all, had been enthusiastic about enforcing the odious Alien and Sedition Laws of 1798 and 1799, and Madison complained of the Marshall Court that it was not activist enough. By interpreting the Necessary and Proper Clause so broadly, the Marshall Court, he thought, had unleashed upon the public the most dangerous branch, the Legislature, and freed it of meaningful restraint. Congressional approval of the Bank of the United States, for example, seems to have weighed much more heavily in Madison's mind than the fact that the Supreme Court had upheld the Bank. Indeed, when Madison finally announced in 1814 that he believed, because of the weight of precedent, that the Bank was constitutional, *McCulloch v. Maryland*[105] had not even been decided.

What would Madison think about the modern debate over "original intent"? He certainly was an advocate for originalism, but in the sense of the original meaning of the document, when viewed against the times in which it was adopted. The kinds of arguments that this approach makes relevant are quite general. They involve broad inferences from the essential structure of the Constitution, from the evils of the 1780s and from the nature of a federal government in general. Through it all, in my view, Madison maintained a generally consistent position. Even when, in his 1791 argument against the Bank, he referred to the failure of a certain proposition at the Convention in Philadelphia, it was not what was said in debate that he cited, but simply the action of the Convention in rejecting a proposal to grant Congress a general power to charter corporations.[106]

To those who would still charge Madison with inconsistency—during his own lifetime he was said to have been on every side of every issue—I would reply that anyone who has seen public service, especially in more than one branch of government, state and federal, and who has lived as long as Madison did, can be made to seem inconsistent in at least some respects. Maybe this is not a bad thing. A person who is completely consistent can justly be accused of having no new thoughts, and, if one is wrong, consistency is hardly a good thing. If Madison did change his view from time to time, we can cite in his favor no less an authority than Cardinal Newman, who remarked that "to improve is to change, and to be perfect is to have changed often."

I can't claim that Madison changed often enough to be perfect, but it does seem to me that he exhibited a healthy sense of practicality in approaching the great constitutional questions that confronted him. Practicality, after all, is not a bad thing in government. If the government doesn't work, if the Constitution is interpreted in such a way as to make it so rigid as to be completely unable to adapt, government will fail of its essential purpose. Maybe those who construe the Constitution could use a little more practicality and a little less theory. However that may be, and even if you think Mr. Madison may have bent a little from time to time and fallen into some degree of inconsistency, I would urge that you judge him with some degree of charity and tolerance. You might even go farther, and use some charity and tolerance in judging those who hold office in our own time.

NOTES

1. See generally Jack N. Rakove, *James Madison and the Creation of the American Republic* (Oscar Handlin ed., 1990).

2. See id. at 1, 181.

3. Letter from James Madison to William Bradford (Nov. 9, 1772), in 1 *The Papers of James Madison* 74, 75 (William T. Hutchinson & William M. E. Rachal eds., 1962).

4. Letter from James Madison to Jared Sparks (June 1, 1831), in 9 *The Writings of James Madison* 459, 460 (Gaillard Hunt ed., 1910).

5. Carroll died in 1832. See Kate Mason Rowland, 2 *The Life of Charles Carroll of Carrollton, 1737–1832*, at 367–68 (New York, 1898).

6. See Rakove, supra note 1, at 10, 15, 18, 31, 42, 130, 133, 146 (noting Madison's public offices: elected in 1774 to Orange County Committee of Safety; commissioned as colonel of county militia in 1775; elected as delegate to Virginia Provincial Convention in 1776; elected to Council of State, advisory board to governor, in 1777; elected to Congress in 1779; elected as delegate to Virginia State Assembly in 1784; reelected to Congress in 1787; reelected to Virginia State Assembly in 1799; appointed Secretary of State under President Thomas Jefferson in 1801; elected U.S. President in 1809).

7. See Jacob E. Cook, *Introduction to The Federalist Papers* at vii, viii–ix (Clinton Rossiter ed., 1961).

8. 5 U.S. (1 Cranch) 137 (1803).

9. See generally James Madison, *Notes of Debates in the Federal Convention of 1787* (Adrienne Koch ed., 1984) (1840).

10. See Rakove, supra note 1, at 76.

11. By a vote of 88 to 80, the Convention rejected Henry's plan to make adoption of the Constitution conditional upon the acceptance of some forty amendments. See id.

12. Drew McCoy, *The Last of the Fathers: James Madison and the Republican Legacy* 18 (1989) (quoting Charles J. Ingersoll).

13. See Rakove, supra note 1, at 78–79.

14. See id. at 80–85 (summarizing Madison's role in launching Congress on its course).

15. For a brilliant description of this process, which no student should miss, see generally Stanley Elkins & Eric McKitrick, *The Age of Federalism* (1993).

16. Kent Greenfield, "Original Penumbras: Constitutional Interpretation in the First Year of Congress," 26 Conn. L. Rev. 79, 80 n.3 (1993) (citing David P. Currie, *The Constitution in Congress: The First Congress, 1789–1791*, at 1–3 (June 12, 1991) (unpublished manuscript)).

17. See Jack N. Rakove, *Original Meanings: Politics and Ideas in the Making of the Constitution* 349 (1996) [hereinafter Rakove, *Original Meanings*]. For a brief overview of Madison's role in the Convention, see generally Jack N. Rakove, "Mr. Meese, Meet Mr. Madison," Atlantic Monthly, Dec. 1986, at 77 (arguing that jurisprudence of "original intent" is not supported by Madison's own thought and actions).

18. See 1 *Annals of Cong.* 385 (Joseph Gales ed., 1789).

19. 11 *Documentary History of the First Federal Congress of the United States of America: Debates in the House of Representatives* 1021 (Charlene Bangs Bickford et al. eds., 1992) [hereinafter *Documentary History*].

20. Id. at 1022.

21. H. Jefferson Powell, "The Original Understanding of Original Intent," 98 Harv. L. Rev. 885, 889 (1985) (quoting Robert McAfee Brown, *The Spirit of Protestantism* 67 (1965)); see also id. at 889–94 (describing influence of Anglo-American Protestantism's anti-interpretive tradition on early constitutional hermeneutics).

22. Greenfield, supra note 16, at 93–94, 94 nn.81–82 (emphasis omitted) (quoting 10 *Documentary History*, supra note 19, at 721–22, 735).

23. 11 *Documentary History*, supra note 19, at 1029.

24. Rakove, *Original Meanings*, supra note 17.

25. Id. at 350.

26. See *Legislative and Documentary History of the Bank of the United States Including the Original Bank of America* 35–85 (M. St. Clair Clark & D. A. Hall compilers, Augustus M. Kelley 1967) (1832) (consolidating transcripts of Senate and House debates on Bank Charter of 1791).

27. U.S. Const. art. I, § 8, cl. 3.

28. U.S. Const. art. I, § 8, cl. 5.

29. U.S. Const. art. I, § 8, cl. 18.

30. See, e.g., James Madison, "Notes on Remarks on the Bank Bill to the House of Representatives" (Feb. 2, 1791), in 13 *Papers of James Madison* 372, 372–81 (Charles F. Hobson & Robert A. Rutland eds., 1981) (arguing that expansive interpretation of Necessary and Proper Clause would destroy essential characteristic of federal government—its composition of limited and enumerated powers).

31. Id. at 374.

32. Id.

33. U.S. Const. preamble.

34. See James Madison, "Report of 1800 on the Virginia Resolutions, Delivered to the General Assembly of Virginia" (Jan. 7, 1800), in 17 *Papers of James Madison* 303, 308–9 (David B. Mattern et al. eds., 1991) (discussing third resolution, which declared that powers of federal government resulted from compact among states); see also Wayne D. Moore, "Reconceiving Interpretive Autonomy: Insights from the Virginia and Kentucky Resolutions," 11 *Const. Comment* 315, 334 (1994) (suggesting that Virginia and Kentucky Resolutions of 1798 and 1799 embraced core principle of state interpretive autonomy in examining allocation of interpretive authority among state and federal governments).

35. See Madison, supra note 30, at 372, 380 (introducing excerpts of debates from Pennsylvania, Virginia, and North Carolina conventions with statement that "[t]he explanations in the state conventions all turned on . . . the principle that the terms necessary and proper gave no additional powers to those enumerated").

36. See Madison, supra note 9; infra text accompanying notes 49–51.

37. See generally 4 *Annals of Cong.* 426–783, 970–1291 (1796) (reporting congressional debates over Jay Treaty).

38. See 1 *Annals of Cong.* 16 (Joseph Gales ed., 1789) ("[T]he Legislative as well as Executive sittings of the Senate were held with closed doors until the second session of the third Congress.").

39. See George Washington, "Message and Proclamation Enclosing the Treaty of Amity, Commerce and Navigation between the United States and His Britannic Majesty (Mar. 1, 1796)," reprinted in 29 *National State Papers of the United States*,

1789–1817, at 106 (Eileen D. Carzo ed., 1985). The House of Representatives appropriated $80,808 for implementing the Treaty on May 3, 1796. See 4 *Annals of Cong.* 1295–98 (1796).

40. See 4 *Annals of Cong.* 759 (1796).

41. See generally George Washington, "Message to the House, Assigning the Reasons Which Forbid His Compliance with the March 24 Resolution (Mar. 30, 1796)," reprinted in 29 *National State Papers of the United States,* supra note 39, at 318.

42. See 4 *Annals of Cong.* 772–81 (1796).

43. See supra text accompanying notes 26–35.

44. Rakove, *Original Meanings,* supra note 17, at 361.

45. 4 *Annals of Cong.* 776 (1796).

46. James Madison, "Notes on Remarks on Jay's Treaty before the House of Representatives (Apr. 6, 1796)," in 16 *The Papers of James Madison* 290, 296 (J. C. A. Stagg et al. eds., 1989).

47. See generally Donald O. Dewey, "James Madison Helps Clio Interpret the Constitution," 15 Am. J. Legal Hist. 38 (1971) (discussing Madison's various approaches to constitutional interpretation).

48. See, e.g., Irving Brant, 3 *James Madison: Father of the Constitution, 1787–1800,* at 436 (1950) (describing Madison's speech to House of Representatives on April 6, 1796, as "lay[ing] down the rule which for the rest of his life enabled him to escape from his 1787 nationalism"). See generally id. at 431–71.

49. See 3 William W. Crosskey & William Jeffrey, Jr., *Politics and the Constitution in the History of the United States* 403 (1980) (recounting instances where Madison attempted to moderate his formerly pro-Federalist views).

50. See 16 *Annals of Cong.* 2628 (1820) (recording "Resolution to authorize the publication of part of the Secret Journal of Congress, Under the Articles of Confederation" of April 21, 1820).

51. See generally Robert Yates, *Secret Proceedings and Debates of the Convention* (Washington, Gov't Printing Off. 1909) (1838).

52. See 3 Crosskey & Jeffrey, supra note 49, at 400–9 (suggesting that Madison deliberately altered his notes on Federal Convention of 1787 to moderate his inconsistent positions regarding states' rights).

53. Letter from James Madison to John G. Jackson (Dec. 27, 1821), in 3 *Letters and Other Writings of James Madison* 243, 245 (New York, R. Worthington 1884).

54. Id.

55. Letter from James Madison to Thomas Ritchie (Sept. 25, 1821), in 3 *Letters and Other Writings of James Madison,* supra note 53, at 228, 228.

56. Id.

57. See Dewey, supra note 47, at 41.

58. Id. at 46 n.26.

59. Leonard Louis Levinson, *Bartlett's Unfamiliar Quotations* 333 (1971).

60. Dolly Todd, a widow, was twenty-six and James Madison was forty-three when they married. See Allen C. Clark, *Life and Letters of Dolly Madison* 25 (1914). Dolly Madison died in 1849. See id. at 449–50.

61. See "Extract from Mr. Madison's Will (Apr. 15, 1835)," in 4 *Letters and Other Writings of James Madison*, supra note 53, at 569, 569.

62. See Elizabeth Lippincott Dean, *Dolly Madison: The Nation's Hostess* 210 (1928) (noting Dolly's difficulties in selling manuscript and eventual purchase by Congress in 1837).

63. McCoy, supra note 12.

64. Id. at 168.

65. Letter from James Madison to Edward Livingston (Apr. 17, 1824), in 3 *Letters and Other Writings of James Madison*, supra note 53, at 435, 436.

66. Letter from James Madison to Thomas Jefferson (Feb. 8, 1825), in 9 *The Writings of James Madison*, supra note 4, at 218, 221.

67. See generally *Eliot in His Time: Essays on the Occasion of the Fiftieth Anniversary of The Waste Land* (A. Walton Litz ed., 1973).

68. See Letter from James Madison to Major Henry Lee (June 25, 1824), in 3 *Letters and Other Writings of James Madison*, supra note 53, at 441, 442 ("[T]he language of our Constitution is already undergoing interpretations unknown to its founders. . . . If the meaning of the text be sought in the changeable meaning of the words composing it, it is evident that the shape and attributes of the government must partake of the changes to which the words and phrases of all living languages are constantly subject.").

69. See Robert Allen Rutland, *James Madison: The Founding Father* 238 (1987) (noting that Madison vetoed bill allocating Bank bonus and dividends to canal and road building because he found such allocation beyond both "necessary and proper" and "general welfare" powers granted by Constitution).

70. Letter from James Madison to Martin Van Buren (July 5, 1830), in 4 *Letters and Other Writings of James Madison*, supra note 53, at 89, 89.

71. Letter from James Madison to Reynolds Chapman (Jan. 6, 1831), in 4 *Letters and Other Writings of James Madison*, supra note 53, at 143, 147.

72. See *James Madison and the American Nation 1751–1836*, at 362 (Robert A. Rutland et al. eds., 1994) (noting that Roane opposed federal courts overturning state court decisions indicating more statute-oriented conception of constitutional authority).

73. Letter from James Madison to Judge Spencer Roane (Sept. 2, 1819), in 3 *Letters and Other Writings of James Madison*, supra note 53, at 143, 146.

74. *McCulloch v. Maryland*, 17 U.S. (4 Wheat.) 316, 406 (1819).

75. Dexter Perkins, *Charles Evans Hughes and American Democratic Statesmanship* 32–33 (Oscar Hundlin ed., 1956) (quoting speech by Hughes).

76. Letter from James Madison to Joseph C. Cabell (Sept. 7, 1829), in 4 *Letters and Other Writings of James Madison*, supra note 53, at 45, 47.

77. Letter from James Madison to M. L. Hurlbert (May 1830), in 9 *The Writings of James Madison*, supra note 4, at 370, 372.

78. Letter from James Madison to Judge Spencer Roane (May 6, 1821), in 9 *The Writings of James Madison*, supra note 4, at 55, 61.

79. See 2 *Annals of Cong.* 1960 (1791) (recording House vote in favor of Bank over Madison's objections); id. at 1769 (recording Senate vote in favor of Bank).

80. See generally Gaillard Hunt, *The Life of James Madison* 201 (1902) (describing Madison's opposition to Bank).

81. See 4 *Annals of Cong.* 346–47 (1811) (recording Gerry's deciding vote in opposition to Bank's charter renewal).

82. See 5 *Annals of Cong.* 174–75 (1815) (recording Senate vote to renew Bank's charter); id. at 1043–45 (recording House vote to renew Bank's charter).

83. See id. at 189–91 (recording Senate consideration of Senate veto and presidential message to Senate).

84. See 5 *Annals of Cong.* 280–81 (1816) (recording Senate vote in favor of new bill); id. at 1343–44 (recording House vote in favor of new bill).

85. See 5 *Annals of Cong.* 189 (1815) (recording veto message from President Madison to Senate, stating that question of constitutionality of Bank was "precluded …by repeated recognitions, under varied circumstances, of the validity of [the Bank], in acts of the Legislative, Executive, and Judicial branches of the Government").

86. "James Madison's Veto Message to the Senate of the United States (Jan. 30, 1815)," in 8 *The Writings of James Madison*, supra note 4, at 327, 327.

87. Letter from James Madison to Charles J. Ingersoll (June 25, 1831), in 4 *Letters and Other Writings of James Madison*, supra note 53, at 183, 186.

88. Id.

89. See Dewey, supra note 47, at 53 (noting that Madison characterized establishment of national bank as "expedient").

90. Id. at 54 (quoting Letter from H. G. Reynolds to James Madison (May 15, 1834)).

91. Letter from James Madison to C. E. Haynes (Feb. 25, 1831), in 4 *Letters and Other Writings of James Madison*, supra note 53, at 164, 165.

92. Letter from James Madison to Marquis de LaFayette (Nov. 1826), in 3 *Letters and Other Writings of James Madison*, supra note 53, at 538, 542.

93. Id.

94. Letter from James Madison to Judge Spencer Roane (Sept. 2, 1819), in 3 *Letters and Other Writings of James Madison*, supra note 53, at 143, 145.

95. Powell, supra note 21, at 941.

96. *The Federalist No. 37*, at 229 (James Madison) (Clinton Rossiter ed., 1961).

97. See generally Edward McNall Burns, *James Madison: Philosopher of the Constitution* 114–15 (1938) (discussing Madison's position on protective tariffs).

98. Letter from James Madison to Joseph C. Cabell (Sept. 18, 1828), in 9 *The Writings of James Madison*, supra note 4, at 316, 333.

99. See generally Burns, supra note 97, at 117–19 (discussing Madison's views on nullification and secession).

100. McCoy, supra note 12, at 133 (quoting Letter from James Madison to Edward Everett (Nov. 14, 1831)).

101. Id. at 135 (quoting Letter from James Madison to Andrew Stevenson (May 2, 1827)).

102. Letter from James Madison to M. L. Hurlbert (May 1830), in 9 *The Writings of James Madison*, supra note 4, at 370, 372.

103. Id.

104. 115 S. Ct. 1624 (1995).

105. 17 U.S. (4 Wheat.) 316 (1819) (upholding Congress's power to incorporate a national bank).

106. See 2 *Annals of Cong.* 1896–97 (1791) (recording Madison's argument that Constitution granted no federal power to incorporate bank).

Chapter 9

Against Constitutional Theory

Richard A. Posner

Constitutional theory, as I shall use the term, is the effort to develop a generally accepted theory to guide the interpretation of the Constitution of the United States. It is distinct on the one hand from inquiries of a social scientific character into the nature, provenance, and consequences of constitutionalism—the sort of thing one associates mainly with historians and political scientists, such as Charles Beard, Jon Elster, and Stephen Holmes—and on the other hand from commentary on specific cases and doctrines, the sort of thing one associates with legal doctrinalists, such as Kathleen Sullivan, Laurence Tribe, and William Van Alstyne. A number of scholars straddle this divide, such as Ronald Dworkin and Lawrence Lessig, and although I mean to keep to one side of it in this lecture, the straddle is no accident. Constitutional theorists are normativists; their theories are meant to influence the way judges decide difficult constitutional cases; when the theorists are law-trained, as most of them are, they cannot resist telling their readers which cases they think were decided consistently with or contrary to their theory. Most constitutional theorists, indeed, believe in social reform through judicial action. Constitutional theory that is strongly influenced by moral theory has additional problems, as I have discussed recently and will not repeat here.[1]

I must stress at the outset the limited domain of constitutional theory. Nothing pretentious enough to warrant the name of theory is required to decide cases in which the text or history of the Constitution provides sure guidance. No theory is required to determine how many Senators each state

This lecture was delivered on October 21, 1997, and appeared in 73 N.Y.U.L. Rev. 1 (1998).

may have. Somewhat more difficult interpretive issues, such as whether the self-incrimination clause should be interpreted as forbidding the prosecutor to comment on the defendant's failure to take the stand,[2] can be resolved pretty straightforwardly by considering the consequences of rival interpretations. Were the prosecutor allowed to argue to the jury that the defendant's refusal to testify should be taken as an admission of guilt, it would be extremely difficult for defense counsel to counter with some plausible explanation consistent with his client's being innocent. So allowing comment would pretty much destroy the privilege—at least as it is currently understood. That is an important qualification. It has been strongly argued that the current understanding is incorrect, that the purpose of the privilege is merely to prevent improper methods of interrogation; and if this is right then there is no basis for the rule of no comment.[3] Maybe, as this example suggests, when fully ventilated no issue of constitutional law not founded on one of the numerical provisions of the Constitution is beyond contestation. But as a practical matter there are large areas of constitutional law that the debates over constitutional theory do not touch and that consequently I shall ignore.

Constitutional theory in the sense in which I am using the term is at least as old as the *Federalist Papers*. And yet after more than two centuries no signs of closure or even, it seems to me, of progress, are visible. The reason is that constitutional theory has no power to command agreement from people not already predisposed to accept the theorist's policy prescriptions. It has no power partly because it is normative, partly because interpretation, the subject of constitutional theory, is not susceptible of theoretical resolution, and partly because normativists in general and lawyers (and as I said most constitutional theorists are lawyers, albeit professors of law rather than practicing lawyers) do not like to be backed into a corner by committing themselves to a theory that might be falsified by data, just as no practicing lawyer wants to take a position that might force him to concede that his client has no case. Neither type of lawyer wants the validity of his theory to be hostage to what a factual inquiry might bring to light. But as a result, constitutional theory, while often rhetorically powerful, lacks the agreement-coercing power of the best natural and social science.

An even more serious problem is that constitutional theory is not responsive to, and indeed tends to occlude, the greatest need of constitutional adjudicators, which is the need for empirical knowledge, as I shall argue using as illustrations the Supreme Court's 1996 decisions forbidding the Virginia Military Institute to exclude women[4] and forbidding Colorado to ban local ordinances that protect homosexuals from discrimination on the basis of their sexual orientation.[5] I know that just getting the facts right can't decide a case. There has to be an analytic framework to fit the facts into; without it they can have no normative significance. But I don't think that constitutional theory can supply that framework. Nor is the design of the framework, as distinct from fitting the facts into it, the big problem in constitutional law today. The big problem is not lack of theory, but lack of knowledge—lack of the very knowledge that academic research, rather than the litigation process, is best designed to produce. But it is a different kind of research from what constitutional theorists conduct.

The leading theorists are intelligent people, and it is possible that their lively debates have a diffuse but cumulatively significant impact on the tone and texture and occasionally even on the outcomes of constitutional cases. (Whether it is a good impact is a different question, and one that cannot be answered on the basis of existing knowledge.) If the theorists do not have a large audience among judges, and I do not think they do, they have a large audience among their own students and hence among the judges' law clerks, whose influence on constitutional law, though small, is not completely negligible. Yet the real significance of constitutional theory is, I believe, as a sign of the increased academification of law school professors, who are much more inclined than they used to be to write for other professors rather than for judges and practitioners. The causes of this academification are beyond the scope of this article, but a particularly mundane cause is simply that there are so many more law professors than there used to be that it has become possible for them to have a nonnegligible audience for their work even if their work is read only by other law professors, as I believe is largely the case with regard to constitutional theory. In addition, as constitutional theory becomes more "theoretical," less tethered to the practice of law, it becomes increasingly transparent to professors in other fields, such as political theory and moral philosophy; and by this means the ranks of the constitutional theorists grow to the point of self-sufficiency. Constitutional theory today circulates in a medium that is largely opaque to the judge and the practicing lawyer.

I. The History and Varieties of Constitutional Theory

The problem in political theory to which constitutional theory is offered as a solution is that our judicially enforceable Constitution gives the judges an unusual amount of power. This was seen as problematic long before the democratic principle became as central to our concept of government as it is now. Hamilton's solution to the problem, drawing on what was already an age-old formalist tradition stretching back to Cicero and shortly to be echoed by John Marshall, was to assert that it was the law that was supreme, not the judges, since judges are (in Blackstone's phrase, but it is also Hamilton's sense) just the oracles, the mouthpieces, of the law.[6]

After a century of judicial willfulness, this position was difficult to maintain with a straight face. The Constitution had obviously made the judges a competing power center. James Bradley Thayer argued in the 1890s that this was bad because it sapped the other branches of government of initiative and responsibility. He urged courts to enforce a constitutional right only when the existence of the right, as a matter of constitutional interpretation, was clear beyond a reasonable doubt.[7] He thought, in other words, that the erroneous grant of a constitutional right was a more serious error than the erroneous denial of such a right, in just the same way that the criminal justice system assumes that the erroneous conviction of an innocent person is a more serious error than the erroneous acquittal of a guilty person. But Thayer didn't explain where he had gotten his weighting of constitutional errors or why it was the correct weighting.

Thayer is the father of the "outrage" school of constitutional interpretation, whose most notable practitioner was Holmes. Holmes's position was not identical to Thayer's; nor were Cardozo's and Frankfurter's positions identical to Holmes's, though there are broad affinities among all four. This school teaches that to be justified in trying to stymie the elected branches of government it shouldn't be enough that the litigant claiming a constitutional right has the better of the argument; it has to be a lot better; the alleged violation of the Constitution has to be certain (Thayer's position),[8] or stomach-turning (Holmes's "puke" test),[9] or shocking to the conscience (Frankfurter's test),[10] or a synthesis of the positions (one supported by Holmes's dissent in Lochner),[11] the sort of thing no reasonable person could defend. The school of outrage is almost interchangeable with the doctrine of judicial self-restraint when that doctrine is understood as seeking to minimize the occasions on which the courts annul the actions of other branches of government. The judge who is self-restrained in this sense wishes to take a back seat to the other branches of government, but is stirred to action if his sense of justice is sufficiently outraged.

I own to considerable sympathy with this way of approaching constitutional issues. And when the outrage approach is tied, as I have just suggested it can be, to the doctrine of judicial self-restraint—a doctrine that is founded on reasons[12]—the approach is no longer as purely visceral as my initial description may have suggested. But I cannot pretend that outrage or even self-restraint furnishes much in the way of guidance to courts grappling with difficult issues. And I could defend the approach convincingly only by showing, what may be impossible as a practical matter to do, that decisions invalidating statutes or other official actions as unconstitutional, when the decision could not have been justified under Thayer's or Holmes's or Cardozo's or Frankfurter's approach, have done more harm than good.

Hamilton-style formalism now has a defender in Justice Scalia.[13] But he lacks the courage of his convictions. For he takes extreme libertarian positions with respect to such matters as affirmative action and freedom of speech on the ground that these positions are dictated not by the Constitution but by the cases interpreting the Constitution.[14] Take away the adventitious operation of stare decisis and Scalia is left with a body of constitutional law of remarkable meagerness—which is not an objection but which requires a greater effort at justification than he has been able to offer. Indeed he has offered little by way of justification other than bromides about democracy. Complaining that the Supreme Court is undemocratic begs the question.[15] The Court is part of the Constitution, which in its inception was rich in undemocratic features, such as the indirect election of the President and of the Senate, and a highly restricted franchise. The Constitution still has major undemocratic features. They include the method of apportionment of the Senate, which results in weighting the votes of people in sparsely populated states much more heavily than the votes of people in densely populated states; the election of the President on the basis of electoral rather than popular votes, which could result in the election of a candidate who had lost the popular vote; the expansion of constitutional rights brought about by the Bill of Rights and the Fourteenth Amendment, which curtails the powers of the elected branches of government; and, of course, lifetime appointment of federal judges who exercise considerable political power by virtue of the expansion of rights to which I have just referred. The Supreme Court is certainly undemocratic in a sense, but not in a sense that makes it anomalous in the political system created by the Constitution, given the other "undemocratic" features that I have mentioned. A further drawback to Scalia's approach is that it requires judges to be political theorists, so that they know what "democracy" is, and also to be historians, because it takes a historian to reconstruct the original meaning of centuries-old documents.[16]

Most constitutional theorizing in this century has taken a nonformalistic direction, unlike that of a Hamilton or a Scalia. We may begin with Learned Hand's argument that the Bill of Rights provides so little guidance to judges that it ought to be deemed (largely) nonjusticiable,[17] and move on to Herbert Wechsler's prompt riposte that constitutional law can be stabilized by judicial evenhandedness, what he called "neutral principles," soon recognized as merely principles. Since principles can be bad as well as good, Wechsler's riposte failed.[18] Focus then shifted to an effort to identify good principles to guide constitutional decision making. Leading candidates include John Hart Ely's principle of "representation reinforcement"[19] and Ronald Dworkin's principle of egalitarian natural justice.[20] These are substantive political principles, and they founder on the authors' lack of steady interest in and firm grasp of the details of public policy. I have complained elsewhere about the egregious underspecialization of constitutional lawyers and theorists,[21] and I don't want to repeat myself. People who devote most of their lives to the study of political theory and constitutional doctrine do not thereby equip themselves to formulate substantive principles designed to guide decision making across the vast range of difficult issues that spans affirmative action and exclusionary zoning, legislative apportionment and prison administration, telecommunications and euthanasia, the education of alien children and the administration of capital punishment, to name just a few current and recent issues in constitutional law.

The constitutional theories propounded by the formalists, by Thayer and his followers, and by Wechsler, were procedural in the sense of offering a method of analysis rather than a master substantive principle in the style of Ely or Dworkin. The formulation of procedural theories has continued. Examples are Bruce Ackerman's "constitutional moments" approach,[22] Lawrence Lessig's "translation" approach,[23] John Rawls's "public reason" approach,[24] and Cass Sunstein's counter to Rawls—his "incompletely theorized" or "judicial minimalism" approach.[25] Ackerman argues that courts should identify political watersheds, such as the New Deal, and accord them the same authority for changing constitutional law as they would accord a formal amendment. This approach requires judges to have the skills of historians, political theorists, and political scientists, so it is open to some of the same objections as Scalia's otherwise quite dissimilar approach. It is also rather too "legal realist," one might even say *realpolitikisch*, in inviting judges to bend law to powerful currents of public opinion, such as those that welled up during the New Deal and are now understood to have been to a considerable degree deeply, even tragically, misinformed.

Lessig argues that just as a good translation is not necessarily a literal one, so keeping faith with the intended meaning of the Constitution's framers may require rulings that depart from the framers' literal meanings. But whether a literal translation is good depends on the purpose of the translation; for some purposes, literal translations are best. Then, too, fidelity to original meanings need not be the sovereign virtue of constitutional interpretation. The real significance of Lessig's approach is that it turns the tables on Scalia by showing that originalism is compatible with what Scalia would think an impermissible flexibility of interpretation.

Rawls is not and does not pretend to be well informed about constitutional law or judicial practice. But his prestige in academic circles is such that his rather offhand suggestion that judges in interpreting the Constitution should confine themselves to what he calls "public reason," defined as the set of considerations that every reasonable person would consider admissible to resolve issues of public policy,[26] has received respectful attention from constitutional theorists. The suggestion, if adopted, would confine judges to a level of generality so void of operational content as to deny them the tools they need to decide cases.

Sunstein takes almost the opposite tack from Rawls, pointing out that people often converge on the resolution of a particular issue, though incapable of agreeing on the principles that determine that resolution. This is importantly true of judges, a majority of whom have to agree on a resolution even if they can't agree on a broad ground that would resolve a host of other issues as well. Sunstein further points out that a "minimalist" approach that eschews broad grounds will reduce the magnitude of the judges' inevitable errors. I like Sunstein's approach, but I see it more as sounding cautionary notes about constitutional theory, in much the fashion of theoretically oriented constitutional commentators who are not themselves propounders of constitutional theories, such as Jack Balkin and Sanford Levinson, than as a theory itself.[27] I have to acknowledge, however, that Sunstein's is close to my own preferred stance, which I call "pragmatic." Pragmatism may seem just another theory, in which event I am contradicting myself in withholding the name of theory from Sunstein's approach. But while in one sense pragmatism is indeed a theory and a constitutional theory when applied to constitutional law, in an equally valid and more illuminating sense it is an avowal of skepticism about various kinds of theorizing, including the kind that I am calling constitutional theorizing.

Although Sunstein's and my approaches are similar, we frequently disagree at the level of application to particular cases. He commends recent decisions by the Supreme Court, including the *Romer* and *VMI* decisions, as commendably minimalist because they avoid (*Romer* more clearly) announcing principles that might overturn a lot of other laws. I consider them wedge decisions, in which the Court takes a first tentative step toward a new abyss, as when the Court moved, and quickly too, without much thought, from the bare holding in *Baker v. Carr*[28] that legislative malapportionment is justiciable to a rigid rule ("one man, one vote") founded on a naive conception of democracy. The decisions that Sunstein commends are minimalist when compared to hypothetical decisions holding that all governmental discrimination against homosexuals is unconstitutional and likewise all segregation of the sexes (in public restrooms, in military units, in college dorms). But from another standpoint they are uninformed adventures in judicial activism; and that is the view I shall be defending.

Sunstein's politics, and I believe his conception of where he would like to see constitutional law heading, are similar to those of Ackerman, Ely, Dworkin, and Lessig. What he understands better than they is that judges, with only a few exceptions, are put off by constitutional theory. Their background is usually not in any kind of theoretical endeavor even if they are former law professors, as a growing fraction of appellate judges are. For even today most law professors are analysts of cases and legal doctrines rather than propounders of general theories of political or judicial legitimacy, the class of theories to which constitutional theory belongs. And even if the judge's background is theory, a theoretical perspective is very difficult to maintain when one is immersed in deciding cases as part of a committee. (This may have been a factor in Robert Bork's resignation from the D.C. Circuit.) The rise of constitutional theory has less to do with any utility that such theory might have for judges than, as I suggested at the outset, with the growing academification of legal scholarship. When Wechsler was crossing swords with Learned Hand, law professors still thought of themselves as lawyers first and professors second and saw their role in relation to the judiciary as a helping one. Nowadays many law professors, especially the most prestigious ones at the most prestigious schools, think of themselves primarily as members of an academic community engaged in dialogue with the other members of the community and the judges be damned.

I am exaggerating. Constitutional theorists want to influence constitutional practice. One cannot read Ely and Dworkin and the others without sensing a strong desire to influence judicial decisions or even (in Dworkin's case) the composition of the Supreme Court—for one remembers his polemic against the appointment of Bork.[29] And Scalia is on the Supreme Court. But to get the richest rewards available within the modern legal academic community a professor has to do "theory," and this tends to alienate the professors from the judges. Sunstein's antitheory is more likely to move judges, but he suffers guilt by association; increasingly judges believe that legal academics are not on the same wavelength as them, that the academics are not interacting with judges but instead are chasing their own and each other's tails. I do not think that Justice Scalia's active participation in the debates over constitutional theory is inconsistent with my claims. He is plainly unmoved by the academics' criticisms of his position; and most of them plainly regard him as an unsophisticated, because academically superannuated, antagonist, one who among other things tacks between theory and practice, using the constraints of his judicial role (for example, the constraint of stare decisis) to bevel his sharp-edged theoretical stance.

II. Toward a New Approach

I would like to see an entirely different kind of constitutional theorizing. It would set itself the difficult—although, from the perspective of today's theorists, the intellectually modest—task of exploring the operation and consequences of constitutionalism. It would ask such questions as, what difference has it made for press freedom and police practices in the United States compared to England that we have a judicially enforceable Bill of Rights and England does not? How influenced are judges in constitutional cases by public opinion? How influenced is public opinion by constitutional decisions? Are constitutional issues becoming more complex, and if so, what are the courts doing to keep abreast of the complexities? Does intrusive judicial review breed constitutionally dubious statutes by enabling legislators to shift political hot potatoes to the courts? What is the effect of judicial activism on judicial workloads and is there a feedback loop here, activism producing heavy workloads that in turn cause the judges to become restrained in order to reduce the number of cases and thus alleviate the workload pressures? Does the Court try to prevent the formation of interest groups that might obtain constitutional amendments that would curtail the Court's power or abrogate some of its doctrines, or to encourage the formation of interest groups that will defend the Court's prerogatives? And what role do interest groups play in constitution making and amending? In the appointment of Supreme Court Justices? In the reception of Supreme

Court decisions by the media and, through the media, the public? Above all, what are the actual and likely effects of particular decisions and doctrines? Did *Brown v. Board of Education*[30] improve the education of blacks? Did *Roe v. Wade*[31] retard abortion law reform at the state level? What effect have the apportionment cases had on public policy? Did the Warren Court's decisions expanding the constitutional rights of criminal defendants contribute to the increase in the crime rate in the 1960s and 1970s and provoke a legislative backlash, increasing the severity of sentences? These questions have not been entirely ignored,[32] but the literature on them is meager, and law professors have contributed very little to it. Exploring these questions would be a more fruitful use of academic time and brains than continuing the two-hundred-year-old game of political rhetoricizing that we call constitutional theory. Some of these questions might actually be answerable, and the answers would alter constitutional practice more than theorizing has done or can do. Thus I am in radical disagreement with Dworkin, who insists that cases in which facts or consequences matter to sound constitutional decision making are "rare."[33]

Which brings me to the *VMI* and *Romer* decisions. I will not claim to have picked these as data for testing my critical and constructive theses by a random process, but it would be easy to pick equally good illustrations from any term of the Supreme Court. What these cases illustrate is that the Court does not base its constitutional decisions on fact. If this is right, it makes it unlikely that what the Court needs is theory, unless telling the Court to pay more attention to social realities can count as a theoretical assertion.

I am not advocating the transformation of litigation into a setting for generating or marshaling social scientific data and for testing social scientific hypotheses. The capability of the courts to conduct scientific or social scientific research is extremely limited, and perhaps nil. But their assimilative powers are greater. I would like to see the legal professoriat redirect its research and teaching efforts toward fuller participation in the enterprise of social science, and by doing this make social science a better aid to judges' understanding of the social problems that get thrust at them in the form of constitutional issues. What the judges should do until the professoriat accepts this challenge and makes real progress in the study of race relations, sexual activity, euthanasia, education theory, and the other areas of social life that are generating constitutional issues these days is an issue that I shall defer until I have explained what seem to me to be the unfortunate consequences of judicial ignorance of the social realities behind the issues with which they grapple.

The Virginia Military Institute is a public college the mission of which is to produce "citizen-soldiers" by bullying methods (the "adversative method," as it is euphemistically called) modeled on the well-known brutalities of the English public schools ("The Battle of Waterloo was won on the playing fields of Eton") and of the traditional Army or Marine boot camp, all being institutions designed to forge male solidarity viewed as the condition of effective military action. VMI refused to admit women (who of course had also been excluded from the institutions on which it was modeled), precipitating the suit. The Court begins its opinion in *United States v. Virginia*[34] by commending "the school's impressive record in producing leaders," but accompanies this bit of polite fluff with the unsubstantiated assertion that "neither the goal of producing citizen-soldiers nor VMI's implementing methodology is inherently unsuitable to women."[35] How does the Court know? And even if the methodology were suitable for women, it wouldn't follow that the school's goal would not be imperiled; one would have to consider the effect of mixing the sexes. Men and women both use toilets, but it doesn't follow that unisex public restrooms are just as appropriate as sex-segregated ones.[36]

The Court's essential reasoning, in invalidating VMI's exclusion of women, is that in the past, men, and many women for that matter, entertained false beliefs about the capacities of women relative to those of men. In ridiculing the mistakes of past generations, however, the Court ignored the possibility that our ancestors' false beliefs about women, whatever the motivation, were the best interpretation of the then-existing scientific knowledge—a point that has been made about Aristotle's belief that a child is (in modern terminology) the clone of its father, the mother being merely an incubator.[37] Moreover, some of the discredited beliefs about women's educational and occupational capacities may well have been true in the then-existing circumstances. When a woman must be pregnant throughout her fertile years in order to have a reasonable assurance of producing a few children who will survive to adulthood, and when most jobs in the economy require brawn, equal employment opportunities for women are not going to be in the cards even if a few exceptional women might be able to take advantage of them. Indignation about historical injustice often reflects ignorance of history—of the circumstances that explain and, yes, sometimes justify practices that in the modern state of society (comfortable, rich, scientifically advanced, push-buttony) would be arbitrary and unjust.

It is flattering to think of ourselves as being the moral superiors of our predecessors, but it is false. And it is sheer illogic (it is the fallacy of naive induction) to argue that if in the past the biological differences between the sexes, so far as those differences bear on aptitudes for various jobs, were exaggerated, those differences must be zero. Not that the Court went that far; but it does convey the impression that it thinks the only differences between men and women are physical. Although the biological differences between men and women in relation to a variety of professional activities were indeed exaggerated at a time when biological science was far less developed than it is today and social conditions far different, the conclusion that there are no relevant differences not only does not follow from history, but is no better than an article of faith. Until recently we did not realize that dolphins communicate with each other by something quite like speech; it doesn't follow that with greater educational opportunities and perhaps a pinch of affirmative action they could learn to speak French. The fact that biology used to be riven with mistake, superstition, and ideology doesn't mean that it's still riven with mistake, superstition, and ideology.

Once the advance of science is conceded, it becomes appropriate to observe that like many articles of faith the "no difference" claim is contradicted by modern science. Modern science suggests that there are inherent differences between the average man and the average woman with respect to aggressiveness, competitiveness, the propensity to take risks, and the propensity to resort to violence[38]—characteristics that, along with the acknowledged differences in physical strength, are relevant to military fitness and performance. When judges are faced with creationists' challenges to the theory of evolution, they reveal themselves to be resolutely scientific in their outlook. But when they are faced with evolutionary biologists' challenge to the pieties of political correctness and radical egalitarianism, they turn pietistic.

I said "average" man and "average" woman. Within each sex, there is a distribution of characteristics, and the two distributions, the male and the female, overlap. Because some women are more aggressive, competitive, and the like, than some men, the adversative methods used by VMI may be more suitable for some women than they are for some of the men admitted to VMI. It could be argued that these exceptional women should be given a chance. But there are two objections. First, the prevalence—the near universality—of qualifying examinations and other set requirements for entry into private schools suggests that a policy of giving everyone a chance to prove himself or herself, in lieu of a preliminary screening for likelihood of success, would be highly inefficient. If only a minute percentage of women, relative to men, are qualified to undergo adversative training, individual consideration of women's applications would yield few benefits. Second, a concern with the consequences of mixing the sexes in the unusual setting of a military academy is unrelated to whether women are able to function as well in that setting as men are.

The Court in the *VMI* case was much taken with the analogy between sex-segregated and race-segregated public educational institutions. Judges can rarely resist analogies, a form of "evidence" (if it can be called that) that is generated by ingenuity rather than by knowledge. Analogies are typically, as here, inexact and often, as here, misleading. Racial segregation was demonstrably a component of an exploitative social system descended from slavery and seeking to preserve its essential characteristics. Sex segregation has a more complex history, one that is not free from elements of oppression but that is also bound up with a desire to limit sexual contact between young people and to tailor education to the difference in life roles between men and women—differences reflecting, as I suggested earlier, fundamental conditions of society that were not less real for having largely dissipated today. Yet even today we do not consider single-sex restrooms to present the same issue that single-race restrooms would.[39]

Even if the history of society's treatment of women is as oppressive and unjust as a majority of today's Supreme Court Justices appear without adequate reflection or inquiry to believe, and is not just a function of limited knowledge or different material conditions of social life, it would not follow that a specific "discrimination," for example in military training, was oppressive and unjust. I would be very surprised to learn that any Justice of the Supreme Court believes that the maintenance of sex-segregated public restrooms violates the Constitution. This means that public segregation of the sexes has to be evaluated case by case and therefore that the Court can get little mileage from ridiculing, as it did at such length, the former exclusion of women from the practice of law and medicine.

Thousands of words into its opinion the Court finally gets to the issue, but lingers there only briefly, for one short, and evasive, paragraph. The issue, as it would appear to a disinterested student of public policy unburdened by commitment to any of the constitutional theories, is whether excluding women from VMI is likely to do more harm to women—whether material, psychological, or even just symbolic (and so perhaps indirectly or eventually material or psychological)—than including them would do to the mission of training citizen-soldiers. The Court says nothing about the first point, as if it were obvious that the exclusion of women from one obscure though distinguished military academy would be the kind of insult to women that forbidding black people to attend military academies would be to blacks or that the exclusion of male homosexuals from the armed forces is to homosexuals by branding them unmanly. That the equal status of women depends to even a trivial degree on their gaining admission to the Virginia Military Institute would be a laughable suggestion, which may be why the Court passed over the question in silence. And for the handful of women who might want to attend VMI the state had set up a parallel institution—a "separate but equal" school that was not in fact equal, as the Court pointed out, ignoring however the fact that it could not be equal, because so few Virginia women want to attend a quasi-military college that it would not make any sense to establish a women's parallel institution as richly supported and maintained as the men's.

If many other public institutions of learning wanted to exclude women, and a decision in favor of VMI would be a precedent enabling them to do so, the harm to women would be greater. But as far as I know or the Court says, no other public institution wants to exclude women. Still, it could be argued that a decision in favor of VMI would be a precedent for the exclusion of women from other military academies and from the combat branches of the armed forces, the branches most likely to favor the "adversative" style of college education. Yet if the national government decided to reduce the percentage of women in the armed forces, it is unthinkable that the Court would stand in its way. The Court always and properly has been timid about intruding into military and diplomatic affairs. These are areas in which the Court is either aware of the limitations of its knowledge and the costs of error or convinced that it lacks the political authority to make intervention stick. It is, as it were, the military irrelevance of VMI that enabled the Court to invalidate a form of military sex discrimination.

As for the possibility that VMI's program would be impaired if women participated, all the Court said is that "[w]omen's successful entry into the federal military academies, and their participation in the Nation's military forces, indicate that Virginia's fears for the future of VMI may not be solidly grounded."[40] In the word "may" lies a noteworthy concession to reality. No one knows what effect incorporating large numbers of women into the nation's armed forces will have on military effectiveness. It is an experiment the results of which may not be known until the nation is challenged in a major war. It is not as if the armed forces had wanted or welcomed the influx of women. The influx was forced upon them by the civilian leadership of the military, responding to political pressure. This does not make it a bad thing. Military professionals, like other professionals (notably including lawyers and judges), tend to be narrow, parochial, and reflexively resistant to change. The racial integration of the armed forces was accomplished in 1948 by civil initiative over military objections, and has been a success. The performance of women in the Gulf War of 1991 was by all accounts excellent. But since then the percentage of women in the armed forces has grown, more and more combat slots have been opened to them, new tensions have arisen, and there is increased grumbling in military and national-security circles. Maybe this explains that telltale "may."

But if simple prudence requires caution about dismantling every vestige of sex segregation in the military, I find it difficult to understand by what rational process the Court could conclude that Virginia was violating the Constitution by excluding women from VMI. The harm to women from the exclusion seems, as I have said, trivial—the entire harm being the difference in the value of a VMI education and the education in the substitute program that the state had created for women multiplied by the very small number of women who would like to attend VMI—and the Court had no basis either theoretical or empirical for thinking that VMI's educational program would not be seriously impaired, disproportionately to the harm to women from exclusion, by the admission of women.

We live in a period of profound peace—or, rather, that is how it appears to people for whom not only the world wars, but the Cold War, are a rapidly fading memory. It is difficult in such a period to take the needs of national defense completely seriously against claims emanating from more contemporary social issues. In such a period the Virginia Military Institute can only seem a quaint vestige and hence an appropriate subject for social experimentation. It seems to me that this is about the sum and substance of the Court's thinking in the VMI case.

But it may be objected that in suggesting that the Court should have weighed the harm to women from exclusion against the harm to VMI's educational program from their compelled inclusion, I am propounding my own constitutional theory, one utilitarian or even economic in character, and thus inviting the same criticisms that I have made of other theorists. Am I not covertly acknowledging that an atheoretical approach to constitutional decision making is impossible? But I never meant to suggest that it is possible to approach constitutional issues free from any predispositions, free, that is, from an approach, or if you will, a theory. I happen to belong to what I earlier described as the school of "outrage," and it is natural for the members of that school to ask about the balance of harms; it is when a governmental policy inflicts severe and seemingly gratuitous injury on a group (women, say, or blacks) that the juices of outrage are likely to flow. I would be inconsistent only if I tried to show that the school of outrage had a truer view of the Constitution than its rivals. I have not tried to show that, and I do not believe that the intellectual tools exist for establishing which of the competing theories of constitutional decision making is the soundest, although it is possible to point out the weaknesses in each theory.

What I do concede is that the Court could not actually have weighed the harm to women from exclusion against the harm to VMI's educational program from their inclusion. The data are missing. The fault, in part anyway, lies with constitutional theory, which claims to offer the courts a data-free method of deciding cases, rather than helping in the discovery and analysis of the relevant data. The first thing the courts have to learn is how little they know. What to do in the face of radical uncertainty is a separate issue, one that I shall come back to.

Justice Scalia's dissent in the VMI case has a different focus from my criticisms of the majority opinion; his focus is on the implications of the Court's decision for single-sex education in general, apart from the military or quasi-military setting. A Court taken with the crude analogy of sexual to racial segregation is unlikely to look with favor on any kind of single-sex education, unless perhaps if the sex is female—and it may be willing to sacrifice the benefits of single-sex education for women on the altar of perceived neutrality. It seems to me that the courts are as poorly equipped to evaluate sex-segregated education in nonmilitary as in military settings.

Judges who do not have a military background doubtless think they know more about education than they do about war and are therefore less willing to cut the political branches of government slack when dealing with educational issues. But do they know enough about education to make intelligent decisions? Little is known about what makes for effective education. The role of resources, of class size, of curriculum, of racial or other demographic sorting or mixing, of extracurricular activities, of technology, of standardized testing, of family structure, of homework—the significance and interaction of these elements of the educational process remain largely unknown. Judges can certainly be forgiven for not knowing what people who devote their lives to a specialized field do not know; it is less easy to forgive them for not knowing that they don't know. Part of a sense of reality, of an empirical sense, of just the kind of sense that constitutional theory does not cultivate, is knowing which areas of social life are charted and which are not, and being willing to follow the chart where there is a chart and to acknowledge when one is embarking on uncharted seas. If even the experts know very little about education, and this after two and a half millennia of serious reflection (beginning with Plato), this implies that we should welcome continued experimentation and diversity.

Brown v. Board of Education is increasingly considered a flop when regarded as a case about education, which is how the Court pretended (presumably for political reasons) to regard it. For there is no solid evidence that it led to an improvement in the education of blacks or even to substantial public-school integration.[41] It is better viewed as a case about racial subordination, whereas the exclusion of women by the Virginia Military Institute cannot be regarded with a straight face as the warp or woof of a tapestry of sex subordination, given the political and economic power of American women.

I shall end with a few remarks about the *Romer* case. This is the second scrape that the Supreme Court has had with homosexuality, the first being of course *Bowers v. Hardwick*,[42] and the most remarkable thing about both judicial performances is the Court's unwillingness or inability to talk realistically about the phenomenon. The majority opinion in *Bowers* and Chief Justice Burger's concurrence treat it as an uncontroversially reprobated horror, like pedophilia, while the dissents in *Bowers* and the majority opinion in *Romer* treat it as a socially irrelevant innate condition, like being left-handed, and Justice Scalia's dissent in *Romer* treats homosexual rights as a sentimental charitable project of the intelligentsia, like the protection of harp seals. The majority opinion in *Romer* finds, sensibly enough, that the constitutional amendment under challenge, which barred local governments from forbidding discrimination against homosexuals, was motivated by hostility toward homosexuality. The Court then holds that hostility is not an adequate justification for treating one class of people differently from another. And that is just about all there is in the opinion. Ignored are the questions that an ordinary person, his mind not fogged by legal casuistry, would think central: why there is hostility to homosexuality and whether the challenged amendment was a rational expression of that hostility.

Many religious people, Christian and Jewish, believe that homosexual activity is morally wrong. There is no way to assess the validity of this belief, and what weight if any such a belief should be given in a constitutional case seems to me an equally indeterminate question. The belief in equality that informs the VMI opinion is as much an article of faith as the Judeo-Christian antipathy to homosexuality,[43] and to suppose that securing equality for homosexuals is part of the meaning of the Equal Protection Clause is equally a leap of faith. In any event, most Americans, whether religious or not, dislike homosexuality and in particular do not want their children to become homosexuals.[44] They are not sure whether homosexuality is acquired or innate, but, unconvinced that it is purely the latter, they worry about their children becoming homosexual through imitation or seduction. They also worry about AIDS spreading from the homosexual to the heterosexual population (although this fear has abated with the peaking of the epidemic). For these and other reasons, most people dislike the flaunting of homosexual relationships and activities. They particularly do not want government to endorse homosexuality as a way of life entitled to the same respect that we accord to heterosexual relationships particularly within marriage. An ordinance forbidding discrimination in housing, employment, or public accommodations on the basis of sexual orientation is naturally viewed as a form of public endorsement of homosexuality.

My own view is that there is compelling scientific evidence that homosexual preference is genetic or at least congenital, and not acquired,[45] so that the fear of homosexual "contagion" from flaunting or public endorsement of the homosexual way of life is groundless. And it is as likely that increasing the rights of homosexuals would reduce AIDS-producing sex among homosexuals as decreasing them would.[46] However, no allusion to the scientific and social scientific evidence bearing on the phenomenon of homosexuality was made in the *Romer* opinion. Therefore, as it stands the Court seems prepared to forbid discrimination against homosexuals even if the Colorado ban on protective legislation for homosexuals is entirely rational discrimination— the equivalent of "discriminating" against airline pilots who have the misfortune to be old or infirm and as a result are grounded against their will.

There are analogies, which may have been in the minds of some of the Justices, between hostility to homosexuals and other, now discredited hostilities, such as anti-Semitism, just as there is an analogy between racial and sexual segregation of public facilities. But analogies, to repeat an earlier point less contentiously, invite inquiry into difference and similarity; they should not be permitted to elide inquiry. Hostility to homosexuals is plainly a different phenomenon from anti-Semitism and has to be analyzed on its own terms, which the Court has refused to do. Some manifestations of that hostility may be so egregious, hurtful, mean-spirited, even barbarous that the courts should invalidate them without waiting to find out a lot about the phenomenon. But merely barring local governments from making efforts to prevent peaceable private discrimination and by doing so to be seen as endorsing the homosexual way of life falls far short of savagery.

My point is not so much that *Romer* and the *VMI* case were decided incorrectly as that the decisions are so barren of any engagement with reality that the issue of their correctness scarcely arises. It is the lack of an empirical footing that is and always has been the Achilles heel of constitutional law, not the lack of a good constitutional theory. But this raises the question of what the courts are to do in difficult constitutional cases when their ignorance is irremediable, though one hopes only temporarily so. Judges don't yet know enough about the role of women in the military, or about the causes of homosexual orientation, to base decisions in cases such as *Romer* and *VMI* on the answers to these empirical questions. Inevitably, the judge's vote in such a case will turn on his values and temperament. Those judges who believe (a belief likely to reflect a judge's values and temperament rather than a theory of judicial review) in judicial self-restraint, in the sense of wanting to minimize the occasions on which the courts annul the actions of other branches of government, will consider ignorance of the consequences of a challenged governmental policy that is not completely outrageous a compelling reason for staying the judicial hand in the absence of sure guidance from constitutional text, history, or precedent. (An important qualification: many constitutional issues can be resolved on the basis of these conventional legal materials.) Activists will plow ahead.

These poles will not meet until much more is known about the consequences of judicial activism and judicial self-restraint. So one thing that we may hope for through the application of the methods of scientific theory and empirical inquiry to constitutional law is the eventual accumulation of enough knowledge to enable judges at least to deal sensibly with their uncertainty about the consequences of their decisions. Ultimately many of the uncertainties may be dispelled. Until that happy day arrives, the most we can realistically ask of the judges is that they be mindful of the limitations of their knowledge. And I do not mean knowledge of constitutional theory.

NOTES

1. See Richard A. Posner, "The Problematics of Moral and Legal Theory," 111 Harv. L. Rev. 1637 (1998).

2. As held in *Griffin v. California*, 380 U.S. 609 (1965).

3. See Albert W. Alschuler, "A Peculiar Privilege in Historical Perspective," in R. H. Helmholz et al., *The Privilege against Self-Incrimination: Its Origins and Development* 181, 203 (1997).

4. See *United States v. Virginia*, 116 S. Ct. 2264 (1996).

5. See *Romer v. Evans*, 116 S. Ct. 1620 (1996).

6. See The Federalist No. 78 (Alexander Hamilton); *Osborn v. Bank of United States*, 22 U.S. (9 Wheat.) 738, 866 (1824) (Marshall, C.J.) ("Courts are the mere instruments of the law, and can will nothing.").

7. See James B. Thayer, "The Origin and Scope of the American Doctrine of Constitutional Law," 7 Harv. L. Rev. 129 (1893).

8. See id. at 144.

9. On Holmes's position, see Richard A. Posner, "Pragmatic Adjudication," 18 Cardozo L. Rev. 1, 2 (1996).

10. See, e.g., *Rochin v. California*, 342 U.S. 165, 172 (1952) (Frankfurter, J.).

11. See *Lochner v. New York*, 198 U.S. 45, 74–76 (1905) (Holmes, J., dissenting).

12. Which I summarize and elaborate in Richard A. Posner, *The Federal Courts: Challenge and Reform* 304–34 (1996).

13. See Antonin Scalia, "Common-Law Courts in a Civil-Law System: The Role of United States Federal Courts in Interpreting the Constitution and Laws," in *A Matter of Interpretation: Federal Courts and the Law* 3, 23–25 (Amy Gutmann ed., 1997).

14. See Antonin Scalia, "Response," in id. at 129, 138–39. He says, "Where originalism will make a difference is not in the rolling back of accepted old principles of constitutional law but in the rejection of usurpatious new ones." Id. at 139. But on his understanding of proper constitutional interpretation, most of the "accepted old principles" were themselves "usurpatious" when first announced, and some of them were first announced in the 1970s and 1980s on the basis of just the kind of nonoriginalist interpretation that he considers usurpative.

15. Cf. Ronald Dworkin, *Freedom's Law: The Moral Reading of the American Constitution* 75 (1996).

16. The shortcomings of lawyers and judges, even of law professors, as legal historians have been noted often. For recent discussions, citing the earlier literature, see Martin S. Flaherty, "History 'Lite' in Modern American Constitutionalism," 95 Colum. L. Rev. 523 (1995); Barry Friedman & Scott B. Smith, *The Sedimentary Constitution* (Oct. 30, 1997) (unpublished manuscript, on file with author).

17. See Learned Hand, *The Bill of Rights* 30 (1958).

18. See Herbert Wechsler, "Toward Neutral Principles of Constitutional Law," 73 Harv. L. Rev. 1 (1959). Criticisms of the article are summarized in Richard A. Posner, *Overcoming Law* 71–75 (1995).

19. See John Hart Ely, *Democracy and Distrust: A Theory of Judicial Review* 87–104 (1980).

20. Expounded in many places, most recently in his article, Ronald Dworkin, "In Praise of Theory," 29 Ariz. St. L.J. 353 (1997).

21. See, e.g., Posner, supra note 18, at 207–14. See id. at 198–207 on the shortcomings of Ely's theory, and Michael W. McConnell, "The Importance of Humility

in Judicial Review: A Comment on Ronald Dworkin's 'Moral Reading' of the Constitution," 65 Fordham L. Rev. 1269 (1997), on the shortcomings of Dworkin's theory.

22. See Bruce Ackerman, *We the People: Foundations* (1991).

23. See, e.g., Lawrence Lessig, "Fidelity in Translation," 71 Tex. L. Rev. 1165, 1166–73 (1993); Lawrence Lessig, "Fidelity and Constraint," 65 Fordham L. Rev. 1365, 1371–76 (1997).

24. See John Rawls, *Political Liberalism* 212–54 (1993).

25. See, e.g., Cass R. Sunstein, *Legal Reasoning and Political Conflict* 35–48 (1996); Cass R. Sunstein, "The Supreme Court, 1995 Term—Foreword: Leaving Things Undecided," 110 Harv. L. Rev. 4, 6–10 (1996); Cass R. Sunstein, *Judicial Minimalism* (Aug. 1997) (unpublished manuscript, on file with author).

26. "[C]itizens are to conduct their fundamental discussions within the framework of what each regards as a political conception of justice based on values that the others can reasonably be expected to endorse and each is, in good faith, prepared to defend that conception so understood." Rawls, supra note 24, at 226; see also John Rawls, "The Idea of Public Reason Revisited," 64 U. Chi. L. Rev. 765 (1997).

27. See, e.g., J. M. Balkin, "Agreements with Hell and Other Objects of Our Faith," 65 Fordham L. Rev. 1703 (1997).

28. 369 U.S. 186 (1962).

29. See Ronald Dworkin, "The Bork Nomination," New York Review of Books, Aug. 13, 1987, at 3, 10, reprinted as "Bork: The Senate's Responsibility," in Dworkin, supra note 15, at 265, 267, 273.

30. 347 U.S. 483 (1954).

31. 410 U.S. 113 (1973).

32. See, e.g., Gerald N. Rosenberg, *The Hollow Hope: Can Courts Bring About Social Change?* (1991); Donald J. Boudreaux & A. C. Pritchard, "Rewriting the Constitution: An Economic Analysis of the Constitutional Amendment Process," 62 Fordham L. Rev. 111 (1993); Isaac Ehrlich & George D. Brower, "On the Issue of Causality in the Economic Model of Crime and Law Enforcement: Some Theoretical Considerations and Experimental Evidence," 77 Am. Econ. Rev. Papers & Proc. 99 (May 1987).

33. See Ronald Dworkin, "Reply," 29 Ariz. St. L.J. 432, 433 (19970.

34. 116 S. Ct. 2264 (1996).

35. Id. at 2269. The Fourth Circuit, in an earlier stage of the case, had based this conclusion on a non sequitur: the success of women's colleges, which are not military and do not employ the adversarial method. See *United States v. Virginia*, 976 F.2d 890, 897 (4th Cir. 1992).

36. The lower court had found "that VMI's mission can be accomplished only in a single-gender environment and that changes necessary to accommodate coeducation would tear at the fabric of VMI's unique methodology." *United States v. Virginia*, 976 F.2d at 897.

37. See Johannes Morsink, "Was Aristotle's Biology Sexist?" 12 J. Hist. Biology 83, 110–12 (1979).

38. See Kingsley R. Browne, "Sex and Temperament in Modern Society: A Darwinian View of the Glass Ceiling and the Gender Gap," 37 Ariz. L. Rev. 971, 1016–64 (1995).

39. I am not arguing that because single-sex restrooms are lawful, VMI should be entitled to exclude women. That would be as illegitimate a use of analogy as the ones that I am criticizing.

40. *United States v. Virginia*, 116 S. Ct. 2264, 2281 (1996) (footnotes omitted).

41. See, e.g., Sonia R. Jarvis, "Brown and the Afrocentric Curriculum," 101 Yale L.J. 1285, 1289–91 (1992) (explaining that there has been minimal progress in equalization of educational opportunity for black children, and that efforts to integrate schools—predominantly through busing—have been met with widespread resistance, white flight, and ultimate resegregation); Steven Spiegel, "Race, Education, and the Equal Protection Clause in the 1990s: The Meaning of *Brown v. Board of Education* Re-examined in Light of Milwaukee's Schools of African-American Immersion," 74 Marq. L. Rev. 501, 503–7 (1991) (finding principles articulated in *Brown* problematic when applied to Milwaukee's attempt to improve education of black children).

42. 478 U.S. 186 (1986).

43. Sanford Levinson remarks (following Michael Perry) upon the double standard that prevails in discussions of the legitimate scope of judicial reasoning: the nonreligious are permitted to make almost any argument they want in support of the positions they take, but the religious are not permitted to make religious arguments in support of their positions. See Sanford Levinson, "Abstinence and Exclusion: What Does Liberalism Demand of the Religiously Oriented (Would Be) Judge?" in Religion and Contemporary Liberalism 76, 79 (Paul J. Weithman ed., 1997).

44. See the summary of polling data in Stephen Zmansky, "Colorado's Amendment 2 and Homosexuals' Right to Equal Protection of the Law," 35 B.C. L. Rev. 221, 245–46 (1993).

45. See Posner, supra note 18, at 572; Richard A. Posner, "The Economic Approach to Homosexuality," in *Sex, Preference, and Family: Essays on Law and Nature* 173, 186, 191 n.26 (David M. Estlund & Martha C. Nussbaum eds., 1997).

46. See Tomas J. Philipson & Richard A. Posner, *Private Choices and Public Health: The AIDS Epidemic in an Economic Perspective* 179–80 (1993).

Chapter 10

The Anatomy of an Execution
Fairness versus "Process"

Stephen Reinhardt

[R]eversal by a higher court is not proof that justice is thereby better done.[1]

The year I graduated from law school, the Warren Court decided *Brown v. Board of Education.*[2] *Brown*, perhaps the most important Supreme Court decision in history, introduced a new judicial era, an era in which the courts became the protectors of the rights of the poor, the disenfranchised, and the underprivileged. The Warren Court—the Warren-Brennan era—will be remembered for that legacy. The Court's decisions were guided by a broad, humanitarian vision of the role of the judiciary and of the Constitution as a living document. The Warren Court expanded concepts of equality, due process, and individual liberty, handing down decisions that redefined notions of justice and fairness.

In the area of civil rights, the Warren Court helped usher in revolutionary and irreversible changes in race relations. It also issued landmark First Amendment decisions such as *New York Times Co. v. Sullivan*[3] and *Engel v. Vitale*,[4] expanding the protections afforded the free press and strengthening freedom from state-sponsored religion. It implemented "one person, one vote" in *Reynolds v. Sims*,[5] changing our entire political system.[6] And in its

This lecture was delivered on October 20, 1998, and appeared in 74 N.Y.U.L. Rev. 313 (1999).

criminal justice decisions, the Warren Court established groundbreaking rules in cases such as *Gideon v. Wainwright,*[7] *Miranda v. Arizona,*[8] and *Mapp v. Ohio,*[9] for the first time implementing some of the Bill of Rights's most fundamental promises and giving life to the Fourth, Fifth, and Sixth Amendments. The rules were as elementary as the one holding that everyone charged with a crime has the right to be defended by counsel. And although Earl Warren had left the Court by 1969, the Warren-Brennan era continued long enough to give us *Roe v. Wade,*[10] which afforded women the most basic of rights, and *Furman v. Georgia,*[11] which for a brief period held the death penalty unconstitutional. At the time, we thought that there was no turning back, that the Supreme Court's transformation of the role of the judiciary would guarantee a new era in constitutional law, an era in which progress would be the rule, forward would be the direction, and the interests and welfare of the people would be dominant.

Today, we face a very different Court, one that has also had a major impact, and one that will be remembered for its own legacy. The Rehnquist Court will be remembered for its stark reversal of the Warren-Brennan Court's expansion of individual rights and protections and for elevating procedural rules over substantive values and limiting rights generally, especially those of racial minorities.[12] It will be remembered for erecting technical barriers that foreclose relief to persons with meritorious constitutional claims. It will be known for reducing access to the federal courts and for placing the interests of the state ahead of those of its citizens. Without formally overruling the liberties and freedoms recognized by the Warren Court, the Rehnquist Court has rendered many of them virtually unenforceable,[13] the exceptions being property rights[14] and, to the surprise of most observers, free speech.[15]

The Rehnquist Court has drawn the line regarding substantive due process, refusing to recognize any new, unenumerated rights[16]—a principle that would have left us without the critical protections of privacy recognized in decisions such as *Griswold v. Connecticut*[17] and *Roe v. Wade.*[18] And one can only contemplate with dread the answer the current Court would have given had it been asked to overrule *Plessy v. Ferguson.*[19]

The Rehnquist Court has placed its greatest emphasis on the expansion of nonconstitutional doctrines such as mootness, ripeness, standing, procedural default, nonretroactivity, independent state grounds, and abuse of the writ. It also emphasizes at every opportunity nostrums such as comity and finality. Under the Rehnquist Court's jurisprudence, these rules regularly prove decisive in limiting the ability of lower federal courts to redress constitutional violations, in shutting the doors of the courthouse to ordinary people. The Court's constriction of rights has been most notable in the criminal justice area: in particular, through assaults on what was once known as "The Great Writ," the writ of habeas corpus—much of it in the name of federalism or, as it used to be known, states' rights. The Rehnquist Court has rendered a number of decisions that prohibit habeas petitioners from bringing claims they did not "properly" raise in state court or in earlier habeas petitions, unless they can overcome an increasingly strict cause and prejudice test[20] or meet an almost impossible "miscarriage of justice" standard.[21] At the same time, the Court has made it easier for states to claim that their courts relied on independent state grounds to reach their decisions and thus to avoid any federal judicial review of their unconstitutional actions.[22] The Court's decisions have also inflated the harmless error and plain error standards beyond recognition, thereby encouraging future violations of constitutional rights.[23] Finally, the adoption of the anomalous *Teague v. Lane*[24] doctrine has foreclosed relief to most habeas petitioners unless they are able to demonstrate that courts generally recognized the particular violation they suffered before their convictions became final. In other words, after *Teague*, habeas petitioners are not entitled to raise claims on the basis of what the Court defines as "new rules."

Today, this maze of procedural barriers compels federal judges to spend up to 90 percent of our time in capital cases and other habeas proceedings trying to determine whether a defendant's rights have unwittingly been forfeited and trying to apply the Supreme Court's arcane and almost impenetrable procedural rules. Unless we conclude that the defendant has somehow surmounted all the Court-created artificial constructs, we cannot even reach what is now usually the easier question: whether the defendant was deprived of his constitutional rights. In recent years, it has become increasingly unlikely that the federal courts can correct constitutional violations occurring in state prosecutions. Frequently, all that is left to a defendant is a claim of ineffective assistance of counsel, which is, of course, one of the most pervasive problems in capital cases.[25] But even a claim of ineffective assistance is often procedurally foreclosed because in the state postconviction proceedings the same ineffective lawyer continues to represent the defendant, or, even worse, the defendant is left without counsel at all. Either way, the ineffectiveness claim almost surely will not be raised in a timely manner and, under the rules adopted by the Rehnquist Court, will be procedurally defaulted.[26] What has been lost in the worship of abstract procedural principles is our concern for fairness and justice—our dedication to the Bill of Rights and the Fourteenth Amendment.

The epitome of this Supreme Court's death penalty jurisprudence is the case of Thomas Thompson, who was executed on July 14, 1998, by the State of California.[27] One year earlier, in August 1997, my court, the U.S. Court of Appeals for the Ninth Circuit, sitting en banc, had issued an exhaustive and forceful opinion vacating Thompson's death sentence and remanding his murder conviction.[28] We held that he had been deprived of effective assistance of counsel on the charge that made him eligible for the death penalty and that the prosecutor's highly improper conduct both at his trial and at the trial of his alleged accomplice violated the Due Process Clause.[29] In short, Thompson had not received anything resembling a fair trial. In April 1998, the Supreme Court vacated our decision, and without uttering a single word of disagreement with our judgment that Thompson's constitutional rights had been egregiously violated, declared, through a now-familiar bare majority of five Justices, that we had committed "a grave abuse of discretion" by hearing Thompson's case en banc.[30]

The Supreme Court's decision that a person could be executed on the basis of a trial in which his fundamental constitutional rights were violated was, sadly, nothing new. By similar five-to-four margins, the Rehnquist Court had previously held that persons could be executed when the constitutional rules violated in their trials had not been "compelled by existing precedent."[31] It also had held that a man could be executed because he could not provide a good enough reason why his winning constitutional claim had been raised in his second habeas petition rather than in his first.[32] Similarly, the Court had ruled that a man could be executed because his lawyer had filed his notice of appeal in the state habeas proceedings three days late.[33]

In *Coleman*, while overturning decades of jurisprudence, the Rehnquist Court explained, in a sentence exemplifying the quality of its concern for individual rights, that earlier Supreme Court habeas decisions were "based on a conception of federal/state relations that undervalued the importance of state procedural rules."[34] "We now recognize," the Rehnquist Court announced, "the important interest in finality served by state procedural rules, and the significant harm to the States that results from the failure of federal courts to respect them."[35] In other words, the Rehnquist Court proclaimed that until the present Justices came along, the U.S. Supreme Court had not been sufficiently perceptive to realize that state procedural rules are more important than fairness, due process, and even justice. If only Justices Warren and Brennan, and other learned predecessors of the current Court, had been possessed of the acuity and judicial wisdom that today's Justices enjoy, we could have devalued the Bill of Rights years earlier.

The surprising thing about the case of Thomas Thompson is that, in contrast to most of the other cases in which the Court refused to entertain the merits of petitioners' claims, there was no contention that any state procedural rule had been violated or that any constitutional principle involved was inapplicable because it was a "new rule," not one generally recognized before Thompson's conviction. No, against all odds, Thompson and his lawyer had scrupulously, and successfully, wound their way through what Justice Blackmun called the "[b]yzantine morass of arbitrary, unnecessary, and unjustifiable impediments to the vindication of federal rights."[36] Yet, once again, the Supreme Court majority refused even to consider whether the petitioner's constitutional rights had been violated. The ostensible reason this time was that the judges on our court had missed a deadline, the state's "final" judgment had become incrementally more final, and, as a result, the en banc hearing we held had been conducted too late. Our decision was null and void. The fact that Thompson would be executed on the basis of an unconstitutional trial was of no consequence to the majority of the members of the Supreme Court.

Perhaps a fuller discussion of what occurred in the Thompson case will help make clearer the sharp differences in judicial philosophy between the current Supreme Court and those who would give substance to the protections afforded all persons by the Bill of Rights and the Fourteenth Amendment. In any event, I believe it to be a tale worth recording.

I. The Trial

Thomas Thompson was convicted in 1983 in a California state court of the first-degree murder and rape of Ginger Fleischli. It was his first criminal conviction. Two years earlier, Thompson had gone out for a night of drinking with a group that included Ms. Fleischli, David Leitch, and Leitch's former wife. Leitch had until recently been Ms. Fleischli's lover, and they had lived together. After the breakup with Leitch, Ms. Fleischli decided to share living quarters with Leitch's former wife. Thompson, who was new to the group, moved in with Leitch as his roommate. At the end of the evening's carousing, Ms. Fleischli and Thompson went to the apartment in which she had lived with Leitch but which Leitch and Thompson now shared. Leitch arrived sometime later that night. By the next morning, Ms. Fleischli was dead. Her body, with multiple stab wounds to the head, was found two days later in a field ten miles away. Suspicion regarding her murder immediately focused on Leitch, because of his prior sexual relationship with her, because he had threatened her in the past, and because he had a history of violence toward women.[37]

The state arrested and eventually indicted both Leitch and Thompson. Its theory was that Leitch wanted Ms. Fleischli dead because he hoped to resume his relationship with his former wife and that he recruited Thompson to join in the killing and disposal of the body. Leitch, the prosecution insisted at preliminary hearings, was "the only person . . . who ha[d] a motive" to kill the victim.[38] At the preliminary hearing, the prosecution presented four jailhouse informants who testified in support of this version of the crime. The informants stated that Thompson had confessed that Leitch had recruited him to help kill Ms. Fleischli because she was interfering with his attempt to reconcile with his former wife. One of these informants testified that Thompson had told him that Thompson had engaged in consensual sex with Ms. Fleischli before Leitch returned home, and that upon Leitch's return, they had killed her.[39] At a subsequent hearing a few months later, the prosecution again argued, "[Leitch] is the only person . . . who has a motive"—that motive being that Ms. Fleischli was "in the way" of a successful reconciliation with his former wife.[40]

The same deputy district attorney prosecuted both Leitch and Thompson.[41] He subsequently testified that his theory of the case never varied throughout the proceedings.[42] Indeed, he advocated the state's principal theory—that Leitch had recruited Thompson to help kill Ms. Fleischli—at the preliminary hearing, at the hearing on the motion to set aside the charges, at Leitch's trial, and at the postconviction hearings.[43]

But when the preliminary proceedings were completed, a surprising development occurred: The prosecutor decided to try Thompson first, and at the Thompson trial he offered an entirely new and contradictory version of the facts. There the prosecutor insisted that Thompson was the sole killer and that his motive was to cover up the fact that he had raped Ms. Fleischli—a theory that was wholly inconsistent with the version he had urged on every other occasion. The prosecutor now argued that Thompson "was the only person in that apartment with Miss Fleischli the night—at the time she was killed."[44] Thompson raped her, he told the jury, and "[b]ecause she said she was going to tell for what he did to her," he spontaneously "killed her to prevent being caught for rape."[45] The prosecutor declined to call any of the four prosecution witnesses the state had presented at the preliminary hearing, all of whose stories directly contradicted the tale he presented at Thompson's trial. Instead, he put on the stand two new and notoriously untruthful jailhouse informants, John Del Frate and the aptly named Edward Fink. The new "snitches" conveniently testified that Thompson had confessed to a version of events that corresponded with the prosecutor's newly developed rape theory.[46] Their testimony provided, in the prosecutor's own words, the "dispositive" evidence that Thompson had raped Ms. Fleischli and murdered her to cover up the crime.[47] The snitches also testified that Leitch was not involved in the murder—that he only discovered that the victim had been killed after he returned to the apartment and found her dead and that his involvement was limited to helping dispose of her body at Thompson's urging.[48] The prosecutor emphasized to the Thompson jury that Leitch was in no way involved in Ms. Fleischli's actual killing, asking "[w]hat evidence do we really have that [Leitch] did anything, had any part [except in disposing of the body]? There is no evidence we have putting him in the apartment that night."[49] He vouched for the new jailhouse informants' credibility: "[T]here's no reason whatsoever they have to lie. There's no motive to fabricate, and [Thompson] couldn't impeach them on one single point."[50] By convicting Thompson of rape as well as murder, the prosecutor succeeded in making him eligible for the death penalty, which the jury and judge then imposed.[51]

Of course, the prosecutor did not stick with this version of the events for long. After Thompson's trial, he returned to the original theory: that Leitch recruited Thompson to help him kill Ms. Fleischli because Leitch wanted Ms. Fleischli dead.[52] At Leitch's trial, the prosecutor did not call the two snitches whose reliability he had vouched for during Thompson's trial and whose testimony he had called "dispositive."[53] Instead, he subpoenaed the witnesses who had testified in Thompson's defense, whose testimony he had sought to discredit at Thompson's trial—testimony that suggested that Leitch, not Thompson, was the murderer.[54] Now, he urged that the jury credit that testimony.

Having obtained Thompson's conviction, the prosecutor returned to the theory he had argued at all the other proceedings, that Leitch's violent history, his past threats toward Ms. Fleischli, and his motive—his desire to remove an obstacle to reconciliation with his former wife—demonstrated that Leitch was the murderer. The prosecutor argued, in direct contravention of his statements to the jury in the Thompson trial, that Leitch was "the only one with any motive for [Ms. Fleischli's] death."[55] And in perhaps the most blatant contradiction of all, he ridiculed the very version of events that he had presented at Thompson's trial, asking whether it would be "reasonable" or "logical" for Thompson to kill Ms. Fleischli, wait for her former lover to return home and discover the murder, and then request his help in disposing of the body.[56] He answered his own question: "No, it didn't happen that way."[57] In short, Thompson did not do what the state told his jury he did. Thompson did not commit the acts for which the state had obtained his conviction, the acts that allowed the imposition of the death penalty.

The incompatibility of the two presentations could not have been more evident.[58] As Judge Betty Fletcher of our court later wrote, "little about the trials remained consistent other than the prosecutor's desire to win at any cost."[59]

The prosecutor's contradictory presentations were so blatantly unethical that, in a wholly unprecedented action, seven former California prosecutors[60] with extensive death penalty experience subsequently filed an amicus brief on Thompson's behalf in the U.S. Supreme Court, arguing that "this is a case where it appears that our adversarial system has not produced a fair and reliable result."[61] This group of top prosecutors included the individual entrusted with the decision whether to seek the death penalty in all capital-eligible cases in Los Angeles County during 1979–91, his counterpart in Sacramento entrusted with the same decision in that county during 1989–95, and the drafter of the California death penalty statute under which Thompson was convicted and sentenced.[62] These highly respected prosecutors severely criticized the egregious conduct of Thompson's prosecutor and observed that "the use of three informants to support one prosecution theory and then two new informants to support another demonstrates how easy it is to manipulate facts when the prosecutor's goal is to win at all costs."[63]

In addition to facing a prosecution that made a fair trial impossible, Thompson found himself defended by an attorney who made the inexplicable decision not to contest the assertion that Ms. Fleischli had been raped, although there was very little evidence that the intercourse had been anything but consensual, and it was the rape charge that made the murder a capital offense. Incredibly, rather than questioning the state's physical evidence or putting on his own forensic testimony, Thompson's defense attorney chose to argue that it was Leitch who had raped Ms. Fleischli.[64] He thus effectively admitted, on his client's behalf, the occurrence of a rape that in all likelihood never occurred—a "rape" that made Thompson eligible for the death sentence.[65] Thompson's counsel also made only minimal efforts to impeach the jailhouse informants who testified that Thompson had confessed a rape and murder to them, failing to discover that both Fink and Del Frate often had testified about purported confessions in exchange for favors from law enforcement officials and were generally regarded as extremely unreliable;[66] that Fink's parole hold[67] had been released after he gave his statements implicating Thompson; that Del Frate's testimony matched inaccurate news reports of the crime; and that even Del Frate's own family knew him to be a "pathological liar."[68] The attorney's failure to contest the allegation that Ms. Fleischli was raped is extremely disturbing in light of Thompson's testimony that he had engaged in consensual sex with her after returning to the apartment and the evidence that Thompson later obtained which casts substantial doubt on the theory that any rape occurred. That evidence includes both forensic testimony and Leitch's own admissions against interest that he observed Thompson and Ms. Fleischli engaging in consensual sex on the night in question.[69]

All in all, Thompson's trial fell far short of minimal constitutional standards in every important respect.[70]

II. The Federal Habeas Petition

After losing his appeals in the California state courts, in 1990 Thompson finally earned the right to present his constitutional claims to a federal court. Thompson filed his petition for writ of habeas corpus in the U.S. District Court for the Central District of California. The case was assigned to Judge Richard Gadbois, a former state court trial judge and an appointee of President Ronald Reagan. Judge Gadbois, who, over a five-year period, read and reread thousands of pages of trial transcripts and held an evidentiary hearing at which he heard additional direct testimony, issued a meticulous and carefully considered 101-page opinion.[71]

Judge Gadbois ruled that Thompson's trial attorney rendered ineffective assistance of counsel as to the rape charge by failing to contest the state's dubious physical evidence and failing to impeach the state's two jailhouse informants.[72] The district court found that this deficient performance prejudiced Thompson in light of the insubstantiality of the evidence that any rape had occurred.[73] The court did not conclude, however, that the prosecutor's use of inconsistent theories reached the level of a constitutional violation.[74] Judge Gadbois's ruling meant that Thompson's death sentence would be vacated, but his murder conviction would stand.[75] The state appealed and so did Thompson.

On June 19, 1996, a three-judge panel of the Ninth Circuit reversed the part of the decision in Thompson's favor.[76] It did so on the ground that any errors made by his lawyer were not prejudicial.[77] The decision gave short shrift to Thompson's arguments, saying, for instance, that the panel "[could not] say that" the informants' testimony "formed a crucial part of the case"[78] even though the prosecutor had called their testimony "dispositive."[79] The panel's essential message was contained in the first sentence of its analysis, where it chanted the Rehnquist Court's mantra: "We are mindful of the limited role of federal courts in habeas review of state convictions."[80] That message of course bore no relation to what the panel actually did in Thompson's case—which was to reexamine, reweigh, and reevaluate the evidence and reject the findings of the district judge. This task is one for which conservative jurists regularly proclaim appellate judges are ill-suited, insisting that such judgments should be left to district judges who, like Judge Gadbois, have conducted the evidentiary hearings. Nonetheless, the panel reached a conclusion contrary to the district judge's conclusion and reinstated Thompson's death sentence.[81]

On August 5, 1996, Thompson filed a timely petition for rehearing and suggestion for rehearing en banc, which was circulated to the judges of our court.[82] Toward the end of September, a judge requested that the panel provide a 5.4(b) notice.[83] A request for such a notice, which is known by the number and letter of one of our internal rules,[84] is ordinarily a precursor to a judge's calling for a rehearing en banc and a signal to the court that the judge is likely to so call.

The procedure by which the full court decides whether to hear cases en banc is provided by statute.[85] As caseloads have proliferated, en banc hearings have become increasingly important.[86] Under our internal rules, if any active or senior judge believes that a decision by a three-judge panel of the court merits rehearing by the court sitting en banc, that judge is entitled to request a vote for rehearing by all the active judges. If a majority of the active judges then votes for rehearing en banc, an en banc court of eleven judges is convened, the case is argued anew, and the en banc court may then issue a decision that supersedes the three-judge panel's decision.[87] An en banc call—that is, a request for a vote on whether to rehear a case en banc—provides a check on unconstitutional executions and leads to reversals in capital as well as noncapital cases.[88]

When a judge requested a 5.4(b) notice in the *Thompson* case, the three-judge panel became obligated to notify the full court after it had ruled on Thompson's petition for rehearing and suggestion for rehearing en banc before the original panel—in layman's terms, after it had considered the losing party's objections and decided to stand by its opinion.[89] Once a judge requests a notice, the other judges who might be concerned about the opinion ordinarily assume that the judge who made the request will take responsibility for the case and, at the appropriate time, will call for an en banc vote or notify the other members of the court that he or she has decided not to make a call, so that any other judge wishing to take up the cause will have the chance to do so.

The *Thompson* panel waited approximately four months, until January 17, 1997, to forward a 5.4(b) notice stating that it had voted to deny the petition for rehearing and to reject the suggestion for rehearing en banc.[90] The sending of that notice triggered a fourteen-day period in which to make the formal en banc call.[91] The fourteen days passed, however, and somehow, for reasons we will probably never fully know, the judge who requested the notice failed to take the next step in time. It is not clear even now how or why the time that our internal rules provided for requesting an en banc hearing slipped by not only that judge—who is, in my opinion, unquestionably the ablest, hardest working, and most conscientious judge on our court—but all the rest of the judges of the court as well. It is not even clear whether the error was entirely human or mechanical, or whether the panel's inclusion in its notice of its intent to amend the opinion played a part.[92]

What is clear is that although more than half the members of the court thought that the issues were sufficiently troubling that an en banc hearing was required, and, although that same majority even thought that we should go to the unusual lengths of recalling the mandate in order to hear Thompson's case en banc,[93] none of us made the call in time. The best explanations seem to lie in our assumption that the judge who had requested the 5.4(b) notice would make the call; in the fact that we receive dozens of e-mail messages a day, many containing brief declarations of formal actions such as the filing of notices and technical orders; in the fact that our system of transmitting such notices is mechanically imperfect;[94] and in the overwhelming volume of the caseload all federal judges face these days, a caseload that often prevents us from being as meticulous in our tasks as we should be.[95] In that regard, I would add only that at the time the *Thompson* case was before our court we were missing one-third of our authorized judges, having just nineteen of our complement of twenty-eight.[96] The critical point, however, is the fact that at least ten of us—a majority of the active judges and the judges who ultimately voted to take the case en banc—failed to make a timely call.[97]

On March 6, 1997, the three-judge panel released an order amending its opinion (in technical, not substantive ways) and again, superfluously, denied Thompson's requests for further proceedings.[98] The day after the order was published in legal newspapers, I became aware for the first time that Thompson's suggestion for a rehearing en banc had been denied and that no judge had sought an en banc vote. I immediately sent a memorandum to the panel.[99] In my opinion, the case necessitated further review. I presumed that if no request for a vote had been made, an error of some type had occurred, and the panel would be willing to grant an extension of time to any judge requesting one, in line with the uniform past practice within our court.

I explained to the panel that I, for one, must have made a mistake in not making the call, that it could have been due to an administrative error that occurred at the time of a change in law clerks, and that after reviewing the opinion I was worried that the panel's decision, along with my mistake, "might lead to the execution of a person who may possibly be innocent and whose constitutional rights appear to have been violated."[100] I closed by asking "whether the panel might be willing to . . . permit me to make a prompt en banc call."[101]

The next day, the judge who had requested the 5.4(b) notice sent a memorandum to the panel, which made it clear that that judge also had not realized that the notice had been circulated.[102] That judge wrote:

> My first awareness that the petition for rehearing and en banc request in this case had been acted on was the receipt of the March 6 amended opinion and order, received yesterday.
>
> I have just received Judge Reinhardt's memo. I second his request. . . . I wonder whether in any event an amended opinion triggers a new 5.4(b) period?[103]

The judge quickly followed up with another memorandum asking: "Was a 5.4(b) notice circulated? Did I miss it?"[104] The initial question whether technical amendments to an opinion would trigger a new en banc period serves only to illustrate how complicated and ambiguous our en banc rules are.[105] Judge Alex Kozinski later suggested, for reasons of his own, that a call might still have been timely in view of the proposed technical amendment. The judge who requested the 5.4(b) notice and I conferred, however, and concluded that under our rules the amendment did not alter the time requirements.

On March 20, Judge Robert Beezer responded on behalf of the three-judge panel.[106] He informed us that "[t]he panel has unanimously agreed that nothing will be done by the panel to extend the time within which an en banc call can be made. We see no reason to delay further consideration of this case by the Supreme Court."[107] This response was remarkable. For the first time of which I am aware, a panel of our court took the extraordinary step of refusing a request by a judge of the court for an extension of time in which to call for rehearing en banc. It refused our request even though no one questioned our explanation that the failure to make a timely en banc call was due to nothing more than human error or some other miscalculation or malfunction. Finally, it did so even though the error was one made by members of the court—not by the petitioner or his attorney—and the result would be that the full court would be deprived of the opportunity to review the panel's decision that a person should die. I was, frankly, shocked by the cold-blooded and uncollegial response of my colleagues. I consulted with the other judge who had joined in my request. The reply came swiftly. There was nothing further we could do. From a practical standpoint, I agreed.[108]

Thompson then, on April 21, 1997, petitioned the Supreme Court for certiorari.[109] It was at that point that the brief of the seven former top prosecutors was filed.[110] The Supreme Court denied Thompson's petition on June 2, 1997.[111] Our court received notice of the denial on June 5 and on June 11 issued the mandate to the district court, an act that subsequently took on enormous significance.

After the Supreme Court denied certiorari, I obtained a copy of the brief that the seven former prosecutors had filed. The strong law-and-order views of the signers were well known to me, as were their reputations for integrity. The brief's description of Thompson's prosecutor's misconduct was startling. I discussed the case with a number of judges on our court, including the Chief Judge, Procter Hug, Jr. One of the judges I spoke with, a former prosecutor, told me that he was personally aware that one of the key jailhouse witnesses against Thompson had a penchant for testifying that he had obtained confessions from others in the jail and that his testimony was generally known to be unreliable. Finally, I spoke with Judge Jerome Farris, a highly respected senior judge who is extremely conservative on criminal justice issues. I sent him a copy of the seven prosecutors' amicus brief. Judge Farris told me that he found the facts to be shocking, if true, and that he thought that we had an obligation to review the case through the en banc process. He was confident that the panel would now accede to a request to let the court rehear the case and that, if not, an overwhelming majority of the court would agree to do so.

Judge Farris's optimism proved unfounded. He sent a memorandum on July 7, less than thirty days after we issued our mandate, in which he asked that he be permitted to call for an en banc vote.[112] The panel swiftly denied his request.[113] The Chief Judge immediately scheduled a vote by the entire court on Judge Farris's request to recall the mandate. Judge Farris offered the following eloquent plea:

> How does injustice happen, and why does it persist throughout human history, are questions that I have long pondered. I've concluded that its primary cause is that most of the strong have little concern for the rights of the weak. Civilization survives because from time to time some of the strong step forward and say "enough." Those who care cannot correct all of the wrongs nor do they owe an apology for those wrongs they cannot impact. However, in my view, they must step forward when the question of appropriate action is presented. In such moments, inaction or indifference—not failure—is the deadly sin.[114]

The debate was interrupted shortly after the panel's denial of Judge Farris's request when two judges, our en banc coordinator and the judge who had until recently been our death penalty coordinator, sent memoranda on July 10 and 11 respectively that temporarily put the brakes on everything— memoranda that were sent with the best of intentions but which led to a decision for which the Supreme Court would later castigate us and impugn our integrity as a court. In the first memorandum, the judge who serves as en banc coordinator informed us of a development in the case: Thompson had filed a new petition in state court and the state courts had resumed their proceedings.[115] The judge urged us to delay any action. The memorandum said:

> [C]onsistent with the [Supreme Court's] exhaustion jurisprudence with which we must live, state and federal courts should not have the same prisoner's life in their hands at the same time. . . . To withdraw the mandate now would appear at the very least to provoke a confrontation with California and its courts that will pull Thompson in two directions.[116]

The judge who had been the death penalty coordinator agreed and urged us to wait until Thompson had exhausted his state court remedies on his second petition before taking any further action on the first.[117] Chief Judge Hug consulted with those of us who had urged immediate action. Aware that the positions of the two coordinators would make it impossible to prevail if an immediate vote were held, the en banc proponents bowed to the coordinators' suggestion. We reluctantly agreed to postpone the vote. In fact, the conflict was not what the two judges had feared. The district court had not yet taken its final action. It had not yet spread the mandate.[118] In practical terms, Thompson's first habeas petition remained before the federal courts. Because the district court still had jurisdiction over that petition, we could have recalled the mandate without intruding on the prerogatives of the state courts. It was in fact the state judicial system that had jumped the gun by resuming jurisdiction over Thompson's proceedings before the federal courts' actions on his first petition had become final. Yet, critical details frequently get lost in the rush of complex death penalty struggles within our circuit, and, as a result, the seemingly reasonable but mistaken view of the two proceduralists prevailed.

So we waited. The California Supreme Court denied Thompson's petition on July 16.[119] Several days later Thompson turned to our court again. He filed a motion to recall the mandate.[120] When the panel finally denied the motion, after a six-day delay,[121] our Chief Judge reactivated Judge Farris's sua sponte call.[122]

Finally, on July 29, less than a week before the scheduled execution, we were able to vote on whether to go en banc to correct the panel's clearly erroneous decision. A majority of the active judges voted to recall the mandate and rehear the case.[123] Oral argument was scheduled for August 1, four days later.[124]

Let me take a moment to assure you that, despite what some Supreme Court Justices and U.S. Senators might think, the Ninth Circuit was not and is not a "liberal" court. At the time the majority of the court decided to recall the mandate, a majority of the judges eligible to vote on the question were appointees of Presidents Reagan or Bush, and they reflected the judicial philosophy of those presidents. That a court composed of a majority of Republican appointees who shared the values of the Rehnquist Court could be considered a liberal body, simply because on occasion it issues a decision that shows respect for human rights or individual liberties, demonstrates just how far the judicial system has come—or gone—from the Warren-Brennan era.[125]

In any event, on August 1, four days before Thompson's scheduled execution, the en banc court heard oral argument.[126] Immediately afterward, we voted seven to four to recall the mandate and reverse the three-judge panel. The opinion was assigned to Judge Fletcher, who circulated a draft the following day, August 2, and filed the final version on August 3.[127] In that opinion, we affirmed the district court's partial grant of Thompson's writ—the order that had reversed Thompson's rape conviction on the ground of ineffective assistance of counsel—and directed that that conviction be set aside.[128] The majority also held that the prosecution's presentation of directly contradictory theories and evidence in the two trials violated the Due Process Clause, and it returned the murder conviction to the district court for further review in light of our decision.[129]

Our opinion noted that the authority to recall our court's mandate had long been recognized as within our discretionary power and had been invoked in numerous other cases presenting extraordinary circumstances.[130] Judge Fletcher wrote: "Our interest both in protecting the integrity of our processes and in preventing injustice are implicated in the case before us."[131] The integrity of our processes had been violated as a result of the inadvertent errors of judges, including myself, who failed to make a timely en banc call, thus allowing the three-judge panel arbitrarily to foreclose review of its opinion by the full court. The threat of injustice resulted from "fundamental errors of law"[132] made by the three-judge panel, which made imminent the execution of a man who had unquestionably been denied a fair trial—a man who was in all likelihood innocent of the crime that made the death penalty possible, if not of all the charged criminal conduct.

Because some judges in the majority insisted that it was inadvisable to expose the details of our internal circuit disputes, the opinion left fairly general the description of the steps that various members of the court had taken in attempting to make an en banc call and the manner in which our efforts had been rebuffed and frustrated. Ultimately, it was precisely this failure to discuss the details of the procedural errors and departures from the court's long-standing practices that enabled Judge Kozinski to put his own spin on "the facts" and to write a separate dissent purportedly describing what had occurred within our court but omitting or mischaracterizing crucial details.[133] Judge Kozinski insisted that "nothing at all unusual happened; the process operated just as it's supposed to."[134] He recounted a version of events that bore little relationship to practical reality. To him, all that had happened was that two judges had missed a routine en banc call, while thirty-five others—all of the remaining active and senior members of the court—had independently determined that the case "did not meet the rigorous standards for en banc review."[135]

Of course, this was neither an accurate nor a fair rendition of the practices of our court or the events that had occurred. Nothing was usual about the *Thompson* case; nothing worked the way it was supposed to. Thirty-five judges clearly had not made the decision Judge Kozinski attributed to them,[136] and a panel of our court had acted in a highly atypical and uncollegial manner. Never before had a panel precluded review of its decision to end someone's life because their colleagues had made inadvertent errors in the timing of an en banc call. The action by the panel was in fact more than unusual; it was unprecedented. While misstatements made in a dissent ordinarily would be of little concern, here the circumstances were different.[137] Judge Kozinski's highly articulate dissents on en banc matters are frequently written with a dual purpose and appear to be aimed at particular members of the Supreme Court. That is why they are often referred to as "cert. petitions." This time there was no doubting my able colleague's objective.[138]

Judge Kozinski's dissent was disturbing for another reason. He argued that because no individual petitioner has a right to an en banc hearing, any "error can be corrected in a future case where the problem again manifests itself."[139] The idea that a court should not concern itself with whether it has erroneously upheld the execution of a human being who is under an unconstitutional death sentence, and who is probably innocent of at least the death-qualifying offense, is disturbing enough. The argument that we need not review en banc because we can resolve the legal issues in another case, after the condemned individual is dead, should shock the conscience of anyone who believes that the objective of our courts is to ensure fairness or justice. In my opinion, Judge Kozinski's dissent called into question the very purpose and legitimacy of our judicial system.[140] Unfortunately, that dissent foreshadowed the approach that the nation's highest court would shortly employ.

Soon after we issued our opinion, the State of California filed a petition for a writ of mandamus with the Supreme Court.[141] Although the Court was in the middle of its summer vacation, the Justices quickly determined to treat the state's request as a petition for certiorari and granted it.[142] The Court's order provided that the Court would not decide whether a condemned man's constitutional rights had been violated, but only whether the Ninth Circuit had the authority to recall its mandate.[143] For a High Court that is supposed to consider only important questions of national concern, this was a strange and most unusual action.[144] As Justice Souter later wrote, on behalf of the Court's four moderate Justices, the Supreme Court took action to solve "a systemic problem that does not exist."[145]

III. The Supreme Court Decision

Given the composition of the Rehnquist Court, the outcome of the *Thompson* case was undoubtedly inevitable.[146] Still, the Court's five to four opinion was a shock to many, both for its hostile, indeed vituperative, tone and for the unprecedented restrictions it placed on the authority of the federal courts to correct their own errors—particularly in cases in which errors result in the most drastic consequence possible. The majority opinion, authored by Justice Kennedy, echoed Judge Kozinski's version of the events within the court of appeals, even quoting his conclusion that "[t]he process operated just as it's supposed to."[147] The majority did not base its analysis upon its reading of the record of our internal correspondence or actions, or on any independent and objective knowledge of the occurrences that had preceded our recall of the mandate; the Justices had no such record before them and were possessed of no such knowledge.

Given the confusion surrounding the events, one might have thought that the Court would not reach such critical conclusions in so cavalier and irregular a manner. But it did. Justice Kennedy simply adopted the erroneous representations of a dissenting judge and incorrectly characterized the procedural errors of the Ninth Circuit as solely a "mishandled law clerk transition in one judge's chambers, and the failure of another judge to notice the action proposed by the original panel."[148] That Justice Kennedy would draw such patently erroneous conclusions is especially surprising. He had served on our court himself, and, in fact, Judge Kozinski had served as his law clerk during a part of that time. Justice Kennedy certainly should have known how our court functions and how our en banc process actually works. Nonetheless, he concluded: First, the failure of two judges to make their views known on time had no practical consequences other than that the court did not receive the benefit of their views, and second, those two judges had then deliberately delayed making an en banc call until they did so just before the execution.

Being one of the two judges, I was in a unique position to know that both of Justice Kennedy's conclusions were wholly incorrect, although I am admittedly not a disinterested or unbiased observer. Still, there are facts that are indisputable—facts that Justice Kennedy and the majority of the Supreme Court simply got wrong. The "only consequence of the oversights" was not, as Justice Kennedy put it, that the two judges failed to contribute "their views to [the] determination."[149] The actual consequence of the errors made by the two judges, and by the majority of the members of the court, was that the court itself was deprived of the opportunity to convene en banc to correct a grievous constitutional error that one of its panels had committed and that a majority of the court desired to correct.

Next, Justice Kennedy's accusation that the two judges deliberately delayed and then made an en banc call just before the execution is false. In fact, the two judges did not make an en banc call at any time. Judge Farris did. And the reason for the critical part of the delay—the part that resulted in the "adverse consequences" Justice Kennedy stressed in his opinion—was not, as Justice Kennedy charged, because the court of appeals "lay in wait,"[150] but, ironically, because the court attempted to follow what two other judges believed to be our obligation to respect the Supreme Court's oft-expressed concerns for comity and federalism.

Notably, Justice Kennedy also failed to acknowledge that our court gave two reasons for recalling the mandate. The first I have discussed sufficiently—the procedural errors in the implementation of our en banc process. The second and more important reason was our desire to correct the serious substantive errors our court had made in an unreviewed panel decision—a decision that would, unless recalled, result in the execution of a human being in violation of the Constitution. This reason the Supreme Court majority never even mentioned.

The Supreme Court's opinion acknowledged the inherent power of courts of appeals to recall their mandates but nonetheless termed our decision a "grave abuse of discretion."[151] The Court, which had never before in its history held that a court of appeals had erred in recalling a mandate, whatever the appellate court's reason for doing so,[152] here ruled that we had seriously erred by taking that action in order to correct one of the most grievous errors a court could make—authorizing an unconstitutional execution. To reach this result, the Supreme Court created a new rule[153] that a federal court of appeals cannot recall its mandate in a death penalty habeas case regardless of the egregiousness of the constitutional error unless the defendant can establish his "actual innocence,"[154] a feat rendered nearly impossible by the stringent requirements the Court has established for meeting that test in other contexts. As Justice Kennedy acknowledged, "in virtually every case, the allegation of actual innocence has been summarily rejected."[155] Recognizing that its opinion departed drastically from prior law, the Court distinguished the *Thompson* case from more "ordinary" recalls of mandates on the ground that Thompson sought relief from constitutional errors in a state criminal trial.[156] Citing other cases in which it had severely limited the right of federal habeas petitioners to raise meritorious constitutional claims, the Supreme Court said that the state court judgment ordering Thompson's execution must be honored because the "finality" of that judgment would deter future crimes, allow the "victims of the crime [to] move forward," and served "to preserve the federal balance."[157] The Court waxed philosophical about the state's interest in the finality of its judgments, an interest which, it said, took on an "added moral dimension" once the mandate issued.[158] Finally, the Court asserted that "[t]his case well illustrates the extraordinary costs associated with a federal court of appeals's recall of its mandate denying federal habeas relief."[159]

And what were those extraordinary costs? In the forty-eight days between the date on which our mandate left the court of appeals for further action to be taken in the district court and the date on which we recalled it—in fact in the entire one hundred twenty days that passed between the date on which we first could have taken an en banc vote and the day on which we actually voted[160]—two things occurred: The state courts prematurely reasserted jurisdiction over Thompson's case and denied a petition that they should not even have been considering, and the Governor of California denied Thompson clemency after a "hearing" that lasted approximately two hours.[161] These two decisions, plus the injury to the state's general, and the victim's particular, interest in "finality," constituted the extraordinary costs involved.

It was those indefinable costs, flowing from the briefest of delays, that, according to the Supreme Court, outweighed the benefit of allowing the courts of the United States to enforce the U.S. Constitution and correct an egregious constitutional error. In my opinion, the Supreme Court's analysis in *Thompson* represents a nadir for the cost-benefit approach to decision making in constitutional cases or otherwise. Most remarkable of all, in making its assessment of the costs, the U.S. Supreme Court never even mentioned the costs to our legal system of allowing the state's violation of the defendant's constitutional rights to go unremedied. It never even considered the costs to society—let alone to the defendant—of permitting a person to be executed on the basis of an unconstitutional trial or for a crime of which he might well be innocent. In short, the Supreme Court never even took into account the interest we all have in upholding the Constitution or the costs we all incur when the federal courts are precluded from performing their basic constitutional functions.

There was another major problem with the *Thompson* decision, a problem that ultimately would make Thompson's execution almost inevitable. By requiring Thompson to meet an actual innocence standard before permitting the recall of the mandate, the Supreme Court imposed a nigh impossible requirement. Thompson certainly had no chance of meeting the standard because in assessing his actual innocence the Court relied for its basic evidence on the record made at a trial in which the fact-finding process was irremediably distorted.[162] In considering that record, the Court did not mention that when the facts were developed Thompson was without the benefit of effective counsel or that the prosecutor's evidence was fatally flawed by his unconscionable and unconstitutional conduct. Instead, the Court weighed evidence that had never been subjected to a true adversarial process, made its own subjective factual findings on the basis of tainted evidence, disregarded the contrary evidence that disproved the theory on which Thompson was convicted, and characterized physical evidence that was, at best, highly questionable, as "ample evidence" of rape.[163] It's no wonder the Court concluded that Thompson could not meet the actual innocence standard.[164]

The *Thompson* case illustrates sharply the values, interests, and concerns weighed in death penalty habeas cases and, to some extent, in habeas cases generally. On the one hand, federal courts consider the state's interest in finality and comity; on the other hand, they consider the interest of the defendant and the public in preserving constitutional values. The various judicial bodies that considered Thompson's claims made dramatically different decisions about the appropriate weight to be afforded the various interests. The district court and the en banc court found Thompson's interest, and society's, in the preservation of life, liberty, and the right to a fair trial important enough to justify vacating an unconstitutional conviction. The original three-judge panel found the most important interest to be preserving the "limited role" of federal courts in reviewing state convictions. Justice Kennedy, on behalf of the Supreme Court majority, found the weightiest interest to be the state's need for finality, even when that need was compromised by only a forty-eight- or one-hundred-twenty-day delay. These decisions, of course, were made in connection with Thompson's first habeas petition—the first and only opportunity Thompson would ever have to vindicate his constitutional rights in the federal courts.

As we can see from the proceedings regarding Thomas Thompson, grandiloquent generalizations about values of finality and comity—grandiloquent formulations of concepts of federalism—are often not so grand when viewed in light of the facts of a particular case and its practical consequences. In Thompson's case, did a short delay really threaten the state-federal structure? Was it really necessary to dismiss without mention the constitutional obligations of the federal courts to ensure due process of law and to adjudicate fairly the legal questions involving the guilt of a man who was in all likelihood innocent of any capital offense, and whose role in a noncapital crime remains dubious and uncertain? Is a state court in which supreme court justices—some of whom have in recent years been recalled for being too "soft" on capital punishment—are subject to popular vote really as well equipped to protect constitutional rights in death penalty cases as a federal court with life-tenured Article III judges?[165] The answers should be apparent to anyone who places the substantive protections of the Constitution above abstract interests in finality and comity. They should be obvious to anyone who does not think that the costs of a brief delay in a court's deliberative process outweigh the importance of human life and the obligation of the federal judiciary to ensure that the states comply with the U.S. Constitution.

IV. The Final Chapter

Given the tone and content of the Supreme Court's decision, the end to the *Thompson* story would come as no surprise. Still, one final chapter remained to be played out. Because our en banc court had voted to grant Thompson's habeas petition, we had found it unnecessary to rule on a separate motion he had filed. In that motion, Thompson had sought a new trial on the basis of newly discovered evidence that the state allegedly had withheld.[166] The evidence consisted of admissions by Thompson's roommate, David Leitch, that he had walked into the apartment the two men shared at approximately 3:00 A.M. the night of the murder and discovered Thompson and Ms. Fleischli engaged in consensual sex.[167] Because the prosecution had built its case against Thompson on the theory that only Thompson had been present in the apartment with Ms. Fleischli that evening, that he had raped her, and that the "rape" had provided the motive for her murder, Leitch's statements constituted critical evidence of Thompson's actual innocence of at least one and possibly both of the charges against him. Leitch's statement directly corroborated Thompson's trial testimony, given over his counsel's objection, that he had engaged in consensual sex with Ms. Fleischli the night she was killed.[168]

Of course, Leitch's statements could not be accepted at face value. His credibility and the weight to be given his information needed testing at an evidentiary hearing, particularly given the inconsistent stories that Leitch had told over the years. However, the fact that this admission was contrary to Leitch's interest, and that it was consistent with the version of events Leitch had reported to his own lawyer at the time of his original trial,[169] provided strong indicia of credibility. Evidence also suggested that the district attorney's office had been aware of this information at the time of Thompson's trial but had failed to disclose it, in violation of Thompson's constitutional rights.[170]

When the Supreme Court overturned our en banc decision, it became necessary for us to perform our final function in the Thomas Thompson case. We reinstated the proceedings regarding Thompson's new trial motion and held oral argument on July 9, 1998—five days before his new execution date. Once again, a procedural barrier, this time erected by Congress and the President, threatened to limit our ability to consider the merits of Thompson's claims.

The new obstacle was a by-product of the Oklahoma City bombing. While Thompson's first habeas petition was under consideration by the courts, two conspirators had committed an infamous crime. They had blown up a federal building, killing 168 people. In the wake of that occurrence, the Antiterrorism and Effective Death Penalty Act (AEDPA) was adopted.[171] The bill was enacted by Congress at the urging of President William Jefferson Clinton. In the AEDPA, Congress and the President enshrined the philosophy and habeas jurisprudence of the Rehnquist Court in statutory law, codifying stringent barriers to review of all habeas petitions, and particularly to second or successive petitions.[172] The two branches of government each sought to appear tougher than the other in the war against terrorists, although no one bothered to explain how limiting the historic right of all state prisoners to habeas relief would help the federal government in the latest of its periodic "wars." Nor did anyone much seem to care. There was an election on the horizon. And, furthermore, when the AEDPA was adopted in 1996, President Clinton had yet to show the first glimmer of interest in curbing prosecutorial excesses that might infringe the rights of persons high or low. In fact, up to that point, President Clinton had not shown any interest in protecting the constitutional rights of any individual accused of wrongdoing.

In any event, under the new AEDPA standard Thompson could not prevail on his motion based on new evidence—whether or not the evidence had been deliberately concealed by the state—unless he could show by clear and convincing proof that no reasonable juror who heard that evidence would have found him guilty of capital murder. Merely to obtain permission to file the motion in the district court, Thompson first was required to establish in the court of appeals a prima facie case of actual innocence by showing facts which if proven would be sufficient to meet the standard.

In my judgment and that of Judge A. Wallace Tashima, a moderate Clinton appointee, Thompson's new evidence met this rigorous prima facie requirement.[173] There was evidence that direct eyewitness testimony existed which, if believed, would establish Thompson's innocence of rape and his ineligibility for the death penalty—evidence that would also directly refute the prosecution's theory of the murder. In our view, such evidence certainly warranted an evidentiary hearing, an opportunity for an objective judge to test its credibility and import using traditional methods of fact finding—especially given the constitutional violations that had tainted the previous findings of Thompson's guilt.

However, most of the judges who had been in the majority when we issued our en banc opinion felt compelled by the Supreme Court's decision—particularly by its unusually strong and specific language regarding the ample evidence of the alleged "rape"—to hold that Thompson could not make the required evidentiary showing of actual innocence.[174] From a practical standpoint, their decision may have been the right one. There was little doubt in their minds or in mine that, were we to rule in Thompson's favor, the Supreme Court would swiftly reverse us once again—and perhaps this time the five-Justice majority would order us whipped or put in the stockade. So the vote against Thompson was nine to two.

The issuance of our court's decision on the new trial motion on July 11, 1998 meant that Thompson's last real avenue for relief had been foreclosed. He was executed three days later. Thompson was the first death row inmate in California since capital punishment had been reinstituted to insist on his innocence through the time of his execution, and he was the first person in the nation ever to be executed on the basis of a trial that an unrefuted decision of a U.S. court of appeals had held to be unconstitutional.

Was Thompson guilty? While I am reluctant to make a judgment of any kind on the basis of the type of evidence adduced before the state trial court, it appears that Thompson may have helped Leitch conceal Ms. Fleischli's body after Leitch murdered her or possibly may have participated in the murder itself.[175] Of course, because Thompson was never tried on the theory that he helped Leitch kill Ms. Fleischli, we will never know whether a jury would have convicted him under such a theory. But even if guilty as an accessory to murder, Thompson was, in my opinion, very likely innocent of the rape charge and therefore not eligible for a death sentence under the applicable law.[176] What the actual facts were will always be unclear. Sometimes, even after a full and fair trial, and regardless of a jury's verdict, doubt remains. Without a fair trial and without a testing for truth through a fair adversary process, we are left only to speculate.

Conclusion

The *Thompson* case has ramifications that go far beyond the particular act of judicial disregard for fairness and justice that led to an execution that should never have occurred. The refusal of the Ninth Circuit panel to grant the request of other judges to extend the time to call for a rehearing en banc could not help but have an effect on the future operations of our court and on the relationships among its members. The decision of Judge Kozinski to quote selectively and publicly from our internal memoranda inevitably will have a similar adverse effect on the way we do business in the future. The brutal attack by Justice Kennedy on the good faith and competence of his former colleagues on the Ninth Circuit may have revealed more about the Justice himself than anything else, but it may also have other ramifications, such as influencing the current deliberations over whether to divide our circuit or, worse, to carve it up into bureaucratic, ineffective divisional units. Most important of all, the Supreme Court decision tells us much about the lack of concern for justice and due process of law that permeates our death penalty jurisprudence.

In *Thompson*, the Court took one further step—its most indefensible thus far—to elevate state procedural interests over concern for human life, over due process of law, and yes, over the Constitution itself. It even went so far as to extend, implicitly, the rule holding defendants liable for procedural errors made by their lawyers[177] to holding defendants liable for procedural errors made by their judges—a bizarre concept indeed. All in all, the *Thompson* case showed the criminal justice system, including both the prosecution and the judiciary, at its very worst.

Perhaps travesties are inevitable if we are to continue to enforce the death penalty. Emotions run high, even among judges. The stakes are different in kind from those in all other cases. The decision as to who deserves to die at the hands of the state is not susceptible to determination by objective, scientific, or uniformly applied rules. Chance and circumstance play the largest role in the deadly death penalty lottery. When the state is out to execute the accused at all costs, and the nation's highest court's primary interest is in establishing procedural rules that preclude federal courts from considering even the most egregious violations of a defendant's constitutional rights, it is time to step back and look at what we are doing to ourselves and to our system of justice.

Although we are not in a period in which we can expect such an examination to result in immediate positive changes, it is nevertheless the duty of the academy and the legal profession to make the record that will be necessary when the pendulum swings. And the pendulum will surely swing—not only with respect to our death penalty jurisprudence, and the harsh and inflexible means by which we today limit the historic writ of habeas corpus, but also with respect to the inimical manner in which the majority of today's judges view individual rights.

Those of us who still believe in the obligation of the courts to ensure fairness and equality for all, who share the concerns that dominated the brightly shining jurisprudence of the Warren-Brennan era, who believe that we are now in a valley in our long legal journey toward justice, may not be around to see the day when our judicial system returns to its state of glory. Obviously, this is not one of the proudest times in our nation's history—for any of our branches of government. It will take time to recover, to undo the damage, to heal the constitutional wounds. In the case of the Supreme Court, given the nature of the appointive process and the practical realities of lifetime tenure, the period required for fundamental change is a lengthy one.

Change will not come easily. It will take hard work on the part of well-trained advocates and creative legal thinkers who refuse to accept the notion that the era of judicial progress is forever over and who will inspire those who learn from their words and deeds. Charles Black, a leading constitutional scholar for the past fifty years, recently suggested that we look to the Declaration of Independence, the Ninth Amendment, and the Privileges and Immunities Clause of the Fourteenth Amendment as sources of unenumerated rights, most particularly the right to a "decent livelihood."[178] Black's ideas are promising and challenging. It may be time, for example, to reconsider the *Slaughterhouse Cases*,[179] which so drastically and wrongfully limited the Fourteenth Amendment[180]—or at least it may be time to do so when we once again have a Court that sees our Constitution as protecting the basic freedoms and liberties of the people, and not primarily as a structure for protecting the interests of the states.

If we have faith in the nature of humanity, if we believe that the course of evolution is progress, if we are truly committed to the principles of liberty, equality, and justice, I am confident that we can return to an era in which the courts serve as the guardians of the values embodied in our Constitution, to an era in which judicial protection of the rights of the poor and the disadvantaged will once again be the order of the day. If we have the will and the determination, we will ultimately prevail.

NOTES

1. *Brown v. Allen*, 344 U.S. 443, 540 (1953) (Jackson, J., concurring).

2. 347 U.S. 483 (1954) (holding that state laws permitting segregation of black and white children into separate schools violates Equal Protection Clause of Fourteenth Amendment).

3. 376 U.S. 254, 279–80 (1964) (stating that, under First and Fourteenth Amendments, state official must demonstrate actual malice to win damage award for defamation claim).

4. 370 U.S. 421, 424 (1962) (declaring official state prayer recited in public schools to violate First Amendment).

5. 377 U.S. 533, 558 (1964) (quoting *Gray v. Sanders*, 372 U.S. 368, 381 (1963)).

6. See id. at 568 (determining that Equal Protection Clause requires that seats in state legislature be apportioned on population basis); see also *Baker v. Carr*, 369 U.S. 186, 237 (1962) (stating that equal protection challenges to voting dilution through arbitrary apportionment is justiciable cause of action under Fourteenth Amendment).

7. 372 U.S. 335, 344–45 (1963) (holding that, under Fourteenth Amendment, state courts must provide counsel for indigent defendants charged with noncapital felonies).

8. 384 U.S. 436, 444–45 (1966) (stating that once taken into police custody, accused must be provided constitutionally adequate safeguards against self-incrimination).

9. 367 U.S. 643, 655 (1961) (holding all evidence obtained in unconstitutional search to be inadmissible in state court criminal trial).

10. 410 U.S. 113, 154, 164–66 (1973) (holding that women have qualified right to privacy under Due Process Clause of Fourteenth Amendment that allows termination of pregnancy absent compelling state interest).

11. 408 U.S. 238, 239–40 (1972) (per curiam) (holding death penalty to be cruel and unusual punishment in violation of Eighth Amendment).

12. The most notable examples have come in the areas of voting rights, see, e.g., *Miller v. Johnson*, 515 U.S. 900, 915–17 (1995) (relaxing standing requirement and applying "predominant factor" test to strike down state redistricting plan); *Shaw v. Reno*, 509 U.S. 630, 658 (1993) (allowing new kind of voting rights claim when

shape of district after redistricting demonstrates race was motivation), and affirmative action, see, e.g., *Adarand Constructors v. Pena*, 515 U.S. 200, 235 (1995) (applying strict scrutiny to federal highway affirmative action program); *City of Richmond v. J. A. Croson Co.*, 488 U.S. 469, 507–11 (1989) (applying strict scrutiny to and striking down city's affirmative action program in construction industry). Some of the Rehnquist Court's decisions diminishing protections for racial minorities were overturned when Congress passed the Civil Rights Restoration Act of 1991, overriding five Supreme Court decisions.

13. The Burger Court, which issued decisions such as *Stone v. Powell*, 428 U.S. 465, 494–95 (1976) (eliminating remedies for Fourth Amendment violations in federal habeas cases), and *Wainwright v. Sykes*, 433 U.S. 72, 86–87 (1977) (tightening procedural default rules), took a step in that direction, but it was only with the elevation of Justice Rehnquist to Chief Justice in 1986 that procedural rules began to become more important than the rights established in the Constitution.

14. See, e.g., *Phillips v. Washington Legal Found.*, 118 S. Ct. 1925, 1934 (1998) (determining interest on funds in Interest on Lawyers' Trust Accounts to be private property for purposes of Takings Clause); *Dolan v. City of Tigard*, 512 U.S. 374, 391 (1994) (applying "rough proportionality" takings standard to invalidate city land-use requirement); *Lechmere, Inc. v. NLRB*, 502 U.S. 527, 540–41 (1992) (balancing employer property rights with employee statutory organizational rights and allowing employer to bar union organizers from property).

15. The Court has stood firm on free speech cases, generally upholding the right. See, e.g., *Reno v. ACLU*, 117 S. Ct. 2329, 2334 (1997) (striking down regulation of indecent material on Internet); *R.A.V. v. City of St. Paul*, 505 U.S. 377, 381 (1992) (invalidating ordinance which prohibited certain bias-motivated expression); *Sable Communications of Cal., Inc. v. FCC*, 492 U.S. 115, 131 (1989) (striking down restrictions on pornographic telephone services); *Texas v. Johnson*, 491 U.S. 397, 399 (1989) (invalidating conviction of individual for burning American flag).

16. See, e.g., *Washington v. Glucksberg*, 117 S. Ct. 2258, 2271 (1997) (refusing to recognize right to die as liberty interest); *Albright v. Oliver*, 510 U.S. 266, 275 (1994) (finding arrest without probable cause not to violate substantive due process); *Michael H. v. Gerald D.*, 491 U.S. 110, 128–29 (1989) (deciding that application of presumption which deprives natural father of recognition of paternity does not violate substantive due process); *Bowers v. Hardwick*, 478 U.S. 186, 191 (1986) (finding no privacy right for consensual homosexual activity). Of course, the Court made a notable exception in *BMW v. Gore*, 517 U.S. 559, 562, 574–75 (1996), in which it held that a "grossly excessive" punitive damage award violated the Due Process Clause of the Fourteenth Amendment.

17. 381 U.S. 479, 485 (1965) (finding that laws prohibiting use of contraceptives unconstitutionally infringe upon protected "zone of privacy").

18. 410 U.S. 113, 154 (1973) (concluding that constitutional right to privacy includes abortion decision).

19. 163 U.S. 537, 550–51 (1896) (upholding constitutionality of separate but equal accommodations), overruled by *Brown v. Board of Educ.*, 347 U.S. 483, 494–95 (1954). In fact, Chief Justice Rehnquist served as a law clerk to Justice Jackson during the Term that *Brown* was decided and wrote a memorandum arguing for continued adherence to the separate but equal doctrine. See Bernard Schwartz, "Rehnquist, Runyon, and Jones—The Chief Justice, Civil Rights, and Stare Decisis," 31 Tulsa L.J. 251, 253–55 (1995).

20. To trace the erosion of the *Fay v. Noia*, 372 U.S. 391, 439 (1963), standard, which allowed review of a petitioner's constitutional claims as long as he did not deliberately bypass state avenues of relief, see *Wainwright v. Sykes*, 433 U.S. 72, 87 (1977) (limiting deliberate bypass standard by requiring petitioner to show cause and prejudice for procedural default at state trial to obtain federal habeas review of constitutional claims); *Murray v. Carrier*, 477 U.S. 478, 490–91 (1986) (applying cause and prejudice standard to habeas petitioner's failure to raise particular claim in state court appeal); *McCleskey v. Zant*, 499 U.S. 467, 493–95 (1991) (extending cause and prejudice standard to determination of "abuse of the writ" through inexcusable neglect).

21. See, e.g., *Sawyer v. Whitley*, 505 U.S. 333, 336 (1992) (requiring "clear and convincing evidence that, but for a constitutional error, no reasonable juror would have found the [defendant] eligible for the death penalty"). The *Sawyer* standard is applied when a petitioner is barred on procedural grounds from bringing his claims but argues that he can show that he is ineligible for the death penalty. I have been unable to find any reported case in which an individual met this standard.

22. Under the current standard, federal courts must often assume that a state court relied on an independent state ground even in cases in which the decisions give virtually no indication of the reason for their dispositions. See *Coleman v. Thompson*, 501 U.S. 722, 740 (1991) (allowing assumption that state court which rejected petitioner's claims must have relied on procedural grounds because state's motion had sought dismissal solely on this basis); *Ylst v. Nunnemaker*, 501 U.S. 797, 803 (1991) (allowing federal court to look to last reasoned state court decision, even if higher state court rejected claims without explanation).

23. See *United States v. Olano*, 507 U.S. 725, 731–41 (1993) (plain error); *Brecht v. Abrahamson*, 507 U.S. 619, 635–39 (1993) (harmless error). In fact, the use of the harmless and plain error standards to frustrate the correction of constitutional errors is the untold story behind the increasing disregard for defendants' constitutional and nonconstitutional rights. The import of those two doctrines is well illustrated by the difference between the Rose E. Bird and Malcolm M. Lucas California Supreme Courts. Under Chief Justice Rose E. Bird (1977–1986), the court reversed 94 percent of the 71 death sentences that came before it on appeal; in contrast, the Malcolm M. Lucas Court (1986–1996) reversed 15 percent of the 212 death penalties it reviewed. While both courts often found errors in the defendants' trial and sentencing proceedings, "[t]he errors the Bird Court justices determined

were 'reversible' were usually regarded as 'harmless' by the Lucas Court justices." John H. Culver, "The Transformation of the California Supreme Court: 1977–1997," 61 Alb. L. Rev. 1461, 1486 (1998).

24. 489 U.S. 288, 310 (1989) (foreclosing applicability of new constitutional rules of criminal procedure in cases which have become final before new rule is announced).

25. Stephen B. Bright's numerous articles on this subject offer compelling discussions of this problem. See, e.g., Stephen B. Bright, "Counsel for the Poor: The Death Sentence Not for the Worst Crime but for the Worst Lawyer," 103 Yale L.J. 1835, 1841–66 (1994) (describing pervasiveness of poor representation, reasons for it, and possibilities for improvement); see also Ruth E. Friedman & Bryan A. Stevenson, "Solving Alabama's Capital Defense Problems: It's a Dollars and Sense Thing," 44 Ala. L. Rev. 1, 6–26 (1992) (discussing problems caused by poor legal representation in capital cases).

26. Under *Coleman*, 501 U.S. at 752–54, ineffective assistance of counsel during state habeas proceedings cannot provide cause for a procedural default because there is no right to counsel at this stage. There may be an exception to this rule when state law guarantees the right to counsel for a state habeas petition; in that case, ineffective assistance may violate a state-created liberty interest and therefore the Due Process Clause.

27. See Eric Bailey, "Inmate Said Goodbyes, Then Died," L.A. Times, July 15, 1998, at A3.

28. See *Thompson v. Calderon*, 120 F.3d 1045 (9th Cir. 1997) (en banc), rev'd, 118 S. Ct. 1489 (1998).

29. See id. at 1048–60.

30. *Calderon v. Thompson*, 118 S. Ct. 1489, 1494 (1998) (Kennedy, J., joined by Rehnquist, C.J., O'Connor, Scalia, and Thomas, JJ.).

31. Most recently, see *O'Dell v. Netherland*, 117 S. Ct. 1969, 1973–74 (1997) (upholding death sentence because requirement of jury instruction regarding parole eligibility was "new rule"). The Court's retroactivity principle derives from another five-to-four decision, *Teague v. Lane*, 489 U.S. 288, 310 (1989).

32. See *McCleskey v. Zant*, 499 U.S. 467, 493–95 (1991) (Kennedy, J., joined by Rehnquist, C.J., White, O'Connor, Scalia, and Souter, JJ.). In this case, the district court had held that the defendant's *Massiah* right to counsel had been violated and that this constitutional claim merited relief. See id. at 476. Moreover, the petitioner's failure to bring the claim earlier was in large part directly attributable to the state's deception. See id. at 526–27 (Marshall, J., dissenting).

33. See *Coleman v. Thompson*, 501 U.S. 722, 727, 752–54 (1991) (O'Connor, J., joined by Rehnquist, C.J., White, Scalia, Kennedy, and Souter, JJ.). The Court held that the ineffectiveness of Coleman's attorney, who had made the fatal mistake, could not excuse Coleman's procedural default because there is no constitutional right to counsel in a state habeas proceeding. See id. at 752–54. The Court reasoned

that "[a]s between the State and the petitioner, it is the petitioner who must bear the burden of a failure to follow state procedural rules. . . . [T]he petitioner bears the risk in federal habeas for all attorney errors made in the course of representation." Id. at 754.

Once again, a comparison to how the Court treats procedural errors by the state demonstrates an inequity in the Supreme Court's doctrines—for while the Court imposes rules on lower federal courts which require us to punish defendants for any procedural errors that they make, despite the fact that habeas petitioners often receive poor legal representation or no representation at all, we are free to ignore the state's errors when its attorneys make similar omissions or mistakes. Thus, although it is very easy for a habeas petitioner to waive an issue by failing to raise it at each appropriate moment, the Court will readily excuse negligence, inattention, or errors on the part of the state. A state that fails to raise a *Teague* objection need not worry—a federal court may still apply it sua sponte. See *Caspari v. Bohlen*, 510 U.S. 383, 389 (1994) (holding that "a federal court may, but need not, decline to apply Teague if the State does not argue it"). Similarly, a state attorney's failure to argue, at the district court level, that a petitioner has not exhausted his state remedies need not preclude the attorney from raising the issue on appeal. See *Granberry v. Greer*, 481 U.S. 129, 133 (1987).

34. *Coleman*, 501 U.S. at 750.

35. Id.

36. Id. at 759 (Blackmun, J., dissenting). It is worth noting that because Thomas Thompson's petition for habeas corpus was filed in federal district court prior to the enactment of the AEDPA, he was not subject to that statute's procedural hurdles. For further discussion of the AEDPA, see infra notes 170–73 and accompanying text.

37. For the facts of the murder, see *Calderon v. Thompson*, 118 S. Ct. 1489, 1494–95 (1998).

38. *Thompson v. Calderon*, 120 F.3d 1045, 1056 (9th Cir. 1997) (en banc) (emphasis added) (quoting pretrial hearing transcript), rev'd, 118 S. Ct. 1489 (1998).

39. See id. at 1055 (recounting informant's testimony).

40. Id. at 1056.

41. See id. at 1055.

42. See id. at 1055 (stating that, "[o]n his own admission, Jacobs [[the prosecutor] never altered his view of the motive and the crime, either before or after he won Thompson's conviction").

43. See id. at 1055–57 (quoting prosecutor's arguments at trials of both Thompson and Leitch).

44. Id. at 1057 (quoting prosecutor's closing argument).

45. Id. (alteration in original) (emphasis omitted).

46. See id. at 1056.

47. See Reporter's Transcript at 2566, *People v. Thompson*, (Cal. Super. Ct. 1983) (No. C-49758) (quoting prosecution's closing argument).

48. See *Thompson*, 120 F.3d at 1056 (referring to informant's testimony).

49. Id. at 1057 (quoting prosecutor's argument to *Thompson* jury) (alteration in original) (emphasis omitted).

50. Reporter's Transcript at 2637, *Thompson* (No. C-49758) (quoting prosecutor's closing argument). Of course, the statement that the informants had no motive to lie was, to use a current term, misleading, because the state had released Fink from jail and dropped his parole hold in return for his testimony. See *Thompson*, 120 F.3d at 1056.

A "parole hold" occurs when a parolee is retained in custody under the administrative authority of the parole authority, usually following a violation of a condition of parole or an arrest for a new crime. See *In re Law*, 513 P.2d 621, 623 n.2 (Cal. 1973) (defining parole hold).

51. The jury recommended the death penalty, and the judge imposed it. See *Calderon v. Thompson*, 118 S. Ct. 1489, 1495 (1998).

52. See *Thompson*, 120 F.3d at 1056–57.

53. Reporter's Transcript at 2566, *Thompson* (No. C-49758) (quoting prosecutor's closing argument).

54. During Thompson's trial, the prosecutor had objected to these witnesses' testimony. Then, as the witnesses left the courtroom following their testimony, he handed them subpoenas for Leitch's trial. See *Thompson v. Calderon*, No. CV-89-3630-RG, slip op. at 66 (C.D. Cal. Mar. 29, 1995).

55. Reporter's Transcript at 2505, *People v. Leitch* (Cal. Super. Ct. 1985) (No. C-49758) (quoting prosecutor's closing argument).

56. *Thompson*, 120 F.3d at 1057.

57. Id.

58. The contradictory nature of these presentations violated the fundamental tenets that govern the performance of a prosecutor's duties. In *United States v. Kattar*, 840 F.2d 118 (1st Cir. 1988), the court commented that, unlike private counsel, who are free to "characterize events in contrasting ways in two separate litigations," a prosecutor's duty "is not merely to prosecute crimes, but also to make certain that the truth is honored to the fullest extent possible during the course of the criminal prosecution and trial." Id. at 127. The prosecution's interest in a criminal proceeding "is not that it shall win a case, but that justice shall be done." *Berger v. United States*, 295 U.S. 78, 88 (1935); accord *Bruno v. Rushen*, 721 F.2d 1193, 1195 (9th Cir. 1983) (stating that prosecutor "has no obligation to win at all costs and serves no higher purpose by so attempting"); Model Code of Professional Responsibility EC 7–13 (1980) (relating that prosecutor's "duty is to seek justice, not merely to convict").

59. *Thompson*, 120 F.3d at 1059.

60. These former prosecutors were: Richard L. Gilbert, Donald H. Heller, Peter J. Hughes, Curt Livesay, M. James Lorenz, Wayne L. Ordos, and Steve White.

61. Brief of Amici Curiae in Support of Petitioner at 4–5, *Thompson v. Calderon*, 120 F.3d 1045 (9th Cir. 1997) (No. 96–8707).

62. See id. at 1–2, 4 n.3.

63. Id. at 7 n.5.

64. See *Thompson*, 120 F.3d at 1052.

65. See id. at 1052–53.

66. See id. at 1053–55.

67. See supra note 50 for a definition of a parole hold.

68. *Thompson*, 120 F.3d at 1054.

69. Leitch's admission was against interest because it established his presence in the apartment before Ms. Fleischli was killed. See *Thompson v. Calderon*, 151 F.3d 918, 934–36 (9th Cir. 1998) (en banc) (Reinhardt, J., concurring and dissenting). For elaboration on the forensic evidence that no rape occurred, see *Thompson*, 120 F.3d at 1052–53. For discussion of Leitch's statements, see *Thompson*, 151 F.3d at 920, 925–26; id. at 934 (Reinhardt, J., concurring and dissenting). For a discussion of the Supreme Court's characterization of the evidence of rape as "ample," *Calderon v. Thompson*, 118 S. Ct. 1489, 1503 (1998), see infra notes 162–64 and accompanying text.

70. While Thompson was sentenced to death, Leitch was not. At his trial, Leitch was convicted of second-degree murder and sentenced to fifteen years to life. He is currently eligible for parole. See Eric Bailey et al., "Protests, Appeals Mark Convict's Last Hours," L.A. Times, July 14, 1998, at A1.

71. See *Thompson v. Calderon*, No. CV-89-3630-RG, slip op. at 2 (C.D. Cal. Mar. 29, 1995) (describing court's involvement over five-year period).

72. See id. at 13, 23–24, 30–31.

73. See id. at 12–13, 23, 100.

74. See id. at 69–70.

75. See id. at 100.

76. See *Thompson v. Calderon*, 109 F.3d 1358, 1369–70 (9th Cir. 1996).

77. See id. at 1366–69.

78. Id. at 1369.

79. Reporter's Transcript at 2566, *People v. Thompson* (Cal. Super. Ct. 1983) (No. C-49758) (quoting prosecutor's closing argument).

80. *Thompson*, 109 F.3d at 1364.

81. See id. at 1370, 1374.

82. See Petition for Rehearing with Suggestion for Rehearing En Banc, *Thompson v. Calderon*, 120 F.3d 1045 (9th Cir. 1997) (No. 96–8707).

83. See *Thompson v. Calderon*, 120 F.3d 1045, 1067 (9th Cir. 1997) (Kozinski, J., dissenting).

84. See U.S. Court of Appeals for the Ninth Circuit, General Orders § 5.4(b) (1997) (on file with the New York University Law Review).

85. See 28 U.S.C. § 46(c) (1994) ("[A] hearing or rehearing before the court en banc [may be] ordered by a majority of the circuit judges of the circuit who are in regular active service.").

86. Justice Kennedy has repeatedly suggested that we hear more cases en banc, most recently in his letter to the White Commission, a commission considering structural changes to the Ninth Circuit. He commented, "[T]he Ninth Circuit does not come close to the number of en banc hearings necessary to resolve intra-circuit conflicts, much less to address questions 'of exceptional importance.'" Letter from Justice Anthony M. Kennedy, U.S. Supreme Court, to Justice Byron R. White, Chair, Commission on Structural Alternatives for the Federal Courts of Appeals 3 (Aug. 17, 1998) (quoting Fed. R. App. P. 35(a)) (on file with the New York University Law Review).

87. See U.S. Court of Appeals for the Ninth Circuit, General Orders § 5.5(d) (1997) (on file with the New York University Law Review).

88. In fact, four times between 1997 and 1998 our court has employed the en banc process to overturn panel decisions denying relief in death penalty cases in which serious constitutional violations had occurred. See *Dyer v. Calderon*, 151 F.3d 970, 985 (9th Cir.) (en banc) (finding denial of right to fair trial when juror lied during voir dire), cert. denied, 119 S. Ct. 575 (1998); *Carriger v. Stewart*, 132 F.3d 463, 479–82 (9th Cir. 1997) (en banc) (holding prosecutor's failure to disclose evidence bearing on key witness's credibility to have denied defendant due process under law), cert. denied, 118 S. Ct. 1827 (1998); *McDowell v. Calderon*, 130 F.3d 833, 837–41 (9th Cir. 1997) (en banc) (finding jury's lack of consideration of mitigating evidence due to trial judge's failure to address jury confusion violative of Eighth Amendment), cert. denied, 118 S. Ct. 1575 (1998); *Jeffries v. Wood*, 114 F.3d 1484, 1490–92 (9th Cir.) (en banc) (holding that extrinsic information conveyed by juror to jury regarding defendant's criminal record violates Sixth Amendment right to confront witnesses), cert. denied, 118 S. Ct. 586 (1997).

89. See U.S. Court of Appeals for the Ninth Circuit, General Orders § 5.4(b)(2) (1997) (on file with the New York University Law Review). The circuit waits for the panel to rule on a petition for rehearing—often for months—because if the panel itself grants a rehearing, an en banc call becomes unnecessary.

90. See *Thompson v. Calderon*, 120 F.3d 1045, 1067 (9th Cir. 1997) (Kozinski, J., dissenting) (noting that request for 5.4(b) notice was made on September 27, 1996 and that notice was issued on January 17, 1997).

91. See U.S. Court of Appeals for the Ninth Circuit, General Orders § 5.4(b)(2) (1997) (on file with the New York University Law Review).

92. See *Thompson*, 120 F.3d at 1067 (Kozinski, J., dissenting).

93. A mandate is the official notice of action taken by an appellate court, directed to the court below, advising the lower court of the appellate court's action and ordering the lower court to recognize, obey, and execute the appellate court's judgment. See 5 Am. Jur. 2d Appellate Review § 776 (2d ed. 1995). Issuance of the mandate occurs when certified copies of the judgment of the court of appeals are received by the district court. See id. § 777. Federal courts of appeals have the in-

herent power to recall a mandate issued to an inferior court and may recall a mandate sua sponte. See id. § 797.

94. An illustration of the imperfection of our system for mechanical transmissions of important communications is provided by events which took place just ten days before delivery of this lecture. Our court was involved in another death penalty proceeding in which last-minute actions were required. We heard telephone argument in the case on a Saturday morning and the majority opinion was prepared and sent to the other two members of the panel via fax late Saturday night. The concurring judge received the opinion at 11:30 P.M. and responded with his concurrence and proposed modifications at 1:30 A.M. Sunday. The dissenting judge included a footnote in his dissent complaining that he had not yet received the proposed majority opinion and that he was forced to write his dissent mid-Sunday morning without knowing the contents of the majority opinion. See *Vargas v. Lambert*, No. 98–99028, 1998 WL 727340, at *12 n.1 (9th Cir. Oct. 11, 1998) (Kleinfeld, J., dissenting). The fact is that the proposed opinion was transmitted by its author to the dissenting judge at the same time that it was transmitted to the concurring judge. Nevertheless, the fax system somehow malfunctioned and the opinion was not received by one of the two judges to whom it was sent. There is no fail-safe method in the current state of the mechanical arts for preventing failures in communication of this nature.

95. In 1997 alone, our court issued over 800 published and 4,000 unpublished opinions. See Report of the Director of the Administrative Office of the U.S. Court, Year Ending 12/31/97, tbl. S-3 (1998). At any given time, it is not at all uncommon for active judges on our court to have a couple of hundred cases in various stages pending before them, as well as emergency motions and other matters that are not part of our regular docket.

96. Federal judges representing every political and jurisprudential philosophy, among them the Chief Justice of the United States and the Chief Judge of the Ninth Circuit, have commented publicly on the fact that the federal judiciary will not be able to ensure that cases are decided fairly and that justice is done unless the extraordinary number of vacancies that currently exist is substantially reduced. See, e.g., Henry Weinstein, "Lack of Judges Leaves Federal Courts Jammed," L.A. Times, May 30, 1997, at A1 (quoting Chief Justice Rehnquist and Chief Judge Hug). Less than two weeks before the delivery of this lecture, a nominee to our court was confirmed after waiting more than forty-one months. Congress recessed, however, without acting on the nomination of Richard Paez, a respected district court judge who was nominated for a Ninth Circuit judgeship almost thirty-three months ago.

97. Despite vigorous opposition by myself and others, and despite the overwhelming vote of the judicial and lawyer delegates to the 1995 Ninth Circuit Judicial Conference, our court maintains a rule prohibiting disclosure of the actual vote totals on whether to take cases en banc. See U.S. Court of Appeals for the Ninth Circuit, General Orders § 5.1(b)(3) (1997) (on file with the New York University Law

Review). For criticism of this practice, see, e.g., *United States v. Koon*, 45 F.3d 1303, 1309–10 & 1309 n.4 (9th Cir. 1995) (Reinhardt, J., dissenting from denial of suggestion of rehearing en banc); *Harris v. Vasquez*, 949 F.2d 1497, 1539–40 (9th Cir. 1991) (Reinhardt, J., dissenting from denial of suggestion of rehearing en banc).

98. See *Thompson v. Calderon*, Nos. 95–99014, 99–99015 (9th Cir. Mar. 6, 1997) (order and amended opinion).

99. See Internal Ninth Circuit Memorandum from Judge Reinhardt (Mar. 12, 1997). This and other internal memoranda are unavailable for public review due to confidentiality concerns.

100. Id.

101. Id.

102. See Internal Ninth Circuit Memorandum (Mar. 13, 1997).

103. Id.

104. Internal Ninth Circuit Memorandum (Mar. 17, 1997).

105. A special committee of judges has been working laboriously for many months to try to correct a number of the procedural ambiguities and problems in our en banc rules.

106. Judge Beezer was the author of the panel opinion. The other members of the panel were Judges Cynthia Holcomb Hall and Edward Leavy. All three were appointed by President Ronald Reagan.

107. Internal Ninth Circuit Memorandum from Judge Beezer (Mar. 20, 1997).

108. The Supreme Court later suggested that we could have moved to suspend the rules at this point. See *Calderon v. Thompson*, 118 S. Ct. 1489, 1499 (1998). However, suspension of the rules requires a two-thirds vote, see U.S. Court of Appeals for the Ninth Circuit, General Orders § 11.11 (1997) (on file with the New York University Law Review), and the procedure has never been employed with respect to the court's handling of appeals or petitions for review, only with respect to nondispositional administrative matters, such as the agenda for court meetings.

109. See Telephone Interview with Missy Pratte, Office of the Clerk of the United States Supreme Court (Mar. 2, 1999).

110. The brief was filed on May 7, 1997. See Brief of Amici Curiae in Support of Petitioner, *Thompson v. Calderon*, 120 F.3d 1045 (9th Cir. 1997) (No. 96–8707).

111. See *Thompson v. Calderon*, 117 S. Ct. 2426 (1997). The Court's denial of certiorari in this case, like in any other, was not a decision on the merits and did not indicate anything of substance. See *Teague v. Lane*, 489 U.S. 288, 296 (1989) (noting that "'denial of a writ of certiorari imports no expression of opinion upon the merits of the case'" (quoting *United States v. Carver*, 260 U.S. 482, 490 (1923) (Holmes, J.))).

112. See Internal Ninth Circuit Memorandum from Judge Farris (July 7, 1997).

113. See Internal Ninth Circuit Memorandum from Judges Beezer, Hall, and Leavy (July 9, 1997).

114. Internal Ninth Circuit Memorandum from Judge Farris (July 14, 1997).

115. See Internal Ninth Circuit Memorandum (July 10, 1997).

116. Id.

117. See Internal Ninth Circuit Memorandum (July 11, 1997).

118. Spreading the mandate is the issuance of an order stated and entered on the record by the district court, noting its compliance with the mandate of the appellate court. See *Integrated Computer Sys. Publ'g Co. v. Learning Tree Open Univ.*, Nos. 93–56656, 94–55799, 1995 WL 444664, at *3 (9th Cir. July 25, 1995).

The district court spread the mandate a week later, on July 14, 1997. It was on this day that the federal decision became final. See *Calderon v. United States Dist. Court*, 128 F.3d 1283, 1286 n.2 (9th Cir. 1997) ("[A] judgment does not become final following appeal until the case is returned to district court, and the mandate is spread." (citing 16A Charles Alan Wright et al., Federal Practice and Procedure § 3987, at 687 n.2 (2d ed. 1996))), cert. denied, 118 S. Ct. 899 (1998), rev'd en banc on other grounds, 163 F.3d 530 (9th Cir. 1998).

119. See *Calderon v. Thompson*, 118 S. Ct. 1489, 1496 (1998).

120. See id.

121. See id. at 1497.

122. See id.

123. See id.

124. A number of the court's more conservative judges signed dissents to the order taking the case en banc. Judge Stephen S. Trott's dissent, joined by Judge Andrew Kleinfeld and later by Judges Ferdinand Fernandez and Pamela Rymer, argued without a hint of irony that our decision to correct internal procedural errors and more fully consider a decision allowing an execution violated "the Eighth Amendment's command that arbitrariness not be a part of the process by which the death penalty is administered." *Thompson v. Calderon*, 120 F.3d 1042, 1044 (9th Cir. 1997) (Trott, J., dissenting). Judge Beezer also authored a dissent, joined by Judges Hall, Brunetti, Trott, Fernandez, Rymer, and Kleinfeld. See id. at 1043 (Beezer, J., dissenting). Judge Rymer filed her own belated dissent. See id. at 1045 (Rymer, J., dissenting).

125. In the little over a year since we voted to recall the mandate, the composition of the court has changed, and a majority of the active judges are no longer appointees of Republican presidents. Nevertheless, the philosophical bent of the court remains unchanged. It is as moderate to conservative as it was before the most recent group of appointments, with a strong emphasis on conservative. This characterization is accurate even without taking into account the changes in status of Judges Betty Fletcher and William Fletcher or the prospective appointment to our court of Chief Justice Barbara Durham of the State of Washington, an arrangement that will help move the court even more squarely into the conservative camp.

126. The members of the en banc court were Chief Judge Procter Hug, Jr. and Judges James R. Browning, Betty B. Fletcher, Harry Pregerson, Stephen Reinhardt, Cynthia Holcomb Hall, Alex Kozinski, Thomas G. Nelson, Andrew J. Kleinfeld, A. Wallace Tashima, and Sidney R. Thomas.

127. See *Thompson v. Calderon*, 120 F.3d 1045 (9th Cir. 1997) (en banc), rev'd, 118 S. Ct. 1489, 1506 (1998).

128. See id. at 1048.

129. Four judges concluded that the prosecutor's conduct constituted an independent reason to reverse Thompson's conviction without any further hearing. Two others agreed that it violated the Due Process Clause but voted to remand to allow the district court to make the initial ruling on whether it was Thompson or Leitch who suffered from this unconstitutional conduct. While it appears fairly apparent from the prosecutor's own comments and from the record as a whole that it was Thompson who was the victim of the unethical conduct, the two judges concluded that it was appropriate to require the district judge to make the initial determination on that point. See id. at 1063–64 (Tashima, J., concurring).

130. See id. at 1048.

131. Id.

132. Id.

133. See id. at 1067 (Kozinski, J., dissenting). Judge T. G. Nelson joined in Judge Kozinski's dissent. Judge Hall, joined by Judges Nelson and Kleinfeld, also filed a dissent, characterizing the recall of the mandate as an attempt to circumvent the AEDPA's prohibition of successive habeas petitions; this dissent also expressed agreement with Judge Kozinski's assessment that Thompson's case presented no circumstances or considerations that were out of the ordinary. See id. at 1064–66 (Hall, J., dissenting). Judge Kleinfeld also authored a separate dissent arguing, incredibly, that the evidence of rape was strong and that Thompson's lawyer was effective. See id. at 1072–75 (Kleinfeld, J., dissenting).

134. Id. at 1067 (Kozinski, J., dissenting).

135. Id. at 1068–69 (Kozinski, J., dissenting).

136. The erroneous nature of Judge Kozinski's representation that no other judge found the case en banc-worthy is demonstrated by the fact that a majority of the court voted for en banc review when the call was ultimately made. Moreover, contrary to the impression left by Judge Kozinski, the practice of the thirty-seven judges on the court at the time was not to review personally each of the over one thousand petitions for en banc review that are filed every year; just as the Supreme Court Justices cannot personally review every petition for certiorari, and eight out of nine of the Justices rely primarily on a memorandum prepared for their joint use by one of the Court's law clerks.

In our court, as I explained earlier, once one judge requests a 5.4(b) notice, the other judges presume that, when the time is ripe, he or she will make the en banc call or give notice to the contrary, obviating any need for each of them to follow all the procedural aspects of the process in every case. In reliance on this practice, other judges refrain from stepping in to issue their own en banc call.

Moreover, Judge Kozinski is demonstrably wrong for another reason when he asserts that thirty-five of the thirty-seven active and senior judges had decided that the case did not meet the standards for en banc review. Many of the senior judges do not even receive the suggestions for rehearing en banc that parties file. At the time Thompson filed his suggestion, only eight of the eighteen senior judges received such filings.

137. There are two other examples of Judge Kozinski's misleading statements and omissions that appear to merit some discussion here. His assertion that the controversy over the missed deadline did not come to the full court's attention until after the Supreme Court had denied certiorari is patently erroneous. The memoranda by the two judges requesting that the panel allow a belated en banc call were circulated to the entire court when they were written, in January 1997, before the mandate had even issued. Additionally, Judge Kozinski speaks of a January 1997 ruling by the en banc coordinator clarifying that January 31, 1997 was the last date for an en banc call. See *Thompson*, 120 F.3d at 1067–68 (Kozinski, J., dissenting). As far as I can ascertain, this memo was not circulated to the full court, but only to the panel.

138. Shortly after publication of what some considered to be a strongly worded concurrence, objecting to and correcting some of the inaccuracies in Judge Kozinski's dissent, I received a letter from a very recent James Madison lecturer. This judge sharply condemned my concurrence, asking why it needed to be so strong since my side had prevailed. Although this jurist is the Chief Judge of another circuit, I had to assume that he was either being disingenuous or completely naive in not understanding both the purpose of Judge Kozinski's actions and the very real danger that the erroneous statements would have an extremely serious and deleterious effect on the ultimate outcome of Thompson's case.

139. *Thompson*, 120 F.3d at 1069–70 (Kozinski, J., dissenting). Justice Souter's dissent also commented on this notion: "[S]urely it is . . . reasonable to resort to en banc correction that may be necessary to avoid a constitutional error standing between a life sentence and an execution." *Calderon v. Thompson*, 118 S. Ct. 1489, 1507 (1998) (Souter, J., dissenting). In actuality, the potential effect of the en banc hearing was greater than the difference between an execution and a life sentence because our reversal and remand on the prosecutorial misconduct issue would likely have led to Thompson's retrial on all charges.

140. Although I vehemently disagree with Judge Kozinski's dissent in every respect—from his unprecedented decision to quote from internal court memoranda, to his misstatement of what occurred within the court's processes, to his view that we can resolve the legal issues affecting *Thompson* after Thompson's death, to his other more fundamental legal conclusions that I believe to be erroneous—I should note that my colleague is an extremely able jurist who is ordinarily not inflexible. In fact, Judge Kozinski's legal talent is extraordinary, and he makes a major contribution to the functioning of our court. The nationwide respect he enjoys is well deserved. As far as I am concerned, Judge Kozinski's dissent proves only that when he goes off base, he really goes way off. Unfortunately, the consequences can be severe.

141. See Petition for Writ of Mandamus, *Thompson v. Calderon*, 120 F.3d 1042 (9th Cir. 1997) (Nos. 95–99014, 99015).

142. See *Calderon v. Thompson*, 118 S. Ct. 14 (1997) (mem.), amended by 118 S. Ct. 16 (1997) (mem.).

143. The Supreme Court initially granted certiorari on two questions: whether Thompson's motion to recall the mandate was an impermissible attempt to evade the restriction on successive habeas petitions and whether the Ninth Circuit had exceeded its power by granting the recall of the mandate. See *Calderon*, 118 S. Ct. at 14; Brief for Petitioner at i, Calderon (No. 97–215). It later amended its grant to add the following third question: "Did the Ninth Circuit, sitting en banc, err in concluding that the three-judge panel 'committed fundamental errors of law that would result in manifest injustice' sufficient to justify recalling the mandate?" *Calderon*, 118 S. Ct. at 16.

The framing of issues is an art in itself, and the way in which questions are posed is often determinative of the outcome of the case. Among constitutional scholars, the best-known example is *Bowers v. Hardwick*, 478 U.S. 186, 191 (1986) (holding Georgia antisodomy law not to violate Due Process Clause), in which Justice White's majority opinion began its discussion by claiming: "The issue presented is whether the Federal Constitution confers a fundamental right upon homosexuals to engage in sodomy and hence invalidates the laws of the many States that still make such conduct illegal and have done so for a very long time." Id. at 190. Justice Blackmun's dissent, in contrast, stated the issue as being "about 'the most comprehensive of rights and the right most valued by civilized men,' namely, 'the right to be let alone.'" Id. at 199 (Blackmun, J., dissenting) (quoting *Olmstead v. United States*, 277 U.S. 438, 478 (1928) (Brandeis, J., dissenting)).

144. Supreme Court Rule 10 states that a certiorari petition "will be granted only for compelling reasons" and specifically articulates the following reasons: the existence of a conflict among federal courts of appeals or state courts of last resort or between lower courts and the Supreme Court on an "important federal question." The rule finally states: "A petition for a writ of certiorari is rarely granted when the asserted error consists of erroneous factual findings or the misapplication of a properly stated rule of law." Sup. Ct. R. 10.

145. *Calderon v. Thompson*, 118 S. Ct. 1489, 1509 (1998) (Souter, J., dissenting). The exercise of the power to recall a mandate in a habeas case is so rare that the Court did not find one prior case to cite. Thus, Justice Souter's statement that no systemic problem existed was a polite understatement.

146. See id. at 1506 (reversing court of appeals and reinstating mandate denying habeas relief to petitioner).

147. Id. at 1499 (quoting *Thompson v. Calderon*, 120 F.3d 1045, 1067 (9th Cir. 1997) (Kozinski, J., dissenting)).

148. Id.

149. Id.

150. Id.

151. Id. at 1494.

152. See 16 Charles Alan Wright et al., Federal Practice and Procedure § 3938, at 712 (2d ed. 1996) ("The power of a court of appeals to recall its mandate once issued has long been recognized. . . . *[N]o formal rules have yet emerged to define and cabin the power.*" (emphasis added)); see also *Hawaii Hous. Auth. v. Midkiff*, 463 U.S. 1323, 1324 (1983) (upholding court of appeals recall of mandate and stating that "[a]lthough recalling a mandate is an extraordinary remedy, I think it probably lies within the inherent power of the Court of Appeals and is reviewable only for abuse of discretion"); *Cahill v. New York, New Haven & Hartford R.R.*, 351 U.S. 183, 184 (1956) (recalling own "erroneous" order "in the interest of fairness"); *Hazel-Atlas Glass Co. v. Hartford-Empire Co.*, 322 U.S. 238, 248–50 (1944) (upholding power to vacate judgment after term has ended when fraud has been revealed).

153. Justice Souter's dissent, joined by Justices Stevens, Ginsburg, and Breyer, pointed out that not only was the rule a new one but that it also departed from the traditional deference granted to a court's "reasonable selection of factors" that justify recalling its own mandate and to the administration of en banc procedures by the courts of appeals. *Calderon*, 118 S. Ct. at 1507 (Souter, J., dissenting). In addition, the dissent found the Ninth Circuit's factors reasonable. See id (Souter, J., dissenting).

154. *Calderon*, 118 S. Ct. at 1502.

155. Id. at 1503 (quoting *Schlup v. Delo*, 513 U.S. 298, 324 (1995) (quoting Jordan Streiker, "Innocence and Federal Habeas," 41 U.C.L.A. L. Rev. 303, 377 (1993))).

156. See id. at 1499.

157. Id. at 1501.

158. Id.

159. Id.

160. If a timely call had been made on January 31, our en banc procedures would have dictated that a memorandum in support of the call be due on February 14, supplemental briefing occur on February 21, and memoranda in support of or against the call be due from all judges by March 14. However, these schedules frequently are extended for substantial periods of time. Thus, while the earliest time at which voting could have been completed was March 31, it would not have been surprising had we not completed voting until May 31 or later. We actually voted to go en banc on July 28.

161. See *Decision in the Matter of the Clemency Request of Thomas Martin Thompson*, July 31, 1997, at 11–12 (on file with the New York University Law Review).

162. The Court also examined, and discounted, forensic testimony and other evidence that Thompson had presented at his state habeas evidentiary hearing,

although its inhospitable view of that evidence was obviously colored by its unquestioning acceptance of the tainted evidence introduced by the prosecution at trial. The Court did not consider recently discovered evidence of Thompson's innocence because doing so would have converted the recall of the mandate into a successive habeas petition under the AEDPA. See *Calderon*, 118 S. Ct. at 1500 (finding that recall of mandate did not contravene AEDPA).

163. Id. at 1503–5 (reviewing evidence of rape).

164. Of course, disregard for questions relating to actual innocence is not a novel principle for the Rehnquist Court, which in *Herrera v. Collins*, 506 U.S. 390 (1993), refused to hold that execution of an innocent individual would violate the Constitution's prohibition of cruel and unusual punishment. See id. at 418–19 (holding that showing of innocence came too late in criminal process to trigger constitutional claim). The Court left the question open but stated that if actual innocence could be a basis for relief without an additional constitutional violation, the standard for showing innocence "would necessarily be extraordinarily high." Id. at 417.

165. For one discussion of the dangers of the politicization of state courts that results from state judges' need to face reelection, see generally Gerald F. Uelmen, "Crocodiles in the Bathtub: Maintaining the Independence of State Supreme Courts in an Era of Judicial Politicization," 72 Notre Dame L. Rev. 1133 (1997).

166. See *Thompson v. Calderon*, 151 F.3d 918, 919–20 (9th Cir. 1998). Thompson filed the motion under Federal Rule of Civil Procedure 60(b), which allows the reopening of cases under certain circumstances, including for newly discovered evidence. See Fed. R. Civ. P. 60(b)(2).

167. See *Thompson*, 151 F.3d at 920.

168. See id. at 934.

169. See id. The lawyer to whom Leitch reported these facts was Ronald P. Kreber. Kreber now serves as a Presiding Judge of the South Orange County District, having been appointed to that post by California Governor Pete Wilson.

170. Thompson's motion to reopen had been denied by the district court just prior to our en banc hearing. Unfortunately, Judge Gadbois, who had been fully aware of the contents of the record and had granted Thompson's original habeas petition, never had the chance to hear the motion. He died before it was filed. Another district judge had stepped in. Judge Dickran Tevrizian decided not to hold an evidentiary hearing and concluded that Thompson's motion did not meet the requirements for a second or successive habeas petition under the newly enacted AEDPA. See *Thompson v. Calderon*, No. CV-89-3630 (C.D. Cal. July 25, 1997) (order regarding petitioner's motion for relief from judgment pursuant to Fed. R. Civ. P. 60(b)).

171. Pub. L. No. 104–132, 110 Stat. 1214 (codified at 28 U.S.C. § 2244 (Supp. II 1997)).

172. See 28 U.S.C. § § 2244, 2254 (Supp. II 1997). States that provide adequate mechanisms for appointment of counsel may impose even more severe time limitations on the filings of prisoners under a death sentence. See 28 U.S.C. § 2263 (Supp. II 1997) (imposing 180-day period for filing).

173. See *Thompson v. Calderon*, 151 F.3d 918, 931 (9th Cir. 1998) (Reinhardt, J., concurring and dissenting); id. at 938 (Tashima, J., concurring and dissenting).

174. See id. at 924–26 (Hug, C.J., joined by Browning, Schroeder, Fletcher, and Thomas, JJ.). Four other judges, who had been in the minority in 1997, concluded that our court did not even have jurisdiction to hear the case, and they would have denied Thompson's motion on that basis. See id. at 926–31 (Kleinfeld, J., concurring in the judgment, joined by O'Scannlain and T. G. Nelson, JJ., and Kozinski, J., in part).

175. Although there was no physical evidence or actual eyewitness testimony that established that Thompson actually participated in the murder, his testimony at trial that he had passed out from a combination of drugs and alcohol and slept through the crime, which took place less than six feet from him, raises a serious credibility question and suggests that he was trying to cover up his own involvement. See *Calderon v. Thompson*, 118 S. Ct. 1489, 1504 (1998).

176. In my view, the physical evidence of rape was uncertain at best. At trial, the prosecution relied primarily on forensic testimony that Ms. Fleischli's wrists, ankles, and palms were bruised in a manner consistent with physical restraint. A police officer testified that the bruising around the wrists was consistent with handcuff injuries, although he acknowledged that he had never seen such injuries on a dead body. However, at his state habeas evidentiary hearing, Thompson presented contradictory forensic testimony suggesting that these bruises were weeks old. Moreover, even if the state's expert were right about the timing of the bruises, they were no more suggestive that Ms. Fleischli had been raped than that she was harmed and restrained in the course of her murder. Similarly, evidence that Ms. Fleischli had been gagged with duct tape and that her shirt and bra had been ripped down the middle and pulled down around her elbows shows violent restraint but not necessarily in furtherance of a rape. Other physical evidence pointed against the conclusion that the sex had been anything but consensual. The state's own witness conceded in his testimony that there was "no anatomical evidence of rape." Ms. Fleischli was found without underwear but wearing tight jeans, which were zipped but not buttoned. A vaginal swab revealed recent semen but infrequent sperm, which may have suggested that Ms. Fleischli douched or washed after sex. (The absence of semen on her jeans ruled out drainage as an explanation; however, the infrequency of sperm could also have occurred if the source had a low sperm count.) Thompson's lawyer failed to pursue this line of investigation. See *Thompson v. Calderon*, 120 F.3d 1052, 1053 n.6 (9th Cir. 1997).

177. See *Coleman v. Thompson*, 501 U.S. 722, 754 (1991) ("In the absence of a constitutional violation, the petitioner bears the risk in federal habeas for all attorney errors made in the course of the representation.").

178. Charles L. Black, Jr., *A New Birth of Freedom: Human Rights, Named and Unnamed* 130–34 (1997).

179. 83 U.S. (16 Wall.) 36 (1873) (eliminating substantive force of Privileges and Immunities Clause of Fourteenth Amendment).

180. See Black, supra note 178, at 28–33, 55–85 (discussing *Slaughterhouse Cases*).

Chapter 11

Women and the Constitution
Where We Are at the End of the Century

Martha Craig Daughtrey

> When an amendment is added to the Constitution it has
> an infinite capacity to bless America if it be wise, and an
> infinite capacity to curse America if it be unwise.[1]

> The basic premise of the Equal Rights [A]mendment is
> that sex should not be a factor in determining the legal
> rights of women, or of men.[2]

[In 1999] the *ABA Journal* published a cover story on the renewed efforts to amend the U.S. Constitution to prohibit discrimination on the basis of gender.[3] As it turns out, the Equal Rights Amendment (ERA) which, if ratified, would have become the twenty-seventh amendment to the Federal Constitution[4]—but which "died" for lack of ratification by three additional states in 1982—was reintroduced in the 106th Congress in 1999.[5] The prospect of a renewed effort to pass the ERA in Congress and to mount ratification campaigns in the fifty state legislatures raises a number of questions that I would like to explore with you this evening.

Setting aside the issue of symbolic desirability for the moment, the most obvious question, of course, is whether such an undertaking is even necessary at this point in our constitutional history. The answer depends on an

This lecture was delivered on October 6, 1999, and appeared in 75 N.Y.U.L. Rev. 1 (2000).

understanding of where we are as the century and the millennium turn, and that, I believe, can only be measured in terms of how far we have come, how far we still have to go, and what would be the quickest and, not incidentally, the safest route to take to reach the goal of gender equality.

I. The Equal Rights Amendment as History

One of the milestones in my legal career was my appointment to the faculty of the Vanderbilt University School of Law in the fall of 1972. When I arrived on campus in September, I was the first and the only woman on the law faculty, undoubtedly the beneficiary of some early affirmative action in hiring, and as the comedienne Minnie Pearl would say, I was "just so proud to be there." I had left behind the fairly narrow and decidedly conservative world of criminal prosecution and had come, I supposed, to a bastion of liberal, politically progressive thought. On my first day at school, I was particularly pleased to be invited to lunch by the two constitutional law professors on the faculty—neither of them "old fogies," both of them only a year or two older than I. As we walked across campus to the University Club, I brought up the subject of the ERA. It had just passed Congress in March of that year and appeared to be steamrolling its way through the state legislatures. What did these constitutional scholars think of the amendment's prospects, I asked, and was stunned at the answer: Not much—an effort to "junk up the Constitution," I was told, that would result in trivializing the field of equal protection. They were solidly against ratification. As I recall, I raised a brief argument in favor of ratification and then fell silent through most of lunch, wondering if the academy was going to be the wonderland of progressive thought that I had imagined it would be. It was not, of course, but after all, no one is quite as naive as a brand-new assistant professor of law. In the end, theirs was the winning position, although the amendment failed, in my judgment, not because of academic arguments about its worth.

In its original form and even in its current stage of development, the U.S. Constitution speaks only in the male gender. Moreover, as Walter Dellinger has pointed out,

> [T]hroughout the process of drafting the Constitution, every draft of every provision used the pronoun "he." It is a commonplace observation that "he" is used in the Constitution in its generic sense as encompassing both genders. This is, of course, technically true. But [one] draft provision casts a very

different light on the Constitution's use of the pronoun "he." For this provision, adopted unanimously for the next-to-last draft of the Constitution, uses the phrase "he or she." Although the pronouns drop out altogether from the final wording of this provision of the Constitution, it is nonetheless extraordinary to find the Convention unanimously adopting a draft provision using the phrase "he or she." At the conclusion of the compromise over navigation and slavery, Mr. Butler moved to insert the following clause: "If any person bound to service or labor in any of the U[nited] States shall escape into another State, he or she shall not be discharged from such service or labor . . . but shall be delivered up to the person justly claiming their service or labor." Throughout the Constitution and all its drafts, "he" is used to refer to President, Vice-President, Senator; "she" appears but once in the evolving drafts of the Constitution, and "she" can be one, and only one thing: a fugitive slave.[6]

The leaders of the nineteenth-century women's rights movement had hoped, of course, that the Fourteenth Amendment's Equal Protection Clause would enfranchise women as well as former male slaves and provide a basis for establishing America's women as first-class citizens in every respect. Given that the word "male," although it nowhere appears in the substantive clause of the Amendment, is used three times in the second section,[7] there was little basis for optimism. Indeed, when Susan B. Anthony was arrested for voting in the 1872 presidential election, she was prohibited by the court from testifying on her own behalf because she was a woman.[8] Equally outrageous is the fact that the trial judge directed a verdict of guilty, giving the jury no option but to convict[9]—a course of conduct, to my knowledge, otherwise unknown to American criminal procedure. (The judge did give Anthony a chance to speak before pronouncing sentence, and—as you might imagine—she said a mouthful.)[10]

It would be another half century before universal suffrage was finally achieved. During that period, Anthony, her stalwart compatriot Elizabeth Cady Stanton, and their followers, having failed repeatedly in their efforts to secure enfranchisement by means of the Federal Constitution, attacked the problem on a state-by-state basis. They had some success in the new western states such as Wyoming and Utah,[11] and with local elections here and there around the country, but the piecemeal approach was costly and largely ineffective. As Carrie Chapman Catt, Anthony's protégée, later described it:

> To get the word male . . . out of the constitution cost the women of the country [more than seventy] years of pauseless campaign. . . . During that time they were forced to conduct fifty-six campaigns of referenda to male voters; 480 campaigns to get Legislatures to submit suffrage amendments to voters;

47 campaigns to get State constitutional conventions to write woman suffrage into State constitutions; 277 campaigns to get State party conventions to include woman suffrage planks; 30 campaigns to get presidential party conventions to adopt woman suffrage planks in party platforms, and 19 campaigns with 19 successive Congresses. Millions of dollars were raised, mainly in small sums, and expended with economic care. Hundreds of women gave the accumulated possibilities of an entire lifetime, thousands gave years of their lives, hundreds of thousands gave constant interest and such aid as they could. It was a continuous, seemingly endless, chain of activity. Young suffragists who helped forge the last links of that chain were not born when it began. Old suffragists who forged the first links were dead when it ended.[12]

Included among those who did not live to see the fulfillment of the suffrage movement was Susan B. Anthony herself, affectionately known as "Aunt Susan." She died at age eighty-six in 1906, fourteen years before the Nineteenth Amendment,[13] the "Susan B. Anthony Amendment," was finally ratified in 1920.[14]

Three years later, in 1923, the original Equal Rights Amendment was first introduced into Congress. The initial language, changed in 1943, provided: "Men and women shall have equal rights throughout the United States and every place subject to its jurisdiction."[15] It had been drafted by the radical suffragist Alice Paul, whose National Woman's Party had split from the ranks of mainstream suffragism, led by Anthony and later by Catt.[16] It was Alice Paul and her sisters-in-arms who chained themselves to the White House gates and were force-fed in prison when their protests took the form of hunger strikes.[17] Once the Nineteenth Amendment took effect in 1920, Paul's followers continued to agitate for the expansion of women's rights, convinced that the vote would not be sufficient to bring about equality between the sexes. The old-line suffragists formed the League of Women Voters, convinced to the contrary that they could rally newly enfranchised women to vote in the reforms they deemed necessary to protect women and children in postwar America.[18] It was an early indication of the dichotomy between the philosophies of "equality feminism" and "difference feminism," which persists to this day.[19]

Some form of the Equal Rights Amendment was introduced in nearly every succeeding session of Congress,[20] but it garnered little serious attention until 1970, a half century after passage of the Suffrage Amendment. That year a renewed effort, influenced by political agitation from the outside, pressed by the Citizen's Council on the Status of Women, and managed on the inside by sponsors Representative Martha Griffiths and Senators

Birch Bayh and Marlow Cook, led to hearings that included testimony urging ratification by several prominent constitutional scholars, including New York University's own Norman Dorsen.[21] Sponsors finally achieved passage on March 22, 1972,[22] principally because politically antagonistic factions within the women's movement were able to coalesce, joined finally by various labor leaders, liberal religious groups, the National Federation of Republican Women—even the League of Women Voters.[23]

Following passage by wide margins in both the House and the Senate,[24] the ERA met with initial success, as states vied to see which could be the first to ratify. Despite the early momentum, however, the amendment fell three states short of ratification at the end of the seven-year ratification period specified in the resolution that accompanied the proposed amendment.[25] Congress then extended the period three years, until June 30, 1982.[26] When no new states had ratified by that date, the amendment famously died,[27] and activists turned their attention to conceivable alternate ways to achieve gender equality—efforts that were already under way across the land.

The alternatives were basically two: piecemeal legislation and extension of the Equal Protection Clause of the Fourteenth Amendment. Viewed from the perspective of the 1970s, neither looked particularly attractive. Until 1971, the year before passage of the ERA, the Fourteenth Amendment had never been invoked successfully in a case involving gender discrimination. Moreover, the prospect of overhauling thousands of individual state and federal laws to protect against the many forms of discrimination existing at that point in the country's history was also daunting. As women's rights activist Florynce Kennedy repeatedly described the challenge, it amounted to winning the Civil War one plantation at a time. Nevertheless, men and women committed to the notion of equality rallied to the challenge and commenced a process of major law reform that continues to this day.

II. Extension of the Equal Protection Clause

It was in the arena of constitutional litigation, however, that the most dramatic changes first occurred, and the success of that litigation can be largely attributed to the ACLU's newly formed Women's Rights Project and to its founder and indomitable director, Ruth Bader Ginsburg. Her first case in pursuit of gender equity, mounted while she was still a law professor at Rutgers, involved a New Jersey law under which schoolteachers who became pregnant lost their jobs. There followed a string of Supreme Court cases in

which Ginsburg was either the prime mover or the force behind the litigation. Of the six cases she argued before the Court during this period, she was
successful in five.

The first of these was the ground-breaking case of *Reed v. Reed*,[28] in
which Ginsburg represented an Idaho mother who applied, unsuccessfully,
to become the executor of her son's estate.[29] So did her ex-husband, and
state law provided that as between persons equally qualified to administer
estates, males were to be preferred to females. In representing Sally Reed,
Ginsburg had a long-term goal to get the Supreme Court to abandon the rational basis test that had always been utilized in sex discrimination cases. Instead, Ginsburg campaigned for a strict scrutiny test, the standard that the
Court had begun to formulate and apply to race-based classifications in the
late 1940s and that had been applied to race discrimination uniformly since
the Court abandoned the "separate but equal" doctrine in 1954.[30] It was undoubtedly clear to her, as it must have been to Thurgood Marshall two
decades earlier, that the barriers would not all fall at once, like the walls of
Jericho. That proved to be the case with *Reed*, in which the Court declined
to apply the higher standard but did reverse the state court's ruling and held
that "a difference in the sex of competing applicants for letters of administration bears [no] rational relationship to a state objective that is sought to
be advanced by the operation of [the Idaho statute]."[31]

Despite the fact that she had fallen short in convincing the Court to treat
gender as a suspect classification, Ginsburg had scored a significant victory—the first successful equal protection challenge on the basis of gender.
As Judge Stephanie K. Seymour so vividly put it: "With the *Reed* decision the
genie was out of the bottle, the toothpaste was out of the tube. . . . '[R]ights,
once set loose, are very difficult to contain; rights consciousness—on and
off the Court—is a powerful engine of legal mobilization and change.'"[32]

Indeed, it was. Two years later, in 1973, Ginsburg was back before the
Court in the case of *Frontiero v. Richardson*[33] and again urged the Court to
apply strict scrutiny to statutes that provided that wives of servicemen were
automatically considered dependents for purposes of obtaining increased
quarters allowances and medical benefits, but that husbands of service-
women were not considered covered dependents unless their wives provided more than one-half of their support.[34] This round, four members of
the Court bought Ginsburg's argument in a strong plurality opinion by Justice Brennan, finding that the statute could not withstand strict scrutiny on
the asserted ground of administrative convenience.[35] Justice Stewart, however, was the "swing vote" in the case and was unwilling to go beyond the

holding in *Reed*, as were three other Justices who concurred separately in the judgment.[36] And, although the Court periodically notes that application of the strict scrutiny standard in gender discrimination cases is still an open question, this split would turn out to be as close to the outright adoption of gender as a suspect classification as the Court would come.

The next case in the series, *Kahn v. Shevin*,[37] represented a setback for Ginsburg. Just a year after her near total victory in *Frontiero*, the Court held, in an opinion authored by Justice Douglas (who had been in the plurality in the prior case), that a Florida statute giving widows but not widowers a five-hundred-dollar exemption from property taxes did not violate equal protection.[38] In the six-to-three decision, the majority held that the challenged statute was designed to further the "state policy of cushioning the financial impact of spousal loss upon the [gender] for which that loss impose[d] a disproportionately heavy burden."[39] Thus, the Court concluded, the distinction in the law rested on "some ground of difference having a fair and substantial relation to the object of the legislation,"[40] in its view a justifiable variation of the rational basis standard applied in *Reed*.

Undaunted, Ginsburg returned to the Supreme Court during its next term, again representing a male client, as she would in so many of the cases she litigated in the 1970s. *Weinberger v. Wiesenfeld*[41] involved another widower, this time one who wanted to raise his infant son himself after his wife had died in childbirth. He applied for and was denied survivor benefits under the Social Security Act because it was strictly a mother's benefit.[42] Perhaps because of the outcome in *Kahn*, Ginsburg changed her strategy in *Wiesenfeld*, arguing not for strict scrutiny but for a "heightened scrutiny" falling somewhere between rational basis analysis and strict scrutiny analysis. Although she won the case for her client,[43] Ginsburg did not succeed in convincing the Court to adopt the intermediate standard that she had presented. Instead, the Court invalidated the provision, which allowed survivors' benefits automatically for widows, but not for widowers on the basis of their wives' covered employment. The Court noted that the "gender-based distinction made by [the statute] is indistinguishable from that invalidated in *Frontiero*" and that it operated "to deprive women of protection for their families which men receive as a result of their employment."[44] Writing for the Court, Justice Brennan did give lip service to the ruling in *Kahn* regarding the weight to be given a "reasonably designed" state policy, but he went on to make clear that "the mere recitation of a benign, compensatory purpose is not an automatic shield which protects against any inquiry into the actual purposes underlying a statutory scheme,"[45] a pronouncement that signaled a retreat from *Kahn* and presaged the Court's subsequent departure from rational basis analysis in the gender discrimination setting.

The breakthrough came in 1976, in a case in which Ginsburg filed an amicus brief but did not argue: *Craig v. Boren*.[46] The substance of the case was certainly not weighty. The equal protection challenge concerned an Oklahoma statute that permitted young women to buy "near-beer" at age eighteen, but restricted men to age twenty-one.[47] Once again, Ginsburg argued in her brief for heightened rather than strict scrutiny, and this time she succeeded where she had failed before. Justice Brennan, writing for a majority of six, interpreted prior holdings of the Court to require that "classifications by gender must serve important governmental objectives and must be substantially related to the achievement of those objectives."[48] The new standard prevails, at least ostensibly, as I shall later note, to this day.

Ginsburg's final victory before the Supreme Court as a lawyer was not in an equal protection case but one decided under the Sixth Amendment's provision guaranteeing the right to an impartial jury. *Duren v. Missouri*,[49] announced in 1979—less than two years before her appointment to the Court of Appeals for the D.C. Circuit—invalidated a Missouri jury selection statute that permitted women to opt out of jury service based on nothing other than their gender.[50] As Ginsburg left the world of lawyering for the rarefied atmosphere of the judiciary, where she would continue to have an impact on the development of equal protection doctrine, her legacy as an advocate for women's rights stood unequaled. As Lynn Hecht Schafran noted at the time of Ginsburg's elevation to the Supreme Court, "I can't imagine how anyone could get from where we were in 1970 to . . . contemporary theories [of gender equality] if Ruth had not done her equal protection work. People forget how things were."[51]

III. The Way Things Were

In preparing for this lecture, I pulled off the shelf in my office the three casebooks that were available for a course I taught on women and the law in the early 1970s at Vanderbilt Law School. The earliest, *Sex Roles in Law and Society*, appeared in 1973.[52] It was authored by New Mexico Law School professor Leo Kanowitz, who, in 1969, had written *Women and the Law: The Unfinished Revolution*.[53] The whole enterprise was so new that there is penciled on the flyleaf of the casebook in my handwriting the dictionary definition of the word "stereotype." Within the next two years, Little, Brown and Company published *Sex Discrimination and the Law*, a casebook by Barbara Allen Babcock, Ann E. Freedman, Eleanor Holmes Norton, and Susan C. Ross, all of whom had litigated in the area of women's rights.[54] Only Babcock was a law professor at the time, at Georgetown University, but Norton had taught and Ross initiated the country's first "Women and the Law" course at New York University School of Law in 1969. Ross later taught the course herself at George Washington University. The third casebook appearing at about the same time was a West publication entitled *Text, Cases and Materials on Sex-Based Discrimination*, by Professors Kenneth M. Davidson, Ruth Bader Ginsburg, and Herma Hill Kay, at Buffalo, Columbia, and Berkeley, respectively.[55]

Undoubtedly, much of the inspiration for the development of these teaching materials can be traced to a conference entitled "Symposium on the Law School Curriculum and the Legal Rights of Women," which turned out to be a truly seminal meeting held at New York University School of Law in the fall of 1972.[56] I was lucky enough to attend and, as a result, to meet virtually everyone writing and teaching in the area of women's rights at that time. It was a pretty heady time: The ERA was gaining steam around the country, and the halls of the academy were filled with talk about strategies for the great transition period following ratification. Looking at the casebooks' tables of contents gives a remarkable snapshot of how much there was to be done. The following recitation hits only some highlights.

Materials on the development of equal protection were key, of course, with explorations of the well-known constitutional trio *Bradwell v. Illinois*,[57] *Goesaert v. Cleary*,[58] and *Hoyt v. Florida*,[59] and the recent appearance on the scene of *Reed* and *Frontiero*. But the casebooks also concentrated on employment law, where adequate enforcement of Title VII[60] and the Equal Pay Act[61] had yet to develop. Job restrictions abounded, some the result of the so-called "protective labor laws" still in existence around the country that generally had the effect of barring women from holding higher paid positions. The existence of segregated "help wanted" notices also perpetuated the problem. Discrimination abounded in pension plans, insurance benefits, what was at the time called workman's compensation, in the Social Security statutes, and, most significantly, in the determination of what constituted a "bona fide occupational qualification," which was the usual defense raised in employment discrimination cases in the 1970s and one that all too often succeeded on the basis of flimsy excuses rather than actual job functions. The fact that some women could and did become pregnant raised barriers for all women workers. "Sexual harassment" as a form of discrimination had not yet been recognized.

In the area of family law, distinctions based on gender and the inequality that resulted were systemic and far-reaching. The casebooks covered the effects of the doctrine of "feme covert"[62] in all its many manifestations, including its effect on grounds for divorce in the virtually universal fault-based system of the era, on a married woman's domicile, her name, her credit rating, the doctrine of interspousal immunity, loss of consortium, the ability of a wife to contract freely, inheritance laws, property settlement, and the right of support following dissolution of the marriage.[63] Inequities abounded not only in property law, but even in community property law. For example, in 1972 when the ERA was passed, and as late as 1980, the Louisiana community property statute, ostensibly giving married women joint ownership of marital property, included this provision: "The husband is the head and master of the partnership or community of gains; he administers its effects, disposes of the revenues which they produce, and may alienate them by an onerous title, without the consent and permission of his wife."[64]

In education, Title IX,[65] which has played such a crucial role in literally leveling the playing field for women, had yet to exert its influence. In 1971, the Supreme Court declined to invalidate a South Carolina scheme that barred men from a women's college that was part of the state university system.[66] Thinking ahead to *Mississippi University for Women v. Hogan*,[67] authored by Justice O'Connor, and *United States v. Virginia*,[68] the VMI decision written by Justice Ginsburg, it is easy to substantiate the claim that having women on the appellate bench makes a difference in the development of constitutional law. Actually, one of my favorite discrimination cases came out of the Sixth Circuit and involved a state university, this one in Eastern Kentucky.[69] During the academic year 1971–72, the school had a curfew that applied only to its women students—known in those days as "coeds"—and that required them to be in their dorms by 10:30 P.M. Monday through Thursday, 1:00 A.M. Friday and Saturday, and midnight Sunday.[70] One of the students, Ruth Robinson, sued, claiming a violation of equal protection. The court responded as follows:

> The State's basic justification for the classification system is that of safety. It asserts that women are more likely to be criminally attacked later at night and are physically less capable of defending themselves than men. It concludes that the safety of women will be protected by having them in their dormito-

ries at certain hours of the night. The goal of safety is a legitimate concern of the Board of Regents and this court cannot say that the regulations in question are not rationally related to the effectuation of this reasonable goal.

The appellant claims that the safety justification is undermined by the shifting curfew for different nights of the week asserting that the streets are no safer at 12:30 A.M. on Saturday than they are at 12:30 A.M. on Wednesday. We hold, however, that the State could properly take into consideration the fact that on weekend nights many coeds have dates and ought to be permitted to stay out later than on weekday nights. A classification having some reasonable basis does not offend the equal protection merely because it is not drawn with mathematical nicety.[71]

Robinson was an easy case to teach. Invariably, someone in the class would raise her hand and suggest that if safety were truly the concern, and if the court was correct in its implication that men were the threat to the women students' safety, then perhaps the men on campus should be subject to curfew and the "coeds" should be allowed to go wherever and whenever they pleased.

Gender restrictions were likewise legally sanctioned in public accommodations, in the military, in criminal law—especially in the area of sentencing—and in many other areas of American life. According to one review of the Davidson, Ginsburg, Kay casebook, "[t]he text contains an insuperable exposition of the fact that our legal system simply has not shown basic fairness to men or women qua persons, and, indeed, that there has been and continues to be a sex-divided legal system on many fronts."[72] For those men and women who were not born until the mid-seventies, these early sex discrimination casebooks would be a revelation. To the rest of us, they are a fascinating reminder of how far we have come in the quarter century since debate about the ERA was last abroad in the land. But I cannot leave the discussion without a few words about the subject I have always found the most intriguing: jury service for women.

IV. Jury Service

In a new study of women and the obligations of citizenship entitled *No Constitutional Right to Be Ladies*,[73] Linda K. Kerber, a professor of history at the University of Iowa, devotes over a quarter of her book to the history of women's jury service in America. That history traces its roots to Blackstone's pronouncement that women were ineligible for jury service due to *propter defectum sexus,* a "defect of sex."[74] In the United States, the Supreme Court indicated in dictum in its 1879 decision in *Strauder v. West Virginia*[75] that states may "prescribe the qualifications of . . . jurors, and in so doing make discriminations" and "may confine the selection to males."[76] More than half a century later, the Supreme Court, in the exercise of its supervisory powers over the federal courts, imposed a cross-sectional requirement in federal jury selection, based, apparently, on a largely unarticulated due process analysis.[77] In *Ballard v. United States,*[78] a 1946 decision, the Court extended the cross-sectional principle to require the inclusion of women in jury venires, but only on federal courts and only in those states in which women were otherwise qualified to serve.[79] At the time, some seventeen states still prohibited women from serving on juries, a situation that was slowly changing as more and more men were drafted into the armed services during World War II. Many others limited women's service. However, it was not until 1975, in *Taylor v. Louisiana,*[80] that the Court identified a constitutional basis for the cross-sectional requirement in the Sixth Amendment.[81]

Hence, as the ERA was being sent from Congress to the states for ratification in 1972, the state of the law with regard to women's jury service was represented by the Supreme Court's 1961 opinion in *Hoyt v. Florida.*[82] The "story behind the story" of *Hoyt* is set out in exquisite detail in *No Constitutional Right to Be Ladies,*[83] and is alone worth the price of the book. It reveals that Gwendolyn Rogers Hoyt was charged in Tampa, Florida, in 1956 with the murder of her husband under circumstances that today would undoubtedly be defended as a response to domestic violence.[84] Although Florida permitted women to serve on criminal juries at the time (several Southern states did not, or similarly restricted service),[85] service was possible only if a woman went to the county courthouse and registered to serve. As a result, at the time Hoyt was tried, 220 women had registered and were theoretically eligible for jury service, along with approximately 10,000 men whose names had been entered on a master list in conformity with prevailing jury selection practices in Hillsborough County—a representation of 2 percent.[86] However, the court clerk had entered only ten women's names on the master list, for an actual representation of 0.1 percent—a ratio of one woman to every thousand men.[87] At trial, Hoyt's attorney objected to the dearth of women in the jury pool, arguing that under the circumstances of the prosecution, it was crucial that his client not be tried by an all-male jury.

Despite the equal protection argument mounted by *Hoyt* in the state courts and on certiorari in the U.S. Supreme Court, none of the judges—all male, we can be sure—heeded the words of Justice Douglas from the *Ballard* decision fifteen years earlier, involving women's service on federal juries, in which he observed:

> The truth is that the two sexes are not fungible; a community made up exclusively of one is different from a community composed of both; the subtle interplay of influence one on the other is among the imponderables. To insulate the courtroom from either may not in a given case make an iota of difference. Yet a flavor, a distinct quality is lost if either sex is excluded. The exclusion of one may indeed make the jury less representative of the community than would be true if an economic or racial group were excluded.[88]

Instead, the Supreme Court upheld the Florida jury statute, noting that it did not "purport to exclude women" from jury service, but merely gave women "the privilege to serve" rather than "impose service as a duty."[89] Thus, the Court held, the statute was not facially invalid, nor did the fact that it operated to produce venires virtually devoid of women constitute an equal protection violation. Justice Harlan explained:

> Despite the enlightened emancipation of women from the restrictions and protections of bygone years, and their entry into many parts of community life formerly considered to be reserved to men, woman is still regarded as the center of home and family life. We cannot say that it is constitutionally impermissible for a State, acting in pursuit of the general welfare, to conclude that a woman should be relieved from the civic duty of jury service unless she herself determines that such service is consistent with her own special responsibilities.[90]

Writing for the Court, Justice Harlan found it unnecessary to decide whether a state might completely bar women from jury service, but he nevertheless noted that the "constitutional proposition" of Strauder's dictum that jury service could be confined to males "has gone unquestioned for more than eighty years in the decisions of the Court."[91]

Ultimately, of course, that proposition would be successfully questioned. When the Court first held in 1972 in *Alexander v. Louisiana*[92] that discrimination on the basis of race violated a criminal defendant's right under the Sixth Amendment, as applied to states through the Fourteenth Amendment, to a grand jury from which no "cognizable" group in the community had been excluded, the Court deliberately pretermitted the question of exclusion on the basis of gender, an issue that had also been raised in the case.[93] Finally, three years later, the Court tackled the issue head on in *Taylor v. Louisiana*[94] and ruled that Louisiana's jury statute, which, like the statute at issue in *Hoyt*, required women to register in order to become eligible for jury service, was in violation of the cross-sectional requirement of the Sixth Amendment established in *Alexander*.[95]

And, three years after *Taylor* invalidated the "opt-in" statute, Ruth Bader Ginsburg convinced the Supreme Court in *Duren v. Missouri*[96] to invalidate Missouri's "opt-out" provision, which allowed any woman, in response to a prominently placed notice on the jury summons, to decline service by returning the summons or by simply not reporting for jury duty.[97] Some two decades later, the final chapter was written. In the 1994 decision in *J.E.B. v. Alabama*,[98] the Court, in a logical extension of *Batson v. Kentucky*,[99] held that "the Equal Protection Clause forbids peremptory challenges on the basis of gender as well as on the basis of race."[100] The tone of the opinion, written by Justice Blackmun, is almost one of surprise, as if the Court had merely overlooked something that should have been obvious all along. Noting that "[m]any States continued to exclude women from jury service well into the present century, despite the fact that women attained suffrage upon ratification of the Nineteenth Amendment in 1920,"[101] the Court said:

> Today we reaffirm what, by now, should be axiomatic: Intentional discrimination on the basis of gender by state actors violates the Equal Protection Clause, particularly where, as here, the discrimination serves to ratify and perpetuate invidious, archaic, and overbroad stereotypes about the relative abilities of men and women.[102]

Although the Court had no difficulty in the jury setting with equating the status of women as citizens with that of African Americans,[103] the Court once again ducked the long-pending question of whether gender should be considered a suspect category for equal protection purposes. A footnote to the opinion reads: "Because we conclude that gender-based peremptory challenges are not substantially related to an important government objective, we once again need not decide whether classifications based on gender are inherently suspect."[104]

The Court then cited *Mississippi University for Women v. Hogan*,[105] a 1982 opinion by Justice O'Connor that is about to bring us full circle to the original question: Taking as a given the need for the Equal Rights Amendment in 1972, at the time of its initial passage, is there any longer a need for the amendment? Or has a gender-neutral millennium truly arrived?

V. Is a Twenty-First–Century Equal Rights
Amendment Necessary?

In its 1982 opinion in *Hogan*, the Supreme Court held that a state-supported university's policy of limiting enrollment in its School of Nursing to females, and thereby denying admission to otherwise qualified males, violated equal protection.[106] The Court split five-to-four in the case, and the deciding vote was cast by the author of the opinion, newly appointed Justice Sandra Day O'Connor. She noted that the party seeking to uphold a statute that classifies on the basis of gender has the burden of "showing at least that the classification serves 'important governmental objectives and that the discriminatory means employed' are 'substantially related to the achievement of those objectives,'"[107] the routine middle ground standard of review in sex discrimination cases. However, O'Connor provided, too, that the burden also requires the establishment of an "exceedingly persuasive justification" for the gender-based classification.[108] This language went unremarked by the dissenters, who were much more interested in a lengthy exposition on the history and virtues of single-sex higher education. But the language was picked up and emphasized by Justice Ginsburg in *United States v. Virginia*,[109] the VMI admissions case decided fourteen years after *Mississippi University for Women*:

> To summarize the Court's current directions for cases of official classification based on gender: Focusing on the differential treatment or denial of opportunity for which relief is sought, the reviewing court must determine whether the proffered justification is "exceedingly persuasive." The burden of justification is demanding and it rests entirely on the State. . . . The justification must be genuine, not hypothesized or invented post hoc in response to litigation. And it must not rely on overbroad generalizations about the different talents, capacities, or preferences of males and females.[110]

In formulating these "directions," had Justice Ginsburg ratcheted up the already "heightened scrutiny" another notch or two? The Chief Justice certainly thought so. Concurring in the judgment and thus producing a seven-to-one decision, with Scalia dissenting and Thomas, whose son was a VMI student, not sitting, Rehnquist pointed to the "exceedingly persuasive justification" language of the Court's opinion and noted that "[i]t is unfortunate that the Court thereby introduces an element of uncertainty respecting the appropriate test."[111]

Justice Ginsburg was most certainly not oblivious to what she had accomplished in the VMI opinion. According to a *New York Times* report:

> [She] recounted in a 1997 speech to the [Washington, D.C.] Women's Bar Association . . . that a year earlier, as she announced her opinion declaring unconstitutional the all-male admissions policy at the Virginia Military Institute, she looked across the bench at Justice O'Connor and thought of the legacy they were building together.

Justice Ginsburg's opinion in the Virginia case cited one of Justice O'Connor's earliest majority opinions for the Court, a 1982 decision called *Mississippi University for Women v. Hogan* that declared unconstitutional the exclusion of male students from a state-supported nursing school. Justice O'Connor, warning against using "archaic and stereotypic notions" about the roles of men and women, herself cited in that opinion some of the Supreme Court cases that Ruth Ginsburg, who was not to join the Court for another eleven years, had argued and won as a noted women's rights advocate during the 1970s.

Addressing the women's bar group, Justice Ginsburg noted that the vote in Justice O'Connor's 1982 opinion was 5 to 4, while the vote to strike down men-only admissions in Virginia fourteen years later was 7 to 1.

"What occurred in the intervening years in the Court, as elsewhere in society?" Justice Ginsburg asked. The answer, she continued, lay in a line from Shakespeare that Justice O'Connor had recently spoken in the character of Isabel, Queen of France, in a local production of *Henry V*: "Haply a woman's voice may do some good."[112]

Did the VMI decision move us to the point that an equal rights amendment might have? Ginsburg herself apparently thinks so. She has been quoted as saying, in an address to the University of Virginia School of Law shortly after the VMI decision was announced, "There is no practical difference between what has evolved and the ERA."[113]

VI. So, Should We "Junk Up" the Constitution?

The advocates of a renewed effort at ratification of the ERA contend not only that women deserve a place in the Federal Constitution, but that amendment of the Constitution is required in order to ensure that we are not forced to retreat on any of the fronts on which progress for women's rights has been so long in coming and so laboriously achieved. They argue that by retaining the language of the failed amendment, the legislative history will remain intact. Moreover, much of the opposition to ratification in the 1970s surely will have dissipated. As the *ABA Journal* reporter points out in an article in the summer of 1999:

> When Congress sent the equal rights amendment to the states for ratification in 1972, ERA opponents warned of dire consequences: co-ed bathrooms, women drafted into the military, the repeal of spousal support laws.
>
> The ERA failed, but the consequences happened anyway. Unisex bathrooms are in college dorms around the country. Women are joining the armed forces—by choice. And modern alimony laws look at sex-neutral factors, such as need and contribution, when determining who should receive support.[114]

The Equal Rights Amendment has the dubious distinction of being one of only six amendments submitted by Congress to the states that have failed at ratification.[115] They were originally among the over five thousand bills proposing amendments to the Federal Constitution introduced in Congress since 1789.[116] Currently, for example, there are a handful of proposed amendments, in addition to the ERA, that are under debate in Congress, in the press, and in the academy. They include a "Ten Commandments" amendment passed by the House of Representatives on June 17, 1999.[117] Its first section provides that "[t]he power to display the Ten Commandments on or within property owned or administered by the several States or political subdivisions thereof is hereby declared to be among the powers reserved to the States respectively."[118] A second section purports to protect "[t]he expression of religious faith by individual persons on or within property owned or administered by the several States."[119] Similarly, the House has passed the so-called "flag burning amendment," giving Congress the power to "prohibit the physical desecration of the flag of the United States."[120] And there are perennial attempts to amend the Constitution to permit prayer in the schools and to ban abortion. It seems to me that there is a legitimate question whether a renewed Equal Rights Amendment would be in very good company if it, too, were to be passed by the House of Representatives, as its House sponsor, Representative Carolyn Maloney (D-N.Y.) proposes.[121]

Perhaps the ERA, resubmitted to the states, would draw little opposition and would be ratified without controversy, as a quasi-dead letter. However, while the "foxhole issue" and the "potty issue" seem to have disappeared from the scene, we can imagine that the forces opposed to gay rights will see the amendment as a threat and vocally and vociferously rejoin the fight against ratification. They would do well to note that in the seven states that have an equal rights amendment in their state constitutions,[122] as well as in the thirteen other states with some provision guaranteeing equality as a matter of constitutional right,[123] society continues to progress without the social, legal, and cultural upheavals that the Stop ERA adherents predicted a quarter century ago.[124]

In conclusion, it is altogether fitting to honor Ruth Bader Ginsburg for her many accomplishments, and for the gumption and the dedication she continues to evidence by pulling on her black robe and showing up for the opening of Court this past Monday, less than three weeks after undergoing major cancer surgery. But while Ruth Ginsburg was busy litigating and deciding equal protection cases, many others in this country were busy in the political arena, fighting the good fight for gender equity on many fronts, committed to bringing about a better world through law reform in the name of constitutional rights and responsibilities. In tribute to them, I could end with a ringing quotation of some kind from James Madison, whose Dolly would certainly smile on us this evening. Instead, I am going to take the liberty of quoting one of the many influential women activists of the 1970s, Jill Ruckelshaus, a cofounder of the National Women's Political Caucus. In 1977, she spoke words that have stayed with me over two decades. She said:

> We are in for a very, very long haul. . . . I am asking for everything you have to give. We will never give up. . . . You will lose your youth, your sleep, your arches, your patience, your sense of humor . . . and occasionally . . . the understanding and support of the people that you love very much. In return, I have nothing to offer you but . . . your pride in being a woman, all your dreams you've ever had for your daughters, and nieces, and granddaughters, your future and the certain knowledge that at the end of your days you will be able to look back and say that once in your life you gave everything you had for justice.[125]

NOTES

1. Equal Rights 1970: Hearings on S.J. Res. 61 and S.J. Res. 231 Before the Senate Comm. on the Judiciary, 91st Cong. 8 (1970) [hereinafter Hearings] (statement of Sen. Ervin) (arguing against passage of Equal Rights Amendment (ERA)).

2. Id. at 298 (statement of Professor Thomas I. Emerson) (testifying in favor of ERA). Professor Emerson's remarks "In Support of the Equal Rights Amendment"

are reprinted at 6 Harv. C.R.-C.L. L. Rev. 225 (1971), along with those of Professor Norman Dorsen and Susan Deller Ross, see id. at 216 (in favor of ERA), and of Professors Paul A. Freund, see id. at 234 (in opposition to ERA), and Philip B. Kurland, see id. at 243 (same), as part of a symposium edition on the proposed constitutional amendment.

3. See Debra Baker, "The Fight Ain't Over," A.B.A. J., Aug. 1999, at 52.

4. In the years since the defeat of the ERA, the last necessary states ratified the current Twenty-Seventh Amendment, which provides that "[n]o law, varying the compensation for the services of the Senators and Representatives, shall take effect, until an election of Representatives shall have intervened." U.S. Const. amend. XXVII. This Amendment was one of twelve proposed by the first Congress in 1789. See Gerald Gunther & Kathleen M. Sullivan, *Constitutional Law* app. A at A-15 n* (13th ed. 1997). Ten of those twelve were ratified and became the Bill of Rights. See id. A sufficient number of states did not ratify the congressional compensation amendment until 1992, a stretch of over two hundred years. See id. Six states had ratified by the end of the eighteenth century; Ohio ratified in 1873. See Michael Stokes Paulsen, "A General Theory of Article V: The Constitutional Lessons of the Twenty-Seventh Amendment," 103 Yale L.J. 677, 678 (1993). The next to ratify was Wyoming in 1978. See Ronald D. Rotunda & John E. Nowak, *Treatise on Constitutional Law* 404 (3d ed. 1999).

5. See H.R. Res. 37, 106th Cong. (1999).

6. Walter E. Dellinger III, "1787: The Constitution and 'The Curse of Heaven,'" 29 Wm. & Mary L. Rev. 145, 153 (1987) (footnote omitted).

7. See U.S. Const. amend. XIV, § 2.

8. See Sandra Day O'Connor, "Speech on 75th Anniversary of Women's Right to Vote," 27 U. West L.A. L. Rev. 7, 11 (1996).

9. See *United States v. Anthony*, 24 F. Cas. 829, 832 (C.C.N.D.N.Y. 1873) (No. 14,459).

10. See Barbara Allen Babcock et al., *Sex Discrimination and the Law* 9–10 (1975) (relating Anthony's impassioned speech given despite obvious hostility from bench).

11. See Eleanor Flexner & Ellen Fitzpatrick, *Century of Struggle: The Women's Rights Movement in the United States* 149–56, 167–70 (1996).

12. Carrie Chapman Catt & Nettie Rogers Shuler, *Woman Suffrage and Politics* 107–8 (1923).

13. The Amendment provides:

The right of citizens of the United States to vote shall not be denied or abridged by the United States or by any State on account of sex.

Congress shall have the power to enforce this article by appropriate legislation.

U.S. Const. amend. XIX.

14. Anthony's last and perhaps most famous public utterance, "Failure is impossible!" came at the conclusion of her remarks at a suffrage rally in Washington, D.C., three days before her death. See Lynn Sherr, *Failure Is Impossible* 324 (1995).

15. S.J. Res. 21, 68th Cong. (1923).

16. See William Henry Chafe, *The American Woman* 112–13 (1972).

17. See id. at 113.

18. It was the League's defense of protectionist legislation that caused the wide postsuffrage split between the two groups of activists. According to one historian:

> [T]he two opposing camps were engaged in a bitter war. One side fought for the exclusive goal of female equality; the other side for social reform. One side believed that suffrage was only the first step in the campaign for freedom; the other that the Nineteenth Amendment had substantially finished the task of making women equal to men. Protective legislation became the crux of the differences between the two groups.

Id. at 119.

19. For a discussion of the principles underlying "equality feminism" and "difference feminism," see generally Carol Gilligan, *In a Different Voice* (1982).

20. See Barbara A. Brown et al., "The Equal Rights Amendment: A Constitutional Basis for Equal Rights for Women," 80 Yale L.J. 871, 981–85 (1971).

21. See Hearings, supra note 1, at 312 (statement of Professor Norman Dorsen).

22. See Flexner & Fitzpatrick, supra note 11, at 322. The final vote in the House was 354 to 24, see 117 Cong. Rec. 35,815 (1971), and in the Senate was 84 to 8, see 118 Cong. Rec. 9598 (1972).

23. The AFL-CIO and the International Ladies Garment Workers Union continued to oppose the amendment. See Babcock et al., supra note 10, at 132–33. Also opposing the amendment were fundamentalist religious groups and the John Birch Society, from which Phyllis Schlafly's Eagle Forum and its STOP ERA campaign later sprang. See Donald G. Matthews & Jane Sherron De Hart, *Sex, Gender, and the Politics of ERA* 59, 67, 153 (1990).

24. The vote in the Senate came despite Sen. Ervin's impassioned recitation of Rudyard Kipling's sentimental verse, "O, Mother of Mine." See 118 Cong. Rec. 9517 (1972).

25. See Baker, supra note 3, at 53.

26. H.R.J. Res. 638, 95th Cong. (1978).

27. It is somewhat surprising that the time restriction on ratification of the proposed twenty-seventh amendment was not seriously challenged. Ironically, the Amendment that ultimately became the Twenty-Seventh was first passed and submitted to the states for ratification in 1789. See supra note 4.

28. 404 U.S. 71 (1971).

29. See id. at 71–72. Ginsburg and her colleague, Mel Wulf, cowrote the *Reed*

briefs, and the case was argued by Allen Derr, local counsel in Boise, Idaho. See id. at 71.

30. See *Brown v. Board of Educ.*, 347 U.S. 483, 495 (1954).

31. *Reed*, 404 U.S. at 76.

32. Stephanie K. Seymour, "Women as Constitutional Equals: The Burger Court's Overdue Evolution," 33 Tulsa L.J. 23, 30 (1997) (quoting Joel B. Grossman, "Constitutional Policymaking in the Burger Years," 86 Mich. L. Rev. 1414, 1416 (1988)).

33. 411 U.S. 677 (1973).

34. See id. at 680. Ginsburg wrote the jurisdictional statement in *Frontiero*, filed an amicus brief for the Women's Rights Project, and jointly filed the reply brief with the Southern Poverty Law Center. Ginsburg, who was given ten minutes of the thirty-minute argument, urged the adoption of strict scrutiny. The principal lawyer for the appellant argued only that the statute was irrational. For background on Ginsburg's role in the case, see Deborah L. Markowitz, "In Pursuit of Equality: One Woman's Work to Change the Law," 14 Women's Rts. L. Rep. 335, 344–46 (1992).

35. See *Frontiero*, 411 U.S. at 690–91.

36. See id. at 691–92. In a separate concurring opinion, Justice Powell, writing for himself, Chief Justice Burger, and Justice Blackmun, also relied on rational basis analysis and added this tantalizing paragraph:

> There is another, and I find compelling, reason for deferring a general cate-gorizing of sex classifications as invoking the strictest test of judicial scrutiny. The Equal Rights Amendment, which if adopted will resolve the substance of this precise question, has been approved by Congress and submitted for rat-ification by the States. If this Amendment is duly adopted, it will represent the will of the people accomplished in the manner prescribed by the Consti-tution.

Id. at 692 (Powell, J., concurring). Justice Rehnquist dissented but did not file a sep-arate opinion. See id. at 691 (Rehnquist, J., dissenting).

37. 416 U.S. 351 (1974).

38. See id. at 355–56.

39. See id. at 355.

40. Id. at 355 (quoting *Reed v. Reed*, 404 U.S. 71, 76 (1971) (quoting *F.S. Royster Guano Co. v. Virginia*, 253 U.S. 412, 415 (1920)) (internal quotation marks omit-ted)).

41. 420 U.S. 636 (1975).

42. Unlike *Frontiero* and *Goldfarb*, see infra note 45, the Social Security Act was strictly a mother's benefit, and it did not rely on establishing dependence. There-fore, the plaintiff was automatically denied the benefit, even though his wife's salary had been greater than his own. See id. at 640–41, 645.

43. See id. at 653.

44. Id. at 642–43, 645.

45. Id. at 648. The *Wiesenfeld* Court noted that "it is apparent both from the statutory scheme itself and from the legislative history . . . that Congress' purpose in providing benefits to young widows with children was . . . to permit women to elect not to work and to devote themselves to the care of children." Id. In 1977, in *California v. Goldfarb*, 430 U.S. 199 (1977), another of Ginsburg's successful equal protection lawsuits, the Supreme Court extended the ruling in *Wiesenfeld* to cover widowers without dependent children.

46. 429 U.S. 190 (1976).

47. See id. at 191–92.

48. Id. at 197.

49. 439 U.S. 357 (1979).

50. See id. at 359–60.

51. David Von Drehle, "A Trailblazer's Step-by-Step Assault on the Status Quo," Wash. Post (Nat'l Wkly. Ed.), July 26–Aug. 1, 1993, at 8.

52. See Leo Kanowitz, *Sex Roles in Law and Society: Cases and Materials* (1973).

53. See Leo Kanowitz, *Women and the Law: The Unfinished Revolution* (1969).

54. See Babcock et al., supra note 10, at v.

55. See Kenneth M. Davidson et al., *Sex-Based Discrimination* (1974).

56. For an article based on a paper presented at the conference, see John O. Johnston, Jr., "Sex and Property: The Common Law Tradition, the Law School Curriculum, and Developments toward Equality," 47 N.Y.U. L. Rev. 1033 (1972).

57. 83 U.S. (16 Wall.) 130 (1873) (denying that Fourteenth Amendment guarantees women right to admission to practice in state courts). Justice Bradley, concurring, opined on the ill-suitedness of the female character to the practice of law: "The natural and proper timidity and delicacy which belongs to the female sex evidently unfits it for many of the occupations of civil life." Id. at 141 (Bradley, J., concurring).

58. 335 U.S. 464 (1948) (finding constitutional statute forbidding women from acting as bartenders, with exception of wives and daughters of male owners).

59. 368 U.S. 57 (1961) (holding that state statute permitting women to serve as jurors only if they explicitly waive their exemption from duty does not violate Fourteenth Amendment); see also discussion infra Part IV (placing *Hoyt* within development of Court's recognition of women's rights to serve on juries).

60. See Civil Rights Act of 1964 § § 701–718, 42 U.S.C. § § 2000e to 2000e–17 (1994).

61. See Equal Pay Act of 1963, 29 U.S.C. § 206(d) (1994).

62. See Black's *Law Dictionary* 617 (6th ed. 1990) (defining "feme covert" as "A married woman. Generally used in reference to the former legal disabilities of a married woman").

63. See Babcock et al., supra note 10, at 561–818; Davidson et al., supra note 55, at 117–418; Kanowitz, supra note 52, at 183–298.

64. La. Civ. Code Ann. art. 2404 (West 1971) (repealed 1979), invalidated by *Kirchberg v. Feenstra*, 450 U.S. 455, 458, 460–61 (1981) (holding that provision violated Equal Protection Clause).

65. See Civil Rights Act of 1964, tit. IX, 20 U.S.C. §§ 1681–1688 (1994).

66. See *Williams v. McNair*, 401 U.S. 951 (1971).

67. 458 U.S. 718 (1982) (holding that state statute excluding males from state-supported nursing school violates Equal Protection Clause).

68. 518 U.S. 515 (1996) (holding that exclusion of women from prestigious military school violates Equal Protection Clause and that violation cannot be cured by creation of parallel women's school).

69. See *Robinson v. Board of Regents*, 475 F.2d 707 (6th Cir. 1973).

70. See id. at 708.

71. Id. at 711.

72. Mary Cynthia Dunlap, Book Review, 27 J. Legal Educ. 120, 124 (1975) (reviewing Kenneth M. Davidson et al., *Sex-Based Discrimination: Text, Cases & Materials* (1974)). The review indicates that gender discrimination casebooks initially met with negative criticism and that, like courses on "Law and Native Americans" or "Race and Police," separate courses on "Women and the Law" were seen at the time by old-line teachers of "standard" law courses, such as Torts and Contracts, as pedagogically illegitimate. See id. at 123–24.

73. See Linda K. Kerber, *No Constitutional Right to Be Ladies* (1998). The book explores the forces behind a legal system that would require women citizens to pay taxes on par with men but deny them the other obligations (and some would say, rights) of citizenship, including voting, jury service, and military service. See generally Shirley S. Abrahamson, "Justice and Juror," 20 Ga. L. Rev. 257 (1986); Barbara Allen Babcock, "A Place in the Palladium: Women's Rights and Jury Service," 61 U. Cin. L. Rev. 1139 (1993); Martha Craig Daughtrey, "Cross Sectionalism in Jury-Selection Procedures after *Taylor v. Louisiana*," 43 Tenn. L. Rev. 1 (1975); Carol Weisbrod, "Images of the Woman Juror," 9 Harv. Women's L.J. 59 (1986).

74. William Blackstone, *Commentaries* *362. The other two principal "defects" were those of liberty and estate. See id.

75. 100 U.S. 303 (1879).

76. Id. at 310. Strauder held that trial by a jury from which members of a racial group have been excluded violates a defendant's right to equal protection when the defendant is a member of the excluded group. See id. at 305–10. In *Hernandez v. Texas*, 347 U.S. 475 (1954), the Court extended the systematic exclusion principle to a group other than one defined by race.

77. See *Glasser v. United States*, 315 U.S. 60, 83–88 (1942).

78. 329 U.S. 187 (1946).

79. See id. at 191–96.

80. 419 U.S. 522 (1975).

81. For a discussion of the convoluted route the Court took to get to *Taylor,* see Daughtrey, supra note 73, at 39–50.

82. 368 U.S. 57 (1961).

83. See Kerber, supra note 73, at 124–94.

84. See id. at 124–27.

85. Alabama did not permit women to sit on juries until 1966. See Daughtrey, supra note 73, at 66 n.284. South Carolina was the last state to allow jury service by women, holding out until 1967. See id.

86. See *Hoyt,* 368 U.S. at 65.

87. See id.

88. *Ballard v. United States,* 329 U.S. 187, 193–94 (1946) (footnote omitted).

89. *Hoyt,* 368 U.S. at 60.

90. Id. at 61–62.

91. Id. at 60.

92. 405 U.S. 625 (1972).

93. See id. at 633.

94. 419 U.S. 522 (1975).

95. See id. at 531–33.

96. 439 U.S. 357 (1979).

97. See id. at 360, 362. A similar statute still existed in Tennessee. See id. at 360 n.6. Alabama, which until 1966 had prohibited women from jury service, revised its law to provide an exemption for women "for good cause." See id. at 359 n.4. Massachusetts allowed the court to excuse any women requesting not to serve in a case involving sex crimes. See id. at 360 n.7.

98. 511 U.S. 127 (1994).

99. 476 U.S. 79 (1986).

100. J.E.B., 511 U.S. at 130.

101. Id. at 131.

102. Id. at 130–31. Contrast this to Justice Blackmun's comments in a dissenting opinion a dozen years earlier, in *Mississippi Univ. for Women v. Hogan,* 458 U.S. 718 (1982), in which the majority invalidated a single-sex admissions policy:

> I have come to suspect that it is easy to go too far with rigid rules in this area of claimed sex discrimination, and to lose—indeed destroy—values that mean much to some people. . . . I hope that we do not lose all values that some think are worthwhile (and are not based on differences of race or religion) and relegate ourselves to needless conformity. The ringing words of the Equal Protection Clause of the Fourteenth Amendment . . . do not demand that price.

Id. at 734–35 (Blackmun, J., dissenting).

103. See J.E.B., 511 U.S. at 136 ("Certainly, with respect to jury service, African-Americans and women share a history of total exclusion, a history which came to

an end for women many years after the embarrassing chapter in our history came to an end for African-Americans.").

104. Id. at 137 n.6.

105. 458 U.S. 718.

106. See id. at 733.

107. Id. at 724 (quoting *Wengler v. Druggists Mut. Ins. Co.*, 446 U.S. 142, 150 (1980)).

108. Id. (citing *Kirchberg v. Feenstra*, 450 U.S. 455, 461 (1981)). *Kirchberg*, by Justice Marshall, invalidated a Louisiana statute giving unfettered control over community property to the husband. See 450 U.S. at 456; see also supra note 64 and accompanying text.

109. 518 U.S. 515 (1996).

110. Id. at 532–33 (citation omitted).

111. Id. at 559.

112. Linda Greenhouse, "From the High Court, A Voice Quite Distinctly a Woman's," N.Y. Times, May 26, 1999, at A1.

113. Baker, supra note 3, at 55. Justice Ginsburg, however, remains an ERA supporter. See David Harper, "Justice Assesses Gender Issue," Tulsa World, Aug. 29, 1997, available in Lexis, News Library, ARCNWS file (quoting Justice Ginsburg on ERA: "[I]t belongs in our Constitution as a norm society embraces. It's what you'd like to teach ninth graders in civics class."); Jeffrey Rosen, "The New Look of Liberalism on the Court," N.Y. Times, Oct. 5, 1997, § 6 (Magazine), at 60 (quoting Justice Ginsburg on ERA: "I would still like it as a symbol to see the E.R.A. in the Constitution for my granddaughter.").

114. Baker, supra note 3, at 53.

115. The six failed amendments are set out in Rotunda & Nowak, supra note 4, at 375–78.

116. See Walter Dellinger, "The Legitimacy of Constitutional Change: Rethinking the Amendment Process," 97 Harv. L. Rev. 386, 427 (1983). For a history of the amendment process, see id. at 427–30.

117. See 145 Cong. Rec. H4486 (daily ed. June 17, 1999).

118. Id.

119. Id.

120. H.R.J. Res. 33, 106th Cong. (1999).

121. See Baker, supra note 3, at 53.

122. Colorado, Hawaii, Illinois, Maryland, Pennsylvania, Washington, and Wyoming. See Colo. Const. art. II, § 29; Haw. Const. art. I, § 3; Ill. Const. art. I, § 18; Md. Const. art. 46; Pa. Const. art. I, § 28; Wash. Const. art. XXXI, § 1; Wyo. Const. art. I, § 3.

123. California, Connecticut, Florida, Iowa, Louisiana, Massachusetts, Montana, New Hampshire, New Jersey, New Mexico, New York, Rhode Island, and Texas. See Cal. Const. art. I, § 31; Conn. Const. art. I, § 1; Fla. Const. art. I, § 2; Iowa Const.

art. I, § 1; La. Const. art I, § 3; Mass. Const. pt. I, art. I; Mont. Const. art II, § 4; N.H. Const. pt. I, art. 1.2; N.J. Const. art. I, § 5; N.M. Const. art. II, § 18; N.Y. Const. art. I, § 11; R.I. Const. art. I, § 2; Tex. Const. art. I, § § 3–3a.

124. They included, in addition to Phyllis Schlafly's Eagle Forum members, representatives from the insurance industry, the armed services, and some labor organizations. There were also groups such as Utah's HOTDOG (Humanitarians Opposed To Degradation of Our Girls) and various offshoots of the John Birch Society.

125. Jill Ruckelshaus, Speech at the National Women's Political Caucus California State Convention, San Jose, California (1977) (on file with author).

___

Chapter 12

Sovereignty in Comparative Perspective
Constitutionalism in Britain and America

Lord Irvine of Lairg

"The American Constitutions," said Thomas Paine, "were to liberty, what a grammar is to language: They define its parts of speech, and practically construct them into syntax."[1] The central role which was played by James Madison, whose memory this lecture commemorates, in the construction of the U.S. Constitution is too well known to require elaboration this evening. It suffices to note that, as one American commentator recently put it, Madison's championing of the amendment of the Constitution was an accomplishment which "entitles him to be remembered as father of the Bill of Rights even more than as father of the Constitution."[2]

In the speech which he made to Congress introducing the Bill of Rights,[3] Madison acknowledged that "paper barriers" have their limitations. But he also observed that, because "they have a tendency to impress some degree of respect for them, to establish the public opinion in their favor, and rouse the attention of the whole community," they are an important means by which "to control the majority from those acts to which they might be otherwise inclined."[4] By thus recognizing the potential of a Bill of Rights, Madison effected for America the constitutionalization of liberty—a process which, in the ensuing two hundred years, many other legal systems rightly have emulated.

I hesitate, however, to categorize the United Kingdom simply as one of those "other" jurisdictions. Of course, ever since Independence, there has

This lecture was delivered on October 17, 2000, and appeared in 76 N.Y.U.L. Rev. 1 (2001).

existed a formal separation between our two systems. But the linkages of legal culture which connect them have proved more resilient. That is hardly surprising, not least because of the shared common law foundation on which modern English and American law both rest.[5] More specifically, many of the rights which were enshrined first in the state constitutions and, later, in the federal Constitution share much in common with the values articulated in English constitutional texts.

For instance, section 39 of the Magna Carta, which provided that "[n]o freeman shall be . . . imprisoned . . . except by the lawful judgment of his peers or by the law of the land,"[6] was clearly a forerunner of the Due Process Clause in the U.S. Bill of Rights.[7] There are equally self-evident parallels between the provision in the 1689 Bill of Rights requiring "that the freedom of speech . . . ought not to be impeached or questioned"[8] and the guarantee enshrined in the U.S. Constitution's First Amendment. More generally, the writings of English philosophers had a fundamental impact on the theory of government which took root in America, as the relationship between the Declaration of Independence and the work of John Locke illustrates.[9]

But in spite of the fact that we share so much in common, there are also obvious differences. My purpose this evening is to focus on one particular point of distinction between the British and American legal systems: the divergence between the American notion of *constitutional supremacy* and the British doctrine of *parliamentary sovereignty*. That distinction has long been viewed as symbolizing a fundamental difference of outlook between the United States and Britain on constitutional matters generally, and more specifically on the status of civil rights in our respective legal systems. I intend to examine the background to that divergence, before going on to suggest that recent developments in the United Kingdom emphasize that the distinction between the two concepts, although real, should not be exaggerated.

I. Parliamentary Sovereignty

Let me begin with the notion of parliamentary sovereignty.[10] The nuances of that principle are the focus of one of the most contentious areas of academic—and, on occasion, judicial—debate in English constitutional law.[11]

The sovereignty principle has not always been rigidly endorsed. In particular, certain judicial dicta from the early seventeenth century questioned whether the courts owed unqualified loyalty to Parliament's enactments. Most famously, in *Dr. Bonham's Case*,[12] Chief Justice Coke said that the common law could "controul Acts of Parliament, and sometimes adjudge them to be utterly void: for when an Act of Parliament is against common right and reason, or repugnant, or impossible to be performed, the common law will controul it, and adjudge such Act to be void."[13] However, by the time he came to write his *Institutes*, Coke's views had become markedly more orthodox, and he accepted that Parliament possessed a "transcendent and abundant" jurisdiction which could not be "confined . . . within any bounds."[14] The correctness of that view was placed beyond doubt by the Revolution at the end of the seventeenth century.[15]

Although there exist myriad definitions of the doctrine of parliamentary sovereignty, the most enduring is that supplied by Albert Venn Dicey, the Victorian jurist and Vinerian Professor of Law at Oxford University. Writing in 1885, he described the Westminster Parliament as having "the right to make or unmake any law whatever," adding, for the avoidance of doubt it seems, that "no person or body is recognized by the law of England as having a right to override or set aside" its legislation.[16] Although much of Dicey's (still influential) work has been criticized by many modern British commentators, I note with interest that, in an authoritative recent book on sovereignty, Jeffrey Goldsworthy concludes that Dicey's definition is still "basically sound."[17] Indeed, for the last three hundred years British courts have not questioned Parliament's capacity to enact any legislation it chooses. As Lord Reid remarked:

> The idea that a court is entitled to disregard a provision in an Act of Parliament on any ground must seem strange and startling to anyone with any knowledge of the history and law of our constitution. . . . [S]ince the supremacy of Parliament was finally demonstrated by the Revolution of 1688 any such idea has become obsolete.[18]

It is true that some British judges now question—extracurially—whether sovereignty theory is apposite to the United Kingdom at the turn of the millennium.[19] In my view these criticisms are misplaced because they fail to appreciate that the notion of sovereignty is, in large measure, a function of the context within which it subsists. I shall argue that it is the evolution of that context which keeps fresh the idea of sovereignty, and which ultimately renders it an appropriate feature of the British constitution at the beginning of the twenty-first century. And I will suggest that it is that same evolutive context which reveals a measure of similarity between the British concept of parliamentary sovereignty and the American theory of constitutional supremacy, although those two ideas are, and will remain, distinct.

II. Constitutional Supremacy

A. The Notion of Constitutional Supremacy

Of course, legislative sovereignty has never been a feature of the U.S. legal system. By 1787, eight of the thirteen colonies had incorporated judicial review into their constitutions. It is ironic that the views expressed by Sir Edward Coke in *Dr. Bonham's Case*, although they had fallen out of favor in England by that time, were relied on in the *Writs of Assistance Case* in 1761,[20] and may have played some part in persuading the colonies to provide for judicial review in their constitutions.

The status of the Constitution as a higher order of law, prior and superior to the powers of the legislative branch, was articulated very clearly by Supreme Court Justice Samuel Chase in the case of *Calder v. Bull* in 1798.[21] "I cannot subscribe to the omnipotence of a State Legislature, or that it is absolute and without controul," said Justice Chase.[22] "An act of the Legislature (for I cannot call it a law), contrary to the great first principles of the social compact, cannot be considered a rightful exercise of legislative authority."[23]

I note, however, that although constitutional review is as central to constitutionalism in America as parliamentary sovereignty is in the United Kingdom, some voices have been raised against it ever since its inception in *Marbury v. Madison*.[24] One such voice was that of Judge John Gibson. In the dissenting opinion which he delivered in the case of *Eakin v. Raub* in the Pennsylvania Supreme Court in 1825,[25] he observed that

> [T]he Constitution is said to be a law of superior obligation; and, consequently, that if it were to come into collision with an act of the legislature, the latter would have to give way. . . . But it is a fallacy to suppose that they can come into collision *before the judiciary.* . . . The Constitution and the *right* of the legislature to pass the act may be in collision. But is that a subject for judicial determination?[26]

Although the jurisprudence of the Supreme Court has provided a clear, affirmative answer to this question, it is striking that the debate about the correctness of *Marbury*—both in terms of its fidelity to the intention of the

Framers and, more broadly, whether it is desirable in normative terms—is still going on, two hundred years after the decision.[27]

B. The Flexible Nature of Constitutional Supremacy

It is certainly not my intention to attempt to evaluate the appropriateness of constitutional review in the United States,[28] although I will have something to say later about constitutional review in the United Kingdom. Instead, my purpose is simply to draw attention to the clear parallel which exists between the ongoing debate in America about the powers of the courts in relation to the Constitution,[29] and the discourse in Britain concerning the desirability of parliamentary sovereignty. Although our respective legal systems begin from different starting points—constitutional paramountcy and legislative supremacy—the two debates address essentially the same questions: How much power should the courts have over the other branches of government? And in what circumstances, if any, is it appropriate for the judicial branch to overrule elected legislators and administrators in order to safeguard individual or group interests?

The fact that this same debate is ongoing within both the British and American legal systems points toward an important fact which is sometimes overlooked. Constitutional supremacy and parliamentary sovereignty are often perceived as concepts which are polemically opposed to one another, given that the former limits legislative power and entrenches fundamental rights, while the latter embraces formally unlimited power and eschews the entrenchment of human rights. However, the better view is that they represent two different parts of a continuum, each reflecting differing views about how the judiciary and the other institutions of government ought to interrelate.

This conceptualization follows (in part) from the fact that the notions of constitutional and legislative supremacy are themselves elastic. For instance, there exists a spectrum of opinions about precisely what constitutional supremacy ought to mean in the U.S. context. Although it is firmly settled that the U.S. Constitution does amount to a superior set of laws which *are* judicially enforceable,[30] this still leaves great scope for flexibility.[31] For instance, by 1858, the Supreme Court had held only two pieces of federal legislation to be unconstitutional.[32] The record of the Court in those early years contrasts sharply with the much more activist approach which was adopted by, for instance, the Warren Court.[33]

Such variation, over time, of the level of activism[34] which is evident in the Supreme Court's decisions reflects (among other things)[35] changing judicial (and societal) conceptions of how the judiciary and the other branches should interrelate—and, in particular, of how the balance should be struck between, on the one hand, judicial intervention and, on the other hand, legislative and executive autonomy. This position is, of course, as inevitable as it is desirable. As Chief Justice Marshall remarked in *McCullough v. Maryland*,[36] constitutions are "intended to endure for ages to come, and consequently, [must] be adapted to the various crises of human affairs."[37] Thus the necessary generality of a Bill of Rights makes it at once both timeless and evolutive. It follows that, while constitutional supremacy is a fixed feature of the U.S. Constitution, the concept is a flexible one, the precise meaning of which is, ultimately, a product of contemporary legal and political thought. The notion of parliamentary sovereignty is, I will argue, similarly elastic.

This flexibility which inheres in the ideas of constitutional and legislative supremacy goes some way toward dispelling the myth that each is the antithesis of the other. Since they are each catholic principles which accommodate a range of views concerning institutional interrelationship, it is meaningless to suggest that they are inevitably opposed to one another. That is why I suggested earlier that the two theories are best thought of as different parts of a spectrum of views concerning how judges should relate to the other branches of government. I will return, later, to these linkages between the two theories.

III. Traditional Points of Divergence

First, however, let me consider in more detail the divergence between the American principle of constitutional supremacy and British adherence to parliamentary sovereignty. There are important clues in the historical context which will help to illuminate the contemporary relationship between the two theories. In particular, I wish to examine some of the key points of divergence which, traditionally, have been treated as preeminent in establishing a clear distinction between them. However, I will also suggest that the tide of history substantially has eroded some of those differences. Certainly, distinctions still remain, but they are more subtle, and less obvious, than once they were.

A. Philosophical Roots

The foremost method by which constitutional and legislative supremacy traditionally have been differentiated is by reference to their philosophical roots.[38] Those roots are relatively clear so far as the U.S. notion of constitutional supremacy is concerned. As Chief Justice Marshall observed in 1821, "[t]he people made the constitution, and the people can unmake it. It is the creature of their will, and lives only by their will."[39] Thus, the state and federal institutions acquire their legitimacy from the popular consensus which the constitutional texts evidence. In this sense, popular sovereignty is the fundamental principle, while constitutional supremacy is its derivative.

Later in this lecture,[40] I will suggest that constitutional primacy is merely one possible derivative of popular sovereignty, and that, viewed in its contemporary setting, legislative supremacy also gives effect to the notion of sovereignty residing in the people. Historically, however, that is not the philosophical foundation on which the principle of parliamentary sovereignty was founded. Some writers suggest that the principle emerged through the translation of religious ideas about authority into a more secular conception of political sovereignty.[41] Whether or not this was so, one point is clear. The origins of the doctrine of legislative supremacy did not lie in a political philosophy which sought to give effect to any conception of popular sovereignty. This is plain, given that it was not until the nineteenth century (at the earliest) that it became possible, with the passing of the Reform Acts, to articulate any sort of normative democratic justification for the sovereign power wielded by Parliament.[42]

From this primary distinction between the models of constitutional and parliamentary supremacy there flowed a number of other differences. Let me mention just two.

B. The Relationship between the Citizen and the State

First, the adoption of constitutional supremacy—and, hence, of popular sovereignty as the fundamental principle—served to place the relationship between the citizen and the state on a very different foundation in the United States from that which obtained in England. In particular, the *dynamic* of the relationship was different. Constitutional paramountcy reflects the notion of social compact, of a population which is engaged in the political process, and upon whose license the continued existence of the institutions of government depends. Thus it invokes the idea of participatory democracy.

In contrast, the concept of parliamentary sovereignty called to mind a more hierarchical structure of superiors and subordinates.[43] Since Parliament's sovereign power did not derive, in the first place, institutionally from the will of the people, there was little or no sense in which that power was felt to be held "on trust" for the community at large.

C. Legal Theory: Positivist and Normative Perspectives

Secondly, the traditional manner of distinguishing between legislative and constitutional supremacy has important implications when it is mapped onto the broader canvas of legal theory. Viewed in its original form, the doctrine of parliamentary sovereignty presented a visage which was relentlessly positivist[44] in outlook.[45] It constituted legal positivism in its paradigm form. By articulating a constitutional theory which demands unqualified judicial loyalty to every Act of Parliament, it appeared to institutionalize the distinction between, on the one hand, legal validity and, on the other hand, considerations of morality.

As the great British judge, Lord Reid, remarked:

> It is often said that it would be unconstitutional for the United Kingdom to do certain things, meaning that the moral . . . [or] other reasons against doing them are so strong that most people would regard it as highly improper if Parliament did these things. But . . . [i]f Parliament chose to do any of them the courts could not hold the Act . . . invalid.[46]

Viewed in this way, the doctrine of parliamentary sovereignty turns the pure theory of legal positivism into legal reality.

Constitutional supremacy, of course, is not amenable to such analysis. The fact that the Bill of Rights enjoys the status of fundamental law precludes a purely positivist approach to adjudication in America. Here, it is impossible to divorce legal validity from considerations of political and social morality. The existence of an entrenched Constitution enjoins an approach which embraces an ineluctable connection between questions of law and questions of morality.

Looked at in this manner, the divide between positivist and normative models of adjudication underscores still further the perceived distinction between the notions of constitutional and legislative supremacy.

IV. A Measure of Convergence?

So much for traditional perceptions. What of present realities? I wish to demonstrate that although the picture I have just painted once may have described accurately the distinction between our two constitutional systems, it is now nothing more than an outdated caricature. In particular, I shall return to the idea which I sketched earlier: that sovereignty, meaningless in abstract terms, is a creature of contemporary political and legal context. I will argue that, once this fundamental point is appreciated, it becomes apparent that the distinction between legislative and constitutional supremacy is real, but markedly more subtle than it once was.

Let me consider some specific features of modern British constitutionalism that fundamentally have changed the context within which the notion of parliamentary sovereignty must be understood and which, as a result, have important implications for any comparison of the principles of constitutional and legislative supremacy.

A. The Modern Basis of Parliamentary Sovereignty

As a matter of legal history, the philosophical foundations on which those two concepts stand have been viewed as the fundamental point of distinction.[47] In particular, the idea that parliamentary sovereignty (unlike constitutional primacy) neither derived from nor depended upon an underlying popular consensus traditionally has exerted a strong influence on English constitutional theory. As Dicey put it, writing at the turn of the last century:

> [T]he courts will take no notice of the will of the electors. The judges know nothing about any will of the people except in so far as that will is expressed by an Act of Parliament, and would never suffer the validity of a statute to be questioned on the ground of its having been passed or kept alive in opposition to the wishes of the electors.[48]

At the beginning of the twenty-first century, the British doctrine of parliamentary sovereignty rests on rather different foundations. In common with most British constitutional developments, the change was evolutionary rather than revolutionary.[49] In particular, it was effected by gradual reform of the electoral franchise. Before 1832, the right to vote in general elections in the United Kingdom was based largely on property qualifications and extended to only 5 percent of the adult population.

The passing of the "Great Reform Act"[50] in 1832 precipitated a period of fundamental reform which lasted for a full century.[51] Even by 1910, however, only 28 percent of the total adult population enjoyed the right to vote.[52] The most far-reaching changes occurred in 1918:[53] Residency (as opposed to property entitlement) became the organizing principle, and, thanks to the sacrifices made by the "suffragettes," women over thirty years of age acquired voting rights.[54]

Those reforms demonstrate the emergence of representative and participatory democracy as the primary principle of constitutional and political theory in Britain. They evidence a paradigm shift in the way the relationship between the state and the individual is conceptualized in the United Kingdom. In this way, the process of electoral reform fundamentally has changed the environment within which parliamentary sovereignty subsists, transforming the doctrine into the vehicle by which the modern commitment to democracy is institutionalized. Thus, the legal sovereignty exercised by Parliament now is viewed as deriving its legitimacy from the fact that Parliament's composition is, in the first place, determined by the electorate in whom ultimate political sovereignty resides.[55]

Indeed, this conception of sovereignty finds clear expression in the principle known as the Salisbury Convention.[56] In 1945, the Labour Party won an overall majority of seats in the House of Commons, yet the House of Lords was dominated by unelected Conservative peers who had inherited their seats. In a debate in the Upper Chamber, the then Viscount Cranborne argued that it would be "constitutionally wrong" for the House of Lords to prevent the manifesto commitments of the elected Government from being enacted into law.[57] That argument was broadly accepted, and the Salisbury Convention thus emerged, according to which the unelected Chamber does not vote against legislation which seeks to give effect to electoral pledges that have been endorsed by the majority of voters.[58]

The present government is pursuing a thoroughgoing process of constitutional renewal.[59] As part of that program, it has abolished the right of hereditary peers to sit in the House of Lords, subject to a temporary right of ninety-two to remain.[60] Although further reform of the Upper Chamber is presently being considered and is not yet firmly settled, the Royal Commission, which recently undertook a thorough investigation of this subject, has recommended clearly that the House of Lords can best fulfill its role as a Second Chamber if it is *not* fully elected.[61] Consequently, the Salisbury Convention, or a modern successor to that principle, will remain necessary in order to articulate the idea that, while the House of Lords has a pivotal role to play both in the legislative process and in holding the executive to account, the *elected* House of Commons is, in the final analysis, the senior partner.[62]

This view of how the two Houses of Parliament should relate to each other, which the Salisbury Convention institutionalizes and which lies at the heart of the present reform program, acknowledges that the legitimacy of Parliament's legislative power is rooted firmly in the will of the electorate, for whom that power is held on trust.[63] This in turn clearly illustrates that the doctrine of parliamentary supremacy, seen from a modern perspective, is properly to be viewed as an expression of the political sovereignty of the people.

We therefore reach the position that the theories of government which obtain in both America and the United Kingdom are founded on the idea of popular sovereignty. The important implication of this is that, viewed from a contemporary perspective, the principles of constitutional and parliamentary supremacy are rooted in the same basic political philosophy which recognizes that government depends, for its legitimacy, on the imprimatur of the people.[64] In this sense, the two theories are distinct species of the same genus. They constitute different methodologies by which the ultimate aspiration—to fully representative, participatory, and therefore legitimate governance—is translated into practical reality.

It is, perhaps, unsurprising that constitutional primacy was the solution which was preferred in the United States, given that the Framers were starting from scratch and wished to constitute the United States on a different footing from that which obtained in the United Kingdom.[65] In contrast, the British constitution is the product of evolution. That defining characteristic of British constitutionalism explains why, in the United Kingdom, the preferred solution has been to retain parliamentary sovereignty, but gradually to change the political and legal environment within which the principle exists. In that evolutive manner, the theory of parliamentary sovereignty, like the principle of constitutional supremacy, has come to represent the primacy which is attached to representative, democratic government, which is surely the most fundamental of all the values which our two countries have in common.

B. Sovereignty, Constitutionalism, and Fundamental Rights

Thus far, I have been concerned with the common foundation which, viewed from a contemporary standpoint, the notions of constitutional and parliamentary sovereignty share. Let me turn, now, to the more specific issue of human rights protection.

I began my lecture by remarking upon the immense contribution which James Madison made to the adoption here of the Bill of Rights. The primacy which, as a result, U.S. law accords to fundamental rights is perceived in other countries as the preeminent characteristic of the American Constitution. It is also regarded as a graphic practical illustration of the perceived fundamental divergence between the theories of parliamentary sovereignty and constitutional supremacy. I wish to challenge the correctness of that perception.

1. Political and Legal Control Mechanisms

It is clear that our respective constitutions begin from different starting points. The U.S. system, through its constitutional texts, articulates a positive approach to human rights: They are marked out, from the very beginning, as sacrosanct. In contrast, the United Kingdom has traditionally adopted a negative approach to fundamental rights. This is based upon the principle of legality: the idea that the citizen enjoys the freedom to do as he or she pleases and that any interference with individual liberties must be justified by law.[66] The primary focus of the British system therefore has been on the legislative process, given that the locus of the citizen's freedom is ultimately traced by Parliament's enactments. Thus arose the notion of the self-correcting democracy, according to which the protection of individuals' rights was effected by the political mechanisms of ministerial responsibility and parliamentary scrutiny. This focus on *political*, rather than *legal*, accountability underscored the distinction between the British and American approaches. The point was captured well by Lord Wright, who remarked that, because "Parliament is supreme," there exist in the British constitution "no guaranteed or absolute rights. The safeguard of British liberty [therefore lies] in the good sense of the people and in the system of representative and responsible government which has been evolved."[67]

However, although it is true that English law traditionally has emphasized political, rather than legal, control of government, this certainly does not mean that it has pursued the former to the exclusion of the latter. English judges have long recognized that, although Britain adheres to a version of the democratic principle which places enactments of the elected legislature beyond judicial control, Parliament "does not legislate in a vacuum."[68] Instead, it "legislates for a European liberal democracy founded on the principles and traditions of the common law."[69] The courts therefore approach all legislation on the well-founded presumption that Parliament intends to legislate consistently with such principles. By such interpretative means, the judiciary has been able to confer a high degree of protection on a range of fundamental norms, such as access to justice,[70] judicial review,[71] and rights of due process.[72]

Consequently, although British courts cannot strike down legislation,[73] they can often, by interpretative means, bring legislation which appears to be inconsistent with fundamental rights into line with them. This emphasizes the point, to which I alluded earlier, that the notion of sovereignty is meaningless unless it is viewed within a particular context. The rule of law, and the values on which it is based, form a fundamental part of the constitutional environment within which the British doctrine of legislative supremacy subsists. In particular, it gives rise to an interpretative framework which is biased strongly in favor of fundamental rights and which thus shapes the context which gives color to Parliament's enactments.[74] Moreover, British courts have long been willing to take account of the European Convention on Human Rights in a number of contexts.[75] For instance, the Convention is used to aid the construction of ambiguous legislation[76] and can influence the development of the common law when it "is not firmly settled."[77] It guides the courts when judicial discretion is exercised[78] and when they are called upon to decide what public policy demands, as well as taking effect in the United Kingdom by operation of European Union law.[79]

The perception of Britain as a self-correcting democracy, in which the rights of the individual are protected entirely by *political* rather than *legal* means, therefore has never been wholly accurate. Like the American principle of constitutional supremacy, the British doctrine of parliamentary sovereignty, understood within its proper setting, embraces both political and legal control of government, although the respective systems strike different balances between those two mechanisms.

2. The Human Rights Act of 1998

It has, however, been clear for some time that the balance struck in the United Kingdom has been premised on an outdated—and exaggerated—view of the efficacy of political accountability.[80] The former Prime Minister John Major remarked in a major speech opposing a Bill of Rights for Britain that "[w]e have no need of a Bill of Rights because we have freedom."[81] This, however, overlooks the fact that constant effort is required in order to ensure that such freedom is preserved in the face of the legislative and executive activity associated with modern governance, both of which are well capable of trampling on basic human rights.

For precisely these reasons, the present government introduced a Human Rights Act.[82] The legislation was enacted in 1998 and, after an intensive period of judicial training and preparation across government, was implemented on October 2, 2000. It places public authorities under a new duty to respect fundamental rights,[83] and requires the government to draw Parliament's attention to any new draft legislation which is likely to compromise civil liberties.[84] Most fundamentally, the Act directs the courts to interpret legislation in a manner compatible with human rights whenever this is possible.[85] And when that is not possible, a "declaration of incompatibility" may be issued,[86] which should lead to the offending legislation being amended by means of a "fast-track" procedure.[87]

The Act does not, however, confer on British courts any authority to quash legislation which is irreconcilable with human rights norms.[88] Nevertheless, the issue of a declaration of incompatibility is very likely to prompt the amendment of defective legislation. This follows because such a declaration is likely to create considerable political pressure in favor of the rectification of national law and because a litigant who obtains such a declaration is likely to secure a remedy before the European Court of Human Rights if a remedy is not forthcoming domestically. Consequently, while British courts will not possess the power to strike down legislation which is incompatible with human rights, their power to issue a declaration of incompatibility is substantial, given that, in pragmatic terms, it very probably will lead to the amendment of defective legislation. In this practical sense, the Human Rights Act does introduce a limited form of constitutional review which is able fully to coexist with the theory of parliamentary sovereignty.[89] It also reconciles the dual democratic imperatives of governance by the majority in a manner which respects minority interests.[90]

3. British Constitutionalism and Legal Theory

I will conclude by considering the broader significance of these developments for the relationship between the principles of constitutional and legislative supremacy. First, however, let me return to a specific point that I raised earlier.

I noted that the sovereignty principle may appear to institutionalize a relentlessly positivist approach to law and adjudication: By commanding unyielding judicial fealty to every enactment of Parliament, it may seem to enshrine legal positivism in its paradigm form, apparently effecting a rigid separation between questions of legality and considerations of morality. To reach such a conclusion would be, however, to misunderstand the meaning of both positivism and sovereignty.

If positivism is simplistically defined as a theory that divorces questions of validity from considerations of morality, then sovereignty is, on any view, positivist in nature. However, the line that distinguishes adjudication on the validity of legislation from questions of interpretation is not watertight. Once this is appreciated, it becomes apparent that the British constitution is able to embrace sovereignty theory without institutionalizing a purely positivist conception of law. The interpretative framework that exists in the U.K. legal order is based on a system of morality that can be traced back to the roots of the common law—which jealously guards the liberty of the individual—and whose most recent manifestation is to be found in the explicit commitment to fundamental rights contained in the Human Rights Act.[91] This reflects an approach which, far from being exclusively positivist, embraces an ineluctable connection between the meaning of law and the framework of values—based preeminently on respect for the rights and liberties of the individual—on which the British legal system is founded.

In this sense, the British and American legal systems both embrace approaches to adjudication which accept a connection between law and morality, albeit that that linkage is given different institutional effect by each system. While the emphasis in the United States is on morality (as it is given expression through the Supreme Court's interpretation of the Bill of Rights) as a determinant of the validity of legislation, the emphasis in the United Kingdom is on morality as a determinant of the meaning of legislation. Thus, while the ultimate objective of connecting law with morality is shared by our respective legal systems, the manner in which that goal is realized differs in order to reflect our distinct constitutional arrangements. This, in turn, reiterates one of my central themes: That, while the principles of constitutional and legislative supremacy *are* clearly different, that divergence is often subtle rather than straightforward. It is to that theme that I finally return.

Conclusion

At first glance, it seems self-evident that American adherence to constitutional supremacy and British attachment to parliamentary sovereignty define a gulf that separates our respective approaches to constitutionalism. My purpose has been to suggest that, while the two theories are clearly different, their divergence in formal terms should not be permitted to obscure a measure of convergence at the level of substance.

This follows because one of the defining characteristics of both theories is that their meaning ultimately is determined by the broader legal and political environment within which they subsist. Although the degree of their conceptual distinction is sufficient to ensure that they do not overlap, their inherent elasticity and context-sensitivity make it unduly simplistic to postulate a bright-line distinction between them. This conclusion applies with equal force both to their underlying foundations and their practical implications.

As I discussed earlier, reform of the British electoral franchise during the nineteenth and early twentieth centuries fundamentally changed the philosophical and political foundations on which parliamentary sovereignty rests, turning the doctrine into the vehicle which, like constitutional supremacy, gives effect to a notion of popular sovereignty. Thus, legislative and constitutional supremacy both institutionalize a theory of government which rests on the same philosophical basis, although they represent different interpretations of how that theory ought to be given effect.

Context is equally central to an appreciation of more practical matters, such as the protection that the theories of constitutional and legislative supremacy afford to fundamental rights. Viewed superficially, the former appears to render human rights absolutely secure, while the latter seems to make them precarious in the extreme. The position, however, is less straightforward in reality. The practical capacity of a written constitution to protect human rights is ultimately dependent upon the broader context within which it exists: "If the judges are not prepared to speak for it, a constitution is nothing."[92] It is the willingness of American judges to give practical effect to the Bill of Rights which has turned an aspirational text into enforceable law.

Equally, the extent to which parliamentary sovereignty renders human rights precarious is a function of the broader constitutional setting. As I argued earlier, the evolution of the context within which sovereignty theory exists has impacted fundamentally upon its implications for human rights protection. In particular, the new Human Rights Act creates an environment within which it is much more difficult, legally[93] and politically,[94] for Parliament to exercise its sovereignty in a manner that is inconsistent with civil liberties.

The fact that the United Kingdom does not embrace constitutional review continues to distinguish our system from that which applies in the United States. But although such differences are important, they should not be allowed to obscure the fact that our respective systems share so much in common. The value of representative and participatory democracy lies at the very heart of both the American and British constitutional orders. And we share an appreciation of the importance of individual liberty whose roots can be traced back as far as the Magna Carta.

Writing in *The Federalist* in 1788, James Madison said that

> The aim of every political constitution is, or ought to be, first to obtain for rulers men who possess most wisdom to discern, and most virtue to pursue, the common good of the society; and in the next place, to take the most effectual precautions for keeping them virtuous whilst they continue to hold their public trust.[95]

Those words ring just as true today as they did two centuries ago. And the commitment to democratic and accountable government that they reflect remains the most fundamental of the many enduring factors that connect constitutionalism in Britain and America.

NOTES

1. Thomas Paine, "The Rights of Man" (1791), reprinted in *Two Classics of the French Revolution* 270, 334 (1989).

2. Leonard W. Levy, *Origins of the Bill of Rights* 34 (1999). For background information on the inception of the U.S. Bill of Rights, see generally id. at 1–43.

3. For the full text of Madison's celebrated speech, see 5 *The Roots of the Bill of Rights* 1016 (Bernard Schwartz ed., 1971).

4. Id. at 1030.

5. See generally Lord Irvine of Lairg, "The Common Origins of English and American Law, Inner Temple Lecture to the Inner Temple, London" (Mar. 22, 2000) (transcript available at http://www.open.gov.uk/lcd/speeches/2000/2000fr.htm).

6. Magna Carta § 39 (1215), reprinted in 1 *The Roots of the Bill of Rights*, supra note 3, at 8, 12.

7. U.S. Const. amend. V; see also id., amend. XIV.

8. Bill of Rights (1689), reprinted in 1 *The Roots of the Bill of Rights*, supra note 3, at 41, 43.

9. See especially John Locke, *The Second Treatise of Civil Government* (J. W. Gough ed., Basil Blackwell 1946) (1690).

10. The work of Sir William Wade remains, for many, the classic exposition of

sovereignty theory in the British context. See H. W. R. Wade, "The Basis of Legal Sovereignty," 1955 Cambridge L.J. 172; Sir William Wade, "Sovereignty—Revolution or Evolution?" 112 L.Q. Rev. 568 (1996).

11. The debate has been prompted both by the implications of European Union membership and, more generally, by a feeling in some quarters that the effective protection of fundamental rights is somehow incompatible with sovereignty theory. For a useful overview of the first aspect of the debate, see P. P. Craig, "The Sovereignty of the United Kingdom Parliament after *Factortame*," 11 Y.B. Eur. L. 221 (1991). On the debate's other dimension, see Geoffrey Marshall, "Parliamentary Sovereignty: The New Horizons," 1997 Pub. L. 1; Richard Mullender, "Parliamentary Sovereignty, the Constitution and the Judiciary," 49 N. Ir. Legal Q. 138 (1998).

12. 77 Eng. Rep. 646 (K.B. 1610).

13. Id. at 652. Similar sentiments were expressed by Chief Justice Hobart in *Day v. Savadge*, 80 Eng. Rep. 235, 237 (K.B. 1614) ("[E]ven an Act of Parliament, made against natural equity, as to make a man Judge in his own case, is void in it self.").

It is worth noting, however, that some historians suggest that Coke was arguing merely in favor of a particular approach to *interpretation*, rather than for a judicial power to *quash* such legislation. See, e.g., J. W. Gough, *Fundamental Law in English Constitutional History* 40–41 (1955). Gough attributes a similar interpretation to the previously quoted passage from *Day*. Id. at 38–39.

14. Sir Edward Coke, *The Fourth Part of the Institutes of the Laws of England: Concerning the Jurisdiction of the Courts* 36 (London, W. Clarke & Sons 1817) (1644).

15. See generally Jeffrey Goldsworthy, *The Sovereignty of Parliament* 142–220 (1999).

16. A. V. Dicey, *Introduction to the Study of the Law of the Constitution* 40 (E. C. S. Wade ed., 9th ed. 1956) (1885).

17. Goldsworthy, supra note 15 at 11.

18. *British Rys. Bd. v. Pickin*, 1974 A.C. 765, 782 (appeal taken from Eng. C.A.).

19. See Sir John Laws, "The Constitution: Morals and Rights," 1996 Pub. L. 622 [hereinafter Laws, Constitution]; Sir John Laws, "Law and Democracy," 1995 Pub. L. 72 [hereinafter Laws, Law and Democracy]; Sir Stephen Sedley, "Human Rights: A Twenty-First Century Agenda," 1995 Pub. L. 386; "Lord Woolf of Barnes, Droit Public—English Style," 1995 Pub. L. 57. For similar sentiments, expressed in the New Zealand context, see Sir Robin Cooke, "Fundamentals," 1988 N.Z. L.J. 158. For rebuttals of the views of Sir John Laws (who is the most enthusiastic judicial critic of parliamentary sovereignty), see J. A. G. Griffith, "The Brave New World of Sir John Laws," 63 Mod. L. Rev. 159 (2000); Lord Irvine of Lairg, "Response to Sir John Laws," 1996 Pub. L. 636.

20. See Maurice H. Smith, *The Writs of Assistance Case* 359–62 (1978).

21. 3. U.S. (3 Dall.) 386 (1798).

22. Id. at 387–88 (emphasis omitted).

23. Id. at 388 (emphasis omitted).

24. 5 U.S. (1 Cranch) 137 (1803). For a useful account of the historical context in which *Marbury* was decided, see Robert G. McCloskey, *The American Supreme Court* 1–34 (2d ed. 1994).

25. 12 Serg. & Rawle 330 (Pa. 1825).

26. Id. at 347–48.

27. For recent contributions to that debate, see Sylvia Snowiss, *Judicial Review and the Law of the Constitution* (1990); Mark Tushnet, *Taking the Constitution Away from the Courts* (1999).

28. It is, however, an interesting question whether the United States would have been a less fair and just society had the courts not assumed the power of constitutional review. Compare Ronald Dworkin, *Law's Empire* 356 (1986) (arguing that judicial review has made U.S. society more just), with Robert A. Dahl, *Democracy and Its Critics* 189–91 (1989) (questioning effectiveness of judicial review to protect human rights).

29. See, for example, the seminal contribution to this debate made by Ronald Dworkin, *Taking Rights Seriously* 131–49 (1977).

30. Academic debate notwithstanding. See supra note 27.

31. Perhaps the most vivid illustration of this flexibility is to be found in the Supreme Court's case law on the constitutionality of racial segregation. As is well known, the Court held in *Plessy v. Ferguson,* 163 U.S. 537 (1896), that the "separate but equal" policy was not incompatible with the Constitution. However, in the celebrated case of *Brown v. Board of Education,* 347 U.S. 483 (1954), the Court came to the opposite conclusion. Chief Justice Warren concluded that the policy deprived the plaintiffs, and "others similarly situated," of the "equal protection of the laws guaranteed by the Fourteenth Amendment." Id. at 495.

32. See *Dred Scott v. Sandford,* 60 U.S. (19 How.) 393 (1857); *Marbury v. Madison,* 5 U.S. (1 Cranch) 137 (1803).

33. For a useful survey of historical and quantitative research on the judicial policies of the U.S. Supreme Court, see David G. Barnum, *The Supreme Court and American Democracy* 74–105 (1993).

34. A discussion of the various meanings ascribed to the term "activism" can be found in Bradley C. Canon, "Defining the Dimensions of Judicial Activism," 66 Judicature 236 (1983). For a comparative analysis of the notion of activism in the fundamental rights context, see Lord Irvine of Lairg, "Activism and Restraint: Human Rights and the Interpretative Process," 1999 Eur. Hum. Rts. L. Rev. 350.

35. Of course, changes in the decision-making trends of the Supreme Court are also influenced by a large number of other factors. The study of such matters forms a discrete discipline in American legal scholarship and is beyond the scope of this lecture. For analysis of the influences which shaped decision making in the Supreme Court during its first two centuries, see, for example, David P. Currie, *The Constitution in the Supreme Court: The First Hundred Years 1789–1888* (1985); David P. Cur-

rie, *The Constitution in the Supreme Court: The Second Century 1888–1986* (1990); McCloskey, supra note 24.

36. 17 U.S. (4 Wheat.) 315 (1819).

37. Id. at 413 (emphasis omitted); see also Alexander Hamilton, "Third Speech at New York Ratifying Convention" (June 28, 1788), in 5 *Papers of Alexander Hamilton* 114, 118 (Harold C. Syrett ed., 1962) ("Constitutions should consist only of general provisions: The reason is, that they must necessarily be permanent, and that they cannot calculate for the possible changes of things.").

38. See generally Roger Cotterrell, "The Symbolism of Constitutions: Some Anglo-American Comparisons," in *A Special Relationship? American Influences on Public Law in the UK* 25, 27–28 (Ian Loveland ed., 1995). These themes are also touched upon by P. P. Craig, *Public Law and Democracy in the United Kingdom and the United States of America* 1, 3–9 (1990).

39. *Cohens v. Virginia*, 19 U.S. (6 Wheat.) 264, 389 (1821).

40. See infra Part IV.A.

41. E.g., John Neville Figgis, *The Divine Right of Kings* 258–59 (2d ed. 1914).

42. See infra Part IV.A for a discussion of reform of the electoral franchise.

43. See Cotterrell, supra note 38 at 39.

44. Space precludes detailed discussion of the meaning of positivism. It is used, in the present context, in a general sense to describe that approach to legal and constitutional theory that treats legal and moral validity as distinguishable issues. E.g., H. L. A. Hart, *The Concept of Law* 185–93 (2d ed. 1994).

45. As one commentator has noted:

No greater testimony exists to the power and resilience of positivism in modern legal thought than the debate between constitutional lawyers about the nature of parliamentary sovereignty. At the root of almost all analyses of the nature and scope of the doctrine lies an unquestioned separation of legal from political principle.

T. R. S. Allan, *The Limits of Parliamentary Sovereignty*, 1985 Pub. L. 614, 614 (footnote omitted).

46. *Madzimbamuto v. Lardner-Burke*, [1969] 1 A.C. 645, 723 (P.C. 1968) (appeal taken from S. Rhodesia).

47. See supra Part III.A.

48. Dicey, supra note 16 at 73–74.

49. For further discussion of the typology of constitutional change in Britain, see Lord Irvine of Lairg, "Constitutional Change in the United Kingdom: British Solutions to Universal Problems, National Heritage Lecture at the U.S. Supreme Court" (May 11, 1998) (transcript available at http://www.open.gov.uk/lcd /speeches/1998/1998fr.htm).

50. Reform Act of 1832, 2 & 3 Will. 4, c. 65, §§ I, IV (Eng.).

51. Additional legislation was enacted in 1867 and 1884 that further widened

the electoral franchise. See Representation of the People Act, 1884, 48 & 49 Vict., c. 3 (Eng.); Representation of the People Act, 1867, 30 & 31 Vict., c. 102 (Eng.).

52. David Butler & Anne Sloman, *British Political Facts 1900–1979*, at 227 (5th ed. 1980).

53. Those changes were effected by the Representation of the People Act of 1918, 7 & 8 Geo. 5, c. 64 (Eng.).

54. In 1928, the franchise was broadened further by extending voting rights to women aged over twenty-one. See Equal Franchise Act of 1928, 18 & 19 Geo. 5, c. 12 (Eng.).

55. A. V. Dicey acknowledged the emergence of political sovereignty alongside the theory of parliamentary sovereignty, see, e.g., Dicey, supra note 16 at 82–85, although he was, perhaps, somewhat reluctant to embrace the full implications of their interaction.

56. Although enunciated in its modern form in 1945 by the then Viscount Cranborne, the principle is known as the Salisbury Convention because it is founded upon the "mandate" doctrine that was developed by the Third Marquess of Salisbury in the late nineteenth century.

57. See 137 Parl. Deb., H.L. (5th ser.) (1945) 47 (remarks of Viscount Cranbourne); see also 137 Parl. Deb., H.L. (5th ser.) (1945) 613–14 (remarks of Viscount Cranbourne).

58. Formulated more precisely, the Convention requires that the House of Lords not oppose bills on their second or third readings. It also is accepted widely that the Upper Chamber should not subject draft legislation covered by the Salisbury Convention to "wrecking amendments" that undermine the fundamental principles on which a bill is founded.

59. For details of the government's reform program vis-à-vis the House of Lords, see generally Modernising Parliament: Reforming the House of Lords, 1999, Cm. 4183, available at http://www.official-documents.co.uk/document/cm41/4183/4183.htm. The reform program also encompasses the conferral of greater protection on human rights; the devolution of governmental power to Scotland, Wales, and Northern Ireland; the enactment of freedom of information legislation; and the establishment of a new strategic authority for Greater London.

60. See House of Lords Act 1999, c. 34, § 2(2) (Eng.).

61. See "A House for the Future," 2000, Cm. 4534, at 7, available at http://www.official-documents.co.uk/document/cm45/4534/4534.htm.

62. The Royal Commission on the Reform of the House of Lords shares this view. See id. at 39–40.

63. The Parliament Acts enacted from 1911 to 1949, which provide, in certain circumstances, for the passage of legislation without the consent of the House of Lords, similarly institutionalize a conception of parliamentary sovereignty that roots its legitimacy firmly in the mandate conferred upon Parliament by the electorate.

64. The arrival of British constitutional theory at this position has led some commentators to suggest that the democratic principle is prior—and therefore superior—to the doctrine of parliamentary sovereignty. See, e.g., T. R. S. Allan, *Law, Liberty, and Justice: The Legal Foundations of British Constitutionalism* (1993); Laws, "Constitution," supra note 19; Laws, "Law and Democracy," supra note 19; "Woolf," supra note 19. As I have indicated elsewhere, that is a view that I do not share. The fate of fundamentally antidemocratic legislation would, in the final analysis, be resolved in the political, not the judicial, arena. See Lord Irvine of Lairg, "Judges and Decision-Makers: The Theory and Practice of *Wednesbury* Review," 1996 Pub. L. 59.

65. For a sophisticated and innovative analysis of the constitutional settlement adopted by the American Founders, see Bruce Ackerman, "The New Separation of Powers," 113 Harv. L. Rev. 633 (2000).

66. The locus classicus of this approach is, of course, the decision in *Entick v. Carrington,* 95 Eng. Rep. 807 (K.B. 1765). The infringement of the individual's rights in that case was held to be unlawful because no legal provision permitted their infraction, and a general plea of "state necessity" was rejected.

67. *Liversidge v. Anderson,* 1942 A.C. 206, 260–61 (1941) (appeal taken from Eng. C.A.).

68. *Regina v. Sec'y of State for the Home Dep't, ex parte Pierson,* 1998 A.C. 539, 587 (appeal taken from Eng. C.A.) (Steyn, L.J.).

69. Id.; see also Lord Steyn, "Incorporation and Devolution: A Few Reflections on the Changing Scene," 1998 Eur. Hum. Rts. L. Rev. 153, 154–55.

70. See, e.g., *Regina v. Sec'y of State for the Home Dep't, ex parte Leech,* 1994 Q.B. 198 (Eng. C.A. 1993); *Regina v. Lord Chancellor, ex parte Witham,* 1998 Q.B. 575 (1997). For a discussion of access to justice and the interpretative process, see Mark Elliott, "Reconciling Constitutional Rights and Constitutional Orthodoxy," 56 Cambridge L.J. 474 (1997).

71. See, preeminently, *Anisminic Ltd. v. Foreign Comp. Comm'n,* [1969] 2 A.C. 147 (1968) (appeal taken from Eng. C.A.), in which the House of Lords vouchsafed, by interpretative means, the availability of judicial review of administrative action.

72. The law of judicial review, which safeguards a broad range of due process rights, takes effect as a consequence of judicial interpretation of enabling legislation, based on the presumption that Parliament wishes basic standards of fairness and rationality to be respected by those agencies upon which it confers power. For a detailed discussion of this "modified ultra vires doctrine" as the juridical basis of judicial review, see Mark Elliott, *The Constitutional Foundations of Judicial Review* (forthcoming 2001); Mark Elliott, "The Ultra Vires Doctrine in a Constitutional Setting: Still the Central Principle of Administrative Law," 58 Cambridge L.J. 129 (1999); see also *Judicial Review and the Constitution* (Christopher Forsyth ed., 2000).

73. Unless it is irreconcilably inconsistent with directly effective European Union law. See *Regina v. Sec'y of State for Transp., ex parte Factortame Ltd.,* [1991] 1 A.C. 603 (1990) (appeal taken from Eng. C.A.).

74. T. R. S. Allan has written extensively about the relationship between parliamentary sovereignty and the rule of law. See Allan, supra note 64; T. R. S. Allan, "Legislative Supremacy and the Rule of Law: Democracy and Constitutionalism," 44 Cambridge L.J. 111 (1985); Allan, supra note 45; T. R. S. Allan, "Parliamentary Sovereignty: Law, Politics, and Revolution," 113 L.Q. Rev. 443 (1997).

75. See 573 Parl. Deb., H.L. (5th ser.) (1996) 1465–67 (remarks of Lord Bingham); Murray Hunt, *Using Human Rights Law in English Courts* 207–61 (1997); Francesca Klug & Keir Starmer, "Incorporation through the Back Door?" 1997 Pub. L. 223, 224–25.

76. See, e.g., *Regina v. Sec'y of State for the Home Dep't, ex parte Brind*, [1991] 1 A.C. 696 (1991) (appeal taken from Eng. C.A.).

77. *Attorney-Gen. v. British Broad. Corp.*, 1981 A.C. 303, 352 (appeal taken from Eng. C.A.) (Fraser, L.J.); see also *Rantzen v. Mirror Group Newspapers (1986) Ltd.*, 1994 Q.B. 670 (Eng. C.A. 1993); *Derbyshire County Council v. Times Newspapers Ltd.*, 1992 Q.B. 770 (Eng. C.A. 1992).

78. See, e.g., *Regina v. Khan* (Sultan), 1997 A.C. 558 (1996) (appeal taken from Eng. C.A.) (exclusion of evidence in criminal proceedings), rev'd sub nom. *Khan v. United Kingdom*, Times (London), May 23, 2000, Law Report, at 18 (Eur. Ct. Hum. Rts. 2000); *Attorney-Gen. v. Guardian Newspapers Ltd.*, [1987] 1 W.L.R. 1248 (H.L. 1987) (appeal taken from Eng. C.A.) (provision of discretionary relief).

79. For the European Court of Justice's case law, see principally Case 4/73, *J. Nold, Kohlen- und Boustoffgroßhandlung v. Commission*, 1974 E.C.R 491; Case 11/70, *Internationale Handelsgesellschaft mbH v. Einfuhr- und Vorratsstelle für Getreide und Futtermittel*, 1970 E.C.R. 1125. For analysis, see, for example, Lord Browne-Wilkinson, "The Infiltration of a Bill of Rights," 1992 Pub. L. 397; Nicholas Grief, "The Domestic Impact of the European Convention on Human Rights as Mediated through Community Law," 1991 Pub. L. 555.

80. See, for example, the substantial number of judgments against the United Kingdom in the European Court of Human Rights. For discussion of the U.K. record before the Court, see A. W. Bradley, "The United Kingdom before the Strasbourg Court 1975–1990," in *Edinburgh Essays in Public Law* 185 (Wilson Finnie et al. eds., 1991).

81. Robert Shrimsley, "Future of the Constitution: Major Pledges to Defend 'Freedoms,'" Daily Telegraph (London), June 27, 1996, at 6, 1996 WL 3960465.

82. Human Rights Act, 1998, c. 42 (Eng.). See generally "Rights Brought Home: The Human Rights Bill," 1997, Cm. 3782, http://www.official-documents.co.uk /document/hoffice/rights/rights.htm; Lord Irvine of Lairg, "The Development of Human Rights in Britain under an Incorporated Convention on Human Rights," 1998 Pub. L. 221.

83. Human Rights Act § 6(1) ("It is unlawful for a public authority to act in a way which is incompatible with a Convention right.").

84. See id. § 19 (requiring government either to make "written statement of compatibility" with Convention rights, or to note its inability to make such statement).

85. Id. § 3.

86. Id. § 4.

87. Id. § 10.

88. In contrast, full constitutional review *does* exist vis-à-vis the enactments of the Scottish Parliament, given that certain matters (e.g., the competence to legislate on reserved matters or in contravention of the European Convention on Human Rights) lie beyond its powers. See Scotland Act, 1998, c. 46, § 29 (Eng.). Nevertheless, the position that obtains in Scotland remains distinguishable from that existing in the United States, given that the Scotland Act does not displace the capacity of the Westminster Parliament to legislate for Scotland on any matter (irrespective of whether it is reserved or devolved). Id. § 28(7). The possibility therefore remains for legislation (enacted by Westminster) to operate validly in Scotland notwithstanding its incompatibility with the Human Rights Act 1998.

89. An approach to human rights that preserves the legislature's ultimate capacity to attenuate them also has been favored by a number of other common law countries. For instance, the New Zealand Bill of Rights Act, 1990 (N.Z.), http://rangi.knowledge-basket.co.nz/gpacts/public/text/1990/an/109.html, requires legislation to be interpreted consistently with fundamental rights, see id. § 6, but leaves the legislature's power to restrict such rights ultimately intact, see id. § 4. Similarly, Section 33(1) of the Canadian Charter of Rights and Freedoms permits legislative derogation from human rights provided that the derogation is explicit. See Canada Act, 1982, c. 11, sched. B, pt. I, § 33(1) (Eng.).

90. See further 582 Parl. Deb., H.L. (5th ser.) 1234 (1997) (remarks of Lord Irvine of Lairg).

91. For a more detailed discussion of the manner in which the Human Rights Act will institute an approach to adjudication that is more explicitly moral, see Irvine, supra note 82, at 229.

92. Sir Stephen Sedley, "The Sound of Silence: Constitutional Law without a Constitution," 110 L.Q. Rev. 270, 277 (1994).

93. This follows because the logical effect of section 3 of the Act is to introduce very clear statutory language as a condition precedent to legislative interference with human rights. See Human Rights Act, 1998, c. 42, § 3 (Eng.) (requiring that, insofar as possible, legislation be read to comply with Convention rights, thereby resulting in clarification of statutory language). The use of such language therefore has become a *legal* requirement that must be satisfied before Parliament is able to infringe fundamental rights.

94. The Act makes it more difficult *politically* for Parliament to qualify human rights because, first, the use of clear language, see supra note 93, and the §

19 statement of compatibility scheme, will draw parliamentary and public attention to the rights implications of draft legislation (and, therefore, will require the government to justify the attenuation of human rights); and second, significant political pressure in favor of amendment is likely to attend a judicial declaration of incompatibility under § 4.

95. *The Federalist No. 57* (James Madison).

Contributors

Richard S. Arnold is a senior judge of the U.S. Court of Appeals for the Eighth Circuit. At the time he delivered the Madison lecture, he was Chief Judge of the Eighth Circuit.

Martha Craig Daughtrey is a judge of the U.S. Court of Appeals for the Sixth Circuit.

Norman Dorsen is Stokes Professor of Law at New York University School of Law, where he codirects the Arthur Garfield Hays Civil Liberties Program and chairs the Global Law School Program. During military service, he assisted in fighting McCarthyism in the 1954 Army-McCarthy Hearings. In 1957–58 he was law clerk to Supreme Court Justice John Marshall Harlan, and he has appeared before the Court in many cases. Among the nine books he has written or edited are *Frontiers of Civil Liberties*, *The Rights of Americans*, and *Our Endangered Rights*. Dorsen was president of the Society of American Law Teachers from 1973 to 1975, president of the American Civil Liberties Union from 1976 to 1991, and chair of the Lawyers Committee for Human Rights from 1996 to 2000. He is the founding president of the U.S. Association of Constitutional Law.

Harry T. Edwards is Chief Judge of the U.S. Court of Appeals for the District of Columbia Circuit.

Betty B. Fletcher is a judge of the U.S. Court of Appeals for the Ninth Circuit.

Ruth Bader Ginsburg is an Associate Justice of the Supreme Court of the United States. At the time she delivered the Madison lecture, she was a judge of the U.S. Court of Appeals for the District of Columbia Circuit.

A. Leon Higginbotham, Jr. was Chief Judge of the U.S. Court of Appeals for the Third Circuit and an Adjunct Professor at New York University School of Law.

Lord Irvine of Lairg is the Lord High Chancellor, United Kingdom of Great Britain and Northern Ireland.

Jon O. Newman was Chief Judge of the U.S. Court of Appeals for the Second Circuit at the time he delivered the Madison lecture. He is now a Senior Judge of the Second Circuit.

Sandra Day O'Connor is an Associate Justice of the Supreme Court of the United States.

Richard A. Posner is a judge of the U.S. Court of Appeals for the Seventh Circuit and Senior Lecturer, University of Chicago Law School. At the time he delivered the Madison lecture, he was Chief Judge of the Seventh Circuit.

Stephen Reinhardt is a judge of the U.S. Court of Appeals for the Ninth Circuit.

Patricia M. Wald was the Chief Judge of the U.S. Court of Appeals for the District of Columbia Circuit at the time she delivered the Madison lecture. She has since served as a judge on the International Criminal Tribunal for the Former Yugoslavia.

Index

References to notes are given as page number followed by n *and note number.*